AN EMPIRE TRANSFORMED

AN EMPIRE TRANSFORMED

Remolding Bodies and Landscapes
in the Restoration Atlantic

KATE LUCE MULRY

New York University Press

NEW YORK

NEW YORK UNIVERSITY PRESS
New York
www.nyupress.org

References to Internet websites (URLs) were accurate at the time of writing. Neither the author nor New York University Press is responsible for URLs that may have expired or changed since the manuscript was prepared.

Library of Congress Cataloging in Publication Data

Names: Mulry, Kate Luce, author.
Title: An empire transformed : remolding bodies and landscapes in the
    Restoration Atlantic / Kate Luce Mulry.
Description: New York : New York University Press, [2021] | Series: Early
    American places | Includes bibliographical references and index.
Identifiers: LCCN 2020015053 (print) | LCCN 2020015054 (ebook) | ISBN
    9781479895267 (cloth) | ISBN 9781479879649 (ebook) | ISBN 9781479857333
    (ebook)
Subjects: LCSH: Great Britain—History—Restoration, 1660–1688. | Great
    Britain—Politics and government—1660–1688. | Great Britain—Social
    conditions—17th century. | Public health—Great Britain—History—17th
    century. | Environmental policy—Great Britain—History—17th century. |
    Great Britain—Environmental conditions. | Great
    Britain—Colonies—America—Administration. | New York
    (State)—History—Colonial period, ca. 1600–1775. |
    Jamaica—History—17th century.
Classification: LCC DA448 .M85 2021 (print) | LCC DA448 (ebook) | DDC
    941.06/6—dc23
LC record available at https://lccn.loc.gov/2020015053
LC ebook record available at https://lccn.loc.gov/2020015054

New York University Press books are printed on acid-free paper, and their binding materials are chosen for strength and durability. We strive to use environmentally responsible suppliers and materials to the greatest extent possible in publishing our books.

Manufactured in the United States of America

10 9 8 7 6 5 4 3 2 1

Also available as an ebook

Contents

AN EMPIRE TRANSFORMED

Introduction

At his Restoration to the throne of England in 1660, Charles II was confronted with domestic disarray and faced a sprawling empire made up of scattered settlements with varied governments and distinct environments. This book investigates how Restoration officials endeavored to recover control and counteract any lingering questions about the king's rightful authority after his long exile by reforming and cultivating environments on both sides of the Atlantic. The king sought to assert his authority by managing targeted landscapes and populations. By supporting and initiating projects of improvement in the early modern landscape, including fen and swamp drainage, forest rehabilitation, urban reconstruction, and garden transplantation schemes, agents of the English Restoration government aimed both to transform environments and refashion the bodies and characters of residents into healthy and well-behaved subjects.

These schemes reflected a growing confidence that both human bodies and characters, and the environments in which they dwelt, were malleable and manipulatable and could be managed and improved by those who aspired to reform society. The proposed alterations of the environment designed to transform the health, temperaments, and behaviors of residents, as well as their prospective wealth, were one subset of a range of activities that contemporaries might have referred to as *improvements*. In the seventeenth century, the improvement of England and its colonies was a common topic of pamphlet and proscriptive writing. These improvements took many forms. Authors touted the social, political, medical, and economic benefits of their improvements. Their texts, which proliferated in the decades after the king's Restoration, reflected a growing belief that plans for reform on a local, national, and even imperial scale, were both possible and desirable.

Whether penning tracts on agriculture, manufacturing, or how to ameliorate the conditions of the poor, authors published a flurry of titles such as *The True English Interest* (1674), *England's Improvement by Sea and Land* (1677), and *Londons Improvement* (1680).[1] When the authors of the print journal of the newly established Royal Society of London for Improving Natural Knowledge included a notice and brief review of Samuel Fortrey's reprinted *England's Interest and Improvement* ([1663] 1673), they praised authors like Fortrey as one of the "Generous persons of *London*, who shew their Love to their Country by devising, proposing and soliciting the best Expedients for the Improvement of *England* and other his Majesties Dominions" through their writings.[2] They acknowledged the imperial scale of improvement schemes such as Fortrey's and praised the affection such authors showed for their country by devising innovative proposals that would also foster the empire's health, strength, and prosperity. When the king established a council "for the better regulating and improving of forreigne Plantations," and when he made plans to "settle and improv ye Island of Jamaica," he similarly turned to the language of improvement to encourage environmental transformations and to secure his sovereighty.[3]

Writers of improvement schemes both before and after the Restoration desired leaders who would be energetic reformers. They claimed England needed only "a propitious and wise Authority" to dedicate time and resources to facilitate improvements.[4] John Evelyn's enthusiastic dedication to Charles II in his book on the problem of air pollution in London praised the king, who "studies only the Publick Good" in order to improve his subjects' "health and felicity."[5] At the Restoration, many hoped that the king would be the powerful and "wise Authority" who could act on their plans and celebrated the possibilities of large-scale interventions by a powerful king as something both possible and highly desirable.[6] They argued that a willing and capable ruler was a precondition to the successful enactment of their improvement schemes. Projects of improvement, however, were not beneficial only to the "health and felicity" of his subjects. By transforming landscapes in ways that prioritized public health, the newly restored king could also buttress his own claims to political legitimacy after the disruptions of civil war, Interregnum, and his own lengthy exile.

Restoration officials feared that a disordered and sprawling empire made up of varied residents and jurisdictional pluralities strained and undermined popular metaphors of the state as a coherent body politic and posed an unwieldy political threat. In 1660 an ad hoc committee tasked with devising the mechanisms of oversight over foreign plantations wondered anew how to overcome the problems posed by such distance and diversity within the empire. When crafting their proposal for the creation of a council dedicated to "regulating and improving" the plantations, its authors suggested the need for greater colonial oversight and centralization. The proposal asserted that the colonists should be reminded of their proper place in relation to London and that they "must hereafter bee brought to understand, that they are to bee look'd upon as united, and Embodied: and that their Head and Centre is heere."[7] They rehabilitated a long-standing analogy by comparing the state to an organic body. Their proposal envisioned a disaggregated body being sutured back together by ships crisscrossing the oceans, which simultaneously enabled the communication or coordination of the limbs or members of empire with the head, which they located in London, and with the sovereign.[8] They recognized that the existence of far-flung territories called into question the proper functioning and cohesiveness of the body politic. The Council of Foreign Plantations commissioners conceived of circulating ships as a means of overcoming the problems of distance by unifying a dismembered—even monstrous—body politic that had been stretched to its conceptual limits by the rapid expansion of the territories under English imperial control.

Writers reflected on the many problems associated with this disaggregated body politic. According to the natural philosopher, physician, and author, William Petty, "The first Impediment of *Englands* greatness is, that the Territories thereunto belonging, are too far asunder, and divided by the Sea into many several *Islands* and Countries; and I may say, into so many Kingdoms, and several Governments." In addition to this geographic spread, Petty warned of "Three distinct Legislative Powers in *England, Scotland,* and *Ireland*; the which instead of uniting together, do often cross one anothers Interest."[9] Not only was the political body dispersed and divided by oceans, but there was little uniformity of governance. Ireland and the Islands of Jersey and Guernsey were under different jurisdictions than England, and the situation was even worse in New England, where "The Government of *New-England* (both *Civil* and *Ecclesiastical*) doth so differ from that of His Majesties other Dominions, that 'tis hard to say what may be the consequence of it."[10]

While Petty identified New Englanders as among the worst offenders and suggested that the better part of the region's residents should be cleared out and shipped to Ireland to repopulate lands much closer to home and nearer to wary authorities, he likewise warned that "the Government of the other Plantations, doth also differ very much from any of the rest."[11] He echoed earlier writers, including an English agent appointed to investigate the government of Massachusetts Bay Colony, who warned that too many people lived under local laws that were "derogatory or contrary to those of England" and should be better regulated.[12] Perhaps the biggest problem that arose from maintaining these divided and distant settlements was the burden of protecting them, Petty mused, because the cost and undertaking of defense inevitably fell to "the chief Kingdom *England*."[13] Officials sought to tackle the problems identified by Petty and others in several ways, including, for instance, by regulating natural resources. Tree rehabilitation projects and the cultivation of naval supplies would help construct the ships necessary to stitch together "soe many remote colonies" and to bring them under a "uniforme inspeccon," so that the king could better assist their "securitie and improvement."[14] The king's interest in "draw[ing] those our distant dominions . . . into a nearer prospect" included the fact that the colonies were "now a greate and numerous people whose plentifull trade and commerce" could "bring . . . treasure to our Excheqr" if properly managed.[15]

The empire's continued expansion during the Restoration compounded problems of governance over a heterogeneous empire that had grown in population and significance since his father's reign. In addition to recently acquired Jamaica, Charles II received Bombay and Tangier through marriage, took New Amsterdam from the Dutch by force, and granted proprietors the colonies of New York, Pennsylvania, East and West Jersey, and Carolina. Not only had colonists "become used to some degree of autonomy" while the English were preoccupied with civil war and experimenting with new forms of government during the Interregnum, but the newly acquired colonies posed additional legal and administrative challenges to a regime that sought greater oversight of the colonies.[16] Restoration officials aspired to impose order and counteract any lingering questions about the king's rightful authority. Despite a recent push among scholars to highlight continuities across the "historiographical divide" marked by the Restoration—and this book includes many such continuities—there were also significant adaptations and innovations to address changing circumstances and unexpected events.[17]

For instance, officials pondered how to rule over newly conquered populations living in the colonies of Jamaica and New York. Catastrophes in the form of plague and fire hit London in the mid-1660s and the debates about how to rebuild the city shaped conversations about urban planning from Kingston to Philadelphia.

As the king sought to secure his power at home and in the colonies, much remained unsettled. One potential source of disorder was widespread uncertainty and confusion over property. Faced with the significant challenge of reassessing and redistributing the Crown, Church and royalists' lands confiscated—or sequestered—by the "usurpers" during the war, the king agreed that Parliament would determine the details of the land settlement. Returning the lands would prove to be a formidable undertaking, and incredibly time consuming, due to the extent to which land had forcibly changed hands in this period.[18] It was a complicated issue and although many royalists turned to the courts, they were frequently frustrated at the slow rate of recovery.[19] Those who had purchased sequestered property vociferously defended their claims. Their voices were influential because many more people had purchased lands than had forfeited them.[20] Meanwhile, the recently completed Down Survey, a survey of Irish land overseen by William Petty to facilitate the redistribution of millions of acres of Irish Catholic lands to English Protestants after Oliver Cromwell's invasion and conquest of the island, likewise fell under scrutiny. The beneficiaries, many of them former soldiers, or those to whom they, in turn, had sold their lands, were unsure of the new king's plans for Ireland.[21] Charles II did not, in fact, reverse the Cromwellian settlement in Ireland, although some minor provisions were made for select individuals to dispute it, which led to drawn-out legal battles.

Confusion over property also unsettled and troubled colonists across the Atlantic. Neighboring towns and colonial proprietors argued over boundaries while colonial charters were recalled by authorities in London for reappraisal and re-approval.[22] This book considers the uncertainties expressed by the Council of Foreign Plantations over plans to settle Jamaica while the island's planters worried that their properties would be forfeited if there was war with Spain. Anxious residents of New York asked representatives of the new proprietor by what tenure they held their lands. Amidst this confusion individual landholders and colonial proprietors sought to strengthen their claims of possession by marking boundary trees and by making improvements.[23] Efforts to secure possession throughout the empire contributed to a "growing archival edifice"

of surveys, "deeds, mortgages and litigation-related records."[24] Proprietors' desires to collect quitrents resulted in a spate of such records,
for instance. Indeed, according to Allan Greer, "the processes of state
formation and property formation went hand in hand."[25] An acceler-
ating paper trail of debates and decisions over land created during the
Restoration lent an aura of credibility to the state.[26] Meanwhile, some
claimants pointed to the improved health of local residents as additional
evidence of their rightful possession, which suggests they believed such
rationales would resonate and further augment their claims in a period
of uncertainty.

By managing targeted landscapes and people the Restoration government sought to assert control over two colonies of conquest, Jamaica
(1655) and New York (1664), colonies that were legally, demographically,
environmentally, and politically unsettled. As a result, these colonies
serve as useful sites to understand better how English Restoration officials sought to assert sovereignty over heterogeneous subjects. In both
colonies, officials looked not only to establish order and legal coherence
but also to transform environments, and in doing so claimed that the
changes would benefit the residents' physical health. In other words,
claiming possession by making environmental improvements was more
than a symbolic political or legal act. Colonial officials also aspired to
remold their new subjects' health and behaviors in sites they believed
required special intervention. Moreover, projects undertaken in the
colonies frequently corresponded to ongoing projects of environmental
improvement and population management unfolding within England,
suggesting that many of the claims about order, health, and political
legitimacy had critical domestic dimensions. The widespread desire for
the return of order, which many people hoped would also restore prosperity, serves as a reminder that the Restoration of the king was also
"brought about as a result of pressure from below," although "not everyone expected the same thing from the restored monarchy."[27]

Despite officials' insistence that the "Severall Pieces, and Collonies"
could be drawn together into "one Comonwealth . . . governd, and regulated accordingly, upon Common and Equall Principles," the metaphors
envisioning the state as a unified, organic body remained strained. More
land, and the introduction of many non-English colonists as imperial
subjects, made it difficult to see how all of the "Pieces" would become
one English body.[28] As a result, individual bodies and landscapes took
on greater importance as sites for promoting or assessing the health of
the polity. This study demonstrates that the health of subjects' bodies

became a particular point of contention and site of contestation. Environmental improvement projects initiated by Restoration officials aimed to improve individual subjects' health and behavior and therefore highlight the dynamic relationship they imagined between place, the porous humoral body, identity, and authority.

Although government intervention in public health is commonly understood as a more recent phenomenon, officials in Restoration England and its colonies saw the health of individual and collective bodies—especially those bodies perceived to be a potential political threat or "infection" of the body politic, such as maroons in Jamaica, the riotous residents of the fenlands in eastern England, or the plague-infected "nasty folks" of London—as coming under the government's purview and fundamentally tied to the health of the state.[29] Assessing subjects' bodies and health also mattered because the appearance of sickly, deformed, or monstrous bodies—or monstrous births—could be ominous, foretelling political turmoil, or they could be a physical manifestation of such upheavals.[30] Through numerous environmental transformations, representatives of an expanding Restoration English empire aimed to refashion perceived outsiders into healthy, virtuous bodies and to constitute ideal political subjects in the late seventeenth-century Anglo-Atlantic. Their environmental improvement projects are evidence of imperial governing strategies that aimed to work, literally, from the ground up and reveal a deeply physical conception of the political subject.

Officials imagined that their intertwined efforts to discipline bodies and promote health and well-being by manipulating landscapes were possible due to prevailing medical theories that held that bodies were remarkably porous and intimately connected to their environment. These early modern European ideas about humoral medicine and health were developed in ancient Greek and Roman texts by the medical writers Hippocrates and Galen, and were later refined by physicians in the Islamic world, including Rhazes, Avicenna, and Averroës.[31] According to humoral principles, every individual was born with a particular balance of the four humors—blood, phlegm, yellow bile, and black bile—which regulated health and complexion. An imbalance or surfeit of these fluids resulted in poor health and an altered appearance. The unique balance of an individual's humors also determined their character or temperament, which could be sanguine, phlegmatic, choleric, or melancholic. An individual's health and disposition were further shaped by diet, exercise, and a range of environmental influences, including climatological and astronomical variations.[32] The qualities of environment, such as the air or soil, engendered any number of characteristics in residents, including imbuing them with diverse cultures and customs. Climate, winds, proximity to the sun, and astronomical events like meteor showers might send pestilence or promote health. Environmental factors might also inspire artistic creativity, boost intelligence, inspire bold or brave behavior, or impart skin hue, or "complexion," to residents.[33] Thus, in this rubric, nature had immense power to shape appearance, health, and behaviors and could be strategically manipulated.

The scrutinizing of individual bodies to draw conclusions about the health of the body politic had immense political significance at mid-century. Royalist writers claimed that both individuals' bodies and the body politic had suffered greatly during the English Civil Wars. They made use of metaphors of a wounded body to make sense of the tumult and violence of the era.[34] According to Nancy Shoemaker, "Turning to body metaphors to provide the explanation of abstract concepts is probably a universal cognitive practice, no matter the culture"[35] A diseased, deformed, broken, and bleeding body politic, much like the wounded bodies of individual participants, required healing and a restored "head," or king, to soothe its wounds. Charles I's natural body, beheaded in 1649, had also left his political body without a head, leaving the "two bodies" of the king unalterably wounded, and "in that same instant, the conventional meaning of the body politic, so numbingly cliché, became radically destabilized."[36] Images of an unwieldy, headless body and of the many-headed hydra of republican rule became powerful metaphors during a chaotic period of civil war, and they took hold in popular culture. Royalists claimed that a body without its proper "head" was prone to chaos and disorder. Too many heads, much like the disorder that resulted from the headless body of a decapitated king, were similarly dangerous to the proper functioning of a natural body and the body politic alike.[37] Not only would the Restoration of the king return the head to the body politic, supporters promised, but he would then turn his attention to healing subjects. In writings, ceremonies, and parades, contemporaries utilized potent metaphors to celebrate the Restoration of the king to the throne of England as akin to a body restored to health.

Using this metaphor, the king's physician, Gideon Harvey, exclaimed that the Restoration of Charles II to the throne of England was the "Soveraign Remedy" that restored the mental and physical health of the nation.[38] Harvey further reflected that although the king's subjects had been "Afflicted with Maniacisms, and Fascinated Distempers of their Minds," his "Blessed Restauration" to the throne had "Cured them."

Harvey's depiction of the king's return as a healing balm to the nation was not only a metaphor. He went on to explain that when Charles II reestablished the "College of Experienced *Physicians*," he preserved the lives of innumerable subjects by making them less dependent upon unlearned "Empirics" who lacked proper training. Meanwhile the "Royal Laboratory sheweth out of what Materials, and in what manner the best Remedies are to be Praepared; So, as You are the Greatest KING, You are the greatest *Physician*," protecting his subjects against "the *Scorvey* of this Age."[39] In other words, he insisted that Charles II's support for the Royal College of Physicians had resulted in better medical knowledge, which promoted his subjects' welfare.

Royalist writers not only emphasized a disaggregated body sutured together by the return of law and order but hailed the return of Charles II as a kind of panacea to an ailing body. When the king sent a letter and his Declaration of Breda to the lord mayor, aldermen, and Common Council of London, he compared the "distraction and confusion" as well as the "misery and suffering" of the civil war and Interregnum to an ailing body. The nation "hath groaned under" "great Troubles and Miseries" akin to "Distempers and Distractions" that "so impoverished and dishonored the Nation" that he hoped "God Almighty will heal the wounds" of the tumultuous era.[40] Many hoped not only that the return of the king would "quiet the confusion" of the previous decades but also that "these wounds which have so many years together been kept bleeding, may be bound up."[41] They promised that the king's return would bring about peace, quiet, order, and good health.[42] Charles II similarly wrote to officials of the navy that upon his Restoration, "God Almighty will heal the wounds, by the same plaister that made the Flesh Raw." He preemptively thanked God for "infusing" those "good Resolutions in your and their hearts" to welcome him back to his rightful place, like a good tonic.[43] According to John Bird, the king was the ideal "Physician to cure those wounds and putrified sores, which our *State-Physicians* (as they have been often called) have made and caused." Bird went well beyond metaphor by claiming that actual instances of diseases like scrofula and rickets had been on the rise during the Interregnum due to the nation's political sins, "so when He our Gracious K. CHARLES II who is now come, hath performed the work he is come to do of *Reformation*, the Disease of the REKETS will be heard of not more in the land."[44] In other words, the Restoration of the king would halt the further spread of the intertwined evils of sin and disease. Restoring order to the macro body politic resulted in the restored health of micro bodies, the bodies of individual subjects.

In his account of the king's coronation procession, John Ogilby touted Charles II's return as facilitating access to rare and healthful medicines located overseas. When the king processed through the city on the day of his coronation in April 1661, his route took him through ornate triumphal arches constructed for the occasion, passing actors in costume personifying or embodying concepts such as Monarchy triumphing over Rebellion.[45] As Charles II passed a second triumphal arch depicting naval scenes, one of the actors would have compared the king to Neptune, or "NEPTUNO BRITANNICO," the sovereign of the seas. His dominion over the oceans, and by turning the "whole Sea" into a "Highway," facilitated trade with the four figures positioned along the arch, the personifications of Europe, Asia, Africa, and America; each figure bore the "Arms of the Companies, Trading into those Parts."[46] Later in the procession actors proclaimed: "Behold . . . Our Prince . . . Brings healing Balm, and Anodynes, To close our Wounds and Pain asswage."[47] Ogilby's script not only hailed the king as the restored head to a confused and disordered body but as the individual best placed to heal subjects' bodies by supporting merchants' overseas trade in spices and medicines.[48]

Meanwhile, Charles II went on to participate in certain healing rituals on a vaster scale than previous kings; he rejuvenated the practice of healing his diseased subjects by laying his hands on those subjects actually suffering from scrofula, known as the King's Evil. He laid his hands on an astonishing number of people. Stephen Brogan estimates that Charles II touched as many as ninety-six thousand scrofula sufferers and indicates that "the key public role of the Stuart monarchs was that of healer, meaning that their religious and medical duties were of paramount importance."[49] During the Restoration the king touched more individuals with scrofula than other English monarchs, which suggests widespread and popular "enthusiasm for royal therapeutics during the Restoration."[50] The king and his officials emphasized the king's ability to heal sickly bodies, in part, as a means of reforming the strained relationship between the Crown and its subjects in response to a period of upheavals and uncertainties.[51] Indeed, as Elaine Scarry has argued, "At particular moments when there arises within society a crisis of belief" such as, in this instance, the belief about the divine right of kings, "the sheer material factualness of the human body will be borrowed to lend that cultural construct the aura of 'realness' and 'certainty.'"[52] By healing his subjects Charles II rehabilitated his legitimacy and authority. Healing bodies was an effective political strategy.

FIGURE I.1. The second triumphal arch depicted Charles II as sovereign of the seas, fostering trade in luxury groceries, spices, and drugs. John Ogilby, *The Entertainment of his Most Excellent Majestie Charles II, in his Passage through the City of London to his Coronation* (London: Thomas Roycroft, 1662). RB 141718, The Huntington Library, San Marino, California.

Royalist writers' emphasis on healing bodies, and their use of body metaphors, not only referenced recent events and literature mourning the martyred body of Charles I, for instance, but tapped into changing ideas about bodies on display in artworks or exhibited and learned in anatomical theaters. Likewise, the empiricism espoused by the Royal Society foregrounded the role of eye-witnessing and the engagement of other bodily senses when gathering facts about nature.[53] As with various early modern political theorists who "grounded their views" in "new claims about the body that flowed from the recent anatomical discoveries and theories," Restoration writers and officials were similarly inspired.[54] Peter Anstey, Ted McCormick, and Jacquelyn Miller have all examined the links between the natural philosophical or medical training and the political writings and policies of a range of individuals, including John Locke and William Petty.[55] This study builds on their insights in order to highlight several Restoration-era reformers' translations of their ideas about natural bodies into their plans to heal the body politic.[56]

Royalists claimed that years of war and violence had ravaged not only bodies but environments, too. They celebrated the return of a king who would proactively cultivate England's landscapes, and offered him a way to further reinvent himself as the rightful steward of the empire. By endorsing improvement projects and tending to the natural "Patrimony" of the nation, the newly restored king, praised as the "prince of planters," further established the basis of his authority by rooting it in his skillful management of nature.[57] Reforestation projects, for instance, were often described as schemes to bring back the symbolic hair—and apparent health and virility—of the body politic.[58] Chartered by the king, the newly established Royal Society published a range of landscape improvement proposals in the *Philosophical Transactions* that they hoped would be "generally beneficial" and would "conduce to the Health, Strength, Populousness and Welfare of these his Majesties kingdoms."[59] Writers proposed, for instance, planting gardens, "fertiliz[ing] barren lands," draining both "bogues" and "infectious Fens, to render the Air wholesome in all the neighbourhood," and replanting trees, including "fragrant Evergreens," thereby sweetening the air. By transforming the "infectious" land and air, writers anticipated that their proposals would inspire "all that have hearty affections for their Native Country and their own Patrimony" to support their work, claiming their projects would improve the land and make it more productive and healthful.[60] While not every plan to cultivate the land sought to transform residents' health, and not all projects to manage bodily health had environmental dimensions, this book examines sites where these aims overlapped. It tracks a particular variant of Stuart political ecology that recognized the human and the natural as entangled and examines the plans they articulated to manage and improve both.[61]

By examining the attitudes and writings of a cohort of elite thinkers who sought to advise officials about the experimental management of domestic and imperial landscapes, this study builds in the work of scholars who investigate the environmental consequences of early modern attitudes and beliefs about nature.[62] Royal Society authors as well as self-proclaimed experts looking for patronage, known as "projectors," were among those writers who offered up a variety of such schemes, which they claimed would transform both people and places around the English Atlantic while also garnering a profit.[63] Their popularity suggests that the English polity, only recently devolved into the violence and incoherence of war, sought new methods and aims of statecraft attentive to healing both people and landscapes.[64] In England and the colonies, the king sought legitimacy by supporting projects of improvement that targeted places and people deemed unhealthy or disordered, which required innovations in governance, not restoration alone.[65]

Administering the dispersed colonies was no easy task, however. After so many years away, the king's knowledge of the American plantations was "abysmal."[66] The knowledge necessary to make informed policy had not been systematically collected by previous regimes. When he was restored to the English throne, Charles II sought to take stock of colonial resources and demography and to assess government activities after his long exile. The Crown's officials aimed to gather knowledge about English colonial holdings in order to familiarize themselves with what natural products might be available and to streamline and tighten control over colonial administration.

In midsummer of 1660, to better facilitate his "ideals of order" for the empire, Charles II appointed ten privy councilors to meet twice a week to concern themselves with the American plantations.[67] That winter the king established the Council of Foreign Plantations, raising the membership numbers from ten to forty-eight.[68] This Council periodically changed, both in form and function, during Charles II's reign. Later called the Lords of Trade and Plantation, its members continued to use questionnaires to better inform themselves about the locations and people over which the English claimed governance.[69] They intermixed queries about the climate and soil of a place with questions about the region's residents, economies, and laws. In questionnaires sent to the

FIGURE I.2. Even as Thomas Hobbes's artificial body offered an alternative to the metaphor of the organic body politic, subjects' natural bodies continued to matter to the state. Thomas Hobbes, *Leviathan, or the matter, forme and power of a commonwealth ecclesiasticall and civil* (London, 1651). Image courtesy of The British Library.

colonies, they cited the king's desire for an "accompt of the Governmt of each Colonie; of their complaints, their wants, their abundance; of their severall growths and commodities."[70] The authors of these circulars, designed to be sent out to colonial governors and others of high standing who could then circulate the queries among their contacts, wanted such thorough information because they insisted there could be no regularized policy, which was the king's aim, without such baseline knowledge.[71] The king claimed he needed the information gleaned from these questionnaires to ensure colonial security and to oversee "improvement."[72] Indeed, the king urged his new Council of Foreign Plantations to seek assistance from "any experienced person, whether merchant, planters, seamen, artificers &c." who might help render the "Dominions usefull to England, and England helpfull to Them."[73]

Meanwhile, the king paralleled the expansion of the empire with the expansion of an empire of knowledge. Each enabled the other. He anticipated that the newly chartered Royal Society would seek "to extend not only the boundaries of the empire but also the very arts and sciences" "for the general benefit of his Majesties dominions."[74] Royal Society members hoped they might provide relevant, useful, and practical intelligence that would be of utility or might aid in English expansion. The king acknowledged that he had incorporated the Royal Society, in part, because their studies might prove useful to him.[75] The Society needed no particular encouragement from the king to imagine an imperial or global dimension to their work. Interests in faraway places appeared early in the Royal Society records. In February 1661 the Society called together a committee with the intention that they might deliberate and compile "proper questions to be enquired of in the remotest parts of the world."[76] But they did not only collect knowledge about the colonies. They also sent questionnaires throughout England to collect and compile the knowledge of the rustic arts from around the country, which suggests that practices to better understand and control imperial places and people inflected their motives and methods of acquiring information from fields and gardens closer to home.

Gathering knowledge about human and natural landscapes was one of the means of rationalizing and consolidating imperial control explicitly articulated by members of the Royal Society.[77] Similarly, the authors of questionnaires developed by the Council of Foreign Plantations hoped to collect and codify knowledge of the people and places of empire and, in the process, help to develop "uniforme" legislation. But the tendency of these numerous questionnaires was to pixilate the landscape, offering peeks rather than the desired vistas. Moreover, the haphazard, and occasionally antagonistic, responses to the questionnaires in the colonies suggest that many did not want to be observed at all. The questionnaires may have been regarded as essential tools by imperial officials who sought to make decisions from the imperial "head," but their desired vision of a coherent body politic largely remained a mirage.[78]

In their proposals for the creation of the Council of Foreign Plantations, authors suggested the necessarily dynamic and symbiotic relationship of protection and loyalty that might draw far-flung colonies and diverse communities into the sphere of English sovereignty. The colonies could expect "Encouragement and Protection" while the Crown could expect accountability, envisioned as the "better ordering and disposing of trade," in the form of payments.[79] A monarch was obliged to protect "both the bodies of subjects and the land they occupied" in order to maintain their allegiance.[80] Restoration officials' deployment of healing languages was an added dimension to this capacious understanding of the meaning of protection and the king's promise to be assiduously "vigilant for their generall Good."[81]

Indeed, assertions that the king should be interested in the "generall Good" of his subjects reveal broad interpretations of the activities that might fall within this category. In the idiom of the day, keeping people alive was essential to national strength, and ensuring the vigor and might of the nation and its inhabitants was certainly one of the king's recognized duties. In the late-seventeenth century, in a period of significant change, Charles II's proposed interventions into subjects' health and the environment offered opportunities for the Crown to gain stability and legitimacy. Royal Society member Reason Melish urged the king to endeavor to boost England's demographic strength because "the strength of a nation consists in the multitude of people, and so likewise its wealth." Beyond numbers alone, Melish determined, those multitudes had to be "rightly Imployed."[82] He suggested that suitable employment included preparing land for arable agriculture. Those lands might then produce more foods and thereby sustain more people, who would go on to turn their own many hands to agricultural labor. This would be an ongoing cycle—of unproductive lands made productive—which could then maintain larger populations. According to Melish, agricultural improvement and national strength went hand in hand.

Because Melish was sure that more people would "add to the strength" of the nation, he thought it should "become the care of those that sit at the helme of Governm^t to use such means as may be thought conducing to encrease the number of our people."[83] He claimed it was the job of Restoration officials to act boldly and presciently to improve the land, and the diets, of a thriving English nation.[84] By acting as a kind of technocrat, the king could engage in "the rational management and optimal exploitation of natural resources" in concert with the management of populations.[85] Similarly, by taking an interest in John Graunt's pioneering demographic study *Natural and Political Observations . . . Made upon the Bills of Mortality* (1662), Restoration officials could use the demographic data about disease and death in the published bills for better managing populations. They admired a book that addressed their intertwined interests of governing people and places.[86]

By investigating rhetoric about the body, this study further reveals a range of anxieties about what happened when bodies traversed the Atlantic, and what happened to English bodies and identities when the English cultivated or consumed commodities from around the Atlantic or the East Indies in England. Were English colonists still English after being transplanted into new soils? Were colonists still English once they had been transplanted to Jamaica, for instance? What about their children and grandchildren, who had never set foot on English soil?[87] Biblical reminders that the dead returned to the dust of the earth from whence they came further reinforced the conceptual links between humoral bodies and soils. If, as people widely believed in the seventeenth century, both plants and human communities were "products of their soil," then what should be done to help settlers maintain their health and identities in newly acquired colonies?[88] Colonization was a deeply embodied and anxious experience.

Legal definitions of what made an English subject did not necessarily operate independently of medical conceptions of what happened to transplanted bodies. Periods of what colonists referred to as "seasoning" was a period of temporary adjustment to a new environment that often resulted in illness. Lingering within words like "seasoning" and "naturalization" were questions about the degree to which transplantation and settlement was a physical process that altered porous bodies, complexions, temperaments, and, quite possibly, individual and political identity and loyalty. To what degree did abstract concepts such as political naturalization, for instance, rely on an understanding of the process by which plants acclimatized to new soils and climates to give it greater conceptual force, and what can the use of such a metaphor reveal about early modern English ideas about the nature of political belonging, particularly given humoral understandings of the body and temperament?[89]

Colonists worried that their malleable human bodies, much like plants, might be transformed in new soils and airs and ruminated on the extent of change. Moreover, if people and landscapes might be cultivated and improved, logic suggests the opposite was also possible, resulting in disordered and degenerated people and places. Officials feared that their plans for the "peopling," "settling," and improving of recently conquered Jamaica, for instance, might be confounded, and made more complicated, by its uncertain legal status, its topographical and climatological variations, and the challenge of transplanting thriving plants and healthy populations alike.[90]

In addition to the possibility that the porous humoral bodies of English colonists might be transformed while living in lands that did not have an "affinity" with the English climate, there was also legal uncertainty about the status of English subjects, and the subject status of their descendants, when they moved permanently across the Atlantic. Although "it was becoming accepted that birth on English soil should be the criteria of whether a person had the rights of an English subject" in the centuries before the English established permanent American colonies, new questions arose in the context of a growing English empire.[91] Lord Coke's judgment in Calvin's Case (1608) confirmed that "persons born abroad were able to acquire the status of a subject" provided at the time of their birth their parents were "under the actual obedience of the king," but it was not entirely clear what this meant "in practical terms," nor did Coke outline how many generations this inherited subject status might last.[92] Thus, whereas scholars have outlined the changing legal definitions of English subject status, this book specifically looks to the environmental and medical discourses that offered alternative ways in which early modern English men and women understood subject status.

New scents might alter attitudes, and unfamiliar foods could also infuse bodies with strength or lead to poor health. Settlers, including the women who would populate the colony with the next generation, knew the success of their endeavors required healthy bodies that had enough to eat. Armies and navies of an expanding English empire likewise required more people to regulate, protect, and facilitate the expanding empire. Yet neither residents of England nor colonists within an expanding English empire were at the mercy or whim of nature alone. English and colonial officials regularly touted their improvement projects as beneficial to residents, including their fertility. By planting sweet-smelling gardens and trees, draining unhealthy swamps, and crafting laws to regulate behavior and lessen the likelihood of infection, officials engaged in practices they claimed were for the benefit of subjects' bodies. As the empire expanded, and as England encompassed and claimed more domestic lands through drainage, contemporaries continually reassessed what it meant to live a distinctively English life and debated the cultural, political, and territorial limits of Englishness. As numerous scholars have pointed out, early modern identities were not fixed traits but, rather, were transformable and associated with a range of material practices.[93] Thus, as Restoration officials grappled with questions about whether or not to integrate non-English inhabitants as subjects within the empire, they simultaneously wondered if English settlers living at such a distance were really still English, politically and physically.[94]

This volume reveals that not all bodies would be welcome in this reconstituted and expanding body politic, nor were all spaces conducive to those bodies or activities deemed acceptably English. In the early modern era, many people found themselves labeled barbarous, animal-like, or otherwise unfit to join the expanding English empire as subjects.[95] Although exclusion was certainly a key feature of community formation in the latter half of the seventeenth century, and this book discusses places and people imagined to be unfit to join the imperial community, it also identifies a range of activities and schemes that highlight how the Restoration government did not limit its efforts to define its political communities with binary categories of inclusion and exclusion alone. Instead, agents of the Restoration government imagined that some people and places might be refashioned, or "new-mold[ed]," into desirable English subjects and absorbed into the expanding body politic.[96] The idea of transforming disparate people and places relied on the belief that bodies, and bodies politic, were malleable, as were the landscapes in which they dwelt. While other scholars may have discussed colonists' practices of scrutinizing bodies to make claims about the successes or failures of their colonial enterprises, this project highlights Stuart ambitions to do so to manipulate targeted communities and landscapes.[97]

The projectors and officials who offered up a variety of schemes that would lead to the transformation and improvement of peoples and landscapes, or who offered the means to remold conquered colonial communities into English subjects, used terminology suggestive of acts of making and remaking that circulated widely in the Restoration era. These metaphors and expressions of concepts like *improvement, restoration, transformation,* and *reformation* were part of a much broader "structure of feeling," or widespread longing, that prevailed in a world that had only recently devolved into the violence and incoherence of war and required new methods and aims of rule.⁹⁸ Although the king had himself been restored, it was difficult to say what it was that had been restored. Much had remained the same, but much had also changed during his exile.⁹⁹ Certainly, many plans of improvement recycled language from earlier generations of writers. But if some midcentury writers expressed a millenarian impulse to bring about "a redemptive future" through social reforms, their enthusiastic pronouncements smacked of sectarian disorder by the king's Restoration.¹⁰⁰ Restoration-era reformers who hoped to avoid suspicion of harboring radical or dissenting views used different language in their proposals. They no longer gestured to universal reform; instead, they promised a range of improvements that would benefit the nation.

An Empire Transformed examines schemes of control articulated by Restoration writers and Stuart officials that took place at the level of garden, field, and fen. The often small-scale nature of their improvement projects, however, still reflected imperial goals. As a result, this study takes seriously Owen Stanwood's claim that, "The story of the making of empire must necessarily be both intensely local and transatlantic in scope."¹⁰¹ This book tracks language operating at two levels, both detailing improvement projects on the ground, in the newly tilled soil of the field, and in the realm of language and concept, elaborated in a range of private and public documents authored, for instance, by officials in London and in the colonies. They wrestled with abstract ideas about the relationship of subjects' bodies to various spaces within the empire. Meanwhile, environmental alterations wrought by ploughs, seeds, drainage ditches, and spades—and the intent to transform the health and lifeways of local residents—can tell us a great deal about the aims and daily processes of empire formation and illuminate or highlight facets of local encounters and settlement that we might otherwise overlook. They also allow us to see when and where residents pushed back against such schemes, by refusing to build required drainage works, for instance.

Alterations made to the physical environment, alongside many unrealized schemes to do so, offer a range of sources in which to read and consider the practices and expectations of English imperial expansion, settlement, and reorganization. Sources, including manuals on gardening and arboriculture, city plans outlining new thoroughfares and green spaces, and proclamations and court orders calling for small- and large-scale drainage works, for instance, are all texts that have helped to define and characterize the archival ground of this study. Medical treatises underscore seventeenth-century ideas about the connection between place and human health, including fears espoused by early modern English men and women about the potentially deleterious effects of new airs and foods on their bodies, even as many still traveled and settled in new places.[102] An examination of the records of various governing agencies, such as the Privy Council, the Lords of Trade and Plantation, as well as legislation formulated by colonial officials, reveals the language authorities used when detailing or demanding the alteration of landscapes, or delimiting social behavior in certain places, often documenting their perceptions of the connection between place, health, and deportment in the process. The records of the Royal Society, the king's "Parliament of Nature," also reveal what people adjacent to the court considered to be their role in collecting useful knowledge in service of the state.[103] In conjunction, these texts reveal how Charles II and his supporters invented roles for themselves by proposing or endorsing schemes of environmental transformation that promised to transform subjects' health as well as restore political order and economic prosperity.

While their plans of improvement rarely unfolded as planned, Ann Laura Stoler encourages scholars to consider what can be gained by "developing historical negatives" in imperial archives.[104] Such archives of failures can reveal "state fantasies" and its "visions of the future."[105] The records also demonstrate that the outsized aims extolled by agents of the Crown often sit alongside records documenting confusion and uncertainty, highlighting the often chaotic reality behind their plans. Even though a number of their projects failed, however, or did not unfold as planned, many of their visions rippled out into the Atlantic world, which had critical implications for the lived experiences of numerous residents within the empire. The chapters in this book are arranged in an order that roughly follows where reformers met with more success in implementing their schemes and concludes with a chapter that investigates a project that was never undertaken, at least not on the scale or in the manner outlined.

The various projects tracked in this book also connect imperial improvement schemes and domestic state-building projects. Although scholars such as Philippa Levine have considered how the "internal colonialism" of Wales, Scotland, and Ireland established patterns for English imperialism abroad and was shaped in turn by those relationships, they have not necessarily considered projects within England itself as part of this story.[106] For instance, proponents of fen drainage in eastern England promised that drainage would reveal immense acreage of arable land; it would be an easily accessible "Florida," or a *new* New World waiting to be revealed in London's backyard.[107] Meanwhile, projectors who schemed to cultivate and process "good sugar" out of apples hoped to "turne England into Barbados."[108] Such statements highlight the need for alternative modes of conceptualizing contemporaries' geographic imaginations within empire.

Indeed, many writers saw continuities between the improvements initiated at home and abroad, or as mutually reinforcing a greater goal. William Petty asserted that the king's expanding empire, in which more settlers cultivated more land and claimed it for England, was inextricably related to the opening up and improving of lands domestically. They were parallel, and sometimes mutually reinforcing, projects. According to Petty, "It is not much to be doubted, But that the Territory Under the Kings Dominions have increased" and that territory under his control now included New England, Virginia, Barbados, Jamaica, Tangier, Bombay, and Dunkirk. Moreover, there was a greater quantity of arable land in England, Scotland, and Ireland due to "the drayning of the ffens, watering of dry grounds, Improving of fforrests and comons," and by the transformation of barren into healthy land. Improvers had also multiplied "severall sorts of ffruits and Garden stuffe" and had made "some Rivers Navigable," so that the "power and Wealth of England hath increased this last 40 years" in these numerous, interrelated ways.[109] In short, Petty estimated that there was more land, more provisions, more people, and more trade. He saw such territorial acquisition and domestic improvement and land reclamation projects as parallel, related stories of English ascendance. Similarly, the *Philosophical Transactions* of the Royal Society touted the numerous landscape improvement projects that spanned the Atlantic, approving the "Dutch Gardiners" who planted "Nurseries" in Scotland and complimenting how Ireland "shakes off her pristin laziness, being now busy in providing fine Linnen . . . tilling more land, and in turning their Mossy grounds into Gardens of Potatoes." Meanwhile, "the very wilderness of *New England* is, on a suddain, become a fruitful Orchard, fenced with Ships of their own building," and "in less time, by the God's blessing, *Jamaica* may be the fairest Garden of the World."[110] The authors surmised that improvement projects spanning the Anglo-Atlantic were interconnected enterprises, and collectively promised prosperity, welfare, and demographic strength.

Concurrent improvement projects undertaken within England and in the Atlantic colonies highlight the need for a wider frame. These points of similarity do not necessarily represent a unified vision of territorial dominance but, rather, point to a series of actions taken to address the relationship of fragmented communities and landscapes to the state. Particular topographies inspired certain kinds of actions. Fears of inaccessible wetlands and of those individuals who called those landscapes home led to drainage projects in English, Irish, and colonial landscapes alike. When Restoration officials considered the fate of Jamaica, they looked to those with experience with islands, particularly islands with warm climes, such as St. Helena, to suggest appropriate plant transplantation schemes. Using a comparative Atlantic lens reveals an ongoing and critical dialogue between domestic and imperial developments.[111]

Due to the rapid acquisition of territory and the conquest of ethnically diverse colonists, Restoration officials formulated innovative responses when reforming the relationship between the monarch and his subjects. Many scholars have disagreed about the capacity of the Restoration government to make good on its aims and emphasize the failure of the Crown to achieve its goals of centralizing and codifying colonial control. Numerous scholars have argued that Restoration-era empire building remained largely on paper, or in the minds of officials, and was not yet a reality. Meanwhile, others have noted the capacious aims of the Restoration court and have elected to focus on those times when Charles II succeeded in asserting greater control over portions of his domains or subjects.[112] One might be tempted to settle the score on the work and legacy of Charles II and his officials by investigating whether the Restoration court succeeded or failed in establishing and enacting coherent policy across diverse terrain. My work, however, builds on Paul Warde's insights that it is not necessarily illuminating to emphasize early modern states' strengths or weaknesses as this collapses "the multiplicity of governmental action" into a stark divide of success or failure. According to Warde, "It is surely permissible for 'the state' to be good at some things and bad at others."[113] This study investigates a period of innovation during which contemporaries reassessed the purpose of colonies, weighed their benefits and drawbacks, and suggested a range of activities in relation to subjects' bodies and particular kinds of landscapes that offer insights into how Restoration officials envisioned and enacted authority within a rapidly changing English empire.

The first chapter of this volume focuses on efforts to rebuild London after a devastating plague in 1665 and a massive conflagration destroyed much of the medieval walled city in 1666. Their debates about urban redesign demonstrate that environmental improvement projects were intended to heal and civilize resident populations. Their schemes sought to restrict the movements and behaviors of "nasty folks," the poor accused of carrying contagion. The sources serve as a reminder that authorities' rhetoric about cleanliness was deployed to forcibly relocate some residents and assert control over different classes of people.[114] Writers and officials published persuasive tracts, proclamations, and poetry reflecting on the new buildings and behaviors they expected in the rebuilt city. Architects of the new London hoped that they might build the new version of the city with proactive attention to human health, increased control over public spaces, and further regulation of individuals' movement and behaviors within the city. Moreover, this chapter highlights how their projects of urban redesign inspired planned cities around the Anglo-Atlantic, including Charleston, Philadelphia, and Kingston.

Beyond London, projectors hoping to reclaim the fenlands similarly grappled with how to remake unhealthy, uncivil residents into healthy subjects residing in well-ordered landscapes. Debates about how to remold and refashion people living in or near wetlands are the subjects of chapters 2 and 3. Chapter 2 examines wetland drainage projects in the fenlands of southeastern England. The chapter details Bedford Level Corporation projectors' efforts to drain, and claim, over three hundred thousand acres of fenlands in the Great Level in the 1660s and examines their assertions that this work would benefit fenland residents. Fen-drainage projectors spoke of transforming the riot-prone, web-footed, hunched, and pale residents of the watery fenlands of eastern England into healthy and productive economic actors. They accused residents of the fens of having been shaped physiologically—and psychologically—by their marshy environs. Their riotous reputations were attributed to the socially isolated and watery landscapes in which they resided. Drainage projectors described the challenging marsh and wetland landscapes of the fenlands as "a wildernesse of water," and asserted such qualities explained inhabitants' status as physical and social outsiders.[115] Inhabitants of the fens did not agree with these characterizations of their homes and in alternative publications emphasized their rich and varied diets and accused projectors of stealing their land. These debates over private property, possession, and authority also feature in the following chapter.

Collectively, chapters 2 and 3 reveal that concurrent drainage projects were undertaken in the colonies and in England, underscoring the need for a comparative Atlantic frame. Chapter 3 examines wetland drainage projects proposed by representatives of colonial New York's new proprietor, James, Duke of York. The governor, Edmund Andros, required local inhabitants to assist in building ditch and drainage works in order to transform the extensive marshland surrounding New Castle, the most prominent settlement along that section of the Delaware River. The new government found the marshlands inaccessible in the best of times, dangerous and impenetrable in the worst. Wetland landscapes along the Delaware physically limited political oversight from New York, whereas drained land enabled access, particularly with the additional construction of bridges and roads. Andros required such infrastructure in the aftermath of his first official appearance in New Castle. Authorities directed newly incorporated residents of the colonial empire, including the Dutch, Finns, and Swedes on the Delaware River, to remake landscapes at the behest of the English colonial government, in English ways.

Chapter 4 follows plans to improve agricultural output, influence consumption patterns, and manage population numbers in England and in the colonies. The Restoration government was aware that the scarcity of food was a likely cause of social and political instability. In order to ensure stability and to increase population size, the king's advisers urged him to manage landscapes and to keep people well fed. Moreover, improvers celebrated the work of cultivation as the means to cultivate the so-called deserving poor as the latter labored to transform wastelands into productive spaces, transforming their own social value in the process.[116] They imagined that pruning, sowing, tilling, and weeding were all means by which men and women might learn, or relearn, the values of duty, work, and civic-mindedness in the wake of wartime disruptions. Those governing England further claimed for themselves the right to intervene in the bodies of English subjects by suggesting, and at times legislating, modes of production, forms of labor, and access to food.

The final chapter considers plans to create two gardens in London and Jamaica on behalf of the king. In 1661 merchants and members of the king's new Council for Foreign Plantations and the East India Company planned the construction of two garden "plantations" on either side of the Atlantic, one in England and the other in Jamaica. The king's advisers requested specimens notable for their flower, smell, and medicinal uses. They imagined that the transplantation and cultivation of medicines would serve to heal the bodies of the king's subjects. They also intended for the soothing aromas to quiet any remnants of the "political disorder" of the previous decades of war and England's experiment with republicanism.[117] Sweetly scented air led to longer-lived, better-tempered, and more virtuous subjects in London. The king anticipated that "alimentary" and scented plants might similarly assist with strengthening and governing Jamaica with specially cultivated "smellscapes."[118] These garden transplantation schemes offer tangible evidence of one approach utilized by the Restoration government to incorporate potentially subversive places and people into the growing English empire. Moreover, discussions about the success or failure of transplanted plants surviving and thriving in a new place offered insight into the potential success or failure of human settlement and naturalization.

This book deploys a transatlantic framework by tracking concurrent domestic and imperial projects of improvement. By highlighting the connections between histories of the body, histories of the environment, and political histories, it offers a new perspective on how the Stuarts sought to consolidate power and manage their subjects in the later seventeenth century, which was an enormous challenge. Officials recognized that a far-flung and growing empire with myriad local climates and a dizzying array of local laws required innovative governing strategies. Potentially destabilizing threats came not only from poorly defined or poorly controlled spaces within the empire but also from unhealthy and unruly bodies. A group of elite thinkers, well-connected merchants, projectors, and officials seeking support from the Crown for their various plans thus drew parallels between unhealthy bodies and a malfunctioning state, and between healthy bodies and a functioning state, and offered advice the king might follow to stabilize his political position.[119] As a would-be healer of bodies and improver of landscapes, the king could offer new justifications for his rule and naturalize his sovereignty in innovative ways. Through projects that manipulated the environment, Charles II and his advisers sought to connect distant, heterogeneous, and scattered settlements and peoples into a stable, governable, and healthy polity during an era of imperial expansion and reorganization.

1 /   Sinful, Sick, and Misbehaving Bodies: Fires, Smoke, and Pestilence in London

In 1665 and 1666 London was hit with two back-to-back disasters. As the poet Jeremiah Wells wrote succinctly in 1667, first God "kill'd th' Inhabitants, then burnt the Town."[1] In 1665 London was struck by a devastating plague. In 1666 much of the medieval walled city and its environs was destroyed by a "most lamentable and devouring" fire.[2] Wells was one of numerous observers who saw in such devastation God's terrifying Judgment. He noted that God must be very angry and that the residents of London were clearly the targets of his just vengeance.[3] Londoners, and the nation more broadly, were left to consider both why God had sent tragedies of such magnitude and how they might stop His destructive wrath from taking aim at them again. While God played an important role in contemporary explanations for the onset of these back-to-back disasters, English men and women likewise considered numerous proximate causes of the plague and fire. Meanwhile, while unexpected, calamitous, and destructive, the fire offered Londoners the opportunity to imagine and discuss what their city could look like, as well as to consider how its inhabitants should move through or interact with a newly built landscape and with one another. Among the numerous schemes elite Londoners authored and designed on rebuilding the City, they offered plans detailing how the city's various communities should be rearranged morally, healthfully, and spatially.

When contemporaries reflected on rebuilding the City of London, they produced persuasive tracts, drew maps and plans, drafted proclamations, and wrote poetry reflecting on the ideal form it should take.

Writers offered a range of advice to the devastated citizens of London. These various sources offer a broad view of what Londoners imagined the purpose of a city to be and how its reconstruction, and the further regulation of the city's infrastructure, might promote public health and a range of additional, intangible ideals. Londoners debated the ideal aesthetic appearance and structure of a city and considered how its residents should interact—or not—within its alleyways, lanes, markets, coffeehouses, and taverns. Therefore, their numerous written productions on restoring and improving London's urban landscape, particularly those transformations intended to moderate the health and living conditions of Londoners, "mediate and thus expose to view the particular social tensions of their times."[4] Elite authors and planners imagined the best ways to regulate the seemingly unregulated poorer residents of the city, including their movements, health, and characters.

When residents debated how to rebuild the medieval City of London, as well as those neighborhoods beyond the walls that had also burned, they considered both the plague and the fire as catastrophic lessons from which they might learn. These devastating disasters inspired proactive planning, new city proclamations, and legislation intended to transform the human and urban built landscapes alike. Writers like Wells celebrated London's quick recovery in the aftermath of devastating plague and reminded readers that just as numbers lost to pestilence had been quickly replaced by recruiting new citizens, or "fresh supplies," to the city, he likewise saw London's potential to recover from the "Ashes" and "ruinous heap" to which it had been reduced by fire. Indeed, Wells imagined that citizens would quickly rebuild the City, and better than ever.[5] Wells and others recognized that urban living, particularly the constructed landscape itself, had exacerbated the effects of plague and fire. For instance, population density in crowded urban spaces increased the chance of contracting an ailment by a close encounter with a sick person on London's busy streets; meanwhile, the materials with which people constructed their homes, and the close proximity of city dwellings, increased the speed and size of the fire, which had consumed all in its path. In other words, the effects of plague and fire were amplified by the modes in which people constructed and lived in the cityscape.[6]

New designs for restructuring the physical layout of the city included projections for the transformations of society.[7] Architects of the new London hoped that the city might be rebuilt with proactive attention to human health, increased control over public spaces, and the further regulation of individuals' movements. In addition to aesthetic pleasure, the new buildings and streets should promote moral rectitude. Before the fire, London was a confused maze of streets, and the buildings were as "deformed as the minds & confusions of the people."[8] Even before the fire, the intellectual and avid horticulturalist John Evelyn had offered numerous visions for a rebuilt London and had written scathingly of the medieval city. After the fire, Evelyn promised that in a few years' time, if those undertaking to rebuild London followed his plans, they would have the reward of witnessing "such a city to emerge out of these sad and ruinous heaps, as may dispute it with all the cities of the World, fitter for commerce, apter for government, sweeter for health, more glorious for beauty; and in sum for whatsoever indeed could be desired to render it consummately perfect."[9] He offered numerous visions of the future city to which he hoped London's rebuilders would aspire.

Many schemes to rebuild London focused on how new construction might influence residents' health and behavior. For instance, commodious streets might provide better ventilation, allowing healthful air into the formerly cramped and narrow alleys. Evelyn and others noted the links between the built landscape and the physical and physiological impact on the city's residents, and reformers sought to reform both human bodies and attitudes alongside the rebuilt urban landscape. Among the oft-mentioned reforms touted by contemporary writers was street paving. These writers insisted that paved roads were easier to keep clean than cobbled stone. Thus the "filth" of the city streets, and their foul odors, might be more preventable, thereby keeping control over one perceived cause of dangerous pestilence: odor.[10] As one of the fundamental elements of a humoral conception of human health, air mattered a great deal to an individual's constitution, mind, personality, and temper.[11] Early modern men and women imagined air as the "sweet ruler that influences the wisdom, power, and appearance of man, of animals, and of plants."[12] Qualities of the air, including smell and temperature, mattered to the residents of early modern England because they understood their bodies as "almost perpetually contiguous" with the "ambient Air" as they breathed it in and exhaled it back out, or as it seeped into the numerous pores covering the body, transforming not only the *Faces* and *Physiognomy*, but also the *Souls* and *Minds* of Men."[13] Salubrious airs could cure, and people often traveled to receive the benefit of such airs.[14] But bad airs, or miasmas, which were often identified as foul smells, could kill.

Thus, it was not only the benefit to human health but a desire to reform Londoners' behavior and to facilitate a new moral order that drove city planners to dream of rebuilding London by featuring green spaces, constructing buildings imbued with architectural grandeur, and laying out majestic, wide streets. Such awe-inspiring construction, made up of straightened streets, and upward-reaching buildings, built toward the heavens, might offer daily reminders of the strength and power of the king and the city's officers who resided, worked, or issued proclamations from such magnificent structures, or rode carriages on the new thoroughfares. Authors claimed that straight roads were conducive to orderly comportment on those roads, which might lead more generally to orderly and well-behaved Londoners.[15]

Evelyn, a founding member of the Royal Society who was later appointed to the Council of Foreign Plantations, emphasized the importance of clear air, visibility, and the necessity of offering calculated views of particular parts of the city for the benefit of both residents and visitors to the city. Such emphasis on visibility points to the dreams of the architects and their patrons to have a better view of—and thereby extend more control over—the residents of the urban landscape, and suggest the state's incipient obsession with visibility and oversight.[16] Broader, parallel streets increased visibility and facilitated control and "publik order."[17] Wide, unimpeded, and paved avenues could also promote trade. In this way, planners imagined a physically reconstructed London to be more accessible, controllable, and profitable. Evelyn further suggested moving smoke-producing industries beyond the walls of the city to preserve Londoners' lungs and enable greater visibility. Various writers deployed imagery of light or sunshine in their works to suggest the importance of viewing and visibility in Restoration London. In his treatise on the rebuilding of London, Samuel Rolle envisioned that the rebuilt city would be "like that more excellent creature, *viz* the Sun, which disperseth clouds and darkness, wheresoever he cometh."[18]

Indeed, the conceptual links between the sun, light, and public order appeared repeatedly in the late seventeenth century.[19] Supporters similarly compared Charles II's Restoration to the English throne to the cloud-dispersing rays of the sun clearing away the roiling clouds of revolution and social upheaval. A king who could see all might control all.[20] The shining, bright brilliancy of the sun, lighting the city and a nation, further alluded to heavenly oversight. If light was associated with knowledge, order, reason, and memory, by contrast darkness was associated with ignorance, confusion, and forgetfulness. In 1670 New York governor Francis Lovelace complained to civil servant and member of Parliament Joseph Williamson that he lived in darkness, "as if we had as well crossed Lethae as the 'Atlantiq' ocean" since he had no news of affairs in London.[21] By linking darkness, distance, and ignorance, Lovelace compared his assignment in New York to the oblivion of the dead in the underworld.

Tracing the rhetoric, plans, and legislation both considered and enacted in the rebuilding of London can thus tell us a great deal about the aims and state-building practices of Restoration officials. During both plague and fire, and in schemes for the rebuilding process, numerous officials sought to extend their reach over Londoners' daily lives by asserting the need for greater control, claiming they did so for the good and safety of the people. Restoration officials seized the opportunity— in the chaotic wake of pestilence and fire—to articulate plans to transform the confused maze of streets, as well as the riotous, heterogeneous residents who traversed them, into well-behaved subjects. In addition to making the city more governable, officials sought to improve the health of the city's residents by staving off myriad disorders.

In the aftermath of these catastrophic events, the king wrested additional control over the City of London Corporation and its ability to define "the freemen of the . . . City," by inviting workers from all over England to assist in rebuilding. Among the many decrees issued in the postfire city, the Rebuilding Act of 1667 "compelled the guilds to lift their restrictions on the employment of skilled craftsmen in London."[22] These incidences reveal the changing relationship between borough corporations and the Crown in the aftermath of disaster.[23] Meanwhile, by intervening in the movements, conduct, and medical practices engaged in by numerous residents of London, and by encouraging physicians to advise on legislation, medical experts were in a position to link the public and private spheres. They achieved new prominence by offering medical advice in print to the king's subjects. Since a strong nation was supposed to be a healthy, populous nation of well-formed subjects, their work was a kind of statecraft.[24] An urban space like London, with its close quarters and direct relationship between medical legislation and the built environment, offers a useful place to underscore the deeply physical conception of the political subject in the early modern English Atlantic.

This chapter examines instances of legislation intended to control the built environment, often accompanied by discussions about how these laws might transform physical bodies and temperaments, thereby altering national health and character. Annabel Brett has argued for the "pivotal role that cities played in the multiple paths to state formation."[25] A close examination of the processes by which officials sought to intervene in the health and moral order of London's residents reveals attitudes and practices debated and tested in urban settings, including in London, elsewhere in England, and around the Atlantic.

Historians have suggested that the myriad discussions about the best ways to rebuild the City of London in the wake of plague and fire, and the designs submitted to do so, likely influenced city-planning ideas around the Anglo-Atlantic world.[26] Recent scholarship on the "urban Atlantic" argues that even when "scaling back" to investigate cities their work reveals "large-scale Atlantic processes" unfolding from a fresh perspective.[27] This chapter suggests that London was an experimental site to test, articulate, and translate ideas about the regulation of urban residents and spaces. Colonial plans for Pennsylvania and Georgia, like the Lords Proprietors' "Grand Modell of Government" for Carolina, paid a great deal of attention to physical layout and regularly articulated the benefits of the proposed layouts to settlers' health and safety.[28] The 1681 plan for William Penn's "green Country Towne" proposed that every house should be placed "in the middle of its plat . . . so that there may be ground on each side for gardens or orchards, or fields" and may have been a response to the back-to-back calamities that Londoners had endured. To those residents who had lived through London's threats of plague, miasmas, coal smoke, and fire, Penn promised a "green Country Towne, which will never be burnt and always wholesome."[29] Penn's rebuke suggested that unlike the overcrowded, congested, smoky, disease- and crime-ridden, and morally suspect city of London, his *wholesome* town would incorporate important lessons learned, and implemented, that would stave off a similar fate. He asserted that the physical layout of Philadelphia was designed to combat the myriad social, medical, and political threats that elsewhere led to disorder and disease. Wider thoroughfares, for instance, solved several problems at once. Broad avenues allowed for more airflow, less congestion, some fire prevention, and fewer dark corners where unobserved dark deeds might be done. Londoners' responses to plague and fire, and their plans to rebuild the city, shaped attitudes toward city planning around the Anglo-Atlantic.[30]

A consideration of sites of urban redesign further suggests that early modern governments were engaged not only in the transformation of colonial "wildernesses" into cultivated gardens when seeking to transform residents of the empire; when promoting political order, social discipline, and public health in London and other urban settings, officials similarly assumed that the spatial dimensions and physical transformations were critical to success.[31] Measures taken to transform colonial people and space resembled plans to promote civic order and public health in London. The parallel processes taken to control disordered places in the colonial and domestic realms suggest that officials' management of the empire and intensified measures to manipulate populations at home shared both goals and the measures taken to achieve them. Many of the same questions about order, health, morality, and improvement drove improvers' schemes, whether in London, Philadelphia, or Port Royal. Moreover, a focus on London reminds us that officials' aspirations to manipulate and transform populations was not limited to colonized spaces and people.

In late seventeenth-century London, varied authorities, including city officials, aldermen, members of the Royal College of Physicians, as well as pamphlet writers with connections to public officials and privy councilors, articulated schemes to govern the daily lives of the inhabitants of London and legislate their conduct and movements by reordering the material landscape. Such actions demonstrate the degree to which the early modern state aspired to intervene in the lives of its subjects.[32] Commentators promised a range of outcomes as a result of those material improvements, including rendering subjects more controllable and governable. Authorities sought to utilize ideas about the connections between place, health, and attitude in order to establish control. Improving London's streetscapes was not merely an abstract notion of improvement but represented interventions by which Restoration officials intended to govern subjects' conduct and express ideological concepts through the built environment. Projects of urban redesign and debates about the relationship of cityscapes to social control and public health reverberated across the empire and were, in turn, shaped by conversations about improving and controlling imperial places and people.

"Foul Bodies" and Plague

The first reports of the plague were issued in the early months of 1665 in the parish of St. Giles-in-the-Fields.[33] At first "it appeared to be only in the outskirts of the town, and in the most obscure alleys, amongst the poorest people," but it spread quickly.[34] The Earl of Clarendon later recounted how many people remained unworried by the appearance of plague in the overcrowded quarters on the edges of the city, imagining they were safely ensconced in wealthier neighborhoods and protected by their individual constitutions and by their manner or mode of living. The social geography of the city placed such undesirable people in contained neighborhoods. But "the ancient men, who well remembered in what manner the last great plague (which had been near forty years before) first brake out, and the progress it afterwards made, foretold a terrible summer." Many began moving their family members to the country even though "their neighbours laughed at their providence, and thought they might have stayed without danger: but they found shortly that they had done wisely."[35] In the face of a widespread and growing epidemic, Charles II and his court decamped to Oxford.[36] On April 30, 1665, the Restoration administrator and Royal Society member Samuel Pepys wrote in his diary that there were "Great fears of the sickenesse here in the City, it being said that two or three houses are already shut up. God preserve us all!"[37]

At the end of the month Pepys visited a coffeehouse, "where all the news is . . . of the plague growing upon us in this town; and of remedies against it: some saying one thing, and some another."[38] Walking in London a week later, on June 7, on "the hottest day that ever I felt in my life," Pepys recorded that he saw more evidence of the plague: "This day, much against my will, I did in Drury Lane see two or three houses marked with a red cross upon the doors, and 'Lord have Mercy upon us' writ there; which was a sad sight to me, being the first of the kind that to my remembrance I ever saw."[39] Officials had marked these doors to indicate the presence of pestilence and to warn those passing by to avoid the infected house and residents, who had all been locked within for six weeks in accordance with plague regulations. As with many passersby, the sight of the plague-marked homes worried Pepys, and he feared for his own health and safety in the presence of contagion. It put him "into an ill conception" of himself and his "smell." He purchased some tobacco to chew on, "which took away the apprehension," because he considered chewing tobacco, particularly its powerful taste and smell, a powerful antiplague measure.[40] In his publication *A discourse of the plague* (1665), Gideon Harvey, later appointed physician to the king in 1675, suggested the use of tobacco for purifying the air and preventing contagion. In fact, it was one of his foremost recommended preservatives for the poor who could not afford his perfumed cordial bags of exotic spices. Harvey wrote that "To smoak Tobacco . . . seems an excellent Preservative" and that "Its judged by many, that Issues conduce to divert the malignity; but chiefly in children and [those with] moyst Constitutions."[41] The specter of death loomed, and many Londoners lived in fear. Those who remained in the city witnessed extraordinarily high rates of mortality among the city's residents, including the deaths of whole families at a time.[42] The summer months of 1665 were the deadliest, but the spread of the plague continued through 1666. While the numbers of the infected and dying had declined by the summer of 1666, hundreds were still dying.[43] Estimated suggest that as many as one hundred thousand Londoners died from the bubonic plague, or approximately one in five residents.[44] Many more throughout England likewise perished as the contagion spread beyond the city.

Such devastating mortality led to several outcomes. Elite writers of treatises about the plague took control of the written narratives about the causes of contagion and indicated that some intemperate, corrupting, and unclean members of the community, and the places where they lived and recreated, were to blame. While there were various cited causes, particularly claims that contagion originated with God, many took the opportunity to write vitriolic statements about the "foul bodies" of the poor and the behaviors of the "Vulgar" inhabitants of London, as if the "nasty folks, as beggars, and others" were to blame for the spread of the God-sent plague.[45] Narratives about the plague were thus "integrally involved in the definition of cultural boundaries and the ordering of social spaces"[46] In these writings, the social body, like the multitude of bodies belonging to that society, was described as threatened on all fronts by filthy, morally degenerate, undesirable vagrants and lower-class rabble, who tended to be spatially contained in certain areas of the city but might penetrate into other areas.

Because they believed that good health involved a complex relationship of environmental factors, daily behaviors or habits, and individual attitude, morality, and outlook, those narrating the events of 1665 at once linked putrid places and people and constructed certain urban spaces and people as dangerous to the community and its collective health. Taverns and alehouses, like gutters and ditches, and houses "crowded with [a] multiplicity of logers and nasty families," were all collectively to blame in many plague tracts.[47] These intricate and overlapping claims about the degeneration of morality and health, and how degeneration reflected issues of class, often focused on particular spatial locations within the city. Moreover, because contagion was often associated with particular people and places, plague regulations increasingly subjected certain residents to heightened restrictions. The interventions promoted by elite writers were taken up by royal, city, and ecclesiastical leaders and directed at particular segments of the population, and at the behaviors and bodies they deemed dangerous to the proper functioning of the body politic. One such set of policies was Plague Orders, which restricted the movement of those infected. Finally, in the aftermath of the devastating fire in 1666 that destroyed much of the medieval city, authorities discussed and addressed some of the claims about the causes of plague in relation to the urban environment during the rebuilding process. For instance, it is likely that calls for paved and widened streets were a means to address some of the perceived causes of plague, such as rotting waste caught between cobblestones.[48]

During epidemics, an individual's health became a public concern. During an epidemic such as the plague, perhaps unlike almost any other early modern health concern, rulers and their officials got involved because of the sheer numbers of people involved, the perceived threats to communal order caused by so many painful deaths and mass burials, and because of the scale of city- and nationwide contagion. Disease disrupted London's "social and spatial order" by refusing to remain in expected places or in the bodies of particular kinds of people.[49] As scholars have noted, by the late seventeenth century epidemics were widely understood to require at least some state intervention, particularly in terms of population control in the form of Plague Orders. As Margaret Healy has argued, "Epidemics, by their very nature demand political responses and provide a good opportunity and rationale for intervention into the lives of others, for the re-ordering of bodies."[50] Officials had the resources available to enforce at least some of the restrictions. Epidemics required officials to reimagine the relationship between illness, bodies, and community.

Moreover, plague infections became narratives of national import in a way that individuals' ailments generally did not. People commonly attributed plagues to God's deadly wrath in response to collective, national sins. In 1665 various writers pointed out that "Our Sins were the Parents of this *Pestilence*" and that it was only through the "most Mighty and Merciful Lord God, in whose hands are health and sickness, who at thy pleasure canst kill and comfort," that individuals, communities, and nations could be collectively cleansed of their sins and sickness.[51] God, imagined as the "best Physician, both of our Souls and Bodies, who canst bring to the Grave, and pull back again, whom thou pleasest," had struck down London because of the residents' "want of Charity, and the neglect of the Poor" of the city.[52] If it was their collective sins that wrought plague, it was by their collective repentance and coordinated behavior that they might stay God's further vengeance. Throughout the Atlantic world, residents offered providential explanations to account for the destruction of wicked, debauched cities. Like Londoners in the aftermath of plague and fire, numerous residents of Port Royal recognized the "terrible Judgement of God" in the earthquake that destroyed the port city in 1692.[53] Sources widely recognized that as an "Ungodly Debauched People" they had brought this destruction upon themselves.[54]

Residents expected state intervention, in part, because of the terminology used to describe and explain how contagion *attacked* or *invaded* people and communities. As Healy has further argued, threats of contamination were regularly described in militaristic terms and thus required equally violent responses. Throughout the early modern era, writers described plagues as attacks on the people of London as an enemy army might attack the city and its residents. Writers "associate[d] urban plague with a city under military siege and suffering enemy despoliation."[55] In the seventeenth century, narratives about plague infection reconfigured some residents as insiders and others as outsiders. Plague attacked the City of London like an enemy threatening to overcome the city by violence. Similarly, venomous and corrupt air threatened to invade the body.

Causes and Cures

According to Gideon Harvey, author of numerous treatises on the medical ailments of the day, the appearance of plagues was commonly related to, or followed, providential signs such as "great Inundations, Stinks of Rivers, unburied Carcases, Mortality of Cattel, Withering of Trees, Extinction of Plants, an extraordinary multiplication of Froggs, Toads, Mice, Flies, or other Insects and Reptils," or even a "moderate Winter, a warm and moist Spring and Summer, fiery Meteors, as falling Stars, Comets, fiery Pillors, Lightenings, &c. A ready putrefaction of Meats, speedy Moulding of Bread, briefness of Small Pox and Measles, &c."[56] And yet, in the instance of the great plague of London in 1665, Harvey found that, much to his surprise, none of these wondrous or mundane signs or events preceded the pestilential infection.

Medical writers disagreed about the signs and causes of plague. According to many physicians, the plague was a result of bad air hovering above filthy and rotting materials, the sort that were found all over early modern London streets. Yet some writers denied this provenance, claiming it was unlikely that a plague of such magnitude was caused by local putrefaction. Instead, the venomous and infectious pestilence was the result of an unhappy configuration of the stars and planets, thereby explaining why the noxious qualities of the air were "so hidden from our senses," as it would not be if it were caused by filth and putrefaction alone.[57] The smellscapes of early modern London were full of putrid smells or rotting materials, human excrement, and scraps of carrion and waste unutilized by those working in various industries throughout the city, like butchers, tanners, and brewers. As writers in favor of planetary misalignment as the cause of infection pointed out, the stink of the city, though wretched, had not been unusual in the early months of 1665. They argued that such stinks might have caused a range of other ailments or compounded the effects of the plague, but bad smells were not the singular cause of the contagion.

If contemporaries disagreed about the cause, they generally agreed that the infection was somehow related to bad air. A prolific writer, Harvey was adamant that the "pestilential venom" that entered people's bodies with such calamitous results was due to contact with "Arsenical fumes."[58] Among the causes of these fumes were the waste products "kitchins" and of "several nasty Trades, as Tallow Chandlers, Butchers, Poulterers, Fishmongers, Dyers, &c." Harvey further blamed the plague on residents' "neglect of cleaning Gutters, Sinks or Ditches, paving the Streets, burying the dead," and failing to remove "Carrion and dead Carcases."[59] Like Harvey, other writers identified rot and smells, particularly the waste of human production and household trash, as particularly problematic. As Roger Dixon wrote on June 16, 1665, it was the rotting meat of butchers that was to blame for so many "calamitous and strange distempers," and he wished that the lord mayor and city magistrates would create and execute laws that would prevent such infection and "would conduce much to the health and safety of the people."[60] According to these writers, without greater control over some industries, and their wastes, Londoners could never be safe. They looked to city officials to act.

Harvey went on to describe how everyday rot and putrefaction, already dangerous to the health and well-being of Londoners, could turn into a deadly killer. Deep in the "womb," of the earth, or in "her close recesses" or "bowels," these varied stinking bodies and filth "do soon kindle and are converted into flaming atoms, by being coagulated in close places, as the pores of the earth of mud."[61] In other words, if the earth could not exchange, or interchange, with the clean air through open "pores" on the earth's surface—because such pores had been blocked by a layer of frost or too much "tough thick mud," for instance—fumes would get trapped within the earth, and the trapped material would then get infected. Like a human body, the earth's body needed to get rid of ill humors and regain balance by expelling them. Trapped for too long under the surface of the earth, as with ill humors trapped in a human body, these fumes or humors became more and more dangerous, fermenting and converting into pestilential fever within. When they did find an opening into the air, the "flaming Arsenical corpuscles," were expelled into the air. Formed deep in the earth by rotting bodies and "filth," the corpuscles were extremely dangerous, forming clouds of contagious miasmas that caused plague in all the bodies that breathed it in or came in contact with it.[62]

The constant contact of human bodies with the environment around them influenced an individual's humoral balance. By inhaling and exhaling air, early modern people believed their bodies were, in every moment, affected and influenced by the air around them. This explains why pestilential airs were so frightening. Miasmas could be very dangerous and were produced by circumstances that had to do with the particularities of unique landscape configurations, human activity, and weather, for instance. Miasmas were particularly dangerous to human health if it was "a close, thick or standing air, (that is not much ventilated) and [in] close places."[63] The close quarters in which Londoners lived led to a dangerous concentration of corpuscles in particular places, which might not have the same deadly effect if encountered in smaller doses or within differently arranged streets or houses. Writers asserted that London's built environment was particularly dangerous because it had many such "close" and unventilated spaces, including tight alleys and crowded taverns.

Anywhere "corpuscles" of plague were emitted and found "floating in the air" posed dangers because these corpuscles were "attracted into the Body, by Inspiration through the Lungs and Nostrils; or otherwise they pierce through one's clothes, and so penetrate into the pores of the intire Body." Although pores all over the surface of the body offered points of entry, there were particularly vulnerable spots that Harvey warned his readers to protect with special care: the wrists, armpits, temples, jugular, and groin. At these locations the "skin is thinnest, and the Arteries most detected, (for the vital spirits seem to attract the air potently through the Arteries)."[64] In other words, veins were closest to the surface at these points. At first, the miasmas entering at these varied points into the body were "not so Energick as to venenate the intire mass of blood in an instant . . . but by degrees, gradually corrupting the blood, and converting its parts into bodies of their own nature," the infection grew stronger, taking over the body.[65] Pestilence invaded individual bodies at their weakest points. It then invaded whole cities.[66]

Because mortality rates were so high once people were infected, many writers focused their attention on prevention. They advised keeping houses, streets, and air clean and keeping them well stocked with varied sweet- or strong-smelling items to counterbalance miasmas. They also advised avoiding large crowds and consuming a variety of medicinal drinks infused with herbs and spices. They appraised London's officials and residents of the best methods to ensure public health: "Keep your Houses, Streets, Yards, back-sides, Sinks and Kennells sweet and clean, for all standing Puddles, Dunghills, and corrupt Moystures, [may] ingender stinking Savours, that may be noisome, or breed Infection," urged one author.[67]

Even those writers who believed that the plague was brought on by dangerously aligned planets and stars, or more immediately by the left-over ashes of comets overhead that "cause the seeds of Pestilence, by their noisome Sulphureous stink," to rain down on unwary humanity, still saw that unclean streets might compound dangers to the body by adding further health risks. Theophilus Garencieres claimed that ill-informed people, believing that household animals like cats and dogs carried the plague, proceeded to "inhumanely butcher Catts and Doggs, and after that leave them in heaps to putrify in the streets, or unburied in fields and ditches, as if the Plague were not sufficient to do its work without the addition of this new Infection."[68] He argued that such unfounded responses compounded the effects of the plague.

Medical writers urged individuals to burn scented fires in every room of their homes, in order to cleanse the air and assist in halting the spread of contagion.[69] Sweet-smelling additions to these cleansing fires helped stave off infection. Thomas Cocke agreed that the best method to ensure self-preservation in the midst of plague was to provision oneself with "Artificiall Fumes and Sents" to counterbalance "the defects" of the air.[70] Plague doctors wore birdlike masks over their faces and in the "beak" were perfumes to keep them healthy as they visited plague homes and the pest houses specially built for the purpose of containing sick Londoners. The relationship between clothes and bodies was complex when addressing the needs of those stricken with plague. Authors regularly advised cleaning and airing out clothes, but they did not necessarily recommend cleansing bodies. Airing out clothes over fires infused with "Frankincese, Juniper, or dryed Rosemary" might counterbalance infection.[71] Harvey agreed that clothes hung before the fire would extract any pestilential air caught in the fibers. He likewise recommended that in the morning individuals should perfume them. He further urged his readers that it would be "commendable" to change clothes once or twice a week, if possible.[72] John Evelyn proposed the construction of an experimental scent ventilator "to convey fresh" fragrance into a room by making a "Tunnell," or funnel, filled with fresh flowers. A bit of wind forced into the tunnel would carry the healing scents into the chamber.[73]

Other health writers offered myriad recipes for concoctions to keep readers free of the plague. Many were preventative measures that involved imbibing steeped and prepared tinctures. They advised not only the use of sweet scents but powerful smells of all sorts, including peeled onions, for their antimiasmic properties.[74] Writers further advised preparing strong-smelling liquids, pastes, or plasters that were more portable or in which handkerchiefs and other wearable clothing items might be steeped and then worn. One writer recommended preparing "The Root of Enula-Campana, steeped in Vinegar, and lapped in a Handkerchief," as "a special thing to smell unto, if you come where the *Sickness* is."[75] Harvey offered how-to guides for numerous pastes, plasters, and accessories that readers might prepare and wear on their bodies, as well as items to carry, such as sweet-smelling cordial bags that contained spices such as cinnamon and were designed to be worn over the heart for the protection of key organs.[76] He suggested people constantly carry perfumes, in perfumed boxes, to smell, thereby "correcting and purifying the air before it is attracted by the Lungs" or, because it was "tedious to be alwaies obliged to hold a perfume to ones nose," to anoint "unguents and oyls" to the nostrils as a hands-free alternative.[77] Of course, as the pestilential air might enter the body through pores, particularly at the dangerously penetrable points at wrists, groin, throat, and armpits, he advised people to take particular caution with those weak spots by wearing "Antipestilential Emplasters."[78] Moreover, he thought a plaster on the stomach might serve to protect the organs, and the brain might be preserved with the use of a "Spice-cap."[79]

Not everyone was so confident. Theophilus Garencieres countered that perfumes provided only a false sense of security against the plague's "spirits," which "hover in every corner of the air, and will seise upon a fearfull man in spight of all the perfumes in the world, though he were shut close in a box."[80] He claimed that fear made a body more susceptible, thereby pointing to individuals' states of mind and attitude as key to preserving health. Even Harvey ultimately agreed that perhaps the only sure method of preserving yourself was to get out of town and breathe new airs. Before a lengthy section on concocting preservatives against the plague, he repeated some age-old wisdom for his readers as the only sure way to stay healthy in the midst of contagion: "Flee quick, Go far, and Slow return."[81]

Although there was a great deal of disagreement about how best to prevent infection, Londoners were desperate for advice, and public authorities sought large-scale solutions for the health of the city. Writers urged city and court officials to act on their suggestions. In 1665 Restoration officials took steps to oversee the health of the city's residents. They understood such measures as necessary to the health of the whole city and, by extension, the nation. The capital of the country, the "mart," of England, would be financially devastated if too many people died or trade ceased to function. Thus, writers urged officials to take proactive measures to contain the contagion.

Harvey urged city officials to take the lead in rendering miasmas impotent. He reflected on an event recorded by Hippocrates in which an island's populace, infected by pestilence, set fire to "a great Wood, which attracted all the Venene Seminaries, and so consumed and amortified them" so that all were saved.[82] And while Harvey acknowledged that there might not be a great wood near London to burn in order to purify the air, he suggested other measures that might offer similar results, such as burning great fires of pitch barrels in infected streets. Harvey encouraged London's officials to burn "*Stinck pots*, or *Stinckers*, as they call them, in Contagious Lanes."[83] Such controlled burnings might cleanse the air and improve public health in affected communities. Perhaps in response to Harvey, or to similar proposals, London's aldermen and mayor ordered bonfires lit in the streets in an effort to combat infection.[84] Pepys noted such public fires in early September.[85]

While medical writers offered readers a variety of means by which they might protect themselves against the plague, they struggled to explain why some bodies were infected and others remained healthy, even if they breathed in the same dangerous air. Physicians explained away the phenomenon as the result of an individual's lifelong habits. As one member of the College of Physicians urged, the best way to avoid the plague was to have "a wholesome and temperate dyet, and a moderate use of the six things called by the Physitians Non-natural, and a heart void of fear, the thing called Contagion being for the most part only a prejacent disposition in the body capable of receiving the Plague."[86] After the worst was over, Clarendon mused that among the many people who had suffered and died of the contagion, many had been women and children, as well as "the lowest and poorest sort of people." As a result, he found that upon his return to London, "few men missed any of their acquaintance when they returned, not many of wealth or quality or of much conversation being dead."[87] In Clarendon's accounting, there was a disproportionate number of the "lowest and poorest" people dead, while those with wealth and wit had so-called qualities that sustained their good health throughout the ravages of the plague year.

Indeed, writers claimed that the "quality" of the body attacked influenced the infection's outcome. In order to understand why some bodies were more susceptible to the contagion than others, Harvey mused that some were predisposed by the "foulness of their bodies, abundance of blood, oppression of the Spirits, aperture of their pores, thinness of texture of body, intemperance, [and] promiscuous converse with all sorts of people, whence the contagion oft lights in Taverns, Ale-houses, &c."[88] In other words, he claimed that individuals' physical characteristics, their location, as well as habits and behaviors altered rates of infection. Like Clarendon, Harvey theorized that the poor were more susceptible and more likely to succumb. Both claimed connections between social class and suffering. Harvey thought that even the prescriptions offered to the poor to preserve their health should be different and tailored to their specific needs as a social group with distinct physical bodies. He argued that the coarse and "foul bodies of the Vulgar" needed a much stronger recipe to promote purging than his daintier, wealthier patients. For instance, repeated vomiting would be necessary for the poor patients because their bodies were so insensitive to cures. "Above all," he wrote, "let them study cleanliness."[89]

Elite treatises regularly targeted individuals whom elites perceived as unclean as the source of interlinked moral and pestilential contagion. Of course, the fact that many of this targeted group did not have the means or the opportunity to "Flee quick, Go far, and Slow return"—and may therefore have been disproportionately exposed and affected—did not seem to matter to their causal explanations. Writers associated the poor with disease, as disproportionately infected with plague, living in cramped and close quarters, laboring in foul-smelling jobs, and engaging in morally corrupt activities that left them more vulnerable to infection.[90] Assigning blame to the diseased poor was a pretext for enacting additional forms of social and physical control. During the height of contagion, fears about the spread of disease led to numerous restrictions, particularly leveraged to control the poor, that were justified as public health initiatives. Officials of the state, the city, and the church, as well as authors of medical treatises, sought to secure public health by establishing certain bodies as diseased and in need of more control.[91] Once they singled out particular groups as "diseased," they quickly subjected those individuals to a range of restrictions to protect the body politic as a whole. As Margaret Healy has argued, "All 'bounded structures' (nations, societies, cities) must imagine their conditions of disunity—problems relating to boundaries, internal structures and the relationship between parts—in much the same way as they imagine the physical body's conditions of disharmony." In the case of London, in the midst and in the aftermath of plague and fire, this disunity was perceived spatially and socially. Healy continued: "When disunity is perceived, a shared set of metaphors is drawn upon to imagine the conditions of well-being and wholeness for both the social field and the individual body—to reconcile one with the other."[92] Numerous writers in London proffered a range of paths to such "wholeness," including delimiting elements of society to certain proscribed spaces.

The connection between sickness and social disruption was deeply ingrained. When so many people fled the town, including the court, the king considered himself in danger from potentially revolutionary or riotous Londoners left within the city. Residents had once turned on his father and might do so to him. To keep control and to promote loyalty, he had gifts crafted specially for those who stayed to keep public order while others fled the plague. Pepys recorded that he personally saw "two or three great silver flagons, made with inscriptions as gifts of the King to such and such persons of quality as did stay in town the late great plague."[93]

Authority, Plague Orders, and Restrictions

After repeated visitations of the plague, early modern states, England among them, designed a range of regulations to deal with its containment.[94] Officials regulated certain bodies more stringently than others.[95] Physicians and pamphleteers suggested a range of resources designed to rehabilitate individuals' disordered bodies and proffered the means of protecting the whole community. Thomas Cocke hoped that his pamphlet *Advice for the Poor by way of Cure & Caution* would reach the poor with the assistance of city officials, suggesting residents "might have but a Paper delivered to them by Publick Authority."[96] Cocke thus suggested that the city publish health guides for the benefit of those citizens without access to a physician's medical care. Towns expelled vagrants or prohibited visitors without papers, claiming that expelling unwanted individual bodies was an appropriate measure to preserve the body politic. Much like purging ill humors from the body, they claimed that they might preserve the health of the community by expelling those unwanted residents whom they categorized as infections. Restoration-era elites also sought to regulate a range of other behaviors, such as preventing attendance at funerals or by suggesting restrictive diets to achieve health. City officials also claimed for themselves the power to regulate certain social spaces—and as a result, regulate morality—by closing places like taverns or brothels in the name of public health. Spiritual advisers, citing passages from the Bible, offered to bring order to disordered souls. If disordered or depressed spirits invited contagion, lifting spirits served to preserve health.[97]

As with their counterparts across Europe, authorities in early modern England sought to contain the spread of the plague.[98] Officials had a capacious sense of their ability, and their right, to regulate individual bodies for the good of the community. They claimed that regulating movement, proscribing consumption habits, and legislating behavior all fell within their purview. They bombarded London's residents with advice and new rules designed to preserve health.[99] The Plague Orders included restrictions on the movement of sick individuals. To halt the progress of the plague, officials marked the front doors of homes containing infected residents and locked them within. Like the doors that caused Samuel Pepys such discomfiture in early June 1665, officials marked the doors of plague victims with red crosses and the words "Lord Have Mercy upon Us." Even those in the home who remained free from infection found themselves locked within and guarded by watchmen to ensure no one entered or exited the house for six weeks. City officials claimed the right to control the movements of all who resided in the house, regardless of infection status, in a highly visible fashion.[100] However, not everyone agreed with this policy. One contemporary wrote scathingly that it was at "the advice of the English College of Doctors" that all the inhabitants of those houses where infection hit were locked within. As a result, many members of the household were likely to perish, and the "family, so dismally exposed, sink one after another in the den of this dismal likeness of Hell."[101]

Locking sufferers within their homes was only one of a range of restrictions regulating individual movement. Officials also asked parishes to prevent people from attending funerals, hoping to stem the spread of infection. London's lord mayor and aldermen issued an order that "no neighbours nor friends be suffered to accompany the corpse to church, or to enter the house visited, upon pain of having his house shut up or be imprisoned," "and further, all public assemblies at other burials are to be forborne during the continuance of this visitation."[102] Such restrictions upset traditional ways of burying the dead and were therefore socially and culturally disruptive to suffering communities. Of course, the constant reiteration of these orders suggests that they were frequently ignored.

Officials also took other steps to halt the spread of contagion. On July 1, the lord mayor of London and the city's aldermen issued orders that the streets be kept clean in an effort to stop the spread of the pestilential miasmas. According to the order, it was "thought necessary, and so ordered, that every householder do cause the street to be daily prepared before his door, and so to keep it clean swept all week long."[103] Moreover, in order to prevent the spread of the plague, public authorities sought to delimit what Londoners could and could not consume. According to Thomas Cocke, "the Colledge in compliance with his MAJESTIES great care of His people, have prohibited the use of all Green, raw Crude and unindigested Fruits, especially Cucumbers, Mellons, and Cherries," whereas "other Fruits moderately used may be permitted." In his pamphlet, Cocke included testimonials from Albemarle and other well-placed supporters, who advised that Cocke's advice ought to be disseminated to all families and the poor by church wardens or parish clerks.[104]

When Londoners sought to pinpoint where and why the contagion began, they frequently pointed to the poverty-stricken and crowded homes and alleys inhabited by London's poor, unsympathetically described as "nasty folks" and "beggars," who could be found in "common Alehouses." Even authors more sympathetic to the plight of the poor still suggested their bodies were ultimately to blame.[105] While the pestilential visitation might have been a result of God's wrath for the bad behavior or moral profligacy of London's residents, the result of dangerously misaligned stars or flaming comets, or of filthy and rotting material emitting contagious miasmas, pamphleteers also imagined a social geography that placed disproportionate blame on particular classes of people, lambasting their characters and behaviors.

As in London, writers offered providential explanations for disasters across the Atlantic world. While they disagreed about first causes, they agreed that the plague visited on London in 1665 was particularly infectious, frighteningly mortal, and threatened the established social order. The specter of death by plague gripped London and its environs for over a year and inspired a rash of treatises and pamphlets promising cures, preventative potions, advice, and explanations. Their authors insisted that their work was "for the Publick Good."[106] Many of the explanations for the contagion came together in a complex knot of concepts relating to cleanliness or cleansing. Keeping clean streets, clean homes, clean bodies, and clean souls were the only ways to prevent infection. Londoners prayed that God, "thou best physician, both of our Souls and Bodies," might cleanse them of their sins.[107] Doctors advised cleansing rooms, clothes, and stomachs. City officials legislated moral and physical cleansing, inside and outside of the home, which they believed was required to heal the suffering city and its inhabitants.

London before the Fire

John Evelyn's satirical text *A Character of England* (1659) conceded that London was well situated on the River Thames, which was incomparably useful to the city's economy, but he otherwise condemned it as a poorly built city of confused, ramshackle, wooden buildings and inconveniently laid-out streets. It had no "modern architecture" and was "badly built."[108] Perhaps worst of all, the view of the city was unimpressive. Wrote Evelyn, "a *City* consisting of a wooden, northern, and inartificiall congestion of Houses; some of the principall streets so narrow, as there is nothing more deformed, and unlike, than the prospect of it at a distance, and its *asymmetrie* within the Walls."[109] Evelyn imagined the asymmetry of its buildings and streets as not only a physical but also a kind of moral deformity. He mused that such irregularities of form were a handicap to the capital city. The "deformed" landscape of the city shaped Londoners, their minds and characters cramped and confused by the poorly planned urban geography. In Evelyn's accounting, the people and their city were mutually constituted and similarly disordered. This was an unfortunate situation, however, because he considered the buildings to be "as deformed as the minds & confusions of the people."[110] He complained that even after bits of the largely wooden city burned down—and fires were a frequent occurrence—streets and structures built as replacements were as poorly designed as ever. After every fire Londoners had the opportunity to rebuild with an eye toward uniformity and symmetry, but that required centralized planning, and no one had emerged to champion such a cause. He lamented the absence of officials with the power to enforce a coordinated plan. He claimed that if a magistrate had both the "power" and "care" to rebuild with principles of uniformity in mind, it would not be such an "ugly Town, pestred with *Hackney-coaches*, and insolent *Carre-men* . . . [and] *Noyse*."[111]

Like Evelyn, various early modern writers claimed that the appearance and arrangement of urban sights and smells offered clues about residents and social order. The physical layout of cities—including the appearance of buildings and the type of construction materials—were reflections of residents' characters and the character of the community. Critics of London's haphazard and narrow lanes assumed that this both reflected, and further promoted, crime, social disorder, and sickness. Associations drawn between the built environment and the moral character of residents also helps to explain why colonists around the Anglo-Atlantic sought to transform urban settings in imitation of an idealized English architectural style; by building and rebuilding, urban residents in the colonies pushed back against claims of moral and physical degeneration while they simultaneously underscored ownership and sovereignty through the construction of permanent dwellings.

Much like English claims that the Spanish had failed to transform Jamaica into a garden and thus failed to truly own it, English writers were similarly critical of prior Spanish buildings and town layout in Jamaica, claiming that the one-story Spanish structures bore a greater resemblance to farmyard stables than homes, even as some quietly acknowledged the low-lying structures might better withstand hurricanes and earthquakes.[112] In Port Royal, those who could afford to do so built new buildings, "many of which are built with Bricks, and beautified with Balconies, after the modern way of building in *London*."[113] Residents proudly proclaimed that Port Royal was "the London of *Jamaica*."[114] Like other port cities around the Anglo-Atlantic, the streets of Port Royal were granted names from London, including Thames and Tower Streets.[115] The brick, multistory buildings located on thoroughfares bearing London street names signaled that the port city was not debauched and peripheral but a civilized, and civilizing, space that bore critical resemblances to the empire's "head."[116]

Like many of his contemporaries, Evelyn also condemned coal-burning industries within London as a particular problem.[117] He suggested planting a variety of sweet-smelling plants that might counteract the influence of the coal smoke, and when the trees and shrubs reached maturity they might be burned instead of coal, thus producing what Evelyn considered to be a less corrosive kind of smoke.[118] Evelyn pointed to the connections between the pestilential coal smoke, poor health, and the riotous tendencies of Londoners. Visitors and residents alike commented on London's clouds of sea-coal smoke. There were days when the clouds were so thick that London resembled nothing so much as "*Hell* upon Earth," the city akin to a "*Vulcano* on a foggy day" covering the city with a "pestilent *Smoak*" that corroded iron, spoiled people's goods, and covered the whole city with a layer of soot. The "horrid smoke obscures our churches and makes our palaces look old. It fouls our clothes and corrupts the waters, so that the very rain and refreshing dew that fall in the several seasons precipitate this impure vapour, which with its black and tenacious quality spots and contaminates whatever is exposed to it."[119] Londoners' lungs also suffered the consequences of this uncontrolled coal-burning within the limits of the city.[120] Medical treatises blamed the inhalation of "sharpe" and pointed atoms of coal smoke for damaging human lungs, linking coal smoke and other dangerous elements in London's airs to the city's high rates of mortality.[121]

Evelyn observed the clouds of soot "so fatally seizing on the *Lungs* of the Inhabitants, that the *Cough* and the *Consumption* spare no man. I have been in a spacious Church where I could not discern the minister for the *Smoak*; nor hear him for the peoples barking." In his account of the city, Evelyn thus presented the falling layers of soot as stifling Londoners' physical and spiritual health. Congregations were unable to hear the words spoken by the minister in church, as swirling soot gathered ominously in the air around them, enveloping the city with physically pestilential and spiritually corrosive smoke.[122] While coal smoke was widely recognized as unhealthy, residents also held more positive associations, linking smoke with industry and prosperity. But that association of coal smoke and industry could signal rampant corruption, greed, and sin. As William Cavert has pointed out, smoke signified many things to Londoners.[123]

After the Great Fire of 1666, reforming enthusiasts like Evelyn saw an opportunity to rebuild London and outlined numerous schemes for new designs and layouts for the city. Steven Pincus has estimated that as many as ten thousand new buildings were constructed in the decade before and after the fire, many utilizing glass. Pincus quoted a returning French visitor to the city in 1685, who reflected, "I find it a different city newly built of brick in place of the one of wood, and badly built, that I left in 1660."[124] Plans to rebuild raised a number of questions about the relationship of morality and social geography to the physical landscape of the city.

While some neighborhoods posed physical risks as sites that bred contagion, others posed political risks. To a degree, the whole city was suspect. The Corporation of the City of London had had ties to republican fomentation, and City magistrates and merchants had broadly supported Cromwell. Its residents posed a threat to the king's residence at Whitehall, in the city of Westminster, just beyond the city walls. The complex local governance of the City made it especially interesting that the king passed a variety of legislation and made a number of proclamations in the wake of plague and fire. Perhaps we might see in his dealings with the City a kind of power grab. One of the king's courtiers wrote that the fire "was the greatest blessing that God had ever conferred upon him, his restoration only excepted: for the walls and gates being now burned and thrown down of the rebellious city, which was always an enemy to the crown," presented him with an opportunity. If he desired, the king might "never suffer them to repair and build up again, to be a bit in his mouth and a bridle upon his neck, but would keep all open, that his troops might enter upon them whenever he thought necessary."[125]

The Great Fire

In the early morning hours of September 2, a fire broke out on Pudding Lane in the house of a baker.[126] As fire consumed the City, residents fled. Much of the medieval walled city continued burning though September 6, leaving behind a city in ashes. Even while the fire still burned, Charles II realized that those who had lost their homes would need food, so that "they who had saved themselves from burning might not be in danger of starving."[127] Without homes to return to, many Londoners gathered in St. George's Fields and Moorefields, "some under tents, some under miserable hutts and hovells, many without a rag or any necessary utensills, bed or board," and "reduced to extreamest misery and poverty."[128] Evelyn reported how he "went towards Islington and Highgate, where one might have seene 200,000 people of all ranks and degrees dispers'd and lying along by their heapes of what they could save from the fire, deploring their losse. . . . His Majesty and Council indeede tooke all imaginable care for their reliefe."[129] Supplies from beyond London were carted into the city for the consumption of those displaced. Likewise, in the days after the fire the king issued proclamations that markets should reopen, even those that had burned down. By reopening markets where they previously stood, the king sought to ensure "That Our Loving Subjects may nevertheless be furnished with a constant Supply of Provisions," so that one disaster did not turn into another: privation, starvation, or social instability.[130]

A month after the fire, the king reviewed the extent of the damage and described the fire as "the most lamentable and devouring fire" that

FIGURE 1.1. Many writers attributed the fire to a justly wrathful God. He destroyed the city because it was the most effective way to awaken residents to their many sins. According to Rolle, "As the face is to the body, so was *London to England*, viz. the beautifullest part of it, and look how men reckon it a great prejudice to their bodies when their faces are marred by any great deformity." In other words, by defacing the body, Londoners would realize the seriousness of their sins. Detail from Samuel Rolle, *Shilhavtiyah or, The Burning of London in the Year 1666* (London, 1667). RB 274038, The Huntington Library, San Marino, California.

"lay to waste the greatest part of the City of London within the Walls, and some part of the Suburbs, whereof more than forescore parishes, and all the houses, Churches, Chappels, hospitals, and other great and Magnificent Buildings of pious or publique use which were within that Circuit, are now brought into Ashes, and become one ruinous heap."[131] Much of the City of London had burned down, while much of London's sprawl beyond the medieval walls, as well as the city of Westminster and the king's palace, remained standing.

FIGURE 1.2. Wenceslaus Hollar captioned his map: "An exact map representing the condition of the late famous and flourishing City of London as
it lyeth in its ruins" after the "dreadfull & lamentable fire." The absences
of structures and homes in the burned area offered a stark visual of the
destruction. Wenceslaus Hollar, *A Map or Groundplott of the Citty of London*
(London, 1667). Image courtesy of The British Library, Crace Collection of
Maps of London, Item Number 53.

In the aftermath of the destruction, two surveyors examined and
reported on the extent of the destruction. Josiah Moore, who had previously been hired by the Crown to drain the Great Level (the subject of
chapter 2) and to attempt to build a mole at Tangier, charted the devastated area alongside Ralph Gatrix. They calculated that the fire had
consumed "three hundred and 73 acres within the wall of the City of
London, and 63 acres, three roods without the walls" and moreover
that "There remains 75 acres three roods yet standing within the walls
unburnt. Eighty-nine parish churches, besides chapels, burnt: eleven
parishes within the walls yet standing. Houses burnt, 13,200."[132] Edward
Waterhous reminisced in *A Short narrative of the Dreadful Fire in London*
(1667) that even if the fire had been planned by England's enemies, they
could not have planned a better locus for the initial spark: "for if all the
Engineers of mischief would have compacted the irremediable Burning
of *London*, they could not have laid the Scene of their fatal contrivance

more desperately, to a probable success than there where it was, where narrow streets, old buildings all of Timber, all contiguous each to other, all stuffed with ailment for the Fire, all in the very heart of the Trade and Wealth of the City."[133]

Clarendon agreed, later describing how the fire had begun in one of the inaccessible and narrow alleys of London, conditions which facilitated the quick spread of the fire. The baker's house was situated amid "little narrow alleys and very poor houses about the place where it first appeared; and then finding such store of combustible materials, as that street is always furnished with in timber-houses, the fire prevailed so powerfully, that that whole street and neighborhood was in so short a time turned to ashes."[134] The human-built topography of the city amplified the disaster. The widespread recognition that the tightly packed wooden homes had likely exacerbated the deadly fire led to questions about how to rebuild London in a more fireproof manner. The materials and methods of London's reconstruction became a matter of state interest and intervention; plans to rebuild should promote the general good and safety of all Londoners.

If they were not already aware, Londoners learned the hard way that the built environment of their city compounded the effects of the fire and risked their health and safety. Just as the plague had taught wealthy Londoners that the best means to avoid illness was to flee the crowded streets of London, fire confirmed, in frightening fashion, the deeply materially interconnected nature of city living. The way individual people moved about the city, where they moved, how they behaved, and how they constructed their homes and shops had the power to influence the many. In this urban space, people, smells, and fires alike crossed social, cultural, and class boundaries, influencing all of its human residents.

In the immediate aftermath of the fire, the king issued various proclamations, as did the lord mayor and aldermen of the city, broadly designed to rehabilitate and reform the physical layout of the city and to transform residents' behaviors.[135] In October, one month after the fire, the lord mayor issued a *Proclamation for Cleansing of City Streets* as well as a *Proclamation for Clearing the City after the Fire*. In early November, he issued a *Proclamation for Punishment of Vagrants and Beggars*. Just as vagrants and beggars came under greater scrutiny in the immediate aftermath of the conflagration, many others also found themselves the targets of fevered accusations and violence at the hands of angry mobs seeking revenge for the fire. Many contemporaries were sure the fire was the handiwork of "popish enemies" who sought the downfall of Protestant England. If the poor and "promiscuous" had been identified as particularly disposed to the plague, and their homes, streets, and places of recreation condemned as the sources of miasma, after the conflagration additional groups were collectively identified as suspect and culpable scapegoats for the devastations Londoners suffered by fire.

Rebuilding London

In the aftermath of the destructive fire, London's residents, city and royal officials, projectors, surveyors, members of the Royal Society, and poets alike considered how best to rebuild. Samuel Rolle described the rebuilding of London as the greatest secular concern of his day, concerning thousands of families.[136] Some saw it as an opportunity to remake the city utilizing architectural models and city-planning ideas under development in continental Europe. Those who devised plans saw an opportunity in the razed city to make the city anew, rebuilding the physical city to fit philosophical, utopian ideals.[137] They offered varied visions of how a "modern" city ought to appear and function.[138] The poet Jeremiah Wells gave voice to the city itself. He imagined that the city, if given human voice, would "thank her cruel fate" because in the aftermath of a destructive fire the city might be rebuilt, with a range of concepts informing the rebuilding. Thus, London should be "Glad to [be] Ruin'd So to be Restored."[139] Indeed, as the poet Simon Ford mused in his poem "Londons Resurrection," "Thy *Ruins* shall prove *Vegetable* too: / And thy scorch't *Stump* to a *new City* grow." He imagined that, like a living organism with the ability to regenerate, London would regrow, vegetable like, renewed and restored. Ford envisioned that this newly grown city would surpass the original. It would be straight and symmetrical, a city "Whose adverse Fronts at equidistant space, / As lines drawn Parallel, their Fellows face."[140]

Wells agreed, and in "On the Rebuilding of London," he suggested that the city might be rebuilt as more "stately," with "larger streets, through which Processions pass."[141] He envisioned that even "in lesser Streets," though they would not be "stately, trim and brave," yet they would be "contented with their meaner fate." These "lesser Alleys" would be "slender, straight, and long." Like "little Riv'lets scatter'd to and fro, to larger Streams they swiftly cut their way," so would the lanes and alleys flow into the streets and grand promenades.[142] In Wells's imagination, the city would be put back into place, but better than before. Just as in this model of nature in which lesser tributaries were "contended" with their place in the natural order of things, so would poorer residents of these alleys be content to return to their newly straightened, and improved, but still "meaner fate."

Like Wells, numerous writers focused on projects such as the widening and straightening of streets as a means to modernize, promote human health and trade, and create stately spaces where processions, with their theatrical pomp and circumstance, might impress London's residents. Ford saw potential in the ruined city to build broader streets.[143] In the old London, the narrow and winding streets had caused innumerable discomforts,

> where Commerce in crowded Throngs was pent,
> or Fires coop'd up had rag'd for want of vent:
> Where obscure Lanes obscurer Facts did hide:
> And Pests by being straitned, spread more wide.

He associated the narrow and "obscure" streets of the old urban landscape as enabling a range of ills, slowing trade, and promoting misdeeds and disease in cramped quarters. Instead, the new city plans and rebuilt streets would be of great utility and benefit to the city's residents, so that

> Traffique in spacious Streets shall now be free,
> And Flames soon spent, or soon supprest shall be.
> Day's Eye each where shall skulking Sinners trace,
> And transient Air infectious streams shall chase.[144]

Sin, infection, and "crowded" streets would thus be better controlled and organized. Meanwhile, the "Buildings thus shall uniformly stand" as "Such Uniformi'ty does our king command." Symmetry, uniformity, and straight lines were everywhere praised by elite writers and schemers as essential elements that should be included in the newly rebuilt London. Uniformity and parallel lines were a means to make legible the formerly sprawling and labyrinthine cityscape as well as bring order to the minds of residents. The sun would shine a light on those residents who carried out untoward or unlawful activities.

In his plans for a rebuilt London, John Evelyn likewise urged architects to enforce uniformity in buildings both great and ordinary, so that "even the very meanest, should exactly respect uniformity, and be more substantially built" than they had been twenty or thirty years earlier.[145] According to Evelyn, rebuilding homeowners needed to "exactly conform to the plot, to the shape of the front, and to such other directions for uniformity and solidity, as his Majesty's Surveyors of Commissioners shall appoint."[146] This was one way to build a community, literally from the ground up, that had some kind of uniformity of appearance and, perhaps, a more orderly and communal ethos. In these plans, Evelyn sought to express a range of political and social ideals through construction, design, and other large-scale material transformations of the urban environment. But perhaps more than any other factor, Evelyn sought wider streets. He urged everyone interested in the form and function of the new city to consider that "in the disposure of the streets due considerations should be had, what are competent breadths for commerce and intercourse, cheerfulness and state."[147] Evelyn declared that in his ideal version of the future London, "I would allow none of the principal streets less than an hundred foot in breadth, nor any of the narrowest than thirty, their openings, and heights proportionable."[148]

Among the plans for the rebuilt city were also schemes to alter and improve the waterways leading into London. Authors like Evelyn argued that the improvements were necessary to promote trade, improve appearance, and ameliorate one of the conditions that led to poor health in and around the city: standing, putrid water. Evelyn proposed widening channels that would allow in considerable vessels. He was particularly keen to improve the waterways running in and around the city and into the Thames because, as things stood, it was dirty, confusing, and unhealthy: "What fractions and confusions our ugly, bridges, and causeways, make," he wrote, "and how dirty, and nasty it is at every ebb, we are sufficiently sensible of; so as next to the hellish smoke of the town, there is nothing doubtless, which does more impair the health of its inhabitants."[149] Better navigation also promised more trade.

While there was a great deal of agreement about particular aspects of the plans for London, there was also much disagreement and different emphases. Christopher Wren's plan for rebuilding London emphasized a regularized, straightened street plan, whereas Evelyn's schematic "laid more emphasis on new parks and squares."[150] Evelyn suggested that officials consider rebuilding London as a kind of garden city with "Spaces for ample Courts, Yards, and Gardens, even in the heart of the city there may be some to the principal houses, for state and refreshment" that might refresh the air.[151] The enthusiasm for rebuilding the City of London is apparent in a letter written by Evelyn in September, in which he described the king and Parliament as "infinitely zealous for the rebuilding of our ruines." But he acknowledged the challenges of rebuilding, writing: "They are now busied with adjusting the claimes of each proprietor, that so they may dispose things for the building after the noblest

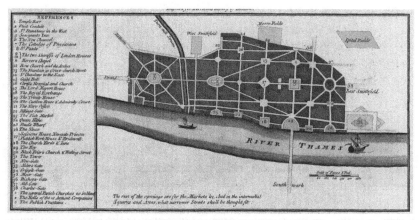

FIGURE 1.3. *Sir John Evelyn's Plan for Rebuilding the City of London after the Great Fire in 1666* (London, 1776). Image courtesy of the Historic Maps Collection, Special Collections, Princeton University Library.

model: Every body brings in his idea . . . and truly there was never a more glorious phoenix upon the earth, if it do at last emerge out of the cinders, and as the designe is layd, with the present fervour of ye undertakers."[152] In order to respect the "claimes of each proprietor," the Commissioners for Rebuilding were instructed to respect property rights, and to ensure everyone was properly compensated if individual property owners were affected by "street-widening schemes," "the uprooting and zoning of particular trades," or the "massive relocation" required by some of the major rebuilding submissions.[153] Before any work could be done, commissioners needed to figure out "to whom all the houses and ground did in truth belong, what term the several occupiers were possessed of, and at what rents, and to whom, either corporations, companies, or single persons, the reversion and inheritance appertained."[154]

While Christopher Wren's design was a major remodeling of the city, Evelyn's plan focused on making the rebuilt London more majestic and regularized.[155] Meanwhile, Royal Society member Josiah Child offered his own plan; he hoped that before any work began, officials would hire a skilled surveyor to produce "an exact plot, according to the geometrical scale of feet," which "ought in the first place to be taken by some able Artist, and in that accurately to be described all the declivities, eminences, water courses &c. of the whole *Area*." He suggested that the "Gent. who performed that of Tangier (according to my conceptions of that plan) might, I suppose, be a very fitting person for that employment."[156] The gentleman in question was none other than Josiah Moore, one of the several "experts" who participated in fen drainage projects in the 1650s and were hired to rebuild the city and reshape its waterways in the following decade.[157] He was involved in post–Great Fire surveying of London.[158] The Duke of York had become his patron several years earlier in 1663.[159] Moore's involvement in multiple projects of "improvement," including the fen drainage covered in chapter 2, reminds scholars not to examine these schemes in isolation.

Contemporaries debated the range of ideas about rebuilding London. Many agreed that first and foremost, the rebuilding should utilize different building materials. As Joseph Williamson wrote in the *London Gazette*, the rebuilt London should be of brick or stone rather than timber.[160] Among the disagreements was how to define the kinds of changes that were desirable and, most importantly, feasible. Henry Oldenburg, secretary of the Royal Society of London, wrote in a letter in September 1666, just after the fire, that "the rebuilding of the citty, as to the model, is still very perplext, there appearing three parties in the house of commons about it." He noted, "Some are for a quite new model, according to Dr Wren's draught; some are for the old, yet to build with bricks; others for a middle way, by building a key and enlarging some streets, but keeping the old foundations and vaults." As he recognized, there was the additional stress of "how to raise mony for carrying on the warre [with the Dutch], and to rebuild the citty at the same time."[161]

In his treatise *Londons Resurrection*, Samuel Rolle agreed that rebuilding London was crucial to its future prosperity and to the welfare of all residents. One was impossible without the other, as trade needed a convenient and well-built place where people might conduct it. In turn, he argued that a reconstructed and prosperous London would lead to innumerable social, cultural, and religious benefits. He, like many of his contemporaries, however, was quick to declare that he saw London's rebuilding not as an inspiration for revolution but as an opportunity to rebuild according to the city's deep foundations. Rolle would show his readers how to achieve restoration "without rasing any one foundation, or fundamental law, and without laying an axe to the root of any tree. . . . I say I have indeavoured to build up a structure of peace, love, and unity upon the foundations that are already laid, without presuming to lay any new ones."[162] He wrote enthusiastically of a deeply conservative, tightly controlled effort that respected London's physical, political, and social roots and insisted that those advising on London's resurrection, even those devising grand schemes, were not revolutionaries.

And yet, projectors aspired to transform the thoroughfares and inhabitants of London, at least on paper. They imagined a rebuilt city with symmetrical homes and widened and straightened streets, which would be the means by which authorities might better survey and monitor the inhabitants as they went about their business.[163] Surveyors, planners, and writers aspired to build an urban environment that could regulate where, when, and how people moved within the city.[164] They intended this rebuilt landscape to facilitate their goals of tightening control over London's citizenry. Straight streets, like idealized military and colonial grids, "facilitated surveillance . . . by eliminating those urban crevices where Europe's human miscellany often sheltered."[165] Straight lines enabled London's elite to monitor human movement and behavior. There are conceptual similarities between the straight urban streets and legislating the straight rows of orchards and agriculture in the colonies. Colonial legislators went so far as to legislate the spacing between trees. Straight lines in cultivated fields were intended as evidence of orderliness in opposition to a colonial wilderness. A similar vision, and a desire to control the disorderly members of urban communities around the Anglo-Atlantic, drove the interest in grid street systems.[166]

In his plans to rebuild the city, Evelyn hoped to highlight particular views. He argued that an individual should not "pass through the city all in one tenor without varieties, useful breakings, and enlargements into piazzas at competent distances, which ought to be built exactly uniform, strong, and with beautiful fronts."[167] He was particularly adamant about one view. According to Evelyn, the road stretching from Fleet to Ludgate "should be no more than might only afford a graceful and just ascent from thence up towards St. Pauls, the only spot in the whole city, where I would plant that ancient and venerable cathedral again."[168] In *London Redivivum*, or London Restored, Evelyn urged that when rebuilding the city the architects should ensure that not only St. Paul's but also parochial churches "might be founded in the centres of spacious areas, piazzazz &c. so as to be conspicuous to several streets."[169] Perhaps by making churches more visible, early modern urban planners hoped for a reciprocal vision: individuals in view of a church may have imagined God's eyes on their daily business as they traversed straightened and well-lit streets. Perhaps the constant views of the church were themselves a form of social control. Evelyn thought that much of the community's social and business life should take place in the proximity to religious centers.[170] It is likely that his scheme to locate much of the community's activities in and near the local church was symbolically and spatially significant.

In Evelyn's scheme, some people would be brought into the heart of the community by arranging streets and open spaces such that people were pulled toward the church and market in the piazza, where they were faced with public institutions of power. Meanwhile, urban redesign could funnel other institutions and people to the physical and theoretical edge of the community. Hospitals, public workhouses, and prisons each should have their own spatial location in the city. According to Evelyn, "the prisons, and Tribunal for trial of criminal offenders, might be built (as of old) near some entrance of the city: about Newgate were a fitting place, as my plot represents it."[171] Prisons and prisoners were both morally and spatially located at the edge of the city in Evelyn's ideal London. He wanted to emphasize the limits of the city, and those individuals associated with those limits. Meanwhile, the state's right and ability to intervene in the lives of individual bodies would be reinforced by the location of its hospitals. Evelyn imagined that the streets on which hospitals were rebuilt "would become one of the principal streets." Meanwhile, "The College of physicians would be in one of the best parts of the town, encircled with an handsome piazza for the dwelling of those learned persons, with the Chirurgeons, Apothecaries, and Druggists in the streets about them."[172] City planning could highlight some activities and hide others.

It was not only keeping the streets clean and clear of noisome, stinking smells but also the facilitation of movement that occupied planners' thoughts. Each High Street in the city should be paved "round or *Causeway* fashion."[173] Planners further aspired to control the movements of people, the time of their movements, and the types of people who might move along those streets.[174] The commissioners for sewers included in their *Act of Common Council by the Commissioners for Sewers, Pavements, &c., Touching the Paving and Cleansing the Streets, Lanes and Common Passages within the City* (1671) a description of the many kinds of people not allowed to utilize the paved streets, and likewise crafted limitations to the types and times of uses. For instance, those who had restricted use of the paved high streets included: "no Beggars or Vagrants, Tankardbearers, Porters, or other persons whatsoever bearing any kind of Burthens on their Heads, Backs, or Arms, Horses, or any kind of Cattel shall be permitted at any time of the day from Six of the clock in the Morning, until Nine of the clock at night, to go on, pass, or be lead upon the flat Pavements in any Street between the Houses and the Posts adjoining the said flat Pavements."[175] There was a great deal of concern to keep load-bearing carts and cars from the paved streets. After

December 10, 1671, no street car or "Brewers Dray" might be drawn by more than one horse within the city, with few exceptions. Meanwhile, the loading and unloading of wagons had to be completed within established hours.[176]

Despite widespread, initial enthusiasm for a range of schemes designed for London's reconstruction, many of the plans were never feasible possibilities. To rebuild according to the models that altered the old street plans would have required taking the time to oversee massive property transfers before building might commence. The Rebuilding Act of 1667 made it clear that officials believed there was neither the time nor the money to adopt most of the changes that had been dreamt up by a range of enthusiastic planners. Instead, the act enabled reconstruction to begin immediately on the old street plans and properties, as "fire had everywhere spared foundations and cellars, occasionally walls; the projects would have involved the destruction of these and so increased the loss." Timelines were also a concern of the act.[177] There were, however, a number of restrictions on rebuilt homes. Structures were to be built using brick and stone, and there were new rules enacted to control the height of buildings. Planners legislating about the design of the new city integrated moral, social, and political theories into the spatial layout of the city.

If city planners did not adopt the more radical schemes for London's new cityscape, many small changes to the urban landscape occurred. Some streets were widened, like Fleet Street, though they were not as wide as Evelyn had suggested.[178] There was likewise a range of improvements in paving streets and in drainage and waste-removal infrastructure.[179] The city enacted a number of preventative measures, hoping to curtail the possibilities of a repeat of the plague or destructive fire in the rebuilt London. In 1668 the Common Council of the Corporation of London issued *An Act for Preventing and Suppressing Fires* detailing ways to prevent another conflagration on the scale of the 1666 fire. Neither did the city want the ramshackle and temporary structures thrown up in the aftermath of the fire to become part of the permanent landscape. On April 6, 1673, the Corporation of London printed broadsides alerting residents of an additional *Act of Parliament for Rebuilding the City* that empowered the lord mayor and Court of Aldermen to "cause all and every the Sheds . . . and other Buildings, which have by License . . . been erected (since the late dreadful Fire) in *Smithfield, Moorfield,* and other void places within the said City . . . to be taken down and removed at or before the 19th day of *September* . . . 1674."[180] In the wake of the destructive fire, various residents received licenses of seven years to build temporary structures while the city officials considered more permanent rebuilding solutions.[181]

While the numerous printed measures and legislation that dealt with the enforcement of street cleanliness were by no means new to postplague and postfire London, it seems likely that the proliferation of printed works on the subject reflected an effort to respond to the perceived causes of deadly contagion and conflagration. The authors of plague treatises had urged public authorities to legislate restrictions on dumping in the streets, and sought out proactive measures to prevent street filth, which they understood to lead to putrefaction and illness. Correspondingly, new measures and legislation took into account such concerns about plague and fire. In 1671 the commissioners of sewers printed an informational booklet for every householder in the city so they might be up-to-date regarding the recent acts concerning street cleaning, entitled *An Act of Common Council by the Commissioners for Sewers, Pavements, &c., Touching the Paving and Cleansing the Streets, Lanes and Common Passages within the City*.[182] According to the commissioners of sewers, the booklet, and the nature of the work it described, was "requisite and necessary to the *Health* and *Trade* of the Inhabitants of this City." The ability to move about, and to do so in good health, was of the utmost importance. Moving unimpeded around the city, and doing so without facing dire health challenges from "noisome" smells and filth, were two of the great challenges of city life. Ridding the city of bad smells was a health measure, especially if foul odors had amplified the effects of the plague.[183]

It seems likely that the memories of this frighteningly mortal contagion, and its perceived causes, were inspirations for many of the specified prohibitions and regulations, such as those advised in *An Act . . . Touching the Paving and Cleansing of the Streets*. As such, the commissioners insisted that city inhabitants, under threat of various financial punishments, should not "lay in the *Streets, Lanes*, or *common Passages* or Chanels within this City . . . any *Dogs, Cats, Inwards of Beasts, Cleaves of Beasts, Fat, Bones, Horns, Dregs*, or *Dross of Ale or Beer*, or any *noisome thing* upon pain of Ten shillings for every offence."[184] Nor might any inhabitant "cast into the *Ditches* or *Sewers, Grates* or *Gullets* of the City, any manner of *Carion, Stinking Flesh, rotten oranges* or *onions, Rubbish, Dung* . . . or any other thing that might stop the course of the same upon pain of forfeiting Forty shillings for every offence."[185] Many of these items were among those listed by contemporary pamphleteers as the cause of the unhealthy airs that led to such catastrophic death the previous decade. Putrefaction, though not universally agreed to be the cause of the 1665 plague, certainly received regular blame. And even authors who pointed to alternative causes still agreed that street filth and rotting animal bodies were the causes of other infections, even if not plague.[186]

This same act crafted regulations for the "Fellowship of Car-men," who were licensed to carry away the "Dung, Soil, Filth, Seat coal-Ashes, and other Dirt" from the streets and from all of the houses of London's inhabitants, provided the inhabitants or their servants took care that the dirt, ashes, and "soil" from their homes "be in readiness for the Car-men . . . either by setting out the same over night in Tubs, Boxes, Baskets, or other Vessels near and contiguous to their Houses." Car-men agreed to year-long terms to sweep and cleanse the streets and to carry the waste collected to common, public lay-stalls.[187] They were to clean the streets each day but Sunday and were generally required to rise early and to be done with their duties by late morning.[188] The lord mayor, aldermen, and Common Council purchased several parcels "of waste Ground" that would become public, common lay-stalls "to be employed for the publick Use and Benefit of the City and Liberties thereof" as well as sites where public stores "for all sorts of Fuel, and for all sorts of Materials for Pitch-ing, Paving, and Cleansing the Streets, and for other Commodities for publick Use" might likewise be stored.[189]

London was not the only city making such alterations to its infra-structure. By the end of the century numerous towns and cities through-out the nation were also paving their "principal streets" "for the benefit of foot-passangers."[190] In his plans for the rebuilding of London, drawn up in 1666, John Evelyn urged planners to consider the best locations for waste receptacles, like these *lay-stalls*, that were both accessible by roads for the ease of removal, and in locations that "would least cumber and infest the town."[191] Evelyn likewise stressed that the streets themselves were among the many problems to be addressed when rebuilding the city. He saw it as an issue that the "Streets should be so narrow and incom-modious in the very Centre, and busiest places of Intercourse; that there should be so ill and uneasie a form of Paving under foot, so troublesome and malicious a disposure of the Spouts and Reformation; because it is hereby rendered Labyrinth in its principal passages, and a continual wet day after the storm is over."[192] Narrow, dark, unpaved streets slowed the circulation of trade and damaged the economy and health of the body politic, much like the sluggish circulation of blood led to poor health.

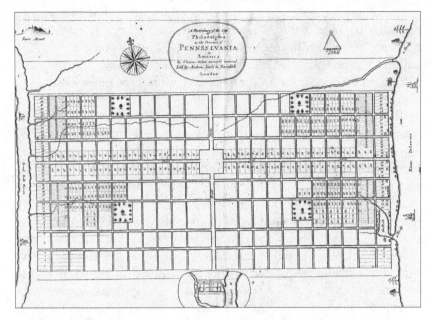

FIGURE 1.4. Thomas Holme included tree-lined parks in the map of Penn's new city. Thomas Holme, *A Portraiture of the City of Philadelphia in the Province of Pennsylvania in America* (London, 1683). Image courtesy of Haverford College Libraries.

The discussions and considerations about how best to rebuild London and prevent such disasters in the future shaped urban design projects around the Atlantic world. When one of Carolina's Lords Proprietors, Anthony Ashley Cooper, 1st Earl of Shaftesbury, designed the "Grand Modell of government" for the colony with the assistance of John Locke; they included detailed instructions for the physical layout of the colony and Charles Town—later renamed Charleston—and advised about its placement with an attention to public health.[193] The Lords Proprietors advised settlers to build "as far up in the country as may be to avoid the ill air of the lowlands near the sea, which may endanger their health at their first coming."[194] Moreover, settlement designs written on June 21, 1672, included instructions that thoroughfares should be "laid out into large, straight, and regular streets."[195] The desire for wider streets in London, and later in Charleston, Philadelphia, Port Royal, and Kingston, was, in part, a response to the disasters. Designers claimed that wider streets were public health measures. More light and greater air circulation could prevent dangerous miasmas and slow contagion. Moreover, Penn promoted Philadelphia as a wholesome town by crafting plans to place each home in an individual plot, surrounded by a bit of green. A town that was too compact was a fire risk. Wider streets might slow a conflagration. That Penn and Surveyor General Thomas Holme had the lessons of London on their minds when they designed Philadelphia is further suggested in the references to London in the description that accompanied Holme's design. He explained that the regular squares would be used by residents like "*Moor-fields* in *London*."[196]

Meanwhile, instructions from the Lords Proprietors to Carolina's settlers drafted May 1, 1671, similarly specified that major thoroughfares should be eighty feet wide, while other streets should still be sixty feet wide.[197] Thomas D. Wilson has suggested that Richard Newcourt's plan for the redesign of London inspired Ashley Cooper and John Locke's designs for Carolina.[198]

Collected among the papers of the merchant, civil servant, and Royal Society member Thomas Povey were "Proposals in order to the Improvement of the County of Albemarle in the Province of Carolina" and "Proposalls concerning building of Towns in Virginia."[199] The anonymous authors of both proposals equated improvement with urban spaces. As in London, they advised construction with brick rather than wood. Indeed, in Virginia, the earth was "proper to make Bricks," and there was a good quantity of stone for building. The author of one of the plans noted the availability of marble for ornamental purposes. If, however, London seemed too crowded, the colonial projectors were more concerned about the dispersed nature of residents in the colonies. In Albemarle County "their disperst manner of living" left them "a disjointed multitude, [rather] than a regular body."[200] Meanwhile, the other author accused Virginian colonists of making only "slowe Improvements." It remained "a Scattered Colonie" that was "uncollected into Bodies, Townes, and Convenient settlements of Trade, Negotiation, and Securitie."[201]

As in London, in Jamaica residents considered how best to rebuild after disaster. After the 1692 earthquake destroyed Port Royal, John Gosse designed the new town of Kingston at the behest of the colony's Council. Gosse's plan included major thoroughfares that were at least fifty to sixty feet wide.[202] Jamaican urban designers had an additional reason to push for wider streets. If buildings toppled during earthquakes, wider streets might save lives. A similar push for wider streets occurred in cities in areas prone to earthquakes, including in Sicily and Peru.[203] Meanwhile, those residents who wanted to rebuild Port Royal instead of relocating

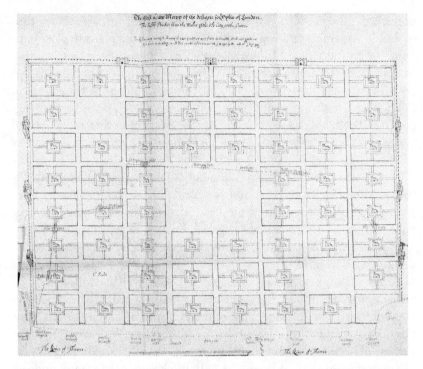

FIGURE 1.5. Richard Newcourt's plan for London included a grid layout with several squares left empty, perhaps as parks, and may have inspired the city plans for Philadelphia. Newcourt informed readers that "the Redd Prickes shew the walles of the old City, & the Gates." Richard Newcourt, *The First Mapp of the Designe for [the] Cytie of London* (1666?), CLC/481/MS03441. Image courtesy of the City of London, London Metropolitan Archives.

to Kingston used a different set of arguments about public health to support their positions. Pointing to the contagion that broke out in the wake of the earthquake among those seeking refuge in Kingston, residents in favor of rebuilding Port Royal claimed it was the location that was "most healthy for their bodys."[204]

In addition to the layout of cities, writers like Evelyn also sought to place certain industries, such as those producing smoke, beyond city limits, or at least downwind of the city. He wrote indignantly that the "Glorious and Antient City . . . should wrap her stately head in Clowds of Smoake and Sulphur, so full of stink and Darknesse."[205] In his descriptions of London before the fire, he pointed to the various activities and practices that produced the coal smoke that choked the city, suggesting that more was at stake than his aesthetic preferences. Indeed, the smoke-filled air affected the individual health, behavior, and social well-being of Londoners. In this instance, too, some of Evelyn's concerns were addressed, and the industries to blame began to be moved to another quarter of the city. Among his postfire recommendations was to remove certain industries:

> For the rest of those necessary evils, the Brewhouses, Bakehouses, Dyers, Salt, Soap, and Sugar-boilers, Chandlers, Hat-makers, Slaughter-houses, some sort of Fish-mongers &c. whose neighborhood cannot be safe (as I have elsewhere showed, and as sad experience has confirmed) I hope his Majesty will now dispose of to some other parts about the river, towards Bow and Wandsworth on the water; Islington, and about Spitalfields &c. The charge of bringing all their commodities into the city would be very inconsiderable, opposed to the peril of their being continued amongst the inhabitants.[206]

Many of the alterations to the built landscape were an effort to rearrange or reinforce the social geography of the city. A home or an institution's placement on a major thoroughfare, or relegated to the edges of, or beyond, the city walls, said much about its place within the social fabric of Restoration London, as did regulations about when and where carts or people might move within the city. Meanwhile, the aesthetic alterations to the built environment, and regulating its wastes and airs, were a means to influence both human health, behavior, and attitudes.

Lady Warwick's Body

In the aftermath of the fire, and amid calls for the rebuilding of London, many writers urged the additional need for reforming the spiritual health of the city.[207] They reminded their readers that no matter how many streets were rebuilt, and no matter how many perfume boxes were prepared by physicians to ensure safe passage in plague-stricken streets, God's vengeance was stronger than any of these human-concocted defenses, and the dual catastrophes of plague and fire had been sent by a justly wrathful God. Writers like Samuel Rolle reminded fellow Londoners that the successful rebuilding of London would require well-made bricks, skilled builders, patrons with deep pockets, and willing magistrates, but they also needed to procure God's assistance, without which all other building successes would be fleeting. According to Rolle, "the great God may be prevailed with to bless and prosper the Building (in which sense he is said to be the builder) *viz.* by our keeping his Sabbaths, relieving his Servants, reforming our ways, and doings that are not good, rebuilding places for his Worship (out of love to Publick Ordinances)" as well as by "seeking his face and favour by Prayer and Fasting."[208]

For most residents, the destruction of London by fire had a very real and intensely personal meaning. At the end of his text on the rebuilding of London, Rolle offered a meditation on the resurrection of bodies, conflating the resurrected city and the resurrection of an individual body. According to Rolle, "I have closed this book with a Discourse of the Resurrection of our bodies, (those houses of clay in which we dwell)" and explained to readers it "is that Article of our Creed, which the resurrection of *London* doth most naturally, and easily put us in mind of, as the destruction of that City, did most genuinely lead us into the thoughts of our own death, and dissolution."[209] He claimed that in his book he attempted to draw out the ways in which personal, spiritual, civil, and national good might all benefit from its insights. Writers likewise encouraged those well beyond London, even if they had not been immediately affected, to meditate on the events and to feel keenly, and intimately, their relationship to the capital city. People throughout England were urged to imagine their fates as tied to that of Londoners, and the nation more broadly.[210]

Writers like Rolle insisted that individual and collective sins brought death and destruction down on the city. London suffered, but it was the responsibility of all those who dwelt in England and Wales (and the border towns between England and Scotland) to feel the weight of these tragedies. They claimed that collective immorality brought about plague and fire. Meanwhile, acts such as praying, fasting, and the weeping of sincere tears might end the destruction and bring about God's forgiveness. These who embraced these deeply embodied and personal acts of meditation and contrition understood them to have the power to alleviate the concerns and consequences described in this chapter.

While the city had a set of problems and concerns unique to its environment, it was also enmeshed within a wider network of political, economic, and ecological belonging. London was connected to communities throughout England and Wales in varied ways. It was the central "mart" that helped to circulate trade, infusing the city with materials and people from beyond its borders, and back out again.[211] It was also the center, or the "head," of the country. Even though many observers noted with worry that the head might have grown too big for the body—and might even be monstrous in size—they still imagined the city to be part of a living organism.[212] When Charles II ordered the whole country, not just Londoners, to fast in the wake of the devastating fire (as well as send money and donations on behalf of residents), he insisted that all were responsible for the devastations, so all had to atone. In this way, fasting became a means by which Charles II highlighted his sense of the personal, economic, political and religious ties between London and the rest of England; what happened to London was everyone's responsibility.

On September 13, 1666, the king issued a proclamation from Whitehall for *A General Fast through England and Wales, and the Town of Barwick upon Tweed* for October 10.[213] On that Wednesday, all of the king's subjects were to observe a day of "Solemn fasting and humiliation, to implore the mercies of God." The proclamation reminded England's inhabitants that "although the afflicting hand of God fell more upon the Inhabitants of this city," yet, "all men ought to look upon it as a Judgment of the whole nation."[214] On that day residents of England, Wales, and the Town of Berwick-upon-Tweed would be united in common supplications and devotions. The king particularly emphasized both the collective punishment and the need for collective supplications, such that "all his Subjects of what Estate or Degree soever" should devoutly observe the day.[215] At a future date the king would publish and supply them, collectively, with "a form of Prayer fit for that purpose." Those who did not observe the day would risk "incurring the utmost severities which can be inflicted upon the wilful breakers and contemners of this his Majesties Royal Command."[216] In the process of acknowledging collective sins, the nation simultaneously engaged in collective fasting. The many hungry bodies of England's residents—each aware of the broader collective that was fasting—imagined their political community, and political belonging, through their bodies.[217] A nation of contrite—but hungry—sinners was imagined into being. In the aftermath of fire, by simultaneously proclaiming general fasts and paving London's streets, Restoration officials engaged in material and abstract community-building processes.

Although various Restoration officials, writers, and the king all claimed that it was God's righteous displeasure for the sins of all of England that brought down disease and flames upon the capital, there were perhaps unexpected consequences to their message that the nation's collective sin was responsible for these devastations. In response to fears over her individual responsibility for plague, fire, and losses in war with the Dutch, Lady Mary Rich, Countess of Warwick, fervently prayed, wept, sighed, and fasted, and imagined that her body and her prayers were capable, in turn, of shaping the fate of the nation.[218] If Charles II and Restoration officials intended to control the message about responsibility and guilt and assert further control over the nation through an insistence on fasting, residents of England may have felt a kind of empowerment by the belief that their actions, thoughts, and bodies had the power to shape national affairs. In this case, Warwick was certain that her fervent prayers and tears were powerful tools to influence England's fate, through reconciling the country to God.

In the morning of July 26, 1666, Warwick awoke and went outside to her gardens to walk and meditate on God. She later wrote in her diary that upon hearing gunshots in the distance she was "much affected" by "consideration of the great sines of this nation."[219] It was these sins that had so "provoked god to punish us with the sorde [of God], and of man, and was very deasirous to be [one of] those who morned and [sighed] for the boominations that was comited in the land," and for her and "own personale sines that had helped, and was a maine [in]gredient to pull doune these miseryes" upon England. In the midst of the Second Dutch War, which lasted from 1665 to 1667, England suffered several dramatic losses at sea, as well as the demoralizing Raid on the Medway. On that July morning Warwick prayed that God might grant her a mourning heart for her sins, and in response, "god was pleased to give abundance of teares, and many groans, and [sighes] for sinn, and much compassion for the poore widowes, and fatherless children that ware made so by this bloody sea fight of which the noyse still sonded in my ears."[220]

Several days later, on a Sunday morning, July 29, 1666, Warwick awoke and "when ready walked in the willdernesse to stur upe my heart to be prepared for the dutyes of the day, then went to my clossett and red in the worde. then went to prayer the heart was excidingly cared out to blesse god for his godnes in praeserveing my famely from sickness, for his plenty."[221] Although the plague had largely subsided in London after its worst months in 1665, it was still killing many, and the contagion had spread throughout the country. On August 1 Warwick selected her own day of fasting for God's further prevention against the plague.

In the evening of September 3, after a dinner during which she hosted "much company," frightening word arrived. She received "newes of Londons being on fire, which much amased and troubled me. and made me pray hartily for that poore distressed plase and people, the fire began the 2d of Sep."[222] The following morning her sister, Lady Ranelagh, went to London, while Warwick walked in her garden so that she might "thinke of the sad miseryes of poor London, and to get my heart affected with them, then reatired and prayed for them. after dinar came the newes of halfe the cityes being burnte doune, and the fire still goeing on to devoure, I fonde my heart mightily affected for the poore sufferers there and reatired into my clossett, and got Mr Smith to pray with me for mercy for that poore city, god was pleased in the prayer to give abundance of teares, and to inable me to send up strong cryes for mercy," and after a short visit with sickly Mr. Clark she returned to her rooms to pray yet again for the "poore city."[223]

The following morning, September 5, she conducted another "fast day." Warwick got out of bed and went outside to her garden in order "to meditate and to consider what I had done in particular to provoke God to punish this nation." Later, back inside, she fervently prayed, confessed her sins to God, and wept "sorely" for her own and the nation's sins.[224] Throughout her diary she constantly imagined that her own sins, and the collective sins of people throughout the nation, had brought tragedies to England's shores. They had individually and collectively sinned against God. The deeply personal and physical responses to the sounds of war, or the news of fire, underscore the intimate way Warwick experienced national news. She imagined a complicated interaction between the material and immaterial worlds. Tears wet on her cheeks and her fasting, hungry body as well as her fervent prayers and meditations were all ways in which her material self and immaterial soul might influence England's future. After pestilence and fire, England's residents imagined London to be a place in need of many kinds of renewal, including spiritual and physical, which were intimately related for observers like Warwick.

If Restoration officials increasingly imagined for themselves a capacious ability to control and transform subjects' physical bodies and political attitudes by altering landscapes—like widening city streets or recommending certain dietary regimes—Warwick's diary provides a glimpse at the flip side of this equation. The subjects of Charles II imagined their fervent prayers and the bodily expressions of grief and guilt had the power to influence England's fate by turning God's righteous anger from their lands.[225]

In 1672 Dr. Woodward reflected that "The Fire however disastrous it might be to the then inhabitants, had prov'd infinitely beneficial to their Posterity; conducing vastly to the Improvement and Increase, as well as the Riches and Opulency, as of the Splendor of this City." He did not doubt that the fire had done a kind of service to the city by demolishing the medieval city and enabling some small modifications of the city's layout and infrastructure. Woodward noted that he "and every Body must observe with great Satisfaction, by means of the Inlargements of the Streets; of the great plenty of good Water, convey'd to all Parts; of the common Sewers, and other like Contrivances, such Provision is made for a free Access and Passage of the Air, for Sweetness, for Cleanness, and for Salubrity, that it is not only the finest, but the most healthy City in the World."[226] The doctor thus highlighted the city's salubrious air, achieved by widening streets. If scholars generally agree that Londoners did not accomplish much in relation to the transformative schemes they had proposed for the rebuilding of London, some residents looked around them and saw a city altered for the better, even if the changes were minor by comparison.

In the aftermath of plague and fire, contemporaries discussed the best methods for rebuilding London and considered the complex relationships between the built environment, population health, and government policy. Many of these discussions and publications about infrastructural changes reflect a capacious, and growing, sense of the government's right and responsibility to intervene in the health and well-being of subjects.[227] In many instances, those rebuilding London took a proactive stance on public health and public order. The Plague Orders, new legislation on rebuilding in the city, orders issued by commissioners of sewers, and advice literature that simultaneously offered the means of managing an individual's bodily health and the health of the social body underscored the ways in which "models of behaviour" and "outward bodily propriety" were intimately tied up with the functioning and health of the body and body politic.[228] It further argues that many of these changes took place in a particular cityscape in which people moved and lived. Changes to London's infrastructure reflect this attention to the moral, humoral, and spatial human geography of the city and shaped plans of urban design around the Anglo-Atlantic.

Meanwhile, the problems facing London during these years were of such a magnitude that Restoration officials sought to extend their political reach over London and its residents. Numerous contemporaries believed that responses to these events required power and money to deal with them quickly and decisively. The people who claimed the power to regulate Londoners' movements, moderate the airs of the city to benefit collective health, and issue proclamations ordering the opening of markets in the immediate aftermath of fire included city aldermen, the City Council, as well as members of the royal court. Plague and fire reconfigured the face of authority in London, at least temporarily. As London rebuilt, Charles II sought to extend greater control over the human and built landscapes of the city as he simultaneously advanced his broader goals of imperial reform. Published discourses of improvement, healing, and remaking demonstrate that English Restoration officials sought new languages of sovereignty in the wake of pestilence, fire, and war. They suggested that the English polity required new methods and aims of statecraft attentive to both landscapes and people.

2 / Taming Fenland Bodies: Draining a Wilderness of Water

In the seventeenth century the bodies of the residents of the fenlands in eastern England were the stuff of legend. Their webbed feet, pallid complexions, and hunched stature seemed to set them as a community apart. It appeared to visitors to the region that their sickly pallor, "ffenny posture," and "turfy sent" were the result of the seasonally swampy land they called home and the unhealthy airs emitted by their murky, marshy surroundings.[1] Negative depictions of fenlanders were not limited to their physical bodies and the dangerous miasmas they inhaled. Descriptions of sickly bodies and high rates of mortality served as denouncements of the diminished moral and spiritual aptitude of residents of the fens. Early modern men and women associated sickness, odor, and sin, often imagining that a people's physical appearance and healthfulness projected their interior morality. In 1663, members of the recently reformed Bedford Level Corporation rehabilitated these intertwined ideas. They built upon, and expanded, existing discourses detailing drainage undertakers' interventions into the fen landscapes, particularly in the region known as the Great Level, or the Bedford Level.

Although an earlier generation of Bedford Level adventurers claimed they had successfully drained the Great Level over a decade earlier, Restoration pamphlets, acts, and references to the fenlands continued to highlight the supposedly poor health of residents in the drowned lands of the fenlands to justify their projects. On the one hand, the appearance of such criticisms was likely because issues with drainage infrastructure, the necessity of repairs, and major flooding questioned broad claims of success. As a result, Restoration projectors once again offered designs for draining the fens while the newly chartered scientific society, the Royal Society, inquired about the "best waies of Drayning Marshes, Boggs, fens, &c."[2] On the other hand, the rhetoric about sick lands and sick people in need of state assistance was a powerful and flexible rhetoric that Restoration officials could rehabilitate, build upon, and apply to a range of settings. Throughout much of the seventeenth century, drainage promoters wrote tracts in support of their projects in which they questioned the very humanity of the inhabitants of the fens by calling attention to their apparent mental, spiritual, and physical deficiencies and pointed to the fenlanders' rude manners and uncivil behaviors as further evidence of the ill effects of the environment on bodily comportment. Pro-drainage projectors pointed to the necessity of remaking such brutish bodies and rotten landscapes, claiming that both could be transformed and incorporated into a healthy and well-functioning body politic.[3] This chapter explores the long history of these claims and investigates why they continued to resonate long after purported drainage success. It further considers how and why Restoration-era commentators embraced rhetoric about the ill health of fenlanders and the need for state intervention on their behalf. When seeking royal support, pro-drainage projectors fashioned claims about taming and curing uncivilized and unhealthy places and people; by supporting their projects, Charles II would have the opportunity to tout his power and healing acumen. Projectors further promised that disorderly, lazy, and "wandering Beggars" of the fenlands would be "set to work."[4]

In order to gain support for their work, drainage promoters suggested that the fen landscapes, much like the residents of the fens, posed a potentially destabilizing threat to the king's fragile authority. Anxiety about the fen dwellers had many causes. They were famous for their riotous behavior, particularly during the recent civil wars.[5] Fenlanders wrote antidrainage screeds, rioted, and tore down drainage works to defend themselves against projectors who sought to turn vast swaths of the fenland commons into private property.[6] Fenlanders could not easily shake off such ascribed character traits. Fenlanders' supposedly unhealthy bodies, the types of activities they engaged in, and the relative inaccessibility of the wetlands they called home (despite claims that they had been successfully drained in the 1650s) were all deemed potential threats to a properly functioning body politic. In his support of drainage, the king's efforts paralleled, in part, those of other monarchs who similarly signaled their "political authority" by engaging in massive landscape transformations, such as the construction of the Canal du Midi or the gardens at Versailles in France.[7] Chandra Mukerji has revealed several such projects of "political territoriality" that served as "a silent demonstration of disciplinary power over the earth" and "pointed obliquely towards techniques of governance that lay beyond the visible and familiar."[8] This chapter situates Restoration-era drainage projects within a broader European context. It also suggests that in England, projects of political territoriality were further justified by drainers' claims that their work also healed and disciplined residents' bodies.

No matter if they were living on or near the coast in salt marshes, farther inland in freshwater peat fens, or on the edges of these wetlands on higher ground, residents had long lived their lives in relative isolation, occupying landscapes largely inaccessible to outsiders during seasonal high waters. And yet, despite being relatively cut off from outsiders, there was a great deal of communication and cooperation among communities of the region and in the development of local forms of land regulation.[9] With its ill-defined boundaries and communities that seasonally operated beyond the control of the state, the fenlands nevertheless remained linked by routes of trade to larger population centers, including London. The ways of life of fenlanders were shaped by their residence in coastal zones, making them ideal subjects to study as part of the "new coastal history," which encourages scholarly emphasis on coasts as "contact zones rather than lines of separation."[10] While drainers may have positioned fenlanders as outsiders, fenland edges and coasts had porous boundaries. Travelers were discomfited by the hybrid nature of the fens, writing about towns that were "an equilibrium Plantation of Earth & water" and therefore neither maritime nor terrestrial.[11] Even as they spun tales of an agrarian future for the drained fenlands, projectors continued to imagine establishing a connection to maritime industries, by cultivating commodities necessary to shipbuilding.

Due to the perceived environmental impact of the fens on human health and character, English writers had long coded watery landscapes as dangerous places where pockets of unruly people dwelt. The challenging landscapes of the fenlands, described as "a wildernesse of water," offered a key explanation for its inhabitants' status as physical, social, and perhaps even spiritual outsiders.[12] Their appearance differed from the residents of other regions of England, and fen society had a different demography than other regions in England, a result of higher rates of child mortality, for example.[13] By draining fenlands, projectors claimed they could refashion the bodies and attitudes of the residents for the better, thereby transforming sickly or deformed outsiders into well-behaved and robust members of civil society. Boundary-subverting landscapes like wetlands, which were neither water nor land, intrigued early modern people for whom place mattered a great deal to a porous human body. Writers discussed the dangers posed to malleable human bodies by wetlands in England, Ireland, and in the Americas. Throughout the Restoration era, scientific societies such as the Royal Society of London solicited and collected stories about the transformative power of waters that turned wood to stone, altered one species of bird into another species, dissolved kidney stones, and cured illnesses. The influence of water and watery places on human bodies was used to explain diverse phenomena, including everything from differing temperaments, manners, and height, to digestive operations.[14]

Waters and wetlands not only influenced individual bodies. Projectors and improvers who wrote in support of draining fens, bogs, and swamps also pointed to the benefits that would accrue to entire communities. Not only would the community receive health benefits from drainage, they claimed, but rude, barbarous, and lazy pastoralists, alongside those who had benefited from the use of wastelands as commons, would be forced to become settled agriculturalists and tenants or day laborers on enclosed estates. Dangerously riotous outsiders (with associations to political movements like the Levellers in previous decades) might be reformed, and thereby neutralized in the process.[15] Moreover, draining advocates regularly described their work as a means of healing or curing sick and suffering fields. Writers of agricultural manuals advised that draining was critical to "Remedying the Diseases" and "Annoyances" of fenny or boggy ground. Indeed, drainage could "cure cold and moist land."[16]

The possibility of transforming and civilizing entire fenland communities by reshaping the surrounding environment had long been touted by adventurers and projectors when offering justifications for their activities. They claimed that their drainage efforts in the fenlands would be a healthful boon to residents, who would no longer suffer from the stagnant, stinking miasmas swirling dangerously above the soggy, fenny grounds. The Bedford Level Corporation shareholders resuscitated and expanded upon these ideas to garner support for their schemes to continue the work of draining the more than three hundred thousand acres of the Great Level. They claimed the dull, heavy, and stultifying airs were nearly suffocating the dull, heavy, and stultified residents of the fens but that these unhealthy airs could be dispersed if Bedford Level

Corporation members were granted the rights, money, and time to complete their drainage schemes.[17] They did not dwell, of course, on the fact they stood to benefit enormously from the vast tracts of arable land they would uncover and lease out, gained at the expense of residents' loss of their fens commons.

Bedford Level projectors promised that their work would improve residents' health, domesticate the people and the place, and facilitate accessibility, travel, and trade in the region. Moreover, they claimed that wetlands were in fact unnatural and the result of the residents' laziness. They claimed they were simply restoring the landscape to its previously dry state.[18] Unimproved, boggy landscapes, left to devolve into their present state, had resulted in a range of unwelcome activities, including unsettled pastoralism. Pastoralism had no place in a culture that prized private property and cultivated fields as an ideal national nature as it implied a failure to domesticate a wild and barbarous landscape and implicated residents' laziness. Richard Franck, a seventeenth-century traveler to Scotland, wrote disapprovingly of a landscape "besieged with Bogs, and barracadoed with Birch trees" and claimed that the "boggy Swamps incommode the Traveller." In Franck's depiction of a militant landscape, bogs and birch trees acted to overwhelm and subvert travelers' aims. Franck further castigated the "Natives" of the region, claiming "in the Winter-Season, [they] employ themselves only to recreate Swine there, because [they are] a People uncultivated in Agriculture."[19] Residents of the fens were similarly stigmatized and portrayed as having only subsistence-based economies, even though their economies and diets were often rich and varied.

Portrayals of uncivil fenlands enabled corporations such as the Bedford Level to justify their schemes as well as their land grabs. They sought to assure Parliament that in addition to a range of economic benefits, the health and collective temperaments of residents of the fens would likewise be transformed, all to the greater benefit of England. Such rhetoric of improvement had long justified a range of schemes that ignored the multiplicity of property claims and communities' access to their commons, even though they raised a host of constitutional questions and issues.[20] For decades, drainage opponents had frequently portrayed their opponents as abusing royal prerogative for personal financial gain, initiating projects that were "destructive to Propriety and the bane of the Commonwealth." According to the author of *The Picklock of the Old Fenne Projects* (1650), Sir John Maynard, the intentions of the drainers were evidence of "the height of Arbitrary Government and Tiranny itself."[21] He directed his anger at the gains of the drainers at the expense of the commoners. The drainers would claim large swaths of land used by commoners as collective pastureland for themselves, turning common land into private land. With little gained and much lost, many fenlanders expressed hostility to the drainage plans.[22] Moreover, the legal history of the fens was complex, and after various acts, grants, and revocations of grants in the decades around midcentury, "the level was left a legal no man's land."[23] If executive favor had once been enough to initiate broad drainage schemes, such as those castigated by Maynard, "neither prerogative courts nor prerogative undertakings were restored at the Restoration."[24]

By supporting drainage projects, Charles II asserted greater control over places and people long associated with social foment. Eric H. Ash has argued for the importance of fen drainage to the process of state building. Fen drainage offered Charles II the opportunity to "demonstrat[e] mastery over . . . valuable specialized knowledge," which "reinforced the legitimacy of early modern states as they consolidated their power and exert[ed] their expanding authority."[25] By claiming a role for the state in managing the nation's natural resources, the king also positioned himself as England's ideal steward. Publications celebrating the successful completion of Great Level drainage, such as Moore's, removed references to the Protectorate and instead added forewords feting Charles II as the good steward who somehow had the forethought to support projects of value to the commonwealth. Meanwhile, whether addressing Oliver Cromwell or Charles II, writers also suggested that "the *State* itself" should undertake some "publick works."[26] While tracking the relationship between fen drainage and state building, this chapter further examines why drainage projectors, like the Dutch drainage projector Cornelius Vermuyden, included claims about healing bodies and landscapes in their proposals.

Wetlands challenged the English and their ideas about governance at home and in Ireland, as well as in the American colonies, in a number of ways, and they took steps to render such spaces, and the people who lived there, legible and controllable.[27] Scholars of the history of the senses have tracked the "revaluation" of the senses in the eighteenth century and the rise of sight as the sense most associated with reason, modernity, and techniques of observation, discipline, and control by emerging states.[28] Among the frustrations voiced about the fens was that it was a "large continent" above which hovered "foggie" air and clouds of "Gnatts" hindering visibility, suggesting challenges to governance.[29] It is also likely that one of the frustrations of watery landscapes that perturbed members of a society increasingly concerned with private property was that such boggy landscapes made it hard to mark boundaries. Not only did wetlands often lack the traditional types of boundary markers necessary to those drawing estate maps or marking properties, such as with fences or trees, but simply accessing the landscape likewise made boundary-marking processes more difficult. In many other regions of early modern England, parishes engaged in an annual procession that marked the borders of the parish by walking the bounds, or, in New England, "beating the bounds."[30] Wetlands, marshes, bogs, and fenlands made this kind of place-making or -marking difficult, if not impossible (especially if you were not dexterous on stilts like fen dwellers were supposed to be).[31] It may be that because challenging fen landscapes were hard to define, they produced anxiety in those who sought to control them. Inaccessible landscapes thwarted the desire to map, demark boundaries, create private property, or transform the earth in ways that were recognizably English. As the historian Allan Greer has argued, on both sides of the Atlantic "the process of state formation and property formation went hand in hand."[32] This formulation suggests that much was at stake if states had no property to regulate and adjudicate to create an "archival edifice" of records to justify its own existence.[33]

This chapter and the following one point to the importance of a comparative Atlantic frame when considering English attitudes toward wetlands. Particular topographies inspired certain kinds of actions by the Restoration state. Fears of inaccessible wetlands and of the individuals who called those landscapes home led to drainage projects in English, Irish, and colonial American landscapes alike. Using a comparative Atlantic lens reveals an ongoing and critical dialogue between domestic and imperial drainage developments. It also reveals personnel involved in domestic and imperial ventures.[34] Moreover, Atlantic-wide debates over how to define improvement (that is, for whom the improvements were intended and who had the right to define them as improvements) raised questions about innovation and prerogative power. As chapter 3 also suggests, protests over drainage projects required by the colonial government along the Delaware River drew on drainage laws in England to fight against officials' labor requirements. Both sets of drainage projects regularly relied on Dutch labor and expertise.

Domestic projectors often used similar rhetoric as colonial officials to justify their projects of improvement, including drainage, or claimed that cultivars planted as a result of improvement projects might facilitate colonial settlements, such as the growing of hemp made into cordage for shipping, in the drained fenlands. At other times, however, they positioned their improvements as an alternative to colonization. They pointed to their projects of improvement within England while simultaneously casting doubt on the utility of colonial holdings. For instance, some fen drainage projectors claimed that by revealing vast domestic lands in England's interiors, their work was more useful to England's strength and power than establishing distant colonies was or could be. Fen projectors claimed that their projects enabled the internal colonization of England because their projects would create a *new* New World of economic possibility.[35] They promised the land reclaimed would be just as productive as that of Virginia, for instance, but simply closer to home. Drainage projects are thus an additional lens into Atlantic-wide conversations and debates about improvement, the nature and limits of political subjecthood, and the proper location and extent of English territory.

Whereas one group of early modern English writers saw agricultural improvement projects as intimately related to colonization efforts and urged the transplantation of plants to and from the Americas to ensure a balance of trade in England's favor, others saw in improvement a viable and desirable alternative to imperial expansion. These latter voices suggested that the ability to intensively cultivate, as well as skillfully plant, desired plants would obviate the need to expand into new lands and extensively cultivate. In *Adam out of Eden, or, An abstract of divers excellent Experiments touching the advancement of Husbandry* (1659) Adolphus Speed declared he intended his work to benefit the public, and he urged his readers to advance the art of husbandry in England. To do this they should "Embrace this opportunity, and reduce these Precepts to practice: England affords Land enough for the Inhabitants, and if men did but industriously and skillfully improve and manure it, we need not go to Jamaica for new plantations."[36] According to Speed, and later Restoration authors, colonial expansion was the result of failed internal improvement. And to early modern observers, new plants, innovative techniques, and proposals could be everywhere they looked, in abundance.

The Fenlands

The whole of the fenlands stretched over approximately seven hundred thousand acres.[37] In addition to the East Midlands, the fens stretched into counties in the east of England, including Cambridgeshire, Lincolnshire,

Norfolk, and Suffolk. The total area of the Great Level, also known as the Bedford Level, prior to major drainage projects at midcentury, was over three hundred thousand acres. The highly varied ecology of the fens consisted of salt marshes near the coasts, peat fens, moors, washes, and major rivers and tributaries crisscrossing the landscape. In a treatise written in 1642, a Dutch drainage projector, Cornelius Vermuyden, described the fens as "broad," "of great extent," "flat, with little or no descent of its owne," and thus this low-lying landscape was regularly inundated with waters.[38] The vast expanse lay near, and at times below, sea level.

Near the coast, in an area called the Wash, lay an estuary zone characterized by the meeting of fresh water emptying into the bay from numerous rivers and saline water washed in from the ocean. It was a constantly changing landscape. Over the centuries the coastline varied greatly, altered by the regular buildup of sand on the coasts, such that some former coastal towns later lay miles inland. At times the tidal mud flats lay deep underwater, and at other times these low-lying flats were exposed, crisscrossed with rivulets, and marked with puddles, stretching for miles. As a result, the landscape of the Wash was a "loose, sandy floor," constantly altered by the ingoing and outgoing tides.[39] Because the fens were often inundated by both incoming and outgoing waters, not everyone appreciated the unique ecology of the Wash. Tracts painted an unflattering portrait of the area. At these low-lying locations, "the Tydes every day bring into the mouth of the Rivers a great quantity" of sand, so that "there is but a few times sufficient Land-water to set the Sands out againe, to keep the Outfall open, insomuch that *Welland* and *Wisbitch* [Wisbech] Outfals are chaoked every Summer." According to the director of works for drainage in the 1650s, Vermuyden, a Dutch engineer who found work remaking the English landscape under Charles I as well as during the Protectorate, this meant "that in processe of time, the outfalls of *Wisbich* and *Welland*, will utterly decay, by the said increase and Sands of the Sea, if they should remaine as now they are, by reason of the daily increase of the Marshes."[40] His visions of "choaked" and "decay[ed]" landscapes suggested the necessity of human hands to make them right. Vermuyden sought to make up for nature's insufficiencies and made a case for his bid to take on the work, and reap the monetary rewards, of remaking the English landscape.

Various rivers wound their way through the fenlands. These included the Welland, Nene, Wittham, and the Great Ouse. Collectively, these rivers had an enormous catchment area. The greater catchment upland and upriver was a landscape characterized by the intersection of many rivers.[41] Mostly broad and slow, these rivers could become rapidly moving with sudden rains or with the change in landscape levels. When Vermuyden assessed the rivers, he similarly claimed that they were choked with vegetation at the lower reaches, where they were "growne full of Hassacks, Sedge, and Reede," and that the rivers were so "full of Weeds" that "the Waters go slowly away from the Lands and out of the Rivers," whereas upriver "they come swift into and upon it out of the upland Counties, where the Rivers have a great fall."[42] Residents had attempted to control, reroute, and alter the courses of many of these rivers since the Roman era, with varied success.

Settlements in the fens were generally in areas that could offer some respite from the deepest waters. They clustered in areas like silt banks, which offered higher grounds for planting and construction. Some residents lived on islands, like Ely, that stayed dry year-round. Still others preferred the higher grounds of the uplands, located inland and at the edges of the fens. But there were scattered settlements throughout the region. These varied ecosystems led to many different kinds of settlements and ways of sustaining life. Those who occupied "half-lands" lived in zones where there was seasonal flooding. There, residents relied on turf-cutting, hay production, and part-time grazing.[43] Fen life and economy were shaped by the varied ecologies found in the region. In the low-lying areas, where there was little natural drainage and where it was flooded year-round, residents made salt and relied largely on fish, fowl, and reed collection. Everywhere they made great use of the natural bounty of the fens. Where it was environmentally feasible, they harvested peat, increasingly popular throughout England as tree resources became rarer.

Drainage adventurers, however, imagined a future when the ecology of the fenlands would be vastly different, when cows, pigs, fields of grains, and a range of agricultural products might be pastured and grown year-round. As things stood, midcentury projectors claimed that the "Soyle of this vast Coutry is Moorish, gathered and growne up higher by the Weeds and Oaze of the waters," and, as a result, "many of them are rich grounds, and all would (if they were well Drayned) be very profitable and become good grounds, especially after they bee burned, manured, and husbanded as such grounds should be."[44] Such quotes suggested that the fens were wasted in their drowned state and called out for improvement. While various drainage efforts had taken place on and off for centuries, the seventeenth-century projectors aspired to reach a vast region and engage in a qualitatively different style of drainage. They promised not only to drain the entirety of the vast Great Level but the "waters to overmaster." The drainage at midcentury aimed to make the region into so-called summer ground, which meant it would be available for planting and harvesting year-round.[45]

Drainage Histories

The Bedford Level Corporation was reconstituted by Parliament in 1663 to ensure the further drainage and future upkeep of the Great Level. Rhetoric about the ill health of the residents in the fens and the "unhealthful, raw & muddy Land" itself had long justified interventions into the fens in earlier eras.[46] Drainage projects were not initiated in the Restoration. Myriad efforts to manipulate and reclaim wetlands had a deep history. From altering the courses of the rivers to constructing local drainage networks, human hands had long sought to channel the water of the wetlands in ways that would suit their needs. There were coordinated efforts to drain the Great Level in the 1630s and again in the 1650s. After the latter effort, adventurers claimed success. In return for pumping money into the project, the investors received land, and lots of it, at the expense of the people who already lived there, as they enclosed commons as a reward for their investments.[47] Improvements and dispossession went hand in hand, as they did in various projects of drainage and enclosure around England.

The first commissions of sewers appeared as early as the thirteenth century. Charged with regulating drainage, they were the first formal organization established by the Crown that could offer recommendations about managing the nation's wetlands and rivers. Yet, even after the establishment of the commission, activities and draining initiatives in the fens were largely privately organized and continued to be of smaller scale than the vast, ambitious projects of the seventeenth century.[48] It was not until the General Drainage Act of 1600 that officials sought investors with the capital to undertake far larger drainage schemes to recover "many hundred thousand Acres of Marshes."[49] In several schemes the monarch was one of the drainage undertakers. On other occasions, the undertakers agreed to save a portion of the land for the king.[50] Many contemporaries praised these large-scale drainage works of the early and mid-seventeenth century. Drainers faced challenging work and local resistance. Indeed, fenlanders questioned the legality of drainage, pointing out that projectors had simply run roughshod over their rights by draining and enclosing their commons. Draining the Great Level further required overcoming technological and financial challenges. Getting so many hands to operate on one task simultaneously required a great deal of organizational effort, money, and experienced drainers with the skills to build various ditch and drainage works that worked in coordination over great distances. Coordinating labor over a sprawling area was daunting.

According to Cornelius Vermuyden, only when Charles I chose to step in and take control did major fen drainage projects become feasible, a claim that no doubt served to ingratiate Vermuyden with the monarch. After serving as director of works in the Hatfield Level in the 1620s, Vermuyden set his sights on the Great Level and crafted a proposal. In that proposal, Vermuyden reminded the king of a conversation in which Charles I lauded the foresight of his father for crafting the General Drainage Act, and "who for the Honour of this Kingdome (as his Majesty told me at that time) would not suffer any longer the said Land to bee abandoned to the will of the Waters, not to let it lye wast and unprofitable."[51] According to Vermuyden, the king could best initiate projects of national interest and overcome local opposition. Vermuyden reasoned, "because the Owners (who are very many) could not agree to doe so great a Worke (the one being willing the other not, the one able to contribute the other not)," the king had stepped in and had "bin pleased to undertake the making of those Lands Winter ground at his owne charge, whereby the said Foure hundred thousand Acres will be made profitable, firme and good."[52] What had been waste, and left to the "will of the Waters," would now be firm land reclaimed by the king.[53] According to Vermuyden, the king was the ideal steward of England's resources and best positioned to decide what was of most benefit to the whole of the nation. He claimed that the king might overcome, or override, individuals' opposition to their loss of property.[54]

Advocates of Crown- and investor-led ventures, and Crown prerogative, saw the piecemeal efforts of the past and the traditional mode by which the commissioners of sewers dealt with fenlands leading only to failure. The commissioners, long charged with local drainage works, traditionally sought to make collective decisions about the required repairs. They likewise relied on the thoughts, advice, and local knowledge of those experienced with ways of life in the fens. For centuries, it was left to local officials "to enforce routine orders for repairs," although they sometimes sought expertise, such as surveyors, "to carry out their more ambitious decrees."[55] When repairs were required, commissioners had the power to tax the community to raise the funds for labor or necessary tools.[56] Eric Ash contrasts these local, conservative efforts to upkeep extant drainage infrastructure with an "interventionist" model proposed by outsiders who ultimately sought to make the whole of Great Level dry land.[57]

The first large-scale efforts to drain the Great Level began in 1630, when the 4th Earl of Bedford, Francis Russell, received the right to drain. In return for venturing money on the scheme, the investors received ninety-five thousand acres. Each adventurer would get a lot encompassing four thousand acres, while the Crown would receive a lot of twelve thousand acres.[58] The scale of the work was massive, and Bedford employed numerous Dutch refugees as laborers. Dutch skill in drainage had impressed much of Europe, including Henry IV, who appointed Humphrey Bradley to "drain and develop marshland across France."[59] The Protestant Bradley began work in 1607. English projectors had long urged readers to imitate "the industrious Netherlander."[60] Ultimately, although Bedford declared the drainage complete, others charged that the adventurers had merely made the lands "winter grounds," meaning that they were only seasonally accessible, not fully drained to support year-round agriculture.[61]

Engaging in substantial drainage schemes risked significant political consequences for the undertakers and the Crown that enabled them to do so because drainage projectors sought to enclose enormous acreage of fenland commons.[62] Scholars have pointed out that the major drainage schemes under the early Stuarts "directly challenged established property rights and ultimately raised wider constitutional issues."[63] These schemes, which the king widely supported, "impinged upon the livelihood of the inhabitants of approximately 1430 square miles of fenland in eastern England," thereby challenging local property rights and commoners' access to their commons.[64] And while the dismissal of fenlanders' property rights was one of many grievances presented to Charles I in the Grand Remonstrance in 1641, fenland residents were also concerned that their ancient "way of life" was broadly "under assault" by outsiders who did not recognize its value.[65] Ultimately, the outbreak of the English civil war caused a variety of disruptions to the work, among them financial, and gave the justifiably discontented residents of the fens the chance to take back some of their land from the projectors and their works.[66]

In the 1650s, Bedford's son picked up where his father had left off after the House of Commons in May 1649 issued "The Act for the draining of the Great Level of the Fens."[67] The act granted the new drainage adventurers seven years to complete the drainage. In this second effort at drainage, initiated by the 5th Earl of Bedford, the aspirational scale of the works was once again simply astonishing. The aims of the drainage adventurers had also changed; in the second effort to drain the Great Level, they aspired not just to "winter grounds" but to year-round dry land. The adventurers secured the assistance of Vermuyden, the same Dutch expert who had designed the drainage works in the Hatfield Level. As many as ten thousand laborers engaged in digging, ditching, and dredging the rivers and sluices, working with spades and hauling displaced soil with wheelbarrows over the wet and uneven grounds.[68] According to Dorothy Summers, some of the multitudes of laborers working on excavating were Scottish prisoners captured in the aftermath of the Battle of Dunbar by Cromwell and forcibly marched south.[69] Among the approximately two thousand Scottish soldiers who survived the extreme conditions of the march, some worked in the fens, while others there were transported as convicts to the American colonies to work as laborers.[70] The addition of the forced labor of political prisoners to efforts to tame the wilderness of water underscores projectors' aspirations to assert control over people and landscapes at the same time. Observers judged the Great Level drainage completed in piecemeal fashion, one area in 1651, another in 1653. By 1656, visitors noted that cultivation was in progress in many of these newly arable lands. A charter of incorporation was next granted to the 5th Earl of Bedford and the adventurers so they could maintain the works over time.

After the Restoration, temporary maintenance acts were put in place until there was time to work out a longer-term solution to the maintenance of the drainage works in the Great Level. In 1663 Charles II issued a new General Drainage Act. The *Proclamation for the Preservation of the Great Level of the Fens, called Bedford Level, and of the Works made for the Dreining of the same* addressed the "Great Level of the fens, called Bedford Level, extending it self into the Counties of Northampton, Norfolk, Suffolk, Lincoln, Cambridge, and Huntington, and the Isle of Ely, or some of them," and praised those previous efforts at drainage that had been undertaken "by our right trusty and welbeloved cosin William Earl of Bedford," as well as the "participants and Adventurers for Dreining of the said Great Level at their very great costs and charges."[71] Charles II praised the work, claiming it was of "publick concernment, and great advantage, benefit, and profit to the whole nation," and therefore an act for the maintenance of such efforts "was made by us with Advice and Consent of the Lords and Commons assembled at Westminster."[72] The new act ensured that the newly founded Bedford Level Corporation regained rights to upkeep and drain the Great Level.

Bedford Level Corporation members were in a long line of English-men who justified their enterprises by proclaiming that their efforts were for the "Interest and Improvement of the nation" as a whole, regularly highlighting the practical application of their work and its value to the country in order to gain support for their projects.[73] In the case of fen drainage, projectors referred to their work as turning wasteland into a dry, cultivatable, productive zone.[74] Bedford Level projectors engaged in pamphlet wars to gain support for their works and to ensure public approval in the following decades. They claimed that they worked for the public good; moreover, they were doing what was best for the people of the fens, whether they appreciated it or not.[75] Those with "dull wits" who could only "judge by sense" did not have, according to the fen-drainage pamphlet authors, the circumspection or elevated awareness required to judge what was good and necessary for their own or the nation's well-being. Bedford Level Corporation investor Samuel Fortrey's *The History or Narrative of the Great Level of the Fenns* (1685) recounted the benefits of drainage and celebrated "heaps of Water turn'd to Land."[76] Fortrey suggested that those who abused the corporation and its works, in writing or by sabotaging the works, were little better than animals with dull wits and were led only by unthinking, bestial sensation, or passion, not by civilized reason. Fortrey described dismissively how inhabitants of the Great Level had made a formal complaint in 1653 detailing how the loss of their fen commons represented a significant loss in income, or at the very least "alleging that it was as much worth before the Draining in *Reed* and *Sedge* as since." Fortrey spent the next several pages dismissing these claims and calculating the benefits of drainage.[77] He offered his own estimates of the value of dry land to prove that draining the lands was the only realistic option.

But who were these "dull wits" so derided? Those living in the fens were famous in contemporary writings for their undomesticated wildness. They were belittled and stigmatized by drainage adventurers as having barely subsistence-level economies. Such a portrayal enabled corporations such as the Bedford Level to justify their schemes, as well as their enormous land grabs. To replace these smaller homesteads, settlement clusters, and vast common lands with large-scale farming techniques, as was occurring in parallel ways through enclosure initiatives elsewhere in the country, was seen as a way to domesticate, and make productive and visible, those portions of England that remained, in many real ways, outside of the control of the state. The association of the civil war with the fenlands was strong for many contemporaries, though some scholars have suggested that many fenlanders were less ideologically committed to one side or the other and were simply more interested in stopping the drainage works at a local level. Their riotousness often had nonpolitical, conservative aims, seeking to maintain their ways of life and customary rights, not to advance a broader political agenda.[78] More recently, Eric Ash has suggested that while fenlanders may not have been trying to "turn the world upside down," "this did not mean that they were unaware of the broader political context or that they lacked a political culture of their own through which they could articulate their interests as against those of the state."[79] Ash further points to drainage as an item included in the Grand Remonstrance to highlight fenlanders' awareness of how their complaints against the abuse of the king's prerogative powers were parallel to concerns held by other communities.[80]

Bedford Level Corporation reports are full of accounts of their attempts to regulate the fenland locals who were "apt to clamour against this Noble Work of Draining and the Undertakers thereof," and who regularly damaged the drainage works.[81] The fact that authors regularly reiterated established regulations against damaging company works or fighting with or threatening employees offers some insight into the variety of ways in which the Great Level inhabitants might have practiced resistance. It is possible to discern the extent of local protests and resistance to drainage through a litany of "lawless" acts listed. Local inhabitants were warned not to alter the dimensions of any river, drain, or sewer, "nor shall [they] Cut, Burn, Cast down, Break up, or do any hurt or damage to any River, Bank, Wash, or Foreland" within the Great Level. Nor could any damage be done, or change made, to the sluices, tunnels, bridges, gates, or rails.[82] If authors thought it prudent to insert and reiterate warnings against damage to company property, we may infer that it was a response to any number of actual, or feared, "lawless" incidents.

Such forbidden resistance again found enumeration in Charles II's *Proclamation for the Preservation of the Great Level of the Fens*, in 1663, based on the 1649 act. According to the proclamation, those who initiated damage to the drainage works risked the "pain of Our displeasure, and such punishment as is due to contemners of Our Royal Commands." Activities that fell under these categories included

all future Attempts, Disturbances, Interruptions, Entries, Forces, Riots, Assemblies, or any other unlawful Act or Acts tending to the disturbance of the publick peace within the said Great Level, or parts adjacent, or the interruption of the said William Earl of Bedford, participants, and Adventurers, their Tenants and Assigns, or of Us or Our Assigns, in the quiet possession and enjoyment of the said ninety five thousand Acres, or any part or parcel thereof, or of, or in any of the Rivers, Dreins, Cuts, Banks, Sasses, Sluces, Tonnels, or any other works made for Dreining of the said Great Level, or interruption, molestation, or disturbance of any their Officers, Agents, or Workmen, in any of their works of the said Great Level, or collecting, or levying any Taxes, or Arrear-Taxes, in order to preserve the said Great Level, until further order. And all our justices of the Peace, Mayors, Sheriffs, and other Ministers of Justice, and all other Our Officers, Military and Civil, and all Our loving Subjects, are hereby required to be aiding and assisting to the said Commissioners of Sewers, and such as they shall appoint, to . . . avoid Our Royal displeasure.[83]

This long list of forbidden activities and injunctions against damaging the works, refusing to pay taxes in support of public works projects, or hurting the "Officers, Agents, or Workmen" engaged in draining the Great Level provides a fairly comprehensive list of the activities of resistance that residents of the fens had either engaged in or the Crown worried they might engage in in the future.

To win over public opinion and maintain support from the Restoration court, projectors attempted to depict those who lived in the fens as both lawless and subhuman, deformed, or sickly, and with the temperaments to match these physical deficiencies. But the residents of the fens did not let such propaganda go unchallenged. In addition to engaging in a range of activities to resist the works, residents also printed treatises that portrayed a very different picture of fen life and highlighted the negative experience of draining. In these tracts, the authors claimed they sought to protect a way of life as well as preserve their land from the aggressive tactics utilized by corporations like the Bedford Company. Indeed, these authors turned the accusation that they were barbaric or animal-like back on their accusers. In *History of the University of Cambridge* (1655), Thomas Fuller wrote of the loss of common land in the fens, eulogizing their loss: "Grant them drained, and so continuing; as now the great fishes therein prey on the less, so the wealthy men would devour the poorer sort of people. Injurious partage would follow upon the enclosure, and rich men, to make room for themselves, would jostle the poor people out of their commons."[84] In *History*, Fuller presented the wealthy adventurers as predators, akin to a large fish devouring the smaller, unprotected fish, leaving them without land and without the means to sustain themselves.

Just as Thomas Hobbes described the "animalization" of man in nature, where "man is a wolf to man," as the outer limits of civil society, so Fuller questioned the right of the projectors to enclose and to cannibalize a way of life by tromping on the rights of the fen dwellers.[85] If vicious animals and cannibals were two types of beings haunting the limits of civil society, then it is clear that both sides in this debate utilized these tropes in propaganda to diminish their opponents. In *The History of Embanking and Draining of divers fens and marshes* (1662), William Dugdale, hired by the Bedford Company to celebrate their accomplishments, also published a fenlander protest song that offered a lyrical ode to life in the fens and a depiction of a way of life that the author claimed was coming to an end. Lives dedicated to fishing, with "boats and rudder," and transport by stilts had all but disappeared to "give place" to cattle.[86] The author lamented that "where we feed in Fen and Reed, they'll feed both Beef and bacon," and through large-scale drainage residents of the fens would become "prey to crows and vermine" without the means to stay alive. According to the singer, drainage adventurers "mean[t] all Fens to drain, and waters to overmaster," and when the land "[was] dry, and we must die," it was "'cause Essex cows want pasture."[87] That humans were being displaced to make room for cattle might have seemed a sensible plan to some of Dugdale's readers, but the song also contained an accusation about valuing grazing rights and cows above the rights of the women, children, and men of the fens, and their ways of life.

The Great Level Reclaimed

In the aftermath of their claimed successes in the Great Level, members of the Bedford Level Corporation advertised the reclaimed fenlands as a viable location for intensive tree and hemp growth, necessary to the naval and shipping industries, and praised the new agricultural prosperity of the region, crowing, "Here thrives the lusty Hemp, of Strength untam'd / Whereof vast sails, and mighty Cables fram'd."[88] According to writers like Samuel Fortrey, it was not only in the colonies that goods necessary for the construction of ships could thrive. Products necessary to building merchant and military ships also grew abundantly in the reclaimed fenlands. An intensified national interest in rehabilitating and adding to England's naval strength and overall shipping power went beyond the direct confrontations of the Second and Third Anglo-Dutch Wars. Perhaps more frightening to many English observers was that the Dutch appeared not only to control the trade routes at sea but were also in control of the varied products and processes necessary for the construction of ships. As one writer noted with frustration, the Dutch bought their hemp in Riga, manufactured that hemp into cloth for sails, and sold it as a finished product to the English, who bought it at high rates. This was a costly, even dangerous, dependency; something had to be done about the nation's lagging manufacturing industry. The author promised that if the English would grow enough of their own hemp and turn it into sailcloth on a scale necessary to meet the nation's purposes, they could compete successfully with the Dutch. Otherwise England had to purchase these finished products, such as linen, canvases, cordage, and nets, from the Dutch. The English worried that England's shipbuilding industry was deeply dependent on their bitter rivals.[89]

Authors urged the manufacture of products for ships in England. They likewise encouraged the Royal Navy, and shipbuilders more broadly, to seek out the raw products for shipping in the colonies. Dependence on Baltic sources for masts could be interrupted at any time by the Dutch; moreover, costs of supplies were a constant anxiety and concern. Against this backdrop writers frequently encouraged domestic replanting and regrowth in order to protect England's naval and merchant shipping futures. There were constant reminders that resources might prove tenuous. For instance, in 1663 Samuel Pepys waged an infamous administrative battle over supply costs related to the navy's contract for masts from the Baltic.[90] It was against this perception of impending crisis that John Evelyn published *Sylva* (1664) and suggested a range of possible means by which England might improve its domestic supplies as well as acquire them from the colonies. Evelyn joined numerous authors of promotional literature from the late sixteenth and early seventeenth centuries who suggested that the American colonies could be the solution to woodland scarcity.[91]

While Evelyn readied *Sylva* for publication, the Bedford Level Corporation promised that the reclaimed fenlands would be invaluable as a great swath of rich soil available for intensive tree and hemp growth, items required to build ships. At the same time, officials sought out tree resources in the colonies. Authors reported that in the colonies there were trees in such abundance that they were even considered a nuisance by some colonists. Evelyn, based on the recommendations by John Winthrop Jr., the governor of the Connecticut Colony and a founding member of the Royal Society, suggested removing those wasteful industries that consumed an abundance of wood, such as glass and metal industries, to the colonies, where "I am inform'd that the New-English (who are become very numerous, and hindered in their advance and prospect of the Continent by their surfeit of the Woods which we want) did about twelve years since begin to clear their High-ways by two Iron-mills. . . . This were the only way to render both our Countries habitable indeed."[92] Thus Evelyn presented what he imagined to be a simple equation: the colonists had too many trees, and England did not have enough. Meanwhile, Evelyn printed John Winthrop Jr.'s reports to the Royal Society recounting the vast number of fir trees, and their associated products, that were available in New England. He reported how a ship carrying "goodly Masts of fir, which I have seen, and measur'd, brought from New England" had arrived in London to widespread admiration.[93]

Bedford Corporation member Samuel Fortrey's cousin, John Josselyn, reported that Maine was "clothed with infinite thick woods," and he published two books on his observations of New England's natural "rarities" after two journeys to the region.[94] As Josselyn wrote, the spruce trees were generally acknowledged to be "absolutely the best Trees in the World" for ship masts and sail yards, and they were plentiful in Maine.[95] By the time Josselyn returned to New England in 1663, Massachusetts was already well established as a trading center for the upland lumber that came from New Hampshire and Maine. While the historian Keith Pluymers has "reconnect[ed] histories of environmental thought and political economy while demonstrating that the political ecology of wood shaped colonial developments across the early modern English Atlantic," by focusing on Virginia and Ireland, a similar confluence also shaped claims about the drained fens' potential to support woodland.[96]

Bedford Level Corporation members tapped into anxieties about wood scarcity and, like colonial promoters, promised that drained lands could support abundant tree growth in service of national wealth and strength. Fortrey's promise that trees and hemp would grow abundantly in reclaimed fenlands was based on his claims that there had been abundant growth in the distant past. According to Fortrey, there had once been a multitude of trees in the fenlands, long before it had been inundated by water, and thus he believed that there might be trees once again. Citing the ancient text of William of Malmsbury, Fortrey argued that the Great Level had once been "a very Paradise . . . bearing Trees, that for their Straight tallness, and the same without knots, str[o]ve to touch the Stars."[97] Such a prelapsarian vision of abundance suggested that the wetness of the fenlands had been an aberration, not its natural state, and that in the wake of reclamation the fenlands might regain its vegetation.

Claims that ancient trees had once grown in what became fenlands or bogs was not unique to Bedford Level adventurers. Reports from the Dublin Philosophical Society (founded in 1683), for instance, recorded evidence from across Ireland that indicated lands that were now bogs had once been covered in trees. Informants reported locating the preserved remnants of immersed giant specimens.[98] One of the ways to express the latent potential of the land and prove that drainage enterprises could produce as promised was to convince investors that land once conducive to such abundant vegetation might be made so again. In this light, bogs, fenlands, and swamps were all wastelands simply waiting to be improved and made once again productive. Inundated lands were not considered to be in their natural state. Instead, it was widely believed that bogs, like fenlands, were the unfortunate and unnatural results of lazy humans living in decaying, postlapsarian, and unimproved landscapes who lacked the skills to uncover and re-create formerly abundant land. Instead, rising waters, left unchecked, had drowned multitudes of useful trees. Once the fenlands, or bogs, were drained and brought back to their perceived *original* state, projectors claimed that the rich soil would be the perfect place for cultivating any number of goods, including hemp and the tall, straight trees heralded by Fortrey.[99]

Authors in the seventeenth century regularly pointed to human failure to explain the existence of watery wastes, coding both land and the people who lived within or beside them as spiritually fallen and barbaric and in need of saving and improving. Evidence of ancient habitations in locations that writers then deemed uninhabitable indicated that the present time was one of decay and was marked by poor stewardship of the land. Contributors to the Dublin Philosophical Society discussing Ireland frequently pointed to evidence of a cultivated and settled past, suggesting an equation for future prosperity by advising an input of English culture, including forms of agriculture, that would produce a transformed and improved Ireland. Among the accounts of Ireland's natural and human histories collected by the Dublin Philosophical Society is "An Account of the manner of Manuring Lands by Sea Shells as practised in the Countys of Londondery & Donegall." The anonymous author of the account declared: "Tis certain Ireland has been better inhabited than it is at present. Mountains that now are covered with boggs have formerly been plowed: for when you dig five or six foot deep you discover a proper soile for vegetables and find it plowed into Ridges and furrowes." Such evidence was observable in a wild mountaine between Ardmagh and Dundalke where the redoubt is built and Likewise on the mountaines of altmore the same as I am inform'd has been observed in the County of Londonderry and Donegall a plowgh was found in a very deep bogge in the Latter and a hedge with wattles Standing under a bogg that was five or six foot deep . . . I have likewise seen Large old Oaks grow on land that had the Remaines of Ridges and furrow and I am told that on the Top of an high mountain in the north, there are yet Remaining the Street and footsteps of a Large Town. in truth there are very few places, but either visibly or when the bogs are Removed there Remains Marks of the Plough which sure must prove that the Countrey was well inhabited. Tis likely that the Danes first and then the English destroyed the people and the old woods. Seem to those that pretend to judge to be about three hundred or four hundred years standing which was near the time that ... the English subdued the North of Ireland and Tis likely made havock of the people that Remained after the Danes were beat out of Ireland.[100]

Writers regularly pointed to an ancient Irish past of extensive and intensive agriculture. They located evidence for this past deep in the bogs that now covered formerly large towns as well as the remains of ridges, furrows, and other "Marks of the Plough." They claimed that an intervention could bring about a restoration of the neglected country. However, the suggestion by this contributor that the English were the cause of the depopulation and woodland depredations offered a potentially subversive counterclaim about who was best suited to reclaim boggy Irish lands.

Accounts of efforts to drain Ireland abound in the Dublin Philosophical Society records. In a letter addressed to the Lord Bishop of Meath, privy councilor of Ireland and vice chancellor of the University of Dublin, an anonymous author wrote that in response to the bishop's "commands to commit to writing such remarks concerning the county of Westmeath as I in my time might have taken notice of," the author had committed some observations to writing.[101] The author noted that residents of Westmeath practiced draining in their husbandry, but although it was "somewhat . . . done amongst us," now more frequently than before, it still fell "far short of what might be and what is necessary for a work so much conducing to publick good.[102] Thus the author saw room for improvements in drainage practices in Westmeath and asserted that even what appeared to be overwhelmingly challenging landscapes might be "bettered by draining," and in the case of the bogs around the Iron Lake, they might be made suitable for pasturage. Draining also uncovered turf so that residents might "cut five hundred in a day" when they could formerly cut none. Draining further enabled a safer and more accessible landscape: "where one could not have walked without hazard; he may now ride securely."[103] The ability to cross safely across wetlands was a critical outcome heralded by the many authors who promoted drainage projects. This author also argued that within the bogs was copious evidence of ancient branches and trees, suggesting "further arguments in confirmation of my former Conjecture that our Iron Lake and our boggs that now bound it were formerly woody pastures."[104] If trees had once grown there, they might do so again and could provide raw materials necessary to the construction of ships.

As with many contemporaries, the anonymous author made implicit links between unimproved landscapes and unimproved human society. When describing the "Customes and Manners" of the residents, the author claimed that the people of Westmeath, "of old were in many Instances Rude and barbarous" and might still be found "howling" at wakes and burials.[105] But the author went on to suggest that "by the long Converse and Domination of our English and by the Care taken by our Ancestors by Statute Laws to abolish the worst and most Rude of their usages the peple are become now more polite and civil and of their own accord are very ready to accommodate themselves in many things to the English modes," and certainly the author imagined lands "bettered by draining" as among those polite and civil transformations.[106]

Indeed, accusations of human ineptitude and laziness were used to justify all manner of actions taken by those who claimed to act on behalf of an intervening state, and projectors used such rhetoric when securing state support. The fenlands, like much of Ireland, were perceived as places whose unhealthy and "intemperate" residents posed potential dangers and had not yet been integrated into the state, posing potential threats.[107] As Charles II and his Privy Council looked to centralize and rationalize a far-flung and growing empire, they simultaneously took steps to reclaim and reorder lands and people within England and Ireland. In eastern England the Bedford Level Corporation not only insisted that the lands they had reclaimed would have a beneficial impact on the nation by making arable what was formerly "waste" but also promised that regulated landscapes bred regulated people, who might be less inclined to rebellion.

Samuel Fortrey, author of *The History or Narrative of the Great Level of the Fenns* (1685) and one of the projectors of the Bedford Level

Corporation who sought to drain the Great Level, assured his readers that the drainage work was for the wider "Publick Good," just as he claimed it was for the local good of the fen dwellers, no matter their varied opinions on the matter. That Fortrey promoted such internal colonization as "of private Profit, and of Publick Store" was not a contradiction to Fortrey.[108] If it had "Begun with vertue, shall with Fortune, end, / For Profit publick thoughts do still attend."[109] In other words, fen-drainage adventurers like Fortrey were in a long line of Englishmen who justified their enterprises by proclaiming that their efforts were for the general benefit of the king's dominions, regularly highlighting the practical application of their work and its value to the country in order to gain support for their projects, even if they stood to gain personally from the ventures.

One of the many arguments deployed by the Bedford Level Corporation in writings intended to gain royal support for their projects, such as Fortrey's text, was that improving the fens would have an inevitable, and positive, impact on the bodies and morals and characters of the people who called it home:

> When with the change in Elements, suddenly
> There shall be a change of Men and Manners be;
> Hearts, thick and tough as Hydes, shall feel Remorse,
> And souls of Sedge shall understand Discourse,
> New hands shall learn to Work, forget Steal,
> New legs shall go to Church, new knees shall kneel.[110]

In Fortrey's *The History or Narrative*, the bodies of the people living in the fens were described as being made up of the assorted properties of the landscape. Their souls were made up of the sedge that grew in their watery surrounds. Moreover, they were portrayed as unruly and without manners, both because the environments in which they dwelt were inaccessible, which prevented oversight, and also because such environments were seen as constitutive of their bodies. Authors such as Fortrey proclaimed that fenland residents possessed "souls of Sedge" and "dull wits" able only to "judge by sense," like animals, and possessed body parts as thick and tough as animal "hydes." Such portrayals enabled him to dismiss their complaints about drainage. He suggested that because they were made up of animal hides and water weeds, they lacked the elevated awareness necessary to judge what was good for them. The drainage adventurers continued to be best placed to make decisions for them.[111] Those with the ability to look from above, not immersed within, the boggy landscape of the fens were the ones best suited to plan the future of the fens. Of course, Fortrey did not acknowledge the rich and seasonally varied foodstuffs residents collected and consumed because it was not, in his eyes, culturally "legitimate" arable agriculture.[112] This was yet another way to suggest that residents were incapable of doing what was in their best interests, thereby suggesting the importance of the Bedford Level Corporation continuing to lead the way toward an improved future.

Projectors celebrated their achievements in controlling and regulating nature, utilizing words such as "muzzled," "tam'd," "govern'd," "reclam'd," "curb'd," and phrases such as, "taught t'obey," and "confin'd as in a Gaol" to describe their work.[113] This dream of jailing the waters, taming and regulating them within man-made, straight ditches, suggests that improvers hoped both landscapes and populations might be remade through this pseudocaptivity and taught to obey.

In overflowing rhetoric, projectors frequently described political and social tumult in watery terms, such as raging seas, storms, and torrents. The residents of the fens, like the waters of the fens, they regularly described as riotous and uncontrollable. Perhaps because water can be so difficult to contain, an overwhelmingly powerful force in the form of enormous waves that batter beaches, or tides that pull inexorably out to sea, water is an especially useful analogy, for instance, to describe collective acts of rebellion. Sir John Denham's descriptions of the overflowing Thames in his midcentury poem "Cooper's Hill" may well represent "the mob-rule that now floods the countryside."[114] In the poem Denham described how, "When a calm river raised with sudden rains" overflows its banks,

> if with bays and dams they strive to force
> His channel to a new or narrow course,
> No longer then within his banks he dwells:
> First to a torrent, then a deluge swells;
> Stronger, and fiercer by restraint he roars,
> And knows no bound, but makes his power his shores."[115]

Such descriptions of water, dangerously unconstrained, likewise appear in pro-drainage literature and suggest that, much like contemporary writers such as Denham, images of water overrunning its banks evoked a range of environmental, social, and political meanings to readers. Specifically, writers frequently accused residents of the fens of destroying ditch and drainage works, allowing the waters to once again inundate the landscape. Meanwhile, fenlanders' protests also used the forces of unconstrained water to make the opposite case. Long after the Bedford Level Corporation claimed to have completed the Great Level drainage and secured their reward in lands and paying tenants, regular inundation by water called such claims into question. One anonymous author penned a satirical ballad lambasting the corporation for its failures and included lines detailing the constant inundation of waters, led by the anthropomorphized "Captain floud," who had successfully stormed and led the waters to overcome the insufficient drainage works. According to the author, Captain Flood had, once again, successfully "brocke ye banck & drownded all ye ffenn."[116]

One of the many claims projectors offered to garner support for their drainage works was that drainage made places more accessible. Compiled among the Dublin Philosophical Society papers is a report by Thomas Phillips on the location and condition of forts in and around Ireland.[117] Phillips suggested that for locals, one of the most significant features of bogs and fens is that they set places apart and made places difficult to access, offering a kind of moat-like protection:

> Towns were thought strong by being incompassed with bogs & Rivers and as great passes, all which I doe find to be quite contrary for ye Improvement of the Countery hath the Bogs and increase daily building and making for the benefit of the severall Counties bordering one upon another so that it will be to no End for his majtie to be at the charge to secure all passes when that there is noe stop or hindrance to be put to ye Improvement of a Countery that is and will be of soe great a value to ye Crowne.[118]

According to Phillips, bogs were "contrary" to improvement, and projects of improvement would be challenging and costly because the bogs seemed to stretch on endlessly. But Phillips suggested that drainage, and securing a way through the bogs, would be of "soe great a value" that the myriad challenges were worth attempting to overcome. We might extrapolate from this report by Phillips and suggest that, like residents of the Irish towns he described, many fenlanders might have valued the inaccessible environments in which they built their homes, which stymied travelers or officials sent to the region.

Centuries earlier the inaccessible and challenging nature of fen landscapes had attracted populations seeking isolation and a place to live a spiritual life. The significant religious centers of the fen region included Thorney Abbey, Ramsey Abbey, and Ely Cathedral. The fens were dotted with nunneries like Catsholme and Crabhouse, as well as monasteries and hermitages, which were all founded in the isolated, watery environ-ments.[119] Like the inaccessible fens, "remote, marginal or liminal places, such as topographical boundaries, river-crossings and bridges, tended to be chosen by solitary ascetics."[120] The myriad environments of the fens were just such locations, marginal worlds that obscured the edges of water and land.

Transforming Fenlanders' Bodies

English projectors had long held critical opinions of residents of watery landscapes in England. As Dugdale asked, "What expectation of health can there be to the bodies of men, where there is no element of good?" He described the air, water, earth, and fire of the region as "cloudy," "putrid," and "noisome."[121] The fens were places of "noisome and stinking vapours, as are indeed prejudicial" to the health of inhabit-ants, "but mostly to such as have been born and lived long in a better air."[122] New residents and travelers to the fens were particularly at risk because their bodies had not yet been seasoned to the region. Travelers also commented critically on the environmental impact on human char-acter. Watery landscapes had long been coded as dangerous places where pockets of unruly people dwelt, such as the inhabitants of the fenlands of England, because they lived in inaccessible and watery places. Rebellious residents of Ireland had long been similarly condemned for retreating to inaccessible "fastnesse of woods and boggs."[123] In England, officials asserted that residents of the fens could be successfully incorporated into the broader political body of the English nation through drainage.

Moreover, in terms of health, there was a great deal of difference between moving and unmoving water. Swift-running water might pro-mote health, whereas slow-moving or stagnant water was associated with miasma and disease.[124] Proximity to water might also be a cause of ill-ness. Living in and around marshlands came with a host of ailments, variously described as marsh fever, ague, or intermittent fever.[125] Travel-ers through the fenlands of Essex had long ascribed the poor health of the region's inhabitants to its peculiar geographical features. The links between water and poor health, travelers especially noted, were "nere the sea coastes . . . and other lowe places about the creekes."[126] Settlers to new places were aware that they needed to be well-informed about the local topography as it was deeply constitutive of health. Proximity to a creek, breathing in the local miasmas that rose up from a marshland and the salt of a seaside wind alike, might influence a person's health, likely for the worse. Places in or near water were often linked with particular ailments and might alter bodies temporarily or more permanently. Localized microclimates near water could contain dangerous miasmas. Scurvy, known as "the plague of the sea," had long been associated with travel, particularly oceanic voyages."[127] Travel writers regularly noted that voyagers who fell sick in transit recovered in a short time upon regaining the land.[128] As one commentator reasoned, scurvy was a disease of mariners and was particularly incident among "such as use the Seas . . . partly from bad Airs, Sea Fogs, sudden Heats and Colds, much Salt Diet." However, it could also affect families "who inhabit near the Seas."[129] Contemporaries hoped that by gathering knowledge about the links between people and particular environments, they could act proactively to improve their health.

Early modern writers and travelers condemned the bodies of fenland residents as pallid, hunched, and sickly in appearance. One traveler to the region, Lieutenant Hammond, described the "ffenny posture" and "turfy" smell of the inhabitants.[130] To outside observers these were the unhealthy and unbecoming attributes of people living in a landscape to which humans were unsuited. Writers regularly asserted that the wetland environment posed dangers to travelers, and residents in particular, because of its powerful influence over both bodies and minds. They associated the air above salt water with scurvy and claimed that even coastal air proximate to the ocean posed regional risks.[131] Outsiders described marshland in deeply uncomplimentary terms. Hammond described passing through "Crowland," a "beastly, nasty Towne" where the residents consumed a "stinking Dyett." He was likewise critical of the "rugged Condition, & debauch'd Manners of the People."[132] Fens negatively affected inhabitants' health, "but mostly to such as have been born and lived long in a better air, as the clergy can attest by sad experience."[133] In other words, natives of the fens suffered, but newcomers with no experience of such "stinking" airs suffered more acutely, even dying from exposure to it.

Observers noted that fen society looked different from the wider English society: population densities were lower, and sex ratios were significantly different from those in English society at large, as men outnumbered women.[134] Writers claimed that the ill health of fen inhabitants had many causes, including marsh fevers. Outsiders did not want to move into the fens. And yet, one group of outsiders regularly expected to relocate to the fens were vicars. Many chose to live outside of their marsh parishes whenever possible, claiming it was the only means to preserve their health.[135] As the historian Mary Dobson has recounted, in their answers to eighteenth-century questionnaires about whether or not each vicar lived in his parish, the responses from the fenlands were disproportionately negative in comparison to those from the country at large.[136] Dobson provides a long list of the responses culled from these questionnaires, including the reasons why eighteenth-century vicars chose not to live in their Essex parishes. The vicar from Wood-ham Ferrers explained his absence: "it being very bad air"; Little Thur-rock: "forced away by sickeness"; Stow Maries: "the air not suffering me there"; Steeple: "in a very unhealthy place"; Stanford Le Hope: "the place it so very Agueish"; Asheldham: "so violently afflicted with the worst of agues and languishing so long under it till our constitutions were almost broke"; East Mersey: "having contracted so ill a state of health"; Greenstead: "frequently taken with agues and feavers"; Tollesbury: "very unwholesome place"; Woodham Mortimer: "for ye sake of my health"; and from West Thurrock: "very unhealthy air in the parish there being salt marshes in it."[137]

Numerous writers described the fens as unhealthy, low-lying land-scapes, and claimed that many residents suffered from chronic illnesses. Contemporaries blamed the smells hovering over the fens and the likeli-hood of dangerous airs entering residents' porous bodies. Author Robert Burton encouraged residents of the fens to leave for the sake of their health: "Who sees not a great difference between *Surry, Sussex*, and *Rumny Marsh*, the wolds in *Lincolnshire* and the Fens. He therefore that loves his health, if his ability will give him leave, must often shift places, and make choice of such as are wholesome, pleasant, and convenient: there is nothing better than change of Aire" to preserve health.[138] Bur-ton claimed that the airs of a place determined both temperaments and health. Dull and heavy air led to dull and heavy people. According to Burton, it was particularly those places that were "full of moores and marshes" where the people were "dull, heavy, and subject to many infir-mities."[139] Air above stagnant water was particularly dangerous.

Meanwhile, the physician Thomas Sydenham described the symp-toms of the chronic illnesses suffered by many fenlanders as well as its phases, which, like the seasonal and tidal waters of the fens, came and went with cyclical regularity. The symptoms had patterns, depending on the type of "ague" under consideration.[140] According to Sydenham, the symptoms in a "quotidian" case came once a day. In "tertian" the symp-toms appeared every other day. Meanwhile, "quartan" was every third day. While most writers attributed the "agues" suffered by fen residents to the rotten air, Hammond described how the "aquaticke" residents of Crowland likewise suffered from "the devellish stinging of their huming Gnatts, which is all the Towne musick they have, as is able to put a man into a waspish feaver."[141] Drainage promoters cited the evident ill health of residents to make a case for drainage. This was because, to the minds of "most who did not live in the affected areas, schemes to drain the marshes were desirable. They promised an end to the disgusting effluvia of the wetlands and the disreputable, sickly societies sheltering therein."[142]

Not only did residents suffer from a variety of chronic ailments that returned with cyclical regularity, and daily breathed in the bad air—or malaria—hovering above the stagnant wetlands, but writers additionally pointed to fenlanders' bodies as misshapen, hunched, or monstrous. Rev. James Brome's *Three Years' Travels in England, Scotland and Wales* (1700) described the people living in the fenlands as "persons so abject and sordid a temper that they seem most to have undergone poor Nebuchadnezzar's fate, and by conversing continually with the beasts to have learned their manners."[143] This reference to the Book of Daniel and the story of Nebuchadnezzar, who was transformed by God into a beast for seven years, offered a mythological account of the supposedly misshapen, web-footed, and beastly bodies of the people who resided in the fens. It is possible that some of the descriptions of fenlanders' bodies may have been related to their modes of transportation during high-water seasons. The stilts utilized for fishing, fowling, or collecting sedge may have been seen as a kind of bodily morphology, as if the tools utilized in these landscapes were an ungainly or unsightly extension of fenlanders' bodies. Indeed, due to the seasonally swampy land they called home, the residents of the fens were popularly believed to have been constituted physiologically—and psychologically—by their environment. If they were to be successfully incorporated into the body politic, English officials supported environmental transformations that would halt such disfiguring customs. Observers had long claimed that the fens transformed those who lived there, leading both to "debauch'd manners of the people" as well as unhealthy, misshapen bodies. As Hammond commented, "I think they be half fish, half flesh, for they drink like fishes, & sleep like hogs, & if the men be such creatures, judge what their women are."[144]

Part of the era's fascination with topographically induced hybrid bodies, particularly those that seemed to bridge the human and the animal in act or form, was that such bodies enabled negotiations about the limits, or boundaries, of political and human communities. For instance, according to Annabel Brett, "Hobbes gets his definitional extremes, his either/or, by animalization—as his own words suggest, a brutalization—of human nature outside the sovereign state, where 'man is a wolf to man.'"[145] If animals were the limits of acceptable human nature, anything or any place that called these boundaries of the human and animal into question was of great interest, including the environments that wrought such changes, and might be remade.

Early modern residents of the Anglo-Atlantic world were familiar with linking types of political and social collectives with the environments that enveloped them.[146] They believed that different climates not only altered health but could affect intelligence, attitude, ingenuity, and even the types of governments established. In print and manuscripts contemporaries such as the members of the Royal Society recorded numerous instances in which topography influenced the appearance and health of the porous human body. Furthermore, within those broader regions, local airs, such as miasmas—near and above swampy, boggy, and fenny landscapes—might lead to further variation in health and behavior.

Such boundary-subverting landscapes intrigued members of early scientific societies, such as the Royal Society and the Dublin Philosophical Society. They discussed and investigated the ways in which seemingly malleable bodies were transformed by the circumstances of birth, or by environmental factors such as the climate, air, or topography. Early modern readers had learned from the works of Hippocrates, such as *Airs, Waters, Places,* the "prevalent illnesses of different locations." Hippocrates wrote that "geography and climate formed the psychological as well as physical characteristics of different populations."[147] Therefore, place mattered a great deal to an individual's health and temperament.[148] Varied topographies affected the "native temperament" of "hearbs and plants" as well as people.[149] Among those landscapes imbued with transformative powers were bodies of water, including wetlands.

Evidence of the power of climate, seasons, and wetland topography to transform physical form was ubiquitous in the early modern Atlantic. One such anecdote, recorded by the Dublin Philosophical Society, reported on a marsh bird, a rail, which altered from "raile" to water hen, and back again, depending on the climate and season.[150] Marshlands were spaces with a peculiar kind of transformative power. As a result of making its home in a marshy landscape that was neither fully water nor land, the rail was believed to shift shapes back and forth depending on the season and, therefore, the water table:

The Irish report that Railes towards winter turn to water Hens, and in the Spring the Water Hens turn to Railes I did for severall years endeavor to Informe myself in this and at last my falconer a little after michaelmas brought me in a bird that had exactly the body of a water Hen and the wings of a Raile and I thought it appeared very plaine that the Raile had moulted the feathers of his body, which came of a darker colour, but had not moulted the feathers of his wings: which confirmed me in the Irish mans opinion Especially considering a Raile is a bird of a short and slow flight, and cannot make his passage out of the Kingdom as Falcons Woodcocks & c tho, yet they are never found in winter among us.[151]

In this case the author supported the claim that marshland rails turn into water hens, and vice versa, by locating a specimen caught midshift, a hybrid bird that had failed to fully transform from one bird into another as it was supposed to do. The unmolted wing of the rail remained in the form of a water hen. This was clear evidence to the anonymous author of this report that, like many bodies, the rail did not have a fixed form but responded quite rapidly and thoroughly to the seasonally altered marshy environment. If there was a lesson to be learned about the rail and water hen, it was that bodies were porous, perhaps frighteningly so. In this case, a bird became a new species altogether in response to new seasons or wetland landscapes.

Like rails and water hens, peoples' health and characters were influenced by the air they breathed and the food they consumed and were similarly subject to seasonal alterations. Natural philosophers wondered at the extent to which nature and natural phenomena had transformative power over human bodies. Evidence abounded in the affirmative. While the rail was one type of hybrid body, it was just one example of many that underscored the surprising malleability of bodies in response to the material world. Such boundary-subverting specimens as the rail and water hen were sought with enthusiasm, in part for the lessons they might impart about the relationship between bodies and places. In Restoration England and its colonies many of the "wondrous" oddities, or "monsters" that captured such interest and attention in fairs, markets, broadsides, and records of the Royal Society were bodies that had been transformed; the porousness and mutability of bodies altered by the circumstances of birth or by environmental factors such as the climate fascinated the public.

Of particular interest were those bodies or specimens that had undergone a transformation, or another type of physical alteration, thereby testing the limits, or boundaries, of form and perhaps function. These changes were often associated with travel into particular climates, changes in season, breathing new or diseased "air," or coming into contact with particular natural objects or type of topography. Further, such wonders were often associated with the varied, transformative properties of water. There are numerous recorded instances of "Remarkable wells," or healing springs. Nehemiah Donnellan related a story of a healing spring to the Dublin Philosophical Society, recounting "that there is on the South side of Loughneagh a Certain portion thereof which is always filled with hot water (as if there were a warm spring under it) and that Captn Nevil Bathed there and was cured thereby of a Rheumatism."[152] Hugh Todd of Oxford University wrote to the Royal Society in 1684 about a medicinal spring outside of Durham that he referred to as a "Treasure of Natural Physick."[153]

Travel to take the waters for their healing properties had become, by this period, a variety of medical tourism in England. Books such as Tobias Venner, *The Baths and Bathe* (1628), and John French, *The Yorkshire Spaw* (1652), promised the healing benefits of spa waters. John Locke wrote to his friend Edward Clarke about the benefits of drinking spa waters. The Duke of Rutland went so far as to pay runners to carry waters from a "spaw" in Derbyshire back to his estate, Belvoir, on various occasions from 1674 to 1675.[154] Whereas once those who could afford it may have traveled to the continent, a domestic industry grew rapidly in the seventeenth century. Proponents reminded English men and women that these home waters were likely more suited to their bodies anyway. Bathing, drinking, and even mere proximity to these healing lakes, wells, and springs was desirable. Scientific societies, including the Royal Society and the Dublin Philosophical Society, arranged for experimentation and requested samples of many of these celebrated waters, hoping to collect and codify the properties of these places.[155] In 1684 William Petty published "Some Queries Whereby to Examine Mineral Waters." He queried whether or not "any Animalcula will breed in it," and if mineral waters acted as better solvents for herbs, roots, and seeds than other water. He wanted to know if they were purgatives, how mineral waters might change the blood of the consumer, and whether mineral waters "swell the Belly, Legg &c." and to what degree.[156]

Meanwhile, in response to a questionnaire from the Dublin Philosophical Society about the healthful properties of "Clonuffee Waters," Mr. King recorded the various trials and experiments to which he subjected the water.[157] But some of its properties eluded him. He marveled that "It quench thirst strangely," and "it brews very well," despite its odd "black-ish color." But most importantly, it produced some of the desired effects one sought in healing waters. If taken with a "handful of common white salt in the first Glass," it "generally purges all."[158] Purgatives were highly desirable, as it was believed the most effective medicines were those that voided "impostumes and other foul stuff." Sweating, bleeding, vomiting, spitting, and otherwise expelling harmful or unbalanced humors was the hoped-for result. Finally, the "Clonuffee Waters" had another signifi-cant consequence. According to Mr. King, "it swells the belly very much so as to oblige a man to enlarge his breecks but this is only for a little time and then it returns to a proportionall lankness."[159] Although such body morphology was temporary, the expansion and contraction of King's girth was just the kind of daily evidence that proved to contemporaries that even in subtle ways bodies were susceptible to environmental and dietary influences and that water had the power to transform.

Yet waters did not always heal. Waters also fostered diseases. There were frightening and powerful waters that could turn substances to stone. The influence of watery places on human bodies could explain diverse phenomena, including everything from differing temperaments and height to digestive operations. Regional and local specificity likewise had implications for the health and character of an individual as well as a community. This flexible and layered notion of the relationship of a per-son to a place made it an enduring idiom, even as the seventeenth cen-tury saw the rise of new and alternative ways of understanding health. Although nature exerted a powerful force, humans imagined themselves able to manipulate it to their needs. Humans might labor to alter the environments in which they, or others, were imbricated. Restoration officials sought to act in an expanded empire of enormous topographi-cal variety. If enough information could be gathered about the ways that watery, marshy, boggy and riverine places transformed people and populations, it might be compiled and codified. It might then be used effectively by those interested in such transformative possibilities. Such a range of uses inspired varied individuals to likewise seek this knowledge and the proscriptive power that came with it. In the early years of the Restoration John Graunt imagined just such an in-gathering and codify-ing role for the Royal Society.[160]

Not only were the bodies of the residents of the fens sickly, but writers described the landscape itself as sickly and in need of medical attention. Wetlands resembled sickly bodies overfull of phlegm, and drainage was akin to removing pus from an abscess. As an anonymous author of a poem detailing the draining of the fens suggested, turning water-logged landscape into dry land was like curing "dropsies" in a situation in which "not one limb was sound" (the term used by early modern physicians when there was too much fluid in the body). The poet went on to draw yet further parallels, claiming soggy fens resembled "the liver rotted, all the vitals drown'd."[161] Describing uncultivated landscapes as sickly, and in need of human attention and improvement had long animated authors of husbandry manuals, who advised cleansing fields of stones and curing "the disease of your fieldes" by weeding or burning unwanted wild vegetation.[162]

"Here's *Florida* Hard By": Revealing New Worlds in the Fens

Although Great Level drainage adventurers like Samuel Fortrey praised the drainage works and suggested that fen drainage, unlike some other far-fetched schemes of colonization, was a solid investment, he had much to gain by celebrating and encouraging projects of reclamation. He asked his readers why anyone would travel far afield or risk one's health and wealth when a botanical paradise could be realized in England's own backyard. His various interests and investments suggested that domestic improvement projects like drainage could complement and facilitate colonization, or they could be an alternative to more risky ventures. In the concluding verses in *The History or Narrative*, his lengthy text in support of drainage, he cautioned colonial adventurers:

> And ye whom hopes of sudden Wealth allure,
> Or wants into *Virginia*, force to fly,
> Ev'n spare your pains; here's *Florida* hard by.

Or, in other words, why go to Virginia or Florida if drainage offered a similarly bounteous, as yet untapped, source of wealth? Fortrey and his cohort of drainage adventurers claimed that large-scale drainage works enabled the internal colonization of England, which was not only a viable alternative to overseas ventures but the more manageable proposition.[163] Fortrey acknowledged that colonies could provide vast wealth but portrayed colonization as unpredictable. For many writers, improvement was the safer route to wealth. If some writers saw internal and transatlantic colonization as complementary in the seventeenth century, not everyone agreed. Instead, several authors pointed to a fraught relationship between improvement and expansion.

Fortrey touted drainage-improvement schemes as the more secure way to access new lands and necessary commodities. His writings intimated that what the nation required was a renewed focus inward on England's own improvement. Yet, although Fortrey was suspicious of unchecked colonial endeavors, he was not against them altogether. While he was invested in fen-drainage works in eastern England, he also patronized voyages to the New World, such as those undertaken by his kinsman John Josselyn, author of two tracts describing the flora, fauna, and human societies in New England.[164] Thus, despite Fortrey's tentative criticisms of colonial endeavors, he might have seen his investments at home and abroad as part of a coherent project. For instance, both ventures provided ready access to specific kinds of goods, such as supplies necessary for the construction of ships. Colonies might also offer goods that could not be procured elsewhere.[165] Fortrey was not the first to express uncertainty about the relationship between internal improvement and colonization. As one correspondent of the midcentury intelligencer Samuel Hartlib—himself a keen advocate of internal agricultural improvement projects—mused, "The improving of a Kingdome is better than the conquering a new one."[166] Sir Robert Southwell wrote to Daniel Finch, 2nd Earl of Nottingham, in 1689 and further warned, "To me it appears wee have already too much Territory abroad, and to get more, were but to drain England of People and to loose at home."[167] Varied writers suggested that colonization was not always the best option. Instead, the people and lands of England, if improved, might be more than sufficient.

England's improvement was, at times, considered to be compatible with, or facilitating, colonization. At other times it was portrayed as a viable alternative to colonization.[168] As Fortrey argued in *Englands Interest and Improvement*, enclosure added value to England because there were certain "ingenious" minds more capable of improving, ordering, and overseeing property than when it had been underutilized as commons. When lands were made more productive, the whole nation was the beneficiary. He claimed that this made enclosure justifiable.

In *The History or Narrative*, Fortrey's treatise on the drainage works in the Great Level, Fortrey recycled and repurposed long-standing motifs about the bountiful productivity of the American plantations and applied them in his descriptions of the reclaimed fenlands. He rehabilitated well-worn themes of abundance and economic opportunity and applied them to his draining schemes in England, breathing new life into them.[169] Although the New World might still have held productive promise, as far as Fortrey was concerned, the American plantations had presented England with as many problems as benefits. By reconfiguring an earlier language of extractive possibilities, Fortrey portrayed the drained fenlands in England as a new colonial frontier and site of economic promise.[170] The landscape and the misshapen, unhealthy, brute-like inhabitants who were portrayed as unwilling or unable to improve the land could both be improved—or removed—by adventurers' efforts.

According to authors like Andrew Yarranton, a prolific writer of agricultural improvement treatises, improvements in farming techniques, such as the addition of nutrients to the soil, new tools, or the introduction and acclimatization of selected plants, might offset or even obviate the need for colonial expansion. Meanwhile, the improvement of wastelands within England, Ireland, and Scotland, such as turning fens and bogs into arable, productive landscapes, was often couched in terms of internal colonization.[171] As Fortrey claimed, the newly productive fens could be just as useful or productive as Virginia or Florida.[172] Opponents of imperial expansion argued that expansion was an unnecessary waste of people, money, and time when there was plenty of room for internal improvement. In Adolphus Speed's *Adam out of Eden, or, An abstract of divers excellent Experiments touching the advancement of Husbandry* (1659), he claimed his work was intended to benefit the public. He urged readers to "embrace this opportunity, and reduce these Precepts to practice: England affords Land enough for the Inhabitants, and if men did but industriously and skillfully improve and manure it, we need not go to Jamaica for new plantations."[173] He echoed the officials who argued that Jamaica was not self-evidently useful and might merely result in a drain of money and men. Because the newly acquired colony could offer no immediate benefit, those writers and officials questioned if future advantages really outweighed current costs.

Adventurers funding internal improvements, such as fenland drainage, similarly questioned the value and necessity of colonization. By focusing on internal improvements, such as draining the fenlands to reveal a new "Florida," Fortrey suggested that England could have all of the benefits of colonization, without the associated challenges, including loss of population, financial risk, or moral ambiguity.[174] Drainers imagined they could provide the material wealth of empire, and avoid trade imbalances, by replanting desired colonial goods in a more accessible location. Much like the later emergence of theories of cameralism in the eighteenth century, wherein the "most basic political goal" of certain countries without their own colonies was "to reproduce the economy of empire and colony" at home in order to avoid the need to import goods, fen drainage adventurers espoused similar rhetoric in the seventeenth century, claiming their work might enhance, or even serve in lieu of, colonization.[175]

Fen drainers contributed to a conversation about whether the way to wealth and power was best accomplished by acquiring more land externally, improving land domestically, or a combination of the two. Some believed that wealth derived from the land was finite and argued that it behooved leaders to look outward and to consider expansion as the appropriate model. Quite simply, for these writers, more wealth required more land. This led supporters to encourage an aggressive imperial policy as wealth and expansion were linked. But expansion was not so simple as merely taking any or all land. Restoration writers like Carew Reynell cautioned that some lands were better than others, especially those lands in alterative climactic zones that offered foods, spices, and other goods that could not be grown in England. These were perhaps the colonies more useful to support because they offered what could not be gained at home. According to Reynell, of all the plantations in America, "the Southern Plantations are the most advantageous to us; and it were well hereafter we planted no more behither Jamaica."[176] Specific colonies might be worth keeping, but advocates of internal improvement were also quick to argue that transplantation and acclimatization could circumvent the need for colonial acquisition.

Fen drainers were quick to remind their patrons and officials that new lands of abundance were not located exclusively in far-flung locales. Imagining the fenlands as an internal continent simply waiting to be uncovered and reconquered from nature had a long history. In 1642 Sir Cornelius Vermuyden praised the king's desire to drain the Great Level, "His now Majesty taking consideration thereof, and fore seeing that these Lands being a continent of about 400,000. Acres, while being made Winter ground would be an unexpected benefit to the Common-wealth of Six hundred thousand pounds per Annum and upwards, and a great and certaine Revenue to all the parties interested."[177] This dream of a *continent* waiting to be revealed by draining reflected contemporaries' claims that the fenlands represented a *new* New World, and this one was in their own backyard, much closer to home.

Charles I had been involved in several earlier schemes to drain the fens, and the Great Level in particular. The king was "enthralled with the grandeur (and profit) of adding a whole new 'country' to his kingdom and dreamed of building a new town in mid-fen, designed by and named after himself."[178] He designed and drew plans for Charlemont himself, intending to link the settlement by a built waterway to the Great Ouse River to ensure agricultural production in Charlemont could be successfully transported to markets.[179] When Lieutenant Hammond passed through "Ely Citty" on the way to Guyhirn, he walked along an "ingeniously finish'd sluice" after coming across "a numerous Company of . . . stout sweating Pioneers hard at worke" digging "to gain ground, and to make ye large Continent of vast, foggie, miry, rotten, and unfruitfull soyle, usefull, fruitfull, & beneficiall, & for the advantage of the Commonwealth."[180] By calling them pioneers of a new continent, Hammond reinforced the perception of "state formation" and "property formation" as mutually constitutive.[181]

Thus, while Fortrey suggested that there was a new "Florida" waiting below the muck of the fens, which was more likely to lead to prosperity than investing in more colonies, numerous contemporaries weighed in on the appropriate relationship between the territorial expansion of the English empire and the improvement of its domestic lands by draining expansive fenlands. Some writers claimed these projects were at odds, whereas others thought colonization and improvement were compatible. For instance, in some of his writings, William Petty asserted that domestic improvements and conquest were incompatible. At other times, Petty espoused opposing views, arguing that the propitious confluence of external expansion and internal improvement together had increased the "power and Wealth of England" over the "last 40 years."[182] According to Petty the increased territories in New England, Virginia, Barbados, Jamaica, Tangier, Bombay, and Dunkirk paralleled and compounded the various improvements that made arable ground accessible and useable within England. The increased acreage internal and external to England, combined with better transportation as well as the introduction of "severall sorts" of fruits and garden items, including the planting of trees, were mutually reinforcing and combined to benefit the whole of the imperial body politic. He claimed that, in addition to increasing the power and wealth of the nation through the varied improvements, the transformation had made the whole of the imperial body "healthy."[183]

John Locke and other late seventeenth-century thinkers were in a long line of legal theorists who claimed that only land that was worked in a way recognized by the standards of European contemporaries, namely, settled agriculture, was properly transformed into private property. Unused land, or poorly utilized or unfenced lands, were subject to forfeiture in this schema. If the biblical injunction to render the land fruitful, or improved, was not followed, then that land could be seized. This was a capacious theory and was used to justify any number of land grabs, including enclosure, drainage, and colonial settlements.

According to someone like Locke, value lay in labor, not just in the land itself. If the land was not being used, or used well, it was subject to forfeiture. In theory, improvers, enclosers, and colonists alike needed only to claim that their work was adding value to the land. Moreover, the "compitent rewards" of risking fortunes and time to recover the fens or set up a distant colony "was absolute title to large acreages of the newly available arable land produced by draining, just as colonial investors received title to lands in America."[184] Thus projectors interrogated the intersection between territorial acquisition, improvement, and possession and analyzed the relationship between them. They debated the comparative benefits of acquiring more land versus the intensive improvement of property already owned. Ultimately, they sought to uncover the means that would best ensure England's improvement, thereby enhancing the nation's wealth, status, power, and health.

Restoration writers regularly compared the country to a body so that rivers were the "veins" of the body of England and needed to be kept clear for the beneficial circulation of trade. Trees, its "hair," provided evidence of the strength or virility of the nation, affected air quality, provided food, and enabled transatlantic colonization. Meanwhile, they described the drainage of fens, bogs, and swamps as something akin to the emetic procedures designed to balance the humors, ensuring the whole body was healthy by attending to its phlegmatic parts. The health and wealth of the country depended on the body politic (the macrocosm) remaining in balance, like a human body depended on a carefully calibrated balance of humors (the microcosm). There was a newfound sense in the exhilarating though unsettled years after the Restoration that the government could and should be willing and able to oversee and maintain the proper functioning of varied "body" parts if one limb were disordered or ill. Although the Great Level adventurers claimed the successful completion of their venture in 1653, it is interesting that writers and Bedford Level Corporation members continued to call for the transformation of unhealthy wetlands into healthy dry land in publications in the following decades. These tracts also call the claims of drainage success into question.

In texts published after the Restoration, writers continued to speak of transforming riot-prone, web-footed, hunched, and pale bodies living in the watery fenlands of eastern England into healthy and productive economic actors, made more fully a part of the early modern political state by massive projects of fen drainage. Because local ecology was believed to be deeply constitutive of physical and physiological characteristics, draining promised to have transformative effects. Arguments in favor of drainage promised the transmutation of the bodies of social outsiders into a community of insiders through the management of bodies of water. This chapter has examined projectors' assertions that they aimed to reshape human societies as well as physical environments. It also reminds us that inhabitants of the fens did not necessarily agree with these characterizations of their homes and in alternative publications emphasized their rich and varied diets and accused projectors of greed, even a kind of cannibalism, not public beneficence.

Although the scale of the fen drainage works was vastly different from that of the drainage projects covered in chapter 3 (fen drainage schemes such as the Great Level covered more than three hundred thousand acres of land, whereas one of the projects of marsh drainage described in chapter 3 was no more than "an English mile"), the enormously varied size of these projects should not encourage easy dismissals of critical parallels. There are telling similarities. The rhetoric of agricultural improvement and the transformation from waste to utility motivated the self-proclaimed improvers in both places. Moreover, in both cases the communities in question were described as a type of outsider, geographically, culturally, temperamentally, and physically. These wetland dwellers on both sides of the Atlantic were threatening to a centralizing English empire. Comparing these two projects of land reclamation enables us to consider an unfamiliar geography of empire, one in which activities in the fenlands in England and the marshlands in North America were in dialogue. Moreover, in both the Bedford Level and in New Castle, Dutch skills at ditch and drainage techniques were called upon. It was these very skills and expertise that encouraged supporters of new naturalization laws to invite skilled Dutch workers into England. As they transformed wet lands into dry lands, they earned the right to stay in England. In both places Dutch hands drained lands that added to the size of the territory of England and its colonies. Their skills in land reclamation through draining were renowned.[185] It seemed the Dutch had succeeded in creating vast wealth out of minimal resources. The Dutch were a constant source of inspiration as well as anxiety for the English, especially the latter when it came to long-distance trade and the control of sea routes to spices and other lucrative specimens in the East Indies. The English also sought to supplant the Dutch in their control over the trade in enslaved people.

However, drainage successes were often fleeting, putting pressure on the claims of the improvers that they were merely returning wetlands to their historically naturally dry condition. In the fens, optimism about reclamation successes gave way, in just a few years, to defeat as lands suffered catastrophic inundations, and it was clear that the Bedford Level Corporation had failed to do what it had set out to do. According to Dorothy Summers, drainage works caused the peat surface to shrink after the water was drained out of it. As the peat level shrank, the drainage works were no longer sufficiently deep in relation to the surrounding surface, leading to further flooding.[186] Proposals to drain the fens were still being published in the Restoration era, including William Dodson's *Design for the Present Draining of the Great Level of the Fens (Called Bedford Level)* in 1665. In the same year, the Georgical Committee of the Royal Society inquired about the "best waies of Drayning Marshes, Boggs, fens, &c.?"[187] Wetlands were difficult environments to control, and the questionable success of these projects of land reclamation challenged the improvers' claims that that these waters or the residents had, indeed, been "muzzled" and "tam'd."

If the fenlands had not been properly controlled and civilized, efforts to civilize residents might have similarly stalled. Drainage, and the upkeep of failing drainage works, continued to preoccupy company members and Restoration officials. Moreover, the debates about drainage and claims about the relationship of different types of waters to the health of residents circulated beyond the fenlands and shaped how officials approached wetlands and the residents of such spaces throughout the Atlantic, including in Ireland and across the Atlantic.

3 / Bodies of Water: The Administration of Nature and the Nature of Administration in the Proprietary Colony of New York

In 1675, a year after the Treaty of Westminster concluded the Third Anglo-Dutch War and once again brought New York under English control, the proprietor, James, Duke of York, took steps to render the settlements and polyglot communities of colonists along the western banks of the Delaware River—made up of scattered Finnish, Swedish, Dutch, Lenape, and English inhabitants—more accessible, controllable, and profitable.[1] During his first official visit to the region, the new governor of New York, Edmund Andros, charged local magistrates and residents to construct dikes and build ditch and drainage works, justifying the required work orders, in part, as measures to promote accessibility and oversight.[2] In addition to the upkeep of roads and bridges that would allow the new English government to traverse the region, he sought to transform some of the marshland surrounding New Castle, the most prominent settlement along the western banks of the Delaware River, from a "generall Nusance" into dry land.[3] When Andros issued the instructions that required inhabitants living nearby to work, the local magistrates who relayed the message were met with varied reactions. Local responses ranged from support, to confusion, to riotous discontent. These mixed emotions came to a head one afternoon in the summer of 1675. A local magistrate named William Tom, who supported plans to construct and repair dikes, recorded a series of events that nearly ended in violence.[4]

Tom complained that the mutinous inhabitants along the Delaware who refused to comply with Andros's drainage orders could not see reason due to their "frenzicall braynes" and implied that despite their oaths, their loyalty to the recently restored English government in New York was debatable. He further implied that their obstinacy and riotousness was, in part, a result of the disordered and swampy landscapes in which they lived.[5] English officials held a range of negative cultural associations for swamps, fenlands, bogs, and other types of wetlands, including their detrimental impact on human manners and health. Moreover, as chapter 2 suggests, the English perceived wetlands as harboring unruly communities living beyond the reach of the state who often failed to cultivate the landscape in ways the English deemed acceptably civilized. The planned transformations of the Delaware's riverine landscapes illuminate an on-the-ground mechanism by which agents of the Restoration court sought to assert authority in a liminal landscape that was both politically and physically ill-defined. Andros, like both previous English governors, sought to make sense of, and intervene in, the places and people who fell within the duke's expansive propriety colony. He and local officials asserted that calming the "frenzicall braynes" of marshland dwellers along the Delaware River was a matter of draining wetlands to uncover the land and the law-abiding subjects too immersed in the metaphorical muck to behave properly. This chapter reveals that James, Duke of York, and his officials held a deeply physical conception of the political subject's body and temperament, and with drainage, aspired to manipulate both. As a result, the construction of dikes and other drainage measures "challenges the association of state power with social and legal structures alone."[6] This chapter further explores why the regulation, or so-called improvement, of the colony's swamps and wetlands was among the first political acts in the region after the English gained, lost, and regained, the Dutch colony.

Successive English governors sought to legitimize tenuous English control in the region by refashioning the landscape, including targeting swamps. As they aimed to establish a new political order by, for instance, requiring oaths of allegiance from non-English inhabitants, they simultaneously sought to ground political changes in the landscape itself. Transforming the material world though improvement projects was, in part, an expression of national identity; as with their contemporaries in England, colonial officials in New York recognized that the colony's landscape served as a stage on which to enact English practices at the unsettled margins of empire.[7] Wetland drainage projects served as "ceremonies of possession" that both dramatized and naturalized English rule in the colony.[8] More particularly, these landscapes became stages on which the proprietor's values and expectations for his colony might be conveyed, replicated, and enacted. In advance of his visit to New Castle to establish a court, Andros's secretary sent a memo explaining how those in attendance should behave, including what lines to say and when to sit or stand. After the residents performed their roles as subjects of the English empire at the site of the new courthouse, public officials instructed them to transform the landscape, thereby "encod[ing]" the new status of the colony and colonists in the ground itself.[9]

English officials celebrated the conversion of so-called wastelands into accessible and productive landscapes and further claimed that such measures benefited residents' health. For instance, in 1669 Governor Francis Lovelace assured the community of Kingston, located on the Hudson River, that the drainage of the "Morasse that lyes under the Towne" would not only improve the land and make it ready for agriculture but would "contribute much to the health of the place."[10] As with new drainage orders issued elsewhere in New York, the English repeatedly claimed that swamplands posed health risks to residents. As a result, their instructions to construct dikes or other drainage works were framed as public health initiatives, and their rhetoric served to further justify their presence in the region. They "improved" the colony, whereas previous regimes had not. In addition to promoting physical well-being, successive governors who issued drainage instructions made sure to highlight the range of benefits that drainage offered residents, including concerns about safety, ease of travel, and the concomitant economic advantages. They planned to unearth better land and people.

While English officials issued instructions to construct dikes and drain low-lying swamp- and marshland in several locations in colonial New York, the events at New Castle left a paper trail that offers a lens through which to examine both the stated impetus to drain as well as residents' varied responses to the English drainage orders in a politically unstable and contested region. The inhabitants of the western bank of the Delaware River were only tenuously integrated into the newly acquired colony of New York, itself only newly part of the empire.[11] The polyglot communities posed a potentially destabilizing political threat because the western banks of the Delaware River were not part of the Duke of York's original grant, which extended only up to the river's eastern banks. New Castle was on the western side, as were many of the communities of Dutch, Swedish, Finnish, and English inhabitants, residents of the former colonies that had once claimed the region, including New Netherland, New Sweden, and New Amstel. Further complicating matters,

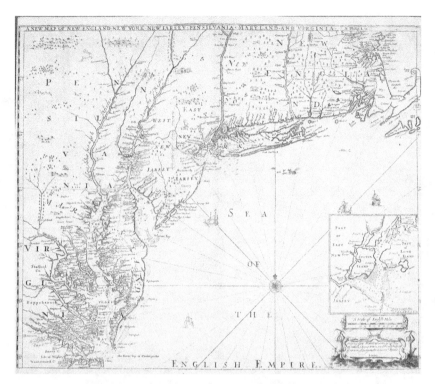

FIGURE 3.1. Philip Lea, *A new map of New England, New York, New Iarsey, Pensilvania, Maryland, and Virginia* (1690). Image courtesy of Lionel Pincus and Princess Firyal Map Division, New York Public Library Digital Collections.

these diverse communities resided at the indeterminate edge of the three proprietary colonies of Maryland, New York, and New Jersey (the latter two were partitioned out from York's original grant that stretched from the St. Lawrence River down to the Delaware Bay, including all or part of what was—or became—Maine, New York, Pennsylvania, Delaware, East Jersey, and West Jersey and included additional claims over the islands of Martha's Vineyard, Nantucket, and Long Island). Moreover, within a decade, residents of the northern Delaware Valley would be incorporated into the new proprietary colony of Pennsylvania (granted to William Penn, the son of Admiral Penn, who had helped secure Jamaica during Cromwell's Western Design and later victualled the navy during the Second Anglo-Dutch War, from 1665 to 1667. The latter resulted in the debt Charles II then cleared with the grant of Pennsylvania).[12] Adding to the

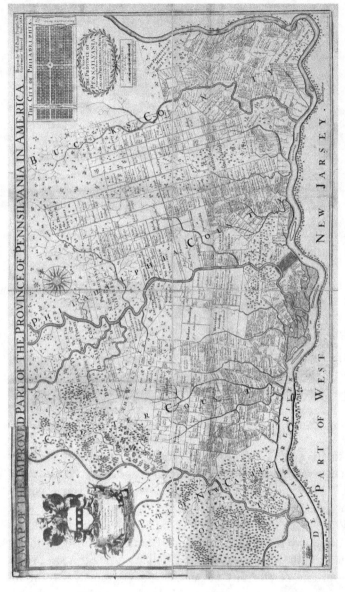

FIGURE 3.2. The residents of New Castle eventually came under the jurisdiction of Pennsylvania, pictured here in the lower left corner downriver from Philadelphia, several decades after the events described in this chapter. Thomas Holme, *Map of the Improved Part of the Province of Pennsilvania in America* (ca. 1705). Image courtesy of The Library of Congress Geography and Map Division.

confusion of overlapping claims were colonists from New Haven who had established the Delaware Company, and other New Englanders who had settled in the area after swearing oaths of allegiance to the Dutch.[13] As a result of numerous overlapping claims and counterclaims, it was unclear if the communities on the western bank of the Delaware River fell within the jurisdiction of the new proprietary colony of New York. The communities were ultimately administered by New York until they were incorporated into Pennsylvania.

According to English officials, several of the marshes surrounding New Castle acted as a hindrance to the settled governance of the English colony because it thwarted stable settlement and ease of access. Elsewhere in New York, as officials sought to settle colonial boundaries, they were also asked to arbitrate local disputes, such as between the towns of Gravesend and New Utrecht, in what is now Brooklyn, in New York City, about the "Bounds and limits of their lands, and particularly about some meadow Grounds."[14] Meadows were often deeply valued lands and held in common.[15] But not all wetlands were valued, and sometimes they resulted in confusion. Wetlands had seasonally shifting and indeterminate edges, which posed a variety of ideological problems. On both sides of the Atlantic, projectors and Restoration officials championed drainage projects as a way to establish clear property boundaries, as well as improve accessibility, civilize the landscape, and transform communities' health and behavior. After draining the fenlands, investors earned money by leasing out their newly gained property. Similarly, proprietors of these colonies relied, in part, on the collection of quitrents if they hoped to gain a profit from the colony.[16] Landlords and proprietors alike required clearly defined private and public property to assess and collect rents.[17] Residents were also keen to define the status of the colony and the status of their property. Among the most pressing questions the residents asked the governor of New York, now that the colony had changed hands, was "by what tenure we hold our land."[18]

Drainage projects also served as a means to assert English sovereignty over the non-English residents in their midst. The newly formed English colonial government found the marshlands inaccessible in the best of times, dangerous and impenetrable in the worst. The swamps, marshes, rivers, and varied tidal- and saltwater ecology found along the banks of the Delaware Bay as well as upriver made travel difficult for those English officials seeking to incorporate the riverside communities into the colony and into the empire. According to Andros, wetland landscapes along the Delaware physically limited political oversight from New York, whereas drained land enabled access, particularly with the additional construction of bridges and highways. Andros further called for such infrastructure after his first official appearance in New Castle. Successive New York governors issued drainage and road upkeep instructions, suggesting both were priorities for English officials and a means by which they asserted power in the region.

It was not only the mix of Native American and non-English colonists, the seasonally limited accessibility of their settlements, or their location at the uncertain edge of various colonial boundaries that made the inhabitants of the Delaware River settlements so worrisome to the new English proprietors. English attitudes toward residents of wetlands were shaped not only by ongoing drainage projects in the fenlands of England but also by new landscapes and people in the colonies. When English officials described the newly acquired lands of the expansive colony of New York, they discussed strategies for dealing with Algonquian-speaking communities residing in the Delaware Valley. According to Amy C. Schutt, early European colonizers referred to the region's indigenous inhabitants as "River Indians" because of their settlement patterns along the Delaware and Hudson Rivers and because of the importance of riverine landscapes to their daily lives and diets.[19] In order to justify their colonization of the region, the English, in what had become a common trope, claimed that the Lenape Indians' seasonal use of the river and supposed lack of permanent agriculture meant that they had not "improved" the land and thus failed to own it. English refusal to acknowledge the agriculture practiced in the region may also have been because Lenape women were the primary cultivators, and agriculture was the domain of women, unlike in English culture.[20]

Moreover, the English regularly created associations between Native Americans and swamps in print. The proliferation of writings on King Philip's War in New England highlighted these links by describing the final battle in the "Dismal Swamp," where Philip and his people sought refuge. In these texts, officials wrote anxiously about swamps as "habitations of cruelty" and as sites associated with Native Americans.[21] Meanwhile, non-English European residents living in colonial settlements along the river were similarly accused of failing to properly cultivate or drain the land, and their supposed failures left them likewise open to accusations that they did not properly own the land.[22]

When English officials looked at the riverine landscapes along the Delaware, they carried with them a variety of associations and beliefs about how marshy environments shaped human bodies and societies.

But colonial officials likewise believed that they, in turn, had the power to shape nature and thus mitigate the impact of the landscape on proximate communities.[23] In other words, while they recognized the transformative effects of wetlands on human health, behavior, and identity, they also imagined the possibilities for mitigating these effects. Agents of the Restoration government expressly hoped to transform subjects by turning watery environments into arable, "civilized" landscapes. In projects that manipulated the marshy environments of the Delaware River, officials sought to articulate a vision of empire that could transform, and possibly incorporate, the heterogeneous subjects into an expanding English empire by draining.[24] However, the English realized that any transformation of non-English European residents into good subjects of the English Crown would be slow. Governor Nicolls counseled patience to officials in their treatment of non-English inhabitants, writing, "wee cannot expect they love us."[25]

Although exclusion was certainly a feature of community formation in the latter half of the seventeenth century, this chapter suggests that in colonial New York, English officials did not limit their efforts to define their political communities with binary categories of inclusion and exclusion alone. Instead, agents of the Restoration government imagined that a range of people and places might be refashioned, or "new-mold[ed]," into desirable English subjects and absorbed into the expanding empire.[26] Part of the original terms of capitulation granted the Dutch the status of denizens after taking oaths of allegiance. Officials permitted them to trade with England and its colonies. The idea of remaking disparate people into English subjects relied, in part, on the notion that bodies, and bodies politic, were malleable, as were the landscapes in which they dwelt. In New York, officials simultaneously instigated transformations in the landscape and devised new laws, believing they were mutually reinforcing. While national differences remained salient features of residents of the Delaware Valley, early modern ideas about malleable bodies suggested the possibility of transformation. Mark L. Thompson has highlighted how, in the early modern era, "national affiliations could be sticky, persistent forms of identification" and that "commonalities of language, religion, history, and place" meant that "national affiliation often adhered to the very character and body of a person as a form of ethnicity."[27] But if ethnicity adhered to the body, it was possible that refashioning bodies might make national affiliations unstick. Discourses about transforming places and people suggest that, at least initially, the English imagined that a wide range of legal, political, cultural, and physical transformations could remake the colony and its residents into ideal subjects of the empire. Much later, the English would believe themselves to have met with some success. In a letter to Peter Collinson in 1750, Peter Logan suggested that the Swedish residents of the Delaware Valley had become "much Anglified as our Term is."[28] But *Anglified* residents remained an aspiration, not a reality, along the Delaware River in the seventeenth century.

This chapter—much like the previous one—analyzes projects of land reclamation as a means to investigate Restoration attitudes toward certain people and places within the Restoration empire and to consider reclamation projects as an assertion of possession and an expression of identity. The "improvement" of landscapes and people was part of a broader—though at times ill-defined—project by which Restoration officials sought to secure the economic and temperamental well-being of subjects at home and abroad.[29] By focusing on the residents of these wetland zones, projectors and government officials sought to claim, or reclaim, bodily health and manners from the vicissitudes of nearby wetlands. In this process, unhealthy bodies—as well as dangerously riotous ones—could be neutralized and naturalized.[30] Unlike the examination of the important economic place afforded saltwater marshes in Concord, Massachusetts, as described by Brian Donahue, or the piecemeal and "profoundly local" drainage initiatives borne out of "demographic pressures" in Acadia, described by Gregory Kennedy, the drainage ordered by the duke's representatives in colonial New York was a metropolitan imposition.[31]

"That Noble and Navigable *River* of *Delaware*"

The wetlands along the Delaware River have changed dramatically since the late seventeenth century. Like the drained "wasteland" surrounding New Castle featured in this chapter, a similar fate awaited many such coastal marshes over the ensuing centuries. Moreover, landscapes along the Delaware were by no means static before European colonization, as the Lenape had long manipulated the environment for their needs. Riverine and wetland environments likewise change over time without human intervention, challenging our ability to understand past landscapes.

As it does today, in the seventeenth century the Delaware River rose in two locations deep in the Catskill Mountains. The east and west branches of the river met at what is now Hancock, New York, and, joined together, they created the boundaries between Pennsylvania and New York, Pennsylvania and New Jersey, and New Jersey and Delaware. At "The Falls" of the Delaware, near what is now Trenton, New Jersey, the river's elevation dropped. Here, the salty tidewater flowing up from Delaware Bay, and the fresh river water flowing from the Catskills, met. Below the Falls, after running much of the length of New Jersey, the river widened, and eventually opened out into Delaware Bay.

Eastern Delaware's geography was largely Atlantic coastal plain, and at its highest elevation the land was not much more than eighty feet above sea level. In many places, the banks of the Delaware River were lined by marshland. The salt and brackish marshes along the coast of Delaware, like those remaining—or rehabilitated—salt marshes today, were flooded two times each day with tidal waters from the bay and the ocean. At the southern tip of Delaware, stretching across the border between Delaware and Maryland, was what we now call the Great Cypress Swamp, covering approximately thirty thousand acres. Colonists marveled at stands of Atlantic white cedar and bald cypress trees.[32]

The Delaware River reached Delaware Bay and emptied into the Atlantic Ocean at what is now Cape May in New Jersey to the north and Cape Henlopen in Delaware to the south. Early Dutch and Swedish settlers along the Delaware referred to the river as the South River and they called the Hudson the North River.[33] These two rivers and the Fresh River—now known as the Connecticut River—drew European settlement and trade to the region. Rivers were often the swiftest transportation routes inland. Colonial powers such as the Dutch West India Company sought rivers that would enable access to inland fur trading.[34] Both rivers were access points for coastal traders and were essential to the schemes of the Dutch and Swedish trading companies that arrived in North America to access the fur trade and other goods from the interior. According to Ted Steinberg, in addition to settling near the rivers, the Dutch "flocked to the more familiar marshy terrain" of meadows and marshland because it reminded them of home.[35] Indeed, many colonists to North America, the English included, recognized that marshlands "were ideal as a place to start" a colony because they provided livestock with hay and new colonists with fish.[36]

Despite centuries of draining and filling in wetlands, there remain as many as seventy-nine types of wetland in Delaware today.[37] These wetlands include both saltwater and freshwater wetlands along the shores of the ocean and bay, the Delaware River, and the banks of its numerous tributaries. As much as a quarter of Delaware can still be defined as wetland.[38] Many of the wetlands in Delaware were seasonal.[39] In the seventeenth century, as today, the landscape changed daily and seasonally along the Delaware River. The tidewaters entered twice daily, pushing water into salt and brackish marshes along the coast, and pushed water upstream, whereby the ratio of salinity decreased. Even in the freshwater tidal marshes, the daily tides pushed more water into marshland along the Christina and Nanticoke Rivers. The town of New Castle was established south of where the tidewater and river met, and it was brackish water that flowed past the settlement on its way to the bay. Estuaries, where fresh water and salt water meet, "are very special environments and, from an ecological perspective, highly productive ones."[40] The colonists described a world of abundance, writing rapturously about oysters that reached a foot in length and describing rivers full of innumerable fish. The Dutch patroon De Vries further celebrated the crabs of the bay as having "the color of our Prince's flag, orange, white, and blue, so that the crabs show clearly enough that we ought to people the country and that it belongs to us." In this way he sought to naturalize Dutch colonization in the colony's natural landscape.[41] The Delaware Indians called the site of New Castle by at least two names, Quinamkot and Tamakonck.[42] Quinamkot described a prominent topographical feature, a "long sandy point."[43] This sandy point no longer exists; the river has been reshaped by centuries of flowing water and human intervention. But the names suggest this "long sandy point" was used for alighting land by boat at New Castle and was perhaps the geological feature, along with the presence of beaver, that first encouraged European settlement at the site.[44]

The southern length of the river opened gradually, becoming the Delaware Bay. The riverbanks and lands adjacent to the river in this region were largely characterized by marshland. In the seventeenth century, water would have been an essential feature of the settlements along the Delaware and its tributaries. Rivers, swamps, marshes, bays, oceans, and the rhythms of daily tidal and seasonal flows influenced the ways the English newcomers thought about and experienced the landscape and shaped how they interacted with the Lenape, Swedish, Dutch, English, and Finnish inhabitants. What the marsh and riverine environment of Delaware meant to these myriad inhabitants, and how they imagined the relationship of their bodies to that environment, is difficult to recover and was enormously varied. Water played an essential role in the daily lives of Delaware's seventeenth-century inhabitants, providing transportation, power, and sustenance. An anonymous pamphleteer celebrated "that Noble and Navigable *River* of *Delaware*," and its nearby tributaries and "*Riv'leis,*" which provided food. They were "abundantly stored with all the species of the *Fish* of *Europe*," as well as local species. Not only did the Delaware River provide an abundance of fish, but the water itself was delectable. The tract's author claimed, "I do not remember, that ever I tasted better water in any part of England, than the springs of this place do yield," and commented approvingly on the swift-running water of the Delaware as superior to the Thames.[45]

Water offers historians a critical lens on the past due to its centrality to human life. Various waters were infused with a range of meanings. Swampy water was not baptismal water; ocean waves differed from fresh springs. Teasing out the myriad meanings of water in a given time and place poses great challenges but offers critical insights. Incorporating interpretive methods, such as phenomenological studies, offers a way to access a fuller understanding of the role played by water in people's understanding of—and embodied relationship to—a place.[46] Although attitudes and individual understanding of water are difficult to recover, what we do know is that the river was central to the lives of those who dwelt on or near its banks and offers a lens to consider the meanings residents and newcomers might have attached to drainage.[47]

Cultural Constructions of Wetlands

For those people who resided near or on the banks of the Delaware River, their lives were shaped by its waters, which were essential to their sustenance, mode of travel, and experience of place. Water altered Delaware's landscape daily. Indeed, the fact of water's constant movement and changeability made it an uncertain legal category in the early modern world. According to seventeenth-century natural law theorists like Johannes Gryphiander, water had the power to destabilize legal categories.[48] Historian Annabel Brett has interpreted Gryphiander's work, writing, "The intercurrent of river and sea allows the physical flux of water the possibility to alter the space of jurisdiction in a way that cannot be assimilated to the human will."[49] She argues that his work highlights the "agency of nature."[50] Human law could not always contain, or account for, the changing nature of water and its processes.[51] Certain landscapes were hard to define legally and physically, but they were also difficult to define culturally. Moreover, English writers and officials were suspicious of the residents of such landscapes, suggesting that they were potentially unstable elements of the body politic due to the local environment in which they resided, an environment that was neither fully land nor fully water.

Wetland topography like swamps, bogs, and fens, much like forests, had long been defined as "refuge[s] for outlaws and a base for dangerous criminals," because such places were relatively inaccessible to the state.[52] Restoration officials regarded residents of seasonally inaccessible places, like New Castle, with suspicion. The English carried negative cultural assumptions about wetlands back and forth across the Atlantic. Colonial officials regularly described swamps and wetlands in deeply uncomplimentary terms. If ideas about the fens shaped English officials' attitudes about wetlands, their perspectives were further shaped by colonial experiences. Colonists like Richard Gilpin wrote anxiously about Algonquian-speaking communities in New England, associating them with swamps. In his treatise of 1677, he wrote, "Our countrymen have noted of the Natives of *New-England*, that the Devil appeared to them in *ugly shapes*, and in hideous Places, as in *Swamps* and *Woods*."[53] Despite the fact that Gilpin wrote about encounters with Algonquian-speaking communities to the North, not in Delaware, Gilpin's freighted rhetoric of diabolism may have shaped officials' perspectives nonetheless.

Other authors claimed that swamps were sites of refuge for Native Americans in times of war. In *A brief description of New-York* (1670), Daniel Denton claimed that Lenape warfare did not involve "pitcht fields." Instead, "when they have notice of an enemies approach, they endeavor to secure their wives and children upon some Island, or in some thick swamp."[54] This constellation of claims appeared in numerous texts printed in London in the seventeenth century.[55] Anglo-American writers regularly drew connections between Indian communities and swamps, and such texts may have influenced how English newcomers and officials understood these landscapes. The English minister Charles Wolley lived in New York from 1678 to 1680 and claimed that Indians' "way of fighting is upon Swamps, i.e. Bogs and Quagmires, in sculking Ambushes, beyond Trees and in Thickets."[56] His use of the term "bog" may have been a reference to Ireland, and this would have infused his observations with additional layers of cultural meaning. In an earlier text, Sir Ferdinando Gorges recounted events from the Pequot War in his text *America painted to the life* (1658), in which the Narragansett speakers refer to their knowledge of how to live and survive in the local swamps as a factor in their favor and a perceived strength of their people in the event of war. In the text, which was published by Ferdinando Gorges, Esq., the grandson of the original proprietor of Maine, Gorges recalls how, as war was looming, Miantinemo, the nephew of "old Cannonicus, chiefe Sachem" of the Narragansett, agreed to "willingly embrace peace with the English" because of their weapons, even though they were "but strangers to the Woods, Swamps, and advantagious places of this Wildernesse."[57] Gorges later recounted episodes from the Pequot War, likely a reference to the massacre at Fort Mystic in 1637, in which the English ambushed the fort and started a horrific fire that burnt the fort filled with Indian women and children. He wrote that any individuals who escaped the violent onslaught of the English found refuge in a nearby swamp. According to Gorges, "the residue flying into a very thick swamp, being unaccessible, by reason of the boggy holes of water, and thick bushes," found temporary safety, while "the English drawing up their company beleaguered the swamp." But because the English were unfamiliar with and unused to this landscape, "and the Indians in the mean time skulking up and down, and as they saw opportunity they made shot with their Arrowes at the English," the English could not follow.[58] In other words, the English were thwarted by the "boggy" and inaccessible landscape, whereas their opponents supposedly felt at home. Meanwhile, elsewhere in his text, Gorges describes swamps as havens for bears. Perhaps Gorges intended to draw an unspoken parallel between Indians and wild animals by suggesting they shared a habitat or other behaviors, in order to ostracize them from a fully human community. Referring to people as animals, or animal-like, was an age-old way to dehumanize them and suggest that they might be dealt with in ways unconstrained by moral or natural laws that might circumscribe the treatment of fellow humans. As a result of the circulation of these printed texts, colonists had been primed to assume that in America, in ways that often paralleled the attitudes toward residents of English fenlands or Irish bogs, those who lived in watery environments might pose certain dangers.[59]

One of the many cultural assumptions English writers and officials held about residents of wetlands was that they were people and communities living beyond the bounds of the state or beyond the reach of the law. The English associated residents of fens and bogs with disruptive and rebellious behavior. In the colonies, they associated swamps with America's indigenous inhabitants and warfare. English officials may not have been surprised, therefore, when the residents of the marshy riverine landscapes of colonial New York behaved in a mutinous manner. When New Castle's residents refused to construct the dikes required by Andros, the English magistrate William Tom compared their rebellious behavior to the supporters of the Long Finn's rebellion several years before.[60] The Long Finn, who was likely a Swede named Marcus Jacobson, conspired in 1669 to return the Swedes to power along the Delaware.[61] While

Jacobson was ultimately shipped and sold into servitude in Barbados, the English were fairly lenient on his coconspirators, fining them instead of using corporal punishment.[62] This way, reasoned Governor Lovelace, the English might halt "ye spreading of ye contagion" without "amputating or cutting of[f] any member to make ye cure more perfect."[63] His language, describing rebelliousness as a kind of infection of the body, and law and order as a means of halting contagion, underscores the point that the English often framed political reform in terms of bodily cures. Metaphors of disease and health mapped easily onto ideas about early modern governance of the body politic.

"Christal Streams" or "Stinking Mud"

In print and manuscript sources, early modern English writers regularly reflected on the relationship of the environment to the appearance and health of their bodies. They wrote disparagingly of miasmas near and above swampy, boggy, and fenny landscapes. Along the Delaware River the residents' humoral bodies—their health and temperaments— were open and responsive to the marshy wetlands in which they resided, including the stagnant airs they breathed and the fish and riverine foods they consumed.[64] The air above salt water had long been associated with scurvy, and even airs proximate to the coast were thought to pose risks to seaside communities. Brackish wetlands along the Delaware River worried the new English proprietors, who were fearful of the health risks. These fears help to explain why drainage regularly featured in instructions to newly established English colonial officials. The architects of these drainage projects worried over stagnant and salty water's influence on the health of the bodies of the region's inhabitants and newcomers.

Thus, in addition to holding critical opinions of the political character of residents of wetland landscapes, such as the fenlands of England, travelers worried about the impact of wetlands on their health.[65] There was something about such unstable, watery landscapes that appeared to contemporaries, in some cases, to lead to unstable people. Perhaps this was because wetlands themselves were daily and seasonally transformed by the regular inundation of waters. As suggested in chapter 2, wetlands were liminal spaces. Many wetlands were seasonally inundated and were therefore neither fully water nor fully land but were instead a kind of hybrid space. These borderlands between types of landscapes, both wet and dry, were spiritually potent and had the power to physically and psychically influence populations. Significantly, early modern men and women expected their bodies to be porous and understood their identities as similarly fluid and transformable. Such boundary-subverting landscapes as wetlands and swamps intrigued early modern people, for whom place mattered a great deal to a mutable body. In England and its colonies people were fascinated and terrified by the ways in which seemingly open and malleable bodies were transformed by environmental factors, water included. English people were especially interested in the effects of wetland landscapes on bodies perhaps because of the range of myths associated with residents of the vast areas of wetlands in England.

One of water's most salient features is its transformability, evaporating into steam or expanding into ice. It is not surprising, then, that early modern writers would focus on the transformative properties of water in "Remarkable wells," or healing springs, or make note of waters that turned substances into stone.[66] Medical tourism included travels to the healing powers of water in places like Bath. As early modern men and women knew well, bodies were susceptible, and watery environments had the power to transform. Baptismal waters transformed souls. Yet, waters did not always heal. Wetlands and marshlands were often uncomfortable and unhealthy places to live. Residents near the Delaware were plagued by mosquitoes and complained of miasmas.[67] After the colonists of New Sweden constructed Fort Elfsborg, they gave it the nickname Myggenborgh, which means "Mosquito Castle."[68] The whine of mosquitoes swarming at night prevented sleep while the endless bites led to swollen, sickly, and miserable soldiers.[69]

Moreover, not all water was equal when it came to colonists' health. Moving water might be healthy, but unmoving, stagnant water posed risks. Daniel Denton, who wrote a promotional tract extolling the virtues of the numerous rivers and streams of colonial New York in an effort to encourage colonists to settle in lands formerly held by the Dutch, claimed that the region's "Christal streams run so swift, that they purge themselves of such stinking mud and filth, which the standing or low-paced streams of most brooks and rivers westward of this Colony leave lying." In other words, New York's healthy, swift-flowing waters might entice new settlers to their sparkling and "Christal" shores. Charles Wolley, a young minister who first traveled to New York with Andros and spent two years traveling through New York, concurred, claiming that "nature kindly drains and purgeth [New York] by Fontanels and Issues of running waters in its irriguous Valleys."[70] The use of "Fontanels" as a metaphor, which was a reference to the medical practice of surgically cutting into the body, or creating ulcers on skin, to purge ill humors out of the land, suggests the ways in which contemporaries understood land-scapes as functioning in similar ways to bodies; both required purgation to stay healthy. Streams with swift currents without blockages, like freely circulating blood, or purging humors by perspiring through pores, signaled health. Meanwhile, those slow-moving waters to the west, "by the Suns exhalation dissipates, the Air corrupted, and many Fevers and other distempers occasioned," which were "not incident to this Colony [of New York]."[71] Denton, like any number of colonial promoters, insisted that whereas their own rivers were swift and healthy, the riverine and wetland environments of *other* colonies were corrupted, stinking, and "aguish." Thus, swift rivers, which were also essential for economic and settlement needs by offering the means of easy transportation and access to routes inland, were often selling points for colonial proprietors seeking to convince settlers of the region's salubriousness.

Proximity to swift-running rather than slow-moving or stagnant water was thus an important consideration for colonists, officials, and proprietors alike. As one anonymous promoter of New Jersey colonization claimed in 1681, even Lord De La Warr, former governor of Virginia—and namesake of the Delaware Bay and River—had wished to remove his colony to the land upon which New Jersey now stood, but he had died before carrying out this scheme of transplanting the Virginia colonists to the north. Had he done so, the author claimed, this would have "prevented the Death of very many Thousands of the English Nation; who have, since that time, found their Grave in Virginia, by reason of the many Boggs, Swamps, and Standing-Waters, which corrupt the Air of the Country."[72] The tract's author blamed the stagnant waters, and thus corrupt air, for the infamously poor health of early Virginians, a claim that continued to haunt the colony at midcentury.

Indeed, promoters of other colonies unfavorably compared the marshy, low-lying lands of Virginia to the unhealthy fen regions in England to convince colonists to choose alternative destinations. The anonymous promoter of colonization in New Jersey offered an unflattering portrait of Virginia, claiming, "I (on my View) disliked *Virginia*; most of it being seated scatteringly, and among *Salt-Marshes* and *Creeks*, worse than *Essex-Thanet* and *Kent*, for *Agues* and *Diseases*; *Brackish-Waters* to Drink and Use, and a Flat *Standing-Water* in *Woods* breed a double Corrupt *Aire*; so the *Elements* are Corrupted."[73] The author dredged up a range of unfavorable qualities associated with Virginia, including swampy marshland, uncivil living arrangements, disease, and death, as well as comparing Virginia to the fenland regions of England.

The author further underscored the deadly combination of swamp below and tree canopy above, which trapped the miasmatic air so that it was doubly corrupted. Meanwhile, referencing scattered settlements suggested that there was not much in the way of a civic life, as residents were "seated scatteringly" and thereby cut off from one another by the marshy landscape in which they made their homes.[74]

But if some writers conceived of a density of trees and overgrowth as posing problems to health and climate, by trapping stagnant air below their canopy, Wolley argued that trees cleansed the air of "malign" qualities. He wrote that the "umbrellas of all sorts of Trees . . . and plants do undoubtedly, tho' insensibly suck in and digest into their own growth and composition, those subterraneous Particles and Exhalations," emanating from "pernicious Lakes," that would otherwise "become matter for infectious Clouds and malign Atmospheres."[75] Moreover, Wolley, unlike many of his contemporaries, did not necessarily see human settlement as a net positive. Instead, he asserted that New York was healthy because of its relatively sparse settlement: "for the longer and the more any Country is peopled, the more unhealthful it may prove, by reason of Jaques, Dunghills and other excrementitious stagnations, which offend and annoy the bodies of Men."[76]

Authors emphasized how human health was remarkably unstable in wetland landscapes and might be further altered by climate and season. Living in and around marshlands came with a host of potential ailments. These were variously described as marsh fever, ague, or intermittent fever.[77] Travelers through the fenlands of Essex had long ascribed the poor health of the region's inhabitants, with their "epidemicall" coughs and pallid hues, due to its "moory soil" and "watry atmosphere." The links between wetness, fog, and poor health were especially noted "nere the sea coastes . . . and other lowe places about the creekes."[78] They were aware that they needed to be well-informed about the local topography as it was deeply constitutive of health. Proximity to a creek, breathing in the local miasmas that rose up from a marshland, or inhaling the salt of a seaside wind alike might influence a person's health, likely for the worse.[79]

Travel writers and medical writers often linked places in or near water with particular ailments. Some places might alter bodies temporarily, others more permanently. Localized microclimates near water could contain dangerous miasmas. Scurvy had long been associated with travel, particularly oceanic voyages, and was known as "the plague of the sea."[80] However, observers regularly noted that voyagers who fell sick in transit recovered in a short time upon regaining the land.[81] As one commentator reasoned, scurvy was a disease of mariners and was particularly incident among "such as use the Seas . . . partly from bad Airs, Sea Fogs, sudden Heats and Colds, much Salt Diet," but it could also affect families "who inhabit near the Seas."[82] Early modern English men and women hoped that by gathering knowledge about the links between health and environment, they might make use of it to preserve health. Colonial promoters realized that they needed people to survive if they wanted their new colonies to thrive.

The young minister Charles Wolley, who traveled to New York on the same ship as Edmund Andros, attempted to explain why the region was colder in the winter than England, despite the more southerly latitude. He explained this phenomenon by offering an analogy. Just as the sharp winters of Venice were "imputed to its vicinity or nigh Situation to the chilly tops of the Alps, for Winds as well as Waters are tainted and infected in their passage," so, too, was the climate of New York shaped by its specific regional topography. New York "in like manner is adjacent to and almost encompass'd with an hilly, woody Country, full of Lakes and great Vallies, which receptacles are the Nurseries, Forges and Bellows of the Air, which they first suck in an contract, then discharge and ventilate with a fiercer dilation."[83] If New York's airs were sharper and colder, however, they were free from the "annoyances which are commonly ascribed by Naturalists for the insalubrity of any Country, viz . . . [any] stagnant Waters, lowness of shoars" or other unhealthy topographical features.[84] Settlers revised their expectations of climate based on ancient theories delineating temperate zones at particular latitudes, because it was clear that such models were inadequate reflections of lived experience.[85]

Writers discussed the influence of watery places on human bodies to explain diverse phenomena, including differing temperaments, heights, and digestive operations. Regional and local specificity likewise had implications for health and character. This flexible and layered notion of the relationship of a person to a place made it an enduring idiom, even as the seventeenth century saw the rise of new and alternative ways of understanding health. However, while nature exerted a powerful force, humans could also manipulate the material world. Armed with knowledge about the ways in which watery, marshy, boggy, and riverine environments might transform health and character, colonial officials could intervene. Drainage works alleviated several related concerns about residents of wetlands. Draining wetlands around colonial New York improved health, rid communities of the "nusance" of wetlands, and offered a justification for the English presence, which was still tenuous and thin on the ground. Remolding "waste" spaces might re-form "waste" people into desirable subjects. Draining swamps that Ferdinando Gorges claimed "harbored bears" and were places of potent spiritual power and refuge for local Indians might alleviate two perceived dangers at once.

"Publique Improvement" in Colonial New York

When English officials sought to secure control, they often turned to the physical world to express their goals and create the infrastructure required to run a colony, by refashioning the landscape. In a letter sent by the colony's secretary, Matthias Nicolls, to the surveyor Walter Wharton on June 22, 1671, he queried, "what publique Improvement may bee made thereabout either by Land or Sea" in an effort to gauge what projects might be undertaken in Delaware.[86] The governor also received proposals regarding potential improvement projects, such as one he received from Captain John Carr, who commanded the military forces in the region, who encouraged him to focus on "clearing the Highwayes, maintaining Fences and other Matters relateing to the Well-Government" of the colony, highlighting how such clearing "may prove of gret use and Benefit for Travelling and Commerce."[87] English officials regularly instructed courts to take issues of travel into consideration, such as clearing and constructing highways and cart ways, "That some way bee made passable between Towne and Towne."[88] Officials similarly instructed villages to care for roads to facilitate the circulation of goods, people, and news.

In 1664 the initial instructions intended for the residents of the formerly Dutch colony followed a familiar pattern throughout New York, and the English allowed residents "the same privileges And upon the Same Terms, which they do now possess" with the only caveat that they "Change their Masters, whether they be the West India Company or the City of Amsterdam."[89] Provided that residents took an oath pledging their allegiance to the English, they would be given the status of "free Dennizen."[90] Indeed, throughout colonial New York, the English encouraged local magistrates to continue their government until instructed otherwise.[91] In some instances, such as in Kingston, on the Hudson River, they did not introduce changes to the Dutch inferior courts until 1669. Although demanding oaths of allegiance was a standard practice, the English recognized that such oaths could be superficial and easily ignored if new circumstances arose.[92] The rate at which the Delaware River valley changed hands in the seventeenth century would have required flexibility from settlers in the region.[93] New York briefly returned to Dutch hands in 1673, before once more reverting to English rule the following year. Perhaps recognizing that such initial "ritual incorporation" of settlers by swearing oaths had limitations, this chapter suggests that the English took further steps to assert control over the topography and polyglot communities of New York.[94] English mistrust that oaths were enough to secure control and anglicize the scattered communities of Finnish, Swedish, and Dutch residents helps to explain the additional measures taken by the English, including the construction and maintenance of roads and the drainage of swamp and marshland. Such transformations to the colonial landscape also point to a capacious sense of what reforms could be imposed by the English, and the expansive conception of what officials might require of new subjects in the colony.

On September 11, 1669, Governor Francis Lovelace sent commissioners north along the Hudson River bearing instructions signed by Lovelace at Fort James in Manhattan. The commission held sessions in the town known by the Dutch as Esopus and renamed Kingston by the English.[95] The following week the commissioners, including Ralph Whitfeld and Captain John Manning, with Lovelace's instructions in hand, read them out loud and allowed for some debate about their contents. Among the first actions required by the commission included the appointment of a surveyor general of highways for both Marblehead and Hurley as well as Kingston. Not only did the commissioners desire an account of the area's highways, but the commission "ordered the Kingston Court to keep village highways passable," suggesting the importance of access to the new English government.[96] Lovelace also sent instructions to construct fences, to "watch [the Indians] closely," and to treat his soldiers kindly while quartering them in their homes. As to the latter, the community at Esopus/Kingston complained that if there were any issues, they were not to blame. They retorted that they had fed the soldiers and washed for them, thus "it is not our fault if we are not dwelling together in amity."[97]

The upkeep and construction of highways featured prominently in the instructions from Lovelace. Among his instructions for Kingston included the "Well Laying of the High-wayes from one Village to another, and keepping them passable."[98] This concern featured regularly in English orders throughout colonial New York, suggesting that the proprietor and his officials were eager to preserve and enhance access to the scattered communities in their newly acquired colony. After allowing for debate and finalizing details about what such an order would entail, the officials affixed the orders to the Kingston town hall, including the "Order for the laying out and keeping passable the High-Wayes and Common Roads" leading through Kingston, Hurley and Marbleton.[99] The order tacked to the door insisted that residents were "obliged . . . to take care that the High-wayes and Common Roads belonging to those three Townes be conveniently layd out and constantly kept passable" and ordered that the "Scout [*schout*] and Commissaryes belonging to Kingston," would be charged with ensuring that the highways and common roads of Kingston were kept passable, and given the "power to Command every person (whom they shall adjudge lyable) to attend to their Orders in the mending of the High-wayes and Common Roads, and to Fyne such as shall neglect their Duty."[100] The new surveyor general of Highways for Kingston, Hurley, and Marbleton, Captain Thomas Chambers, would supervise the *schout* and commissaries to ensure they did their duties and had the power to fine, in "Skeppl[es] of wheat," those who did not.[101]

Throughout the new colony, English officials wrote laws regulating the highways and common roads of New York. A month after Lovelace signed the instructions for the commissioners bound for Kingston, the General Court of Assizes met in New York and crafted some "Additions and Amendments" made to the laws of the colony. They, too, referenced the importance of keeping the highways clear of debris. The court chastised "divers young persons" for "cutting downe and felling Chestnutt Trees" too near to the colony's roads. Not only was timber wasted, which was yet another problem to be addressed, but as a result of such thoughtless felling "often times the highways are blockt up by the falling of the Trees crosse the way." As a result, the court ordered everyone to use any felled trees and to "take Care they do not any way hinder or block up the Said High Wayes under the Penalty of forty shillings for every such Offence or Corporall punishment."[102] Such addendums to the colony's laws highlight how movement and accessibility were priorities for the English governor and those he represented.

One of Governor Lovelace's purposes in keeping the roads clear and passable was to establish a mail service. In a letter from Lovelace to Connecticut's governor John Winthrop Jr., he affirmed the centrality of highway routes to English aspirations to connect their scattered colonies. As Lovelace wrote to Winthrop, a mail service would ensure "all publique occurences may be transmitted between us, together with severall other great conveniencys of publique importance, consonant to the commands laid upon us by His sacred Majestie, who strictly injoins all his American subjects to enter into a close correspondency with each other." Indeed, a regular mail service carried along cleared and interconnected highways was the "means to beget a mutual understanding." The scheme to "promote a happy correspondence" between the colonies would further "so universall a good work." The route was scheduled to begin operating in 1673, but that same year the Dutch retook New York, and the proposed monthly mail service was postponed.[103]

Although roads and highways were of great "publique importance" as a means to allow for "a close correspondency" between individual towns and colonies, the same "Speciall Court" held in Kingston in September 1669 included additional instructions designed to transform the local topography. The court also required the inhabitants of Kingston to "take care that the Morasse that lyes under the Towne be drayn'd; whereby the Place will not only be Improovd to be better; But it will contribute much to the health of the place."[104] There were several implications wrapped up in Lovelace's instructions to drain. First, by stating that drainage was an improvement, the governor offered up a logic deployed by many English colonists before and after him. Initiating "improvements" to the landscape was regularly used as the means by which the English sought to justify their claims to American lands and the simultaneous dispossession of Native Americans.[105] By claiming land was unimproved and underused, or that it was lying in waste, the English deployed an interpretation of the "Roman law of the first taker," which suggested that they might claim any lands they improved.[106] In other words, if no one had labored to improve it (in ways the English recognized or acknowledged), the land was subject to forfeiture. The English deployed similar logic against the Spanish in Jamaica, as will be discussed in chapter 5, and they used a similar argument against the Dutch. Moreover, the claims to "improvement" echoed religious sentiments. The English regularly asserted that improvement was a biblical injunction, a requirement to turn a fallen, postlapsarian world back into the Garden of Eden that their progenitors had lost.

In his instructions to Kingston's residents, Lovelace claimed that drainage would also improve their health. Here, too, was the innovative claim that the English regulation of the landscape might improve the health of residents, offering further justification for their authority in New York. Framed as a public health initiative, Lovelace offered yet another avenue to justify English sovereignty in a conquered colony. After reading the drainage instructions aloud, the commissioners allowed for some debate. After they discussed "every Particular," they affixed the finalized instructions to the town hall.[107] The town would face a fine of "one hundred Skepples of Wheat" to be sent to "his Majesty" if the "Morass be not drayed by the last of November."[108] The instructions affixed to the town hall reiterated many of the points made in the initial instructions and further claimed that "The Draining the Swampish or Morasse Ground lyeing and adjoying the Towne" would be for the "Publique Good." The final instructions used even more vehement language, proclaiming that drainage "would very much conduce to the health of the place, and the Improvement of soe much ground which is rendered at present almost useless." In the second draft, drainage would "conduce"— not simply "contribute"—to residents' health.[109] The final version also added language about how the "Swampish" land to be improved was, at that time, "almost useless."[110] Here, again, emerges the unspoken accusation that the Dutch had failed to perform an essential public good by not rendering the land useful. The "as yet unperform'd" drainage project had left the residents with "almost useless" land that was also a public nuisance and health risk.[111] While the size and scale of the "Morass" remains unclear, it served a rhetorical purpose. Its drainage served as a symbolic act to further justify English authority in a place where the English presence was thin on the ground. The English could now point out how they had not only defeated the Dutch to acquire New York by conquest, but they had improved lands that lay unimproved during Dutch rule and that their activities would be conducive to residents' comfort and health.

However, in an Extraordinary Session held by the *schout* and commissaries on September 23, 1669, on the same day officials affixed the drainage orders to the town hall, they crafted a reply to the governor's missive. They answered that it was "impossible" to do the work required "because no laborers are to be had, yea, hardly enough to attend to our own land, because many people went from this place to the new villages."[112] It seems likely that they were referencing the depopulation that occurred in the aftermath of what is known as the Second Esopus War, between the Dutch and the Esopus, a tribe of Lenape people, in 1663. While there was not a "mutiny" in Kingston, as there would be in New Castle the following decade, in both cases residents resisted English orders to drain.[113]

It would be wrong, however, to suggest that a concern for the fate of swamps and marshlands was only a top-down affair, used by the English to justify or enhance their authority in newly acquired New York. In other instances, we see communities in New York reach out to English officials to secure their support for "improvements" in or around local swamp or marshlands. Communities may have done so for a range of reasons. They

may have manipulated English officials' eagerness to "improve" or legislate over colonists' property—litigating about property enabled colonial
officials to highlight their important roles in the community—and redirected this enthusiasm for their own ends.[114] It is also possible that communities shared English officials' fears over the dangers of swamplands.
An example of a community that sought English approval to deal with
the "damage" caused by local swampland was the village of Breuckelen
(a Dutch village in what is now the borough of Brooklyn in New York
City). On November 17, 1671, residents of the village of Breuckelen peti-
tioned the governor for the title to unfenced marshland located in their
community. They claimed that "a certain piece of land or woodland . . .
whereunto appertains a certain swamp or marsh" had been left unoc-
cupied "for the past 15 or 16 years" because "the proprietor has gone to
Holland or Patria, so that the aforesaid land or marsh tends therefor to
the great prejudice and damage of the commonalty, insomuch as many
horses and cows have been lost in the aforesaid marsh, the same not
being enclosed."[115] Because this unenclosed marshland caused a great
deal of "mischief" and "damage," the petitioners requested "that with
his Honor's approbation the aforesaid land and marsh may be given and
granted to some of our actual Inhabitants who ask to enclose the said
marsh, so that they possess and may make use of it in right ownership. It
is, therefore, our request to you, Right Honorable Governor, to grant it to
our Commonalty so that we may be relieved from such damage."[116] The
constable and overseers signed the request.

The petition was successful, and on January 5, 1672, Breuckelen's
residents agreed to confiscate "the land formerly belonging to Mr. Carel
Gabree." They then "Resolved to apply to the Hon. Sessions of purchase
the fee of said land and adjoining marsh and swamp for a certain sum,
and thereunto authorized in person Dirck Storm and Jan Cornelisse
Buys and Dirck Janssen" to do so. Finally, they unanimously resolved to
purchase the land for three hundred guilders.[117] Finally, on July 12, 1673,
Matthias Nicolls, colonial secretary, gave the representatives a certificate
of purchase for the confiscated lands. He explained that the governor had
entrusted him to deal with the request for the "Lott of Land and Meadow"
within Breuckelen's precincts.[118] Nicolls acknowledged that the land
had been confiscated in the "Last Warre, and lay neglected and unfenct
to their great prejudice."[119] By reaching out to the English governor, it
would appear that the residents of Breuckelen used the goals and preju-
dices of the governor, and the growing imperial apparatus, to achieve
their own ends. Crown agents arbitrated in favor of local demands at the

behest of local actors. In this instance, the residents of Breuckelen likely intended to make use of the valuable marshland for pasturage.[120] The community of Kingston opposed the instructions imposed by the governor and declined to drain. In Breuckelen they purchased the unfenced "swamp or marsh" lands in order to fence it and make use of it. Local negotiations over the fate of local swamp and marshlands subvert any easy top-down narrative about a regime bent on centralizing authority through the regulation and manipulation of the landscape. This was a process negotiated in individual villages across colonial New York.[121]

It seems likely that another reason the English were so concerned with draining is thus made visible by reading the drainage instructions in conjunction with another regular English demand. The new English proprietors also ordered that "the bounds of every Towne and Parish be perambulated" and property boundaries settled as a result. The court wanted to know the "exact bounds" of the various towns along the Hudson and likewise required that individuals "settle" their lots and prove their ownership or risk forfeiting the lands to the king. In other words, they were required to renew patents.[122] Knowing who owned which lands helped officials assess quitrent rates. Every inhabitant had to pay His Royal Highness two shillings and six pence worth of "corne" as quitrent annually for every hundred acres.[123] Taxes could not be assessed if property bounds and ownership remained unknown. As a result, there were financial reasons to establish clear boundaries. If marshlands and swamplands prevented clearly marked boundaries, they subverted the goals of the colony's proprietor and officials.

Draining in New Castle, 1675

On June 4, 1675, a rowdy crowd gathered around magistrates from New Castle who had traveled to the Lutheran Church at Crane Hook, on the Delaware River, to make an announcement. The day nearly ended in a riot. They were responding to events that had transpired the previous month. On May 13–14, during his first official visit to New Castle, the new governor of New York, Edmund Andros, held a special court session during which he issued an order requiring the inhabitants of New Castle to assist in building highways and cart ways. To do so required the town to first do something about Captain Carr's low-lying meadow at the northern end of town as well as Hans Block's "Low Ground or Swampe" on the south side of the town.[124] In the court proceedings, officials referred to wetland locations as a "generall Nusance to this place

FIGURE 3.3. The small town of New Castle was one of the most prominent settlements on the western banks of the Delaware River. It was located near where the tidewater of the Delaware Bay met the fresh water flowing from the north. Detail from Philip Lea, *A new map of New England, New York, New Iarsey, Pensilvania, Maryland, and Virginia* (1690). Image Courtesy of The Lionel Pincus and Princess Firyal Map Division, The New York Public Library Digital Collections.

and Country as it now lyes."[125] Indeed, Carr's meadow, because there was "neither bridge nor fitting way to passe," had resulted in the "great ruan" of the town.[126] The court also mandated that the town create ditch and drainage works on the southern edge of town. The magistrates later determined that the dikes running along Block's swamp first had to be repaired and strengthened before the town could even begin to accommodate the governor's orders to construct a highway. The magistrates decided that "each and every male, who belongs to the district of New Castle, shall begin work next Monday" and report for at least two mandatory workdays to construct the dikes and sluices, or pay for their absences.[127] One of the purported purposes of drainage works was to resolve the contention that these swamps hindered the movement of the local townsfolk. These drainage works were also part of a broader effort of the new government in New York to make their journeys from town to town more "convenient." The new English government worried about how to reach many of the settlements on the west side of the Delaware, which hindered effective political oversight. These challenging and seasonally inaccessible landscapes limited English administrators' control over the Finnish, Swedish, Dutch, and English inhabitants of the formerly Dutch colony and they worried such landscapes stymied trade and communication between towns.[128]

Supporters of the drainage works claimed that as things stood, to travel to Swanwyck, a town only one English mile away, the inhabitants either had to cross through the mire, which was a dangerous proposition, travel around Block's swamp by sailing on the river, or walk around its perimeter, thereby traveling five or six miles through the woods.[129] The magistrates claimed their orders to drain would help travelers avoid the "peril and danger" of traversing the colony in the winter, when ice made the river impassable. When the frozen river prevented an easy journey, travelers walked through the woods, which was rendered too dangerous if and when they were at war with the local Indian population.[130] As this constellation of associations suggests, the English newcomers linked ideas of improvements to claims of accessibility and control, while also imagining and rationalizing Indian dispossession.

Officials argued that drained land enabled access, particularly with the additional construction of bridges and roads. Andros likewise required such infrastructure. In addition to drainage works, the court session Andros hosted in May had also required the construction of highways and bridges and had recommended the presence of a ferryboat at The Falls in an effort to make the area more accessible to the town's inhabitants, as well as improve accessibility for the king's representatives going about their business in the region.[131] In this way, the new English officials intended to bring order to what they viewed as disordered landscapes and scattered communities. One of the purposes of this improved infrastructure was to render the settlements along the Delaware more controllable. Highways and bridges enabled the transportation of goods, communication, and information, and assisted the influx of new settlers. These projects would also allow the rapid transmission of laws, and the representatives of those laws, with more ease.[132] The colony's proprietor, James, Duke of York, was eager to settle and take control of the landscape in and around New Castle and its inhabitants and to reassert his legitimacy. With the colony only recently returned to English hands in the preceding months, he sought a way to settle, and transform, the landscapes and residents of his new colony, hoping to make it profitable. Exerting political control over newly acquired residents of an expanding English empire was, in part, about making "improvements" to the region's topography.[133]

The special court convened at New Castle because it was the principal settlement in the region, referenced in letters as "ye strength of ye Rivr."[134] The English divided the settlements on the west side of the river into three court districts. The court that met at New Castle covered a district that stretched from the Cristina River to Bombay Hook. New Castle was located on the Delaware River, just across the water from the vast tract of land granted to James, Duke of York, by his brother in 1664, which included land and settlement in what is now Maine, New York, New Jersey, Pennsylvania, and islands off the coast of Massachusetts. The land on which New Castle stood, however, was in dispute, as it was not part of the original grant to James. At this inaugural monthly court session in New Castle, the court had ordered, prior to constructing bridges and highways, that Captain Carr's "Meadow Ground shall bee apprized by indifferent Persons and the Towne to have the refusall, but whosoever shall enjoy it shall bee obliged to maintaine sufficient bridges and wayes through the limitts thereof, with a Cartway."[135] In other words, if residents wanted to enjoy the meadow as commonage, they had to help with the construction and upkeep of improvement infrastructure. The new magistrates selected the appraisers. New Castle magistrates chose two appraisers while the Upland Court selected the other two.[136] After inspecting the marshlands in question, they "judged the marshland to be of no value."[137]

With the "impartial" opinions in hand, the magistrates of New Castle decided that they could not immediately construct the governor's highway because the work "can not be carried out unless an outer-dike with sluices is first built along the water," and as a result "they therefore order herewith that each and every male, who belongs to the district of New Castle, shall begin work next Monday on the aforesaid outer-dike and continue to work until the aforesaid outer-dike has been completed."[138] Martin Cerritsen, Pieter de Witt, and Hendrick Sybrants were selected to be in charge of this significant undertaking, as the dike would be "ten feet wide at the bottom, five feet high and three feet wide at the top." After the initial construction, the upkeep would fall to the townsfolk of New Castle, while the "country people shall thereafter not be obligated to work (without being paid for it)." While the inhabitants of New Castle would be responsible, they would also benefit from the enterprise on "the condition that they shall also derive the profits from the aforesaid marshland and have it as their own."[139]

While these projects would unfold to the north of town, the magistrates also decided that it was in the "public interest" to repair and strengthen the existing outer-dike and sluice on the edges of Hans Block's marshland. Although this dike and sluice "shall this time only be repaired and built up by each and every male who lives in the district and under the jurisdiction of New Castle," in future, the repairs would be the responsibility of the Dutch magistrate Block and his heirs. Unlike the meadow to the north of town, this land would remain in the hands of the Block family.[140] Block had requested "assistance in repairing his Ditch itt being the Common and nearest foot way from this Towne to Swanwick Crane Hook and parts adjacent."[141] But this did not sit well with the inhabitants of the district of New Castle. According to the clerk of the court of New Castle, William Tom, on the day in June when the magistrates read their decision aloud to the nearby community of Crane Hook, assembled in the Lutheran church, the largely Finnish residents angrily surrounded the magistrates. According to Tom, they gathered in "such a mutinous and tumultuous manner" and "somme having swords some pistols others clubs with them such dispitefull language." As the protesters of the drainage works later pointed out in written petitions to Andros, they were wholly unwilling to assist with the drainage of Block's valley marsh. They were determined "nott to be slaves to Hans Blocks perticular Interest."[142]

Petitioners from Christina Creek and Crane Hook later explained that though they were willing to "repaire the Kings high waye" as well as "to make and secure the Dick for a foott passage over the river side with a soficient sluice to draine the water outt of the flye [valley]," the same was not true of Block's dike.[143] The petitioners maintained that they were perfectly willing to construct dikes and highways "for the Concernes of the King and publique" or for the "Conveniency of the towne," but they were wholly unwilling to labor for Block, one of the newly appointed magistrates. They maintained that repairing Block's dike, even if it was necessary to construct the mandated highway, was "not a publique butt privett Concerne."[144] They pointed out that the original work order had promised that if the town worked to ditch the "small piece of Swampe on the Souths[ide] of the Towne," they would be able to "enjoy it."[145] The meadow formerly belonging to Captain Carr would become common land, to be used and enjoyed by all, but this was not the case with Block's meadow.[146] The petitioners pointed out that "without the privelige" of enjoying the "flye of Hans Block," they were "nott any way willing to repaire the Dick."[147]

Among the protesting inhabitants of Crane Hook mentioned by Tom included Jacobus Fabritius, the "preister," Jacob Vander Veer (whom magistrates later claimed had "alwayes ben a Troublesome, mutinous person and one of a turbulent spirit from the beginning always Contending with and opposing authority" while living a life "more that of Indian than Christian"), John Ogle (an Englishman), Pieter de Witt, Barnard Egbert, Thomas Jacobsen, Iuryan Boatesman, Mathys Smith (written elsewhere as Matthias Mathiasson de Vos), and Evert Henrickson.[148] In his own letter to the governor, Block claimed that a belligerent John Ogle had vocally denied that the community was willing to assist in either project, even if they later protested that they were only against draining Block's private property. Instead, claimed Block, Ogle had asserted, "We neither intend to build Hans Block's dike nor the other dike." Another man, "Mathys Smith," spoke up, siding with Ogle: "The man speaks the truth and what he says we all say," and then added "more foul words."[149] At that, the constable, Captain Cantwell, struck Smith with a cane for his retort. At that point, Fabritius also asserted his support of Ogle. When Cantwell attempted to grab ahold of the two ringleaders, Fabritius and Ogle, and bring them aboard a boat bound for New York to hold them accountable for their actions, the crowd surrounded the boat, "somme crying fatt them fatt them." As Charles T. Gehring has pointed out, this was likely Tom's efforts to capture the Dutch: "Vatt hem aen," or, "seize it." Afraid of how far it might escalate, the magistrates released the two local ringleaders to appease the growing crowd.[150]

Meanwhile, in his own account to the governor, William Tom claimed that all of these townspeople were in "such a humor" because they were "drunke," and had "frenzicall braynes," which is how he accounted for their mutinous behavior. He implied that such riotous behavior was a result of unsound minds, or humors, or else they would not have disagreed with the recommendations made in their best interest. In frustration, he wrote how it was "impossible for us to get . . . Justice according to the best of our Knowledge when all our accions shalbe disputed by a plebeian faccion which will not only force us to leave the bench but will expose the Country to greate charges when upon every occasion there frenzicall braynes pleases what wee determine there according to your honors order and instruccions," especially because the "Sweeds and Fynnes being such a sort of people that must be Kept under else they will rebel and of that nation these here are the worse sort as by instance the Long Fynne."[151] The "Long Finn" was a reference by Tom to rumors of a planned insurrection that had been started in Kingston, New York.

Marcus Jacobson was known as the Long Finn, and in 1669 he was the source of rumors of a Swedish plot to take back what they had lost in the Americas. The rumors led to his arrest and trial in New Castle.[152] Jacobson was ultimately sold into servitude in the West Indies. Tom used this incident in order to make his case for taking a hard line against the protesting inhabitants of the district around New Castle. He called those in disagreement with the new magistrates "mutineers" and requested that the governor send soldiers to keep the peace.[153] Several days after the initial confrontation, Block ran into Ogle on the street. Block pointed out that "we had had the confirmation of our order put up on the church." Ogle replied, "I think as much of your order as this dirt on the street" and kicked at the dirt with his feet.[154]

Tom intended his description of a mass of Swedes, Finns, and Dutch with their clubs at the ready to underline the vast gulf between their supposed ignorance, drunkenness, and "frenzicall braynes" and the rational, law-enforcing officials like himself. Tom argued that they were irrational, lacking in reason, and did not know what was best for them. He implied that disordered landscapes led to disordered brains and disordered subjects. Tom's reference to humors suggests a medical imbalance. It was a common rhetorical move to suggest that a community's health and character, their humors, were shaped by the natural world. As the traveler Jaspar Dankers would later write about a congregation in New York: "We therefore went, and found there truly a wild wordly world. I say wild . . . because most all the people who go there to live, or who are born there, partake somewhat of the nature of the country, that is peculiar to the land where they live."[155] In his comments he ascribed the wildness of the social body to the wildness of the place. Moreover, much like magistrates' claims that one of the dike mutineers, Jacob Vander Veer, was mutinous and troublesome because of living a life more "Indian than Christian," Dankers similarly mused that those who lived "in the interior of the country somewhat nearer the Indians are more wild and untamed, reckless, unrestrained" and otherwise worryingly transformed by both the company they kept and the wilderness in which they resided.[156] Almanac author Daniel Leeds similarly worried about the untamed wilderness of New York and its effects on residents' behavior, explaining, "such is the influence of this Wilderness on the inhabitants who are born here [that] it inclines them to an *Indian* way of living."[157] His son, likewise an author of almanacs, attributed the unsociable behavior of residents of colonial New York to the environment, in this instance the weather. When the chilly "North-west" wind blows, it "blows us sharply one against another, Friend against friend, and brother against brother."[158] English officials claimed their work, including that of drainage, would have both a healthful and civilizing effect on the land and the people.

Meanwhile, much like the Long Finn rebellion, the dike mutiny may have been sparked, in part, by anxiety about land and a conflict about labor. Several years earlier, the Long Finn had gained supporters for his anti-English stance and had purportedly claimed the Swedes had "suffered from the English, and how they, partly by treachery, partly by force took from them one big piece of land after another."[159] Anxiety about the meaning of work orders may also have played a role. After all, the terms on which tenants held their leases on the patroonships of New Netherland included three days of service owed to the patroon, as well as a requirement to upkeep roads.[160] It is possible that their angry claim that they would "nott be slaves" was a rejoinder that they were not anyone's tenant and did not owe any individual their labor.[161]

When Captain Carr wrote to the governor and his council with some proposals of what work must be done in the town of New Castle, among his suggestions was clearing up any confusion "about Publique Charges . . . as also for clearing ye High wayes, maintaining ffences & other mattrs relateing to ye Well-Governmt of that place be reinforced by yor Honor approbacon."[162] By noting that these concerns first arose "at and about ye time of ye Tryall of ye Long ffinn," Carr's text suggests a long-standing connection between efforts by the English to secure money for public works, including the construction of highways, and non-English residents' mutinous behavior. This suggests that events in New Castle followed some of the same patterns, as debates about what constituted a public good and how to determine related costs or labor were already connected in Carr's missive. Moreover, in the same text, Carr hoped the governor might acquaint New Castle's residents "by what tenure they hold their lands." His query suggests that English residents were similarly uncertain about how they held their lands and expressed some anxiety over it.[163]

Disagreements over the fate of Carr's and Block's swamplands, and the relative responsibilities assigned to residents for cost and upkeep of the new dikes and sluices, cast light, in part, on the tensions between the largely non-English inhabitants of New Castle and the surrounding communities and the schemes of the English colonizers. Andros and his local contacts justified their work requirements as necessary improvements, public health initiatives, and a reclamation of wastelands. But court-defined improvements are not necessarily considered improvements by those affected by the changes. Tension over the fates of these meadows may also have included the difficulty in distinguishing between profitable and unprofitable lands, which was to a certain extent, of course, a judgment call. And what qualities defined the expert who could make these decisions? Low-lying meadows may have been a nuisance to some, while productive to others. Records suggest that there was a disagreement about the relative use of the meadows and wetlands by the very fact that the court also found it necessary to appoint judges to ascertain the "use" value of the lands in question. The court-assigned experts found them to be of "no use."

As scholars have pointed out, marshes, meadows, and other variable wetland landscapes ranged in use-value. In many communities, meadows were valued as excellent places for grass growth, which could also be turned into hay, and necessary to feed animals. Writers distinguished between productive and unproductive wetlands. Samuel Clarke wrote that in New England there is "little cold spewing Land, no Moorish Fens, nor Quagmires: The lowest Grounds be the Marshes, which are ovrflown by the Spring-Tides: They are Rich Ground, and yield plenty of Hay, which feeds their Cattel," and "near the Plantations there are many Meddows never overflowed, and free from all Wood, where they have as much Grass as can be turned over with a Sithe, and as high as a mans middle, and some higher" so that the cattle were larger, produced more milk, had more calves, and were "freer" from disease.[164] In 1670 Daniel Denton echoed these sentiments, describing how English animals carried to colonial New York were healthy "by reason of the large and spacious Medows or Marches wherewith it is furnished, the Island likewise producing excellent English grass."[165] Brian Donahue's careful exposition of the adaptive stewardship of farmers in colonial Concord reveals that the first English settlers were drawn to the area by the wetlands, which they considered "a great blessing."[166] Far from draining or filling in this invaluable common land, farmers carefully managed the Great Meadow and its grasses, which they used for hay. According to Donahue, "Agrarian life in Concord, as in many other colonial New England towns, revolved around hay meadows and their management."[167] It seems likely that the court needed to make a formal statement about the nonutility of the lands because marshlands were so often highly desirable as places for hay consumed by cattle, among other uses.

Anger about the drainage works had yet another critical dimension. As one angry inhabitant pointed out, they were "nott to be slaves" to the needs of any individual, nor to New York or to England.[168] The genesis of this anger revolved around the fact they did not have a say in the schemes, yet residents were required to labor or pay a tax equivalent to their labor. In addition, as many inhabitants argued, they refused to put in the time and money to these so-called public-work projects if they would not benefit from the work. In this instance, Hans Block's private interests would benefit from public money and labor. It was a long-held custom, for instance, in fen drainage projects in England, that only those people who would obtain a tangible benefit from the drainage could be taxed. The Statute of Sewers had long been in place to enforce this custom.[169] Inhabitants countered Andros's orders. Forcing them to work to improve lands owned by particular individuals, such as Hans Block, was against both long tradition and the law. The magistrates, however, argued that the path along Block's land was the "common" and "nearest foot way," suggesting an alternative definition of what was a public or common good.[170]

A similar complaint had been made a decade earlier, on Long Island, when residents complained that they been "inslav'd" under Governor Nicolls's "Arbitrary Power," which he "[exer]cize[d] more than the King himselfe," by the rates imposed by the English to collect sums for public works and public charges. Captain John Underhill wrote to Governor Nicolls in the spring of 1666 to inform him of the "Slander" of "malicious men" who complained about the warrants issued to gather the rates. Nicolls then demanded Underhill send him the names of those who had "opened their venomous hearts so freely to you." According to Nicolls, such mutinous and treasonous speech must be punished because "the late Rebellion in England, with all the ill consequences thereof, began with the self same steps and pretences. By defaming his Majesties Government, to Corrupt and Steale away the hearts of his Majesties Subjects."[171] For Nicolls the Civil War and Restoration of Charles II were immediate reminders of the recent histories of such debates. Dutch residents' anger at the rates imposed upon them and calling them a form of enslavement resemble those arguments made several years later in Crane Hook, when the community disagreed over what constituted a public benefit. Nicolls, like the New Castle magistrates, wrestled with local communities over who should bear the burden of the public charge and what constituted a public good.

Not only do these events offer a window into the Restoration government's efforts to regulate the non-English inhabitants of the empire through the manipulation of the environment through public works projects, but they also offer evidence of James's innovations as a colonial proprietor. Alterations to the landscape reflect his conception of his rights, even duties, as a colonial proprietor. Indeed, James had an expansive sense of what his government in New York might require of its inhabitants. The drainage demands show that his representatives were willing, on some occasions, to ignore the laws of England in New York. When designing the Duke's Laws for New York, the Duke of York and his colonial agents collected the law books of other colonies and sought to cobble together a new set of codes derived from those they liked while excluding those they did not, intending to learn from what they perceived to be the mistakes of the past. The Duke's Laws were the result of this work. His grant had not required James to create a representative assembly. Instead, he created a governor's council. He thought elected assemblies were "dangerous" and disordered because they "assume to themselves such priviledges wch provfe destructive to, or very oft disturbe, the peace of the government wherein they are allowed."[172]

To contemporaries, to make an improvement was to assert rightful ownership. In this construction, unused lands and poorly utilized lands were theoretically subject to forfeiture.[173] It was a capacious theory and was used to justify any number of land grabs, including enclosure, the enormous acreage acquired by projectors in the fenlands, and in colonial settlements.[174] Colonial officials deemed the creation of arable lands an improvement on the natural state of nature, and as a result, drainage was a means to claim possession. Part of the eagerness to settle and "improve" the land was due to the contemporary understanding that this was one of several ways to lay claim to land. It is likely the duke was so quick to require particular sorts of improvement projects because he was staking an ideological claim to his "natural" rights to an unsettled and legally unstable area.[175] The residents of the western shores of the Delaware River found themselves at the uncertain edge of Maryland, New York, and New Jersey. In the end, they would become part of Pennsylvania. But in the meantime, it is possible that these improvement projects were a strategy by York to lay claim to those settlements not technically within the bounds of his grant. One means to incorporate the land and people along the western banks was to promote improvements, and thereby possession.

Remolding Landscapes and People

In a letter Robert Smythe wrote to Edward Byllynge, governor of West New Jersey from 1680 to 1687, which was printed within a collection of letters in 1681, Smythe urged the governor to gaze across the Delaware River to "a very good Tract of Land" which, if he settled it with "good Neighbours, and under a right Authority, would be vastly Advantageous." Smythe imagined how Byllynge might lay claim to these advantageous lands if he put them under "right Authority." He acknowledged it was already settled by a considerable number of "*Swedes, Findlanders, and Dutch*" who might, over time, and "through a good Government over them . . . become very good Neighbours, at least, much better than at present they are." While generally unimpressed with the current residents of the western banks, Smythe thought they might prove malleable if the English established a strong government over them. Smythe continued, musing, "I think it was highly your Advantage, that you found few or no Inhabitants settled in New-Jersey; so that you had none to *new-mold, displace, or remove, contend or quarrel with* [my italics]."[176] Here we see the range of strategies that Smythe suggested a new government might deploy to deal with populations that were already living in a place it desired to control. If Byllynge were to extend his reach across the Delaware and take up control over the settlements on the west side of the river, he *theoretically* had a range of options when dealing with residents (of course, England had already made Dutch residents denizens, so some of the options Smythe enumerated were theoretical, not actual). In Smythe's accounting, residents could be displaced or removed, or they might be subdued after a contention or quarrel. They might also, like landscapes, be "new-mold[ed]."[177]

Once again we see how improved landscapes were seen as being able to bring about improved citizens. One of William Penn's earliest comments on the inhabitants of Delaware, only several years later, was a condemnation of their failure to properly cultivate fruit trees. He blamed their long isolation among the Lenape Indians for their agricultural failures.[178] In Daniel Denton's *A brief description of New-York* (1670) he similarly condemned the Native American and previous European inhabitants of the region alike for their agricultural failures. Like others, he was surprised that the rich lands in and around New Castle "should be no better inhabited" considering the rich soil, healthy climate, and ease of river travel.[179] He contended that the Dutch government had made any number of errors in their control of the region that had inhibited its planting and stunted its growth. He argued that they were always in danger from Indians, but they were afraid of starting a war in case they lost access to the "*Bever*-trade," "which was the main thing prosecuted by the *Dutch*." This single-mindedness, he argued, made them ignore necessary cultivation.[180] Of course, what these commentators did not consider was that the Dutch "failure" to plant might have been a Lenape design. As recent scholarship on the area has suggested, the Dutch had tried to practice large-scale agriculture in the Delaware Valley, but the Lenapes quickly destroyed the colony. Although they would not allow large-scale planting, they did allow trade. The features of the Delaware Valley were thus shaped by Lenape as well as Dutch preferences, and the negotiation of the conditions of Dutch settlement.[181]

To suggest that someone had failed to improve or to cultivate a landscape was a comment on their civility, or, more specifically, their lack thereof. The fact that the inhabitants along the Delaware River had not done a better job of improving the landscape, doing little to "reduce" the landscape in order to cultivate and embellish nature, implied that their rights to the land were in doubt, as was their civility. As the English were already primed to see people in wetlands as politically riotous and uncivil (due in part to conversations in print about the fens), anyone who did not make improvements was easily discounted; they were animal-like people who lived beyond the bounds of civil society.

English officials believed that if residents along the Delaware were to be successfully incorporated into the empire, it was necessary to teach them how. In advance of his first official visit to New Castle and the new Bailiwick court, Edmund Andros sent an elaborate set of rules about how to behave during the special court that convened in New Castle on May 13 and 14, 1675. Plans for this day had been long in the making, and there was much business on the agenda. Secretary Richard Nicolls had sent ahead a schedule for the day, instructing the inhabitants and attendees on how to act on this auspicious occasion. He provided a step-by-step guide to help them act the part of ideal English townsfolk: "At the first meeting of the Court, The Cryer is to make Proclamacion and say O yes, O yes, O yes: Silence is commanded in the Court, whilst his Royall Highnesse Governor, Councell and Justices, are sitting, upon paine of Imprisonment."[182] This guide contained careful, detailed instruction on how to behave and had been sent ahead to ensure that this first court session with Andros went smoothly. After they learned the lines of this courtroom drama, the court dictated instructions to manipulate and reconstruct the physical environment around New Castle. Both Nicolls's instructions on how to enter a courthouse and behave as prescribed, as well as Andros's prescription for alterations and improvements in the landscape, were similarly sites in which physical, political, and cultural control could be performed and enacted. The bodies of the Dutch, Swedish, Finnish, and English inhabitants along the Delaware would perform new roles against new backdrops, acting like English subjects until they became them. Although Lenape invitees were also welcomed to the court session, the English did not appear to consider Lenape residents as people who might be "new-mold[ed]" into subjects. The English invited several Lenape chiefs to attend this first court session, but as allies, not subjects.

The English officials planned to request a formal friendship status. Perhaps because they believed that Lenape relationships with the Dutch were pretty good, at least in terms of trade, the English hoped this goodwill would carry over in their favor.[183] Like the Long Finn and his concern about English greed for land, Lenape sachems had similarly accused the English of grasping for land. In a letter from William Tom and Peter Alrich to Governor Lovelace in 1670, they had urged Lovelace to visit the Delaware, "treate with the Sachems," and convince them not to go to war with the English. The Indians were prepared to go to war because "they say where the English come they drive them from there lands and bring for instance the North Virginia and Maryland and feare if not timely prevent[ed] [the English] shall doe so here."[184]

As scholars have argued, landscapes offer views into the "constructions of national identity."[185] According to Burden and Kohl, "A place (the English countryside) is a spatial practice . . . encoded with aesthetic, cultural, and social relations" that include "class and power."[186] Landscapes were thus a powerful place for ceremony, political theater, and identity formation. The ability to manipulate nature was an assertion of natural right, a symbolic and material claim to power, particularly in an unstable postwar period. The ability to cultivate nature, or reclaim land by which to enable cultivation, was an argument made by many contemporaries in support of Charles II's right to rule. As other scholars have noted, landscapes were a "built metaphor" and undergirded a belief that "managing plants and managing people were not, after all, very different from each other."[187] Restoration interest in environmental manipulation has largely been understood in these highly symbolic terms.

But what occurred in New Castle was more than an expression of symbolic power. The theatricality of the courtroom performance—that included instructions on when to stand, when to speak, and what to say—combined with the environmental changes dictated by those courts, ultimately came together in a full-throated effort to claim control and display power in a place where their hold was tenuous. The scripts, stages, and scenery were all designed to remake or remold the participants into English subjects while simultaneously renaming towns, introducing new laws, and requiring oaths of allegiance.[188] It was a visual and highly symbolic drama, but the transformation was also about tangible changes made to the spaces in and around New Castle described in this chapter. These comprehensive steps taken by the English took seriously the role of place, and the physical experience of place, in the construction and assertion of identity and power. By renaming towns, improving residents' health through drainage, and constructing cart ways that connected communities and facilitated trade, the English sought to create a sense of place and to construct their own civic vision, grounding their conception of what it meant to be a subject of the English empire in the landscape itself.

The overlapping boundaries and the uncertainty over how best to incorporate the land and residents along the western banks of the Delaware River resulted in disputes between the several colonies' proprietors. Imperial officials struggled with how to define the boundaries of such uncertain spaces and sought to articulate the political status of the varied residents. Ultimately, like the other regimes that had swept over the region, the English granted favorable rights to the polyglot communities, provided they took oaths of allegiance.

Although the English may have hoped to transform residents and ultimately planned to remold residents into something more "Anglified," the choice of marshland drainage as one avenue to accomplish this metamorphosis may seem, perhaps, an odd one. After all, in the early modern world it was probably the Dutch who were best known for the system of dikes that had enabled them to reclaim approximately two hundred thousand acres from the sea in the early decades of the seventeenth century.[189] They also undertook a range of drainage projects in their North American colony, including digging canals to drain "Blommaert's Vly" on the southern edge of Manhattan in 1643, one the earliest mentions of Dutch drainage works in the colony.[190] English governors' insistence on drainage suggests the possibility of the persistence of Dutch ways in accomplishing these projects. While scholars such as Ted Steinberg have noted the English penchant for filling in the soggy lands of New York instead of draining them, and this is certainly the case both contemporaneously and in later decades, this chapter reveals that the English also gave numerous orders to drain.[191] Meanwhile, as Steinberg has argued: "Dutch influence over the landscape persisted. The rivers emptying into the Hudson on the western side of what is now New York continued to be called *kills* as opposed to the English equivalent, *brooks*. *Bays* remained *reaches*."[192] Indeed, no matter how "Anglified" the region might become,

Restoration officials remained deeply troubled by the potential "ill consequences" of mutinous and treasonous speech of residents of the empire that might lead to rebellions like "the late Rebellion in England," or, what they worried might be the return of external imperial enemies in the form of flotillas sailing into New York to claim or reclaim it.[193] This chapter acknowledges the persistence of non-English identities and ways of living on the land while also highlighting English officials' attempts to remold them.

The English aspired to transform landscapes and, in the process, to transform bodies and behavior. Not all spaces, bodies, or behaviors were deemed acceptably English to be welcomed into the expanding English empire. Lingering suspicious about foreign "nations" in New York were cause for concern. We tend to consider the legal mechanisms by which non-English residents were incorporated into the English colony, but in addition to requiring oaths, the English sought additional measures to transform the residents into acceptable subjects, and the landscape into something properly English. The degree to which such pockets of unruly people living in inaccessible and watery places might be transformed alongside their environments was a critical question. Undergirding Charles II's efforts to bring the "loose and scattered" peoples and places of the empire under unified control were local "improvements" such as drainage, the construction of roads, and courthouses made of brick. Officials intended that the upkeep and construction of interconnected roadways would facilitate movement, trade, and regular mail services. Such infrastructure required accessible and traversable landscapes. In colonial New York, drainage facilitated these imperial plans. But drainage did more than merely connect towns and colonies that were otherwise inaccessible, useless, or beyond the control of imperial officials. In their orders to drain, English officials also anticipated that they might transform the health and manners of colonial New York's residents in the process.

Along the banks of the Delaware River, individuals likely related to the land in many ways. They may have related to it politically, understanding themselves as subjects within a territorial polity.[194] Perhaps they viewed their relationship to the land as economic, legal, or cultural as, indeed, "place has infinite meanings and morphologies."[195] It is also possible that they related to the landscape physically and medically. In the early modern era people considered how their bodies were connected to the environment, understanding that the local wetland ecology was deeply constitutive of their individual humors and might have transformative effects. English officials promised to improve the health of communities through drainage, as well as to rid them of swampy nuisances. When officials justified projects to transform the landscape, they claimed that places and people might be "new-mold[ed]" and "Anglified" during the process. Modifying the landscape countered the potential threat posed by non-English residents of the unsettled colony. Drainage was one means of defining the scope of English rule over distant, heterogeneous landscapes and people.

Although one of the projects of marsh drainage on the outskirts of New Castle was no more than "an English mile," the fact that new legislators demanded drainage here, as elsewhere, is telling. Supporters of drainage works utilized rhetoric about agricultural "improvement" and the transformation of land from waste to utility to support their actions. Disagreements about the appropriateness, fairness, and utility of the drainage were overcome by claims that insisted that the improvement of wastelands for the reclamation of accessible, arable lands was a necessary public good. "Improvement" was both a powerful and flexible rhetorical tool that could address local wetland meadows, on the one hand, and entire fenland regions on the other. On the banks of the Delaware River, the myriad communities who dwelt there were described as a type of outsider; politically, geographically, culturally, and temperamentally—if not physically—these wetland dwellers on the outskirts of the distant American plantations were seen as threatening to a centralizing English empire. At the Restoration Charles II sought to define imperial consolidation legally and physically, as did the Duke of York in his new colony. This chapter has also suggested that the persistence of humoral medical theories meant that colonial officials traversing the newly acquired colony of New York frequently explained and understood their interventions in the landscape, both draining marshlands and constructing highways, as shaping bodies as well as bodies politic. This chapter reveals Restoration era officials' efforts to impose a political ecology along the Delaware River that differed from the relationships other scholars have revealed between colonists, wetlands, and meadows in other places. For instance, Brian Donahue has revealed the ongoing importance of salt marshes to communities in New England. Gregory Kennedy has also pointed out the value of meadows to early colonists in Acadia. While much of the local wetlands were filled in over time, according to Kennedy, this was done at a slow pace, by individual families and neighbors, not by fiat or by drainage companies.[196] This chapter follows drainage projects initiated by the representatives of the colony's proprietor, and their claims that drainage was a matter of public health and safety.

After civil war, and in a region that had changed hands several times, political stability in the empire could not be taken for granted. Officials sought to ensure stability and to initiate projects of improvement. Like postlapsarian landscapes, and human bodies, social and political bodies trended toward degeneration, rot, corruption and instability. This trend could be reversed only by active intervention in these physical, and metaphysical, worlds. Bodies and bodies politic were not homeostatic and needed regular infusions of tonics and laws to keep balanced, particularly as the empire expanded. Waterlogged worlds were one such decayed and wasted space that might be reformed and cured, for instance, by purging ill humors out of the land with drainage. This chapter has been an effort to think about what a certain kind of imperial project looked like on the ground, and the kinds of actions taken by those who opposed them.

The claims of "improvement," however, were constantly undermined by the real places and people and by the daily and seasonal ways that elements of the landscapes constantly remade "improved" landscapes. Water is powerful and difficult to control with confidence. In the end, many drainage successes were fleeting, putting pressure on the claims of the improvers that their alterations to either landscapes or polities were of lasting significance. Only two years after the drainage works were implemented in New Castle, the new magistrates composed a letter to Andros that recounted how "The Dyke and Sluce being by a Storm Lately broke and mutch out of Repair Capt. Colier and Capt. Cantwell have therefore Ingaged the payment for the Remakeing of the Same againe the t'Charge thereof amounting to about 800 gilders." Although Collier and Cantwell had agreed to lay out the costs for the repairs, they intended to get repaid. All residents were to "pay pro Rato towards itt To have their parts but those whoe Refuse, to Loose their Commanadge."[197] Those who would not pay to assist in upkeep would lose their share of access to the common lands reclaimed from the Delaware wetlands.[198] Time and again colonists learned that wetlands were difficult environments to control, and the questionable success of these projects of land reclamation challenged the improvers' claims that these landscapes, and the nearby residents, could be remade into ideal English subjects.

4 /   Improving the Body: Agriculture, Food, and Population Size

Food was one of the primary means by which a leader might symbolically reinforce the idea that he or she was capable of protecting subjects, as ample food supply symbolized wealth, power, and legitimacy. As a result, banqueting and other ceremonial aspects of food were key elements of the art of governance. Charles II consumed many meals in the public eye, meals that included unusual and highly prized items, such as pineapples, that he shared out among some of his courtiers. John Evelyn had the opportunity to taste "that rare fruit called the King-Pine" off of the king's own plate and wrote about the event in his diary. In the early modern era the pineapple was considered a kingly fruit and was often described thusly because of its delicious, almost heavenly, taste.[1] Only kings and their close associates had the chance to eat pineapples in London in the mid-seventeenth century because few specimens survived the long voyage across the ocean, and European gardeners were unable to grow pineapples until the end of the century with the development of greenhouses. Charles II consumed exotic items like pineapples, which were described enthusiastically by travelers to the West Indies and carried back for a very lucky few to sample, to display his reach, power, and magnificence.[2]

The pomp and circumstance of such ostentatious consumption was a ritual of display intended to prove Charles II's ability to provide sustenance for his court and country. It was important to Charles II that even in exile he should maintain an enviable table, borrowing heavily to ensure that his household ate well. According to Anna Keay, this theatricality was actually a necessity in exile when little separated Charles II from his subjects other than the quality of his clothes and the sumptuousness of his table. The king sought to appear magnificent, even in exile. After regaining the throne, he fed select subjects in highly visible ways to encourage domestic stability and to secure his position.[3] Feeding courtiers rarities reinforced the king's legitimacy, and serving exotic foods like pineapple underscored Charles II's claims to power over colonial territories, and even over nature itself.[4] The dishes on the king's table were therefore about power and showmanship and legitimated his right to rule. The king associated himself with exotic pleasures that offered sensory delight, which emphasized his wide reach and magnificence.

Not only was he concerned with the quality of the foods consumed, but the quantity was an important aspect of establishing legitimacy, too. Leaders around the Anglo-Atlantic world grappled with similar associations between authority and access to food. Horror stories of death and starvation had long circulated alongside colonial promoters' claims of abundance and astonishing fertility in the English colonies.[5] More recently, in England, wartime ravages to villages where soldiers fought or were quartered during civil war led to widespread deprivation and further suffering. Bad harvests due to weather conditions from 1646 to 1651 further exacerbated the problem.[6] Midcentury authors, many of them parliamentarians and their supporters, promised a better world and offered agricultural solutions to solve various social ills. Some of these writers saw in acts of gardening and agricultural improvement a way to rehabilitate a fallen world and return the earth (and the commonwealth) to a prelapsarian, Edenic state.

Whether they had theological or more prosaic aims, writers churned out improvement literature, much of it highlighting horticultural and agricultural improvement, focusing on how to turn wastelands into arable lands to produce more food for consumption and sale. On January 18, 1659, author and later member of the Royal Society, John Beale, wrote a letter wondering at the hundreds of new kinds of "pleasant or wholesome drinkes, & more kinds of bread & foode" that he had the opportunity to write about. He was astonished by the "amplification of Gods Table for the releefe of Mankinde." Indeed, new foods and commodities such as "Coffa, Thee, &c" had entered English diets even before he had the opportunity to write about them. In all of this, he mused, he saw evidence of the "Mystery of Gods providentiall expedition in increaseing knowledge, commerce, & mutuall accomodations, all over the world."[7]

His enthusiastic references to new foods masked the reality of widespread anxiety over new consumption habits.[8] Meanwhile, after the Restoration, writers continued to tout agricultural improvement projects as the best means to promote "the Common Good" and ensure national strength, at least in demographic and economic terms.[9] They associated food stability with political stability. Restoration officials recognized that they might capitalize on anxieties over food access by arguing that it was the Stuarts, not Oliver Cromwell or his supporters, who were best placed to restore order and ensure that subjects were well fed.

Even during the Protectorate, royalist authors of recipe books hailed the exiled royal family and their associates—such as Charles I's former physician, Theodore Mayerne—for providing the reading public with "Kitchin-physick" recipes, and suggested they were the proper caretakers of subjects' health.[10] While referencing the "Approved Receipts and Experiments in Cookery," which were copied from Mayerne's manuscript, the anonymous author of a cookbook published in 1658 claimed that the "Art of Cookery, and Teaching men to eat, not like Caniballs, but like men, is none of the lowest Requisites in a well-governed Commonwealth." By citing Mayerne in the title as well as in the text, the author not so subtly associated eating well, maintaining bodily health, civility, and good government, with the Stuarts.[11] Another well-known recipe book published in this period, W. M.'s *The Queens Closet Opened. Incomporable Secrets in Physick, Chirurgery, Preserving, Candying, and Cookery; As they were presented to the Queen* (London, 1655), similarly underscored its association with the Stuarts and drew connections between the queen and healing, cooking, and the domestic arts.[12] After the Restoration, officials, agricultural writers, and members of the Royal Society—particularly those thirty-two Royal Society Fellows who were members of the newly established "Georgical Committee" in 1664 who resolved "to compose a perfect History of Agriculture and Gardening"—continued to discuss and debate farming, gardening, and the introduction of new and more diversified diets as a matter of national importance.[13] Many royalists carried home new tastes after their time living in exile.[14] Among their concerns were locating healthful and flavorful plants, especially if money might be made by cultivating and selling them. They also sought to solve seemingly intractable social ills, such as poverty and hunger, by ensuring access to sufficient food.

After the Restoration, supporters asserted a connection between having enough to eat and eating well with the king, as a way to legitimize his position. Historian Michael A. LaCombe points to the long-standing centrality of food "to any image of an effective leader" in the English Atlantic and argues that the breakdown of authority in early colonial settings was often associated with officials' inability to ensure their community's access to food or its orderly distribution.[15] The Restoration government was aware that the scarcity of food was a likely cause of social and political instability and looked to stave it off.[16] When William Petty looked back and pondered the causes of civil war, he argued that the violence was partly the result of hunger among the poor, or, in other words, "allowing Luxury in some, whilst others needlessly starve."[17] People without food often act out of desperation. His arguments have been echoed by scholars, who argue that "Food supply was the Achilles heel of the early modern state; short of religious war, nothing so menaced the state as food shortages and the resulting social upheavals."[18] Restoration officials, like many leaders before them, regulated and legislated access to grain, such as limiting exports. Chartered by the king, the Royal Society published a range of proposals to inspire agricultural innovation and the cultivation of new food. They anticipated that their myriad agricultural and gardening plans would be "for the common benefit of their Countrey" and would "conduce to the Health, Strength, Populousness and Welfare of these his Majesties kingdoms."[19]

Local communities also had long developed responses to food scarcity. Officials established a range of initiatives at the village level, such as poor laws, to respond to bad harvests and seasons of dearth as well as to address longer-term conditions of poverty. These laws were regularized and routinized in the early modern period.[20] Scholars suggest that by the end of the seventeenth century, threats of crisis-level famine had generally disappeared from England as "the implementation of poor laws became universal, or nearly so," though famine conditions hit Scotland in the 1690s, for instance.[21] Locally raised taxes ensured that communities could ameliorate the worst ravages of poverty, particularly hunger. Despite the existence of some social safety nets, however, much work remained to be done. But government officials, writers, and residents of England and its colonies disagreed about who was responsible for public welfare and what improvements could best alleviate hunger.[22]

Authors of literature on the "Rustick Art[s]" promised to teach their elite, land-owning readers the latest innovations in gardening and farming.[23] One observer acknowledged the rapid publication and circulation of improvement literature in the 1660s and 1670s, noting that "books of husbandry are sold off as fast as the press can print them," but complained that a quantity of texts did not result in quality advice since they often injudiciously included "anything that seemed new and probable."[24] In addition to publishing new techniques in husbandry, these treatises introduced new foods and flavors to diversify diets and advised about food preparation and preservation. Whether they promised panaceas for hunger in the consumption of Jamaican chocolate or advised the planting of thousands of fruit trees in English hedgerows as curative food for the poor, authors contributed to broader debates about who should initiate projects of improvement and suggested that public hunger and health should be a matter of state interest.[25]

One explanation for the appearance of so many proposals, and even some legislation, purporting to address hunger or boost population size was the oft-discussed connection between demographic strength, a healthy economy, and geopolitical power. Robust, well-fed subjects could fight, if need be, against England's enemies.[26] Recipe books promised cures for sterility and infertility by the consumption of everything from globe artichokes to liquids with infusions of American-grown sassafras.[27] Whereas sixteenth-century writers expressed fears of overpopulation, by the mid-seventeenth century many authors instead feared English underpopulation and took steps to address their anxieties. A preoccupation with the nation's demographic strength was due, in part, to the acknowledged role that population played in securing colonial claims against a backdrop of intense imperial rivalries.[28] The English symbolically secured sovereignty in the Americas, lands which colonial promoters claimed were lying in "waste without any improvement," by planting gardens, and building houses and fences, by which they might "replenish the earth and subdue it." Such work required many hands. Moreover, by bearing children, women might further obey the biblical injunction to "increase and multiply" and act as agents of colonization while doing so.[29] The perceived connections between propagation and securing dominion helps explain why so many colonial propagandists emphasized the benefits of the colony's environment, and some of its groceries, to women's fertility.

Improvers celebrated the work of cultivation as the means to likewise "cultivate" the "deserving" poor as they transformed the land from wastes to productive spaces, transforming their social value in the process.[30] Able-bodied people who were without work were described as "waste" people. Writers proposed that if such people could be properly managed, both *waste* lands and *waste* people could be made useful to the nation through labor.[31] Similarly, transported prisoners sent to the American plantations might rehabilitate their economic and moral

selves while cultivating the soil. After all, tillage and the arts of planting were supposed to have been "Adams imployment in Innocency," and
authors had long pointed to the moral, physical, and economic benefits
of planting fields, gardens, and orchards.[32] By pruning, sowing, tilling,
and weeding, English men and women might learn, or relearn, the values of duty, work, and civic-mindedness. The centrality of agricultural
labor to English ideas about improvement and property help explain
why agricultural metaphors were widely used when articulating the
ideal relationship of authority figures, whether God or the king, to the
governed. God was regularly figured as a husbandman. In *A Treatise of
Fruit Trees* (1653), Ralph Austen reminded readers of John 15, lines 1–2:
"I am the true Vine, and my Father is the Husbandman. Every branch in
me that beareth not fruit he taketh away: and every branch that beareth
fruit, he purgeth it, that it may bring forth more fruit."[33] Writers like
Austen described moral reformation in deeply physical terms. The language of cultivating individuals and society was co-opted by the state to
describe or justify relationships between the state and its subjects, as well
as individuals and the land.

Authors of agricultural improvement treatises, authors of recipe
books, members of the Royal Society, and colonial governors alike were
deeply interested in the specific type of food introduced, transplanted,
and prepared, as well as the labor required to cultivate and trade them.
Foods were essential to life but also had deeply symbolic meanings and
were believed to be crucial to both individual and national identity and
of critical economic importance. Consequently, there were many reasons why controlling the quantity and variety of plants cultivated and
consumed mattered to Restoration officials. Officials saw in agricultural
improvement projects the means to simultaneously cultivate healthy
bodies, robust economies, and secure social order within the growing
English empire.[34]

Planting Fruit Trees "For the Benefit of the Poor"

Among Charles II's many struggles in the months and years after his
Restoration was how to assert the legitimacy of his authority with the
specters of civil war and his beheaded father looming in the recent past.
If his subjects had killed his father, what stood in the way of another
such overthrow of government? One way to assert his rightful place on
the throne was by adopting various symbols to emphasize his natural
stewardship of England. Taking the oak tree as a symbol of his reign, for

example, went well beyond memorializing his evasion of the armies of Oliver Cromwell in its shady boughs.[35] Oak was a favorite of the shipbuild-ers who facilitated an increasingly interconnected empire. Moreover, these long-lived specimens of the plant world represented order, stabil-ity, and durability in a seemingly uprooted world. Trees were rooted to the ground, and their branches lengthened and stretched toward the sky and could be imagined to represent the connections that existed between past and future generations, like the lineage or family tree of the Stu-art kings. As symbols of stability and longevity, numerous landowners, including the king, planted orchards, avenues, and hedgerows with trees. The increased popularity of arboriculture after the Restoration resulted in tree-lined walks and promenades with massive bowed limbs hanging overhead. They offered a promise of stability in the wake of the instabili-ties of war. They also emitted sweet smells. In *Sylva* (1664), John Evelyn advised planting the sweet-smelling "Virginian Acacia" to provide shade for the king's new "Plantation" in St. James's Park.[36] Known for their "intensely fragrant" blooms, Evelyn noted that the French already used them to adorn their walks.[37] Such planned avenues lined with stately, sweet-smelling trees grew in popularity among the gentry.[38]

But the king's claims went well beyond symbol and metaphor. To make good on his claims of natural stewardship, he and his advisers sought knowledge about England's wood reserves and encouraged mem-bers of the Royal Society, among others, to offer ideas about conserv-ing and replanting trees. A far-flung empire required ships that could carry goods, soldiers, and officials and that served practical ends. The king's advisers sought information about England's forests, as well as tree resources in the colonies, and how such woodlands might best serve the state, including fruit trees. Like advisers in other European countries who drew similar connections, Evelyn equated tree rehabilitation and national strength.[39]

Writers often expressed fears of instability and disorder in environ-mental terms, such as the destruction of trees, particularly fruit-bearing trees. As one commentator assessed the landscape of Ireland after the war, much of the damage was irreparable: "Orchards before the wars in many parts there were good ones but . . . thirtie years peace will not . . . repaire the ruins of the war [because] most have bin destroyed and the rest over grown."[40] Not only had the war ruined orchards, claimed the author, but the reverberations would likely be felt for decades, as trees, with life spans even longer than those of humans, took many years to recover from such destruction. The devastation of orchards was especially damaging to the king's subjects because they lost a source of food, further compounding the ravages of war.

John Evelyn's *Sylva* (1664) was a celebrated collaboration between the Restoration government and the Royal Society. He claimed his text was a response to the principal officers and commissioners of the navy, who desired knowledge about England's tree resources and how to better improve upon them. Evelyn was one of numerous authors to urge proactive measures, calling on the king to implement a systematic plan to rehabilitate England's timber resources. According to Evelyn, very little could contribute as much to the power, wealth, and safety of the nation as "Cultivating our decaying Woods": "For, as no Jewel in your Majesties resplendent Crown can render you so much Lustre and Glory as your regards to Navigation; so, nor can anything impeach your Navigation, and the Reputation of That, whiles you continue thus careful of your Woods and Forests."[41] Evelyn thus encouraged the king to continue to be a thoughtful steward of England's tree resources, which, he intimated, demonstrated Charles II's fitness to rule over England.

By contrast, Evelyn's text portrayed Cromwell as a rapacious abuser of England's forests and tree supplies, thereby implying he had been unfit to rule over England and its natural resources. Indeed, Evelyn blamed the current shortage crisis on the "Usurpers, and injurious Sequestrators" of the commonwealth for the evident depredations of the nation's forests.[42] According to Evelyn, the commonwealth government had no respect for the country's ancient and venerable trees. In St. James's Park they planned to cut down the "Royal Walk" of elms, "That living Gallery of aged Trees," and sell them for money, like they did elsewhere on formerly royal lands. He claimed that under Cromwell the depredation of trees was everywhere apparent, and "so dishonorable and impolitic a waste of that Material, which being left intire, or husbanded with discretion, had prov'd the best support and defence" of the nation.[43] Cromwell's poor management of England's trees, royalists like Evelyn argued, put the nation at risk.

Evelyn claimed that the king, in contrast, supported measures to reforest England, thereby proving himself the best supporter and defender of the nation. Evelyn's depiction of these disparate styles of caretaking trees was, of course, meant to point to essential differences in the styles of governance between Cromwell and the king. The treatment of trees stood in for a range of political and cultural meanings, such as a long-term investment and a promise for the future. By extension, in Evelyn's text, replanted trees were symbols of the hoped-for longevity and stability of the restored Stuarts. Evelyn equated the Restoration and the return of the proper steward of England's human and natural resources. He predicted that England would be reclothed with the cover of trees, which were so necessary to England's wealth, power, and well-being. As garden historians have noted, arboriculture took particular hold after the Restoration. For instance, grand avenues, lined by trees, became increasingly popular on landed estates in this period.[44] Perhaps, like the king, the landed gentry realized the symbolic power of a landscape dominated by stately, long-lived trees as evidence of order and stability. But Evelyn claimed that, in addition to improving the "glory and wealth of a Nation," trees might further provide travelers with shade and fruit.[45] Such trees could serve multiple ends. Their towering presence asserted an estate's permanency, and landowners claimed their trees would benefit the nation, serving as ready timber, fuel, and food resources should the need arise.

After outlining a variety of historical statutes with which previous English governments had attempted to manage woodland resources, and which he dismissed largely as failures, Evelyn offered his own scheme for ensuring that England had the number of trees necessary for present and future use. If every person "worth ten pounds per annum, within his Majesties Dominions, were by some indispensable Statute oblig'd to plant his Hedge-rows with the best and most useful kinds of them," such measures would ensure an afforested future for England.[46] Perhaps acknowledging that not all property owners would plant trees in their hedgerows in response to his call to action, Evelyn urged the appointment of officers who would "have a more universal Inspection, and the charge of all the Woods and Forests in His Majesties Dominions." This work of inspection could be performed by local deputies "skillful in Husbandry," who could offer advice to those unfamiliar with planting trees. Such an individual might reverse long-standing neglect by "a vigilant and industrious Checque."[47] This individual would report to a "Superiour Officer, or Surveyor [who] should be accomptable to the Lord Treasurer, and to the principle Officers of His Majesties Navy for the time being."[48] Such an officer would have wide-ranging authority and had to be knowledgeable about trees. If the king wanted to be "our glorious Prince SOVEREIGN OF THE SEAS," his regulation of forestry resources was prudent and necessary.[49]

Two years earlier Evelyn had presented many of his ideas about improving England's tree resources in manuscript form to the Royal Society. In "Proposalls and Reasons for the Improving, & advancing of Planting, humbly tendered to the Lords & Comons in Parliament

Assembled," he suggested first and foremost the planting of fruit trees.[50] This was because "it is well knowne by longe experience, that the work of Planting fruit trees & other trees in this nation, is of very great Profitt, & advantage to all people," but particularly to the poor, because there were so many ways to make use of the fruits as food, drink, and medicines. Because planting trees was of such obvious advantage, he proposed "That a Law may be made for planting of fruit trees, and other trees most pfitable."[51] He reimagined fruit trees as a means of providing for large numbers of the landless poor. Planted at public charge, fruit trees could serve as a social safety net, and he believed their cultivation ought to be a matter of state interest. He claimed that planting fruit trees would be a boon to the nation because "people may have a great part of their meate & drink out of their hedges with small paines." Nor would such plantations particularly disrupt profits from grain, hay, or pastures because they would not take up much room. Such trees would be conducive to the health of England's inhabitants, as "it is knowne, & concluded" by physicians that cider "is the most healthfull liquor: not only preserving from, & curing divers diseases in mans body, but also very much conducing long life."[52] Similarly, when members of the Royal Society sent queries to contacts in colonial Virginia, they asked whether or not colonists had planted orchards of "wholesome fruit."[53] Around the Anglo-Atlantic world, planting orchards were conceptualized as a means of solving a variety of intractable ills, including providing for the poor, the infirm, and the widowed.[54] Charles II might secure his position as the caretaker of his subjects' health by supporting proposals that called for the careful management of England's fruit trees.

In addition to fruit trees, other trees should be planted: "for Timber, ffuell, & other uses the same proportions may be observed, as in ffruit-trees: And hereby also great advantages may be made to the nation." This was crucial because "there hath beene of late yeares, a great wast, & destruction of wood, & timber; so that without this care there will not be a sufficient supply for necessary uses in time to come." On top of these myriad benefits, Evelyn further postulated that the planting of trees would likewise regulate the climate of England, so that the "fields would be much warmer in winter and cooler in somer, [than] when they lye open, And consequently Corne, Cattle, & other commodities will ... come on the better, to the great advantage of all."[55]

Evelyn was not the first to offer up plans for tree rehabilitation projects in England.[56] Richard Corne had spent two decades in Normandy and had been impressed with their fruit tree cultivation; in 1625 he wrote a treatise suggesting how to introduce fruit culture throughout England.[57] There is also some evidence that individuals did not merely write about planting trees but actually planted them. For instance, the Earl of Southampton recorded his plantation of "many thousand fruit trees" within his "hedgerows, demonstrating the current strong enthusiasm for fruit as food for all."[58]

Outside of England, fruit trees took on additional meanings. The ability to cultivate the landscape in ways deemed properly civilized was a metric regularly deployed by the English to justify colonization. As N. Dowdall wrote in a manuscript description of County Longford in 1682, the improvements made by English landholders in Ireland often featured fruit trees. Throughout his text he made an implicit argument that well-ordered orchards, like culture, civility, and the English, arrived in Ireland hand in hand.[59] For the newer English residents of Ireland it was a means by which they might justify their residence and colonization of Irish land. They celebrated their arrival as heralding a new era of agricultural "improvement" in Ireland. The author of *The Improvement of Ireland* similarly argued that the lack of Irish orchards "hath been a defect of wonderfull stupidity from all ages, even from the first inhabitants of the Island."[60] Claims that the Irish had failed to invest in tree cultivation, whereas the English made that investment, were an attempt to represent their colonization as justified.

Among the vast changes to the Longford County landscape noted by Dowdall were those initiated by Arthur Forbes, Lord Viscount Granard, "who hath improved it to a very great degree by reducing much of Red bog into firm and good Land," on which he planted orchards, and hop yards, "and hath by such industry managed the soyle that it boardeth all sorts of Plants and flowers that are sett or sowed . . . now growing . . . in great verdure."[61] Therefore, in place of bogs, there was now "great verdure," including fruit trees. Like his "fair and spacious House, with Lovely gardens of Pleasure enclosed by High Stone Walls against which great Plants of Fruit of all sorts grows," the rearranged landscape fit an English ideal. In addition to "delightful Gardens" Dowdall praised the groves and orchards of the Earls of Longford as especially noteworthy.[62] The orchards and groves afforded "great variety of Trees, & flowers," which were planted with "industry," thereby civilizing that parcel of Irish landscape. Dowdall thus implied that the former residents of the land had not possessed such celebrated skills in arboriculture and lacked the means and desire to enhance the land. This common trope portrayed their displaced Irish predecessors as indolent and lazy, lacking the circumspection and industry necessary to embark on long-term improvements to the land. In this way, trees were imagined to be "agents of personal and sociopolitical transformation."[63] They represented the stewardship of the English, stability, and an investment in the distant future, in ways that other perennial plants might not. Dowdall further celebrated Sir Connell Horall, who had "wrought much Improvement" by "Inclosure, orchards, [and] Gardens," and wrote approvingly of all the former Cromwellian soldiers who were now property holders. According to Dowdall, "all such souldiers as had lotts in this County have all improved on theire proportions soe that the Country is much better then ever it was." In the place of "much Red bogg" in the west, there were new orchards.[64] Soldiers first subdued the people, then sought likewise to subdue the land.

The author of the manuscript treatise the *Improvement of Ireland* reserved a special kind of distaste for those elite and "antient" Old English families who had not improved their lands: "And here I cannot but reflect: that It taste[s] of the Savage, to see an antient estated Family continue to live in the Country on their Lands: yet without tolerable Habitation: without the Decorums of Garden and pomaryes: without meadows and inclosed Pastures . . . without in fin any thing that may speak a gentile and wise Economy." According to the author, their failures to make "improvements" heralded by the age called their social position, and even their loyalty, into question. The New English in Ireland, meanwhile, were "imbued with notions of progress, improvement, reformation and profit making, which led to the colonial subjugation of the great majority of the Irish population."[65] They celebrated, among other things, their ability to bring a timeless, ancient, and barbaric culture into a modern era. Savage cultures lacked the ability to think about the long term, only the short term. Such claims of shortsightedness on the part of the Irish, like their failure to invest in trees, were yet another way to justify English colonization and control of Ireland. Another report from Ireland, written by the Reverend John Keough on March 14, 1683/4 in Stokestown ("near Elphon"), detailed the landscape of the counties of Roscommon and Connaught. Keough claimed that while there were very few plant products in these counties that would be of interest, many "may grow here if Labour were employed about it and there are some Gentlemens gardens fraught with trees and herbs of the best sort ordered by ye skill of Gardeners."[66] Contributors to the Dublin Philosophical Society, like Keough, chastised the supposed indolence of the Irish. Arboriculture became one of many instruments designed to anglicize Ireland.[67]

The ability to improve upon local nature was an argument about the naturalness of political or personal possession. To contemporaries, to make an "improvement" was to assert rightful ownership. Lands that were not up to a certain standard of cultivation could be subject to forfeiture. Cultivation, particularly on a grand and expensive scale, was heralded as evidence of the cultured and civil gardeners as opposed to wild and uncivilized others.[68] In the wake of the Restoration, the king, his officials, and colonial governments each asserted that they were legitimate, in part, because they were able to manipulate nature to the advantage of the local population or to the whole nation, particularly by increasing the food supply. Knowledge, in this case to increase the production of food by legislation or improvement, was an argument for their natural right to power. The king supported various reforms to agriculture, viticulture, and arboriculture as evidence of his political legitimacy because he sought to manipulate nature to the nation's advantage, positioning himself as the symbolic head of a bountiful national table, securing food supplies, like crisp and healthy apples, for his subjects.

"Wholsom & Pleasant for Foode": Eating Right in the Restoration

William of Newburgh's twelfth-century manuscript *History of English Affairs* includes the extraordinary story of two children, a brother and sister, who emerged from pits on the outskirts of what is now Woolpit, Suffolk, in East Anglia.[69] The appearance of the children astounded the residents of Woolpit who first encountered them, wandering and confused, near the ditches. Most remarkable to the townsfolk was that the boy and girl's skin and clothing were completely green. Moreover, they spoke a language no one could understand.[70] The townsfolk brought them back to the village. For days they would not eat, until someone happened to bring in green beans, and the two eagerly consumed the vegetables. According to Newburgh, over time, the children learned to eat other foods. Perhaps most extraordinarily, their skin lost its green hue as their diet changed. And as their green skin faded, they began to speak the local language. Both children were eventually baptized. However, only the girl went on to survive and thrive, marrying a local man and bearing children, reportedly still alive at the time of Newburgh's writing. Her brother, who never quite learned to fit in, died.[71] According to Jeffrey Jerome Cohen, "the medieval lexicon of race did not allow for hyphenated terms," such as sometimes-green, sometimes-white children. It was for this reason that the green children so troubled Newburgh's narrative, and twelfth-century England more broadly.[72] Allusions to the tale resurfaced in seventeenth-century texts, including a popular science fiction account of lunar travel by an English bishop named Francis Godwin, which followed the protagonist, Domingo Gonsales, to the East Indies, St. Helena, the Canary Islands, and the moon. It was an itinerary—excluding the moon, of course—that resembled travels undertaken by East India Company ships that rendezvoused at St. Helena en route to England. The renewed popularity of the story of green children from another world resurfaced and resonated against a backdrop of intensifying movement, migration, and trade with distant places and its lessons about cultural and bodily transformation.[73]

The tale instructed readers that immersion in a new physical environment, alongside new dietary and social practices, led to a range of transformations, underscoring the malleability of human bodies and culture. While Newburgh's account offered many possible explanations for the multiple transformations undergone by the green strangers, food clearly played a critical role in the story. Indeed, the tale lays bare the central relationship of food to both the physical condition and appearance of the individual, as well as the formation of community. While food is a fundamental bodily need, and caloric and nutrient intake is necessary to survival, its meanings can also be deeply subjective and infused with layers of cultural significance. Beyond ensuring "basic subsistence," choices about consumption "couple selfhood with collective experiences."[74] Food choice has long played a crucial role as the means by which an individual might understand and perform their affiliation and belonging.

In the early modern era, people believed their health and temperament alike were shaped by the consumption of foods and drinks, as various items were chewed, swallowed, digested, circulated by blood, and incorporated into the body. Natural philosophers and physicians concluded that as food was digested it was "transmuted" into flesh, blood, and "seed."[75] And "as the Blood is, so is the State of the Body, either healthful or distemper'd," suggesting that diet had an immediate and direct impact on well-being, particularly due to its influence on blood.[76] The early modern "Exchange model," by which "Food is ingested and excreted, air is inhaled and exhaled, fluids are taken in and expelled" underscored the body's porousness.[77] Foods may have been consumed daily, a constant requirement to sustain life, but it was the choices people made about food that were significant as symbols of community, class, religion, health, and as expressions of regional or national belonging. Because foods could transform the body into a "healthful or distemper'd" state, there was considerable overlap in the conception of foods and medicines; both could adjust the balance of the humors in the body.[78] Foods had their own characteristic humors that could be calculatedly consumed or avoided, depending on the needs of individual complexions or temperaments, which ranged from sanguine, choleric, melancholic, to phlegmatic. Thus, the preparation and consumption of foodstuff "was never neutral because the qualities, or characteristics, of foods were translated into corresponding physical, mental, moral, and spiritual qualities of the eater."[79] Food was one of a range of ways by which a person might regulate their own imbalanced or porous body as it interacted with the outside world. In John Archer's treatise, *Every man his own doctor* (1673), he instructed all eaters to understand their "own Constitution and Complexion" as well as the "Nature" of foods "whereby every Man and Woman may understand what is good or hurtful to them" before selecting their own individualized diets according to their own humor.[80]

The lessons of the story of the green children, and similar tales of food and bodily transformation, resonated in the seventeenth century. The case was a useful barometer of anxieties about difference, set off, in part, by the movement of colonists around an expanding empire and the consumption of new foods and drinks.[81] Moreover, early modern English men and women grappled with a dizzying array of goods carried by ships back to London and other ports. English writers on Jamaican natural history after English conquest of the island in 1655 pointed to a range of medically efficacious commodities from the island already in daily use in London.[82] The consumption of goods from far-flung lands challenged residents of England to wrestle with concerns about the transformative effects of their consumption habits. While consumers embraced many new foods, drinks, and medicines, they also expressed lingering anxieties about whether or not they were simultaneously importing unwanted, foreign influences alongside the commodities they desired.[83] Broadsides, poems, and treatises warned English consumers, for instance, of the potent dangers lurking in their coffee. Sipping "Syrrop of Soot" cast coffee drinkers under a "Turkish Spell" such that "Men and Christians" turned into "Turks."[84] The dangers of coffee, such publications cautioned, included the possibility that drinking "new liquors" would result in religious conversion: "When coffee once was vended here, / The Al Koran shortly did appear," warned one verse.[85] Writers reacted to the growing popularity of coffee in England. If the first coffeehouse appeared in Oxford in 1650, they soon dotted London's urban landscape; there were at least eighty coffeehouses by 1663.[86] They were popular meeting places for Londoners, Royal Society members included, but Charles II's government regarded coffeehouses with suspicion due to "their associations with England's radical past."[87] One observer claimed that coffee and sedition arrived in England together, "when the palates of the English were as fanatical as their brains."[88] The king's suspicions about coffeehouses helps explain why he issued *A Proclamation for the Suppression of Coffee-Houses* (London, 1675). Anxieties about what imported food and drink, like coffee, might do to malleable English bodies and identities replicated earlier antitobacco screeds from the first decades of the seventeenth century, which accused smokers of inhaling and exhaling dark clouds of smoke "that might transform Englishmen into Africans by altering not the surface of the body, but instead its very core."[89] Of course, publications espousing deep suspicions about the transformative effects of new commodities can be found alongside evidence of their enthusiastic adoption.

In the seventeenth century, Londoners considered their city the "Emporium of the World." Ships carrying people, and laden with goods, were unloaded on London's docks.[90] The place of origin of slips, seeds, plants, and dried specimens, in addition to spices, fabrics, and other luxuries, fascinated English consumers. Many of the goods and plants were understood to carry traces and qualities of their place of origin. According to Alix Cooper, early modern Europeans were deeply interested in the provenance of new consumer goods. Indeed, "Literally thousands of treatises were published over the course of the early modern period debating the merits of particular substances, from local beers or wines to exotic tinctures. In almost every case, the geographical origins of each item, as well as its prospects for replication or naturalization," were of particular and absorbing interest to their potential consumers.[91] As goods streamed in from all over the world, some writers even looked to the skies as the next horizon for new botanical rarities. They wondered about the likelihood of life on other planets or on the moon and mused about whether "the green children came thence, which Nubrigensis speakes of," citing Newburgh's story.[92] Interest in life on other planets, including the lunar vegetation that Robert Hooke, Royal Society Fellow, claimed to have witnessed through his telescope, fascinated writers and thinkers of the era, who even imagined the possibilities of lunar colonizing and botanizing and considered the lucrative potential in transplanting exotic moon plants back to earth.[93]

Yet, there remained a range of concerns about consumption, and the medical utility, of foreign products. Food, as consumers were well aware, might change green children to white, or the reverse. Writers expressed uncertainty about how exotic specimens would agree with individual humors. While distant realms offered the lure of the fantastic, there remained questions about the potentially detrimental impact of foods and medicines cultivated in foreign soils and climes. Moreover, some medical doctrines suggested that God would have created cures to local ailments in the local environment, inspiring naturalists to investigate nature closer to home.[94] Indeed, as Samuel Hartlib noted, "Where any Endemicall or Natural disease reigneth, there God hath also planted a specifique for it."[95] Thus, eating and drinking foreign or unfamiliar substances, for health and pleasure, could be fraught with anxiety. Transplanting specimens added additional layers of confusion. What wanted or unwanted characteristics would new airs, waters, and soils imbue in transplanted commodities? As chapter 5 investigates, officials scheming to transplant East Indian spices to Jamaica had to confront the possibility that naturalizing foreign plants into new soils might alter the nature of the plant, adding or subtracting key qualities. Despite these reservations, the possibilities of new and potentially useful and lucrative plant life obtained from distant shores often overrode their fears.

Such questions of transplantation were also of essential importance to English colonists setting out for new climatic zones and unfamiliar soils. Many wondered if they could successfully transport English foodstuffs to new environments. This was a key concern, as colonists were already anxious about what new climates might do to their temperaments and health.[96] Indeed, food played a significant role in colonists' ideas about how to mitigate the potentially dangerous effects of new environments on their bodies and communities. As Rebecca Earle has asserted about the role of food in early modern Iberian colonization: "[It] was much more than a source of sustenance and a comforting reminder of Iberian culture. Food helped make them who they were in terms of both their character and their very corporeality."[97] Early modern English colonists similarly sought to safeguard their porous bodies when they ate new foods in the colonies or consumed commodities carried into England. Eating new foods, or foods poorly prepared, might result in unforeseen ailments. For instance, in his treatise on chocolate, still relatively new to English consumers in the wake of Jamaican conquest, William Hughes sought to discount the widespread belief that consuming cacao kernels without grinding them first could cause "obstructions" in women, who might "become Lencophlegmatical, and look of a whitish colour."[98] Anxieties about unhealthy phlegmatic complexions caused by unground cacao kernels, like tales of the green children of Woolpit, must have pricked at the back of their minds as men and women sat down to meals with unfamiliar foods. Colonists also likely wondered about the effects of new foods on new shores. What would happen to their humors and complexions? Would they change hues? Would women become more or less fertile? They were well aware that consuming local foods might impact them in a range of ways that they could not yet conceive.

Foods had the power to transform the body into a "healthful or distempered" state by adjusting the balance of the humors in the body.[99] Moreover, as John Archer, *Every Man His Own Doctor* (1673), and Thomas Tryon, *The Good Housewife Made a Doctor* (1690), would have agreed, food and medicine were frequently synonymous, and both regulated humoral bodies. This is apparent in manuscript recipe books in which recipes for food and recipes for medicines were frequently interleaved.[100] Foods had their own humors, which individuals had to consider when preparing or consuming them. Different bodies required different foods. Or, as John Worlidge wrote in his text celebrating cider, "as the Climates and Scituations of Countries, and the humours and dispositions of the Inhabitants differ, so have they their various and different Drinks and Liquors, and their Diets, Habits, & c."[101] In other words, cider made from apples cultivated in English orchards was the liquor best suited to English bodies. Recipe writers reassured cooks that herbs and spices could be used to magnify or negate certain humoral qualities of the meals in preparation so as to render them more healthful to the individual consuming the dish. As a result, food was a way by which people could reestablish bodily balance or consume foods that were best suited

FIGURE 4.1 (opposite page). John Worlidge celebrated the value of propagating fruit trees. Not only would planters refresh themselves by walking through the wholesome airs of orchards, but by eating apples instead of meat they would also prolong life. He hoped that his book would offer guidance so that even those of "vulgar Capacities" could plant with success. John Worlidge, *Vinetum Britannicum: Or, A Treatise of Cider, and Such Other Wines and Drinks that are Extracted from All Manner of Fruits Growing in this Kingdom* (London, 1676). RB 121071, The Huntington Library, San Marino, California.

Red streak

to their complexions. Each body was a constantly fluctuating vessel, ensuring that dining "was never neutral."[102]

Many writers offered the means by which to preserve health and prolong life by altering or regulating diet. Various spices had first been introduced into the English diet due to the belief that they were medicines. For instance, sugar was believed to be medicinally efficacious well into the eighteenth century.[103] Restoration writers were likewise interested in how best to preserve the health and bodies of their fellow diners. One of the founding members of the Royal Society's Georgical Committee, John Beale, wrote numerous letters to correspondents encouraging the cultivation of apple orchards, enumerating what he believed to be national foods and drinks, and recommending a "hortulan diet."[104] Beale also wrote to the Royal Society in the hope that they could encourage the king to support agricultural experimentation in order to stave off future famine.[105] Indeed, the "best meate in the world," he declared, was "trodden under foote" and ignored because people lacked knowledge of an "Adamiticall diete."[106] In 1668 Daniel Cox announced to the Royal Society that "the preservation of Health and Prolongation of Life may be procured by Food & physic derived only from Vegetables"[107] in order to advocate that greater care and attention should be paid to the study of plants and plant consumption. He was not the only one to suggest that a simpler diet of vegetables secured health and long life. William Temple advocated for "fruits and plants [rather] than flesh which easier corrupts."[108] John Evelyn's *Acetaria, A Discourse of Sallets* (1699) similarly advocated for the health benefits of a vegetable diet. Evelyn's earlier work likewise reflected on the value of apples and cider as ideal food and medicine for the poor. John Milton, Isaac Newton, John Ray, and Thomas Tryon also took an interest in vegetarianism and its potential benefits to their health.[109]

The quality of the food consumed mattered because it "could induce dramatic perturbations in both [the] physical and emotional condition" of bodies.[110] Food was therefore an avenue toward manipulating political subjects' minds and bodies. Beliefs in the transformative power of food further explains why new foods could cause consumer anxiety and explains why that information mattered to the state. When the Connecticut governor, alchemist, and natural philosopher John Winthrop Jr. composed his treatise on corn, "Of Maiz," and presented it to the Royal Society on December 31, 1662, he explained that throughout the plantations colonists regularly consumed corn and that it was a wholesome, as well as a good-tasting, food.[111] But English colonists had not always been so equanimous about the grain. Although earlier colonists had avoided corn at all costs, assuming that the consumption of corn was one of several factors leading to the transformation of their bodies into Native American bodies, it was an important crop in many colonies by the second half of the seventeenth century.[112] Colonists may have preferred wheat, but it was not always feasible to plant, due to environmental, technological, or labor constraints. Wheat was labor intensive and required farming equipment that was not readily available, particularly in early phases of North American colonization.[113] In the southern colonies, as Lorena S. Walsh has pointed out, "wheat was difficult to harvest, laborious to thresh, and plagued by a low grain-to-seed ratio. It also required a complex milling process that could be supported only by a relatively dense population. All told, wheat was a poor crop for 'pioneer communities.'"[114] It might not have been a practical crop, but it remained a desirable commodity as a marker of civilization, and an aspirational ideal. In the northern colonies, wheat was more readily available. Winthrop's discussion and reportage on American corn was in response to requests from the Royal Society, who hoped to gather knowledge about "foreign" husbandry. As one contemporary urged, "Ingenious Gentlemen and Merchants, who travel beyond the Sea, [should] take notice of the Husbandry in those parts," and Winthrop's treatise reflected such interest among the Royal Society membership. Winthrop wrote his treatise for the Royal Society as the Georgical Committee simultaneously solicited information about agricultural practices around England.

Winthrop's defense of corn may also have been, in part, to claim the colonists' new appetites as natural and healthy, staving off accusations that colonists suffered physical and social degeneracy in American climes and in the company of Native Americans. He celebrated corn to prove its healthfulness to detractors, particularly in England. According to Winthrop, corn remained popular even in the northern plantations where English and Dutch colonists grew "plenty of wheates and other grayne," claiming, "this sort of corne is still much in use there, both for bread, and other kinde of foode made out of itt." He argued that John Gerard, who had written in his *Herbal* (1597) that corn was difficult to digest, offered little nourishment, and was thus not fit for human consumption, was clearly misinformed. Instead, argued Winthrop, it "is wholsom & pleasant for foode, of which greate variety may be made out of it."[115] Since Winthrop Jr. was one of the few Fellows of the Royal Society from the colonies, his discussion of corn and other matters with other members of the Royal Society served multiple purposes. As the historian Walter

W. Woodward argues, Winthrop's scientific engagement with the well-connected members of the Royal Society was a means to secure patronage, and perhaps even the ear of the king. In London to negotiate for a new royal charter for Connecticut in the wake of the Restoration, his scientific interests became the means of engaging in informal diplomacy on behalf of the colony.[116]

The Royal Society's interest in corn was based, in part, on the feasibility of transporting corn to England and its suitability to English bodies. Winthop Jr. was not the first to celebrate the virtues of corn on the other side of the Atlantic. Among the Hartlib Papers, a collection of documents associated with the midcentury intelligencer Samuel Hartlib, are proposals to transport corn to Scotland, which recount how first "Hugh Lamy went into Scotland" to present several schemes to the Scottish Parliament. One proposal "concern[ed] the improuement of husbandry and the bringing in of the use of the Indian Corne into Scotland." Another proposed the "settlement of a plantation wel armed and policied in the Indies. All wch was offered for the publick and particular good and especiall relief of the poore."[117] The intention of these plans, according to their French Huguenot designer, was to serve the public, particularly the poor, and to facilitate population growth.[118] Hugh L'Amy argued that transplanting corn would benefit not only the poor but also the "owners of the ground and the f[a]rmers," as they would have a new grain to sow, to the benefit of all. According to L'Amy, the internal improvement of Scotland's husbandry and a new plantation in the West Indies were mutually reinforcing. The plantation would make available "al manner of commodities [fitt] for this life" and would "sett up also a stronge trade." Transplanting and cultivating corn could also offer food in times of scarcity. L'Amy and his partner Peter Le Pruvost next sought to initiate a similar set of schemes in England. Unfortunately for the Frenchmen, some officials never replied to their proposals, and others merely laughed. And yet, others agreed that "Indian Corne" was a crop well suited to serve the poor and hungry in times of dearth and a way to stave off social disruption. While these transplantation schemes foundered, agricultural writers and projectors maintained an interest in learning more about the cultivation and consumption of new foods, including corn.

Winthrop acknowledged that colonists' knowledge of corn was derived from Indian practice and skill. He recounted how they timed their planting by observing when a certain tree sprouted leaves or when a certain fish returned to the rivers. He recorded their methods of planting, offering enough detail to assist those unfamiliar with corn in growing it, when to weed, and how to store the harvested corn.[119] He recorded how, when the Indians made the corn into food, they had myriad methods of preparation. It might be boiled until tender and added to dishes of fish or venison as an accompaniment. On other occasions "they bruise it in a mortar & then they boyle it and make good food of it." On yet other occasions "they beate it small and make a kinde of bread of it baking it under ye embers," but the "comon way of dressing of itt" was to thrust it "amongst the hot embers and continually stiring of it yt it will be thoroughly parched, without any burning but be very tender, and turned almost quite the inside outward, wch wilbe almost whyte, and flowry" after the kernels had popped. The popped corn was then sifted from the ashes and beat in mortars into a fine meal. They consumed corn prepared in this way at home and during travel, "being putt up into a bag for their journey being att all tymes ready and may be eaten either drye or mixed wth watter: they find it [an] extremely wholsome diet." The English also used this finely ground corn as a flour substitute to make bread.[120] His careful descriptions remind us of how often the English assimilated to indigenous ways of cultivating and consuming crops.

Winthrop also wrote about corn as a kind of bread replacement. Finding a suitable grain that might produce a bread-like food was essential to many new colonists, a trait they shared with Spanish colonists. As Rebecca Earle has revealed, Spanish colonists' "culinary models were largely inherited from the Greco-Roman world, in which wheat, wine and oil had constituted not only the most prestigious foodstuffs but also the very essence of civilization."[121] Whether or not corn could fulfill this critical role was uncertain, but Winthrop argued that in its numerous guises corn was "a food very pleasant and wholesome, being easy of digestion and is of a nature diareticall and cleansing and hath no quality of bynding ye body as ye herbal suposeth but rather to keepe it in a fit temperature." Winthrop further praised it—when prepared in a method that left corn boiling the whole day, then cooling it and adding it to milk—as a meal that "may be taken as well in sickness as in health even in feavers and other acute diseases." According to Winthrop, a doctor Wilson imported dried corn for the use of his London patients. Among its numerous uses, moreover, corn was even used in the colonies as a grain to make beer. While in London Winthrop prepared some of his corn beer for members of the Royal Society, at their request.[122] Meanwhile, Winthrop also wondered if the sweet stalks might produce some sugary substance, so that New Englanders might have a commodity with which to compete with the sugarcanes of the Caribbean.[123]

While the reputation of corn changed over time, in part due to the efforts of colonial advocates like Winthrop Jr., the fears associated with the consumption of a range of other plants remained difficult to assuage. Despite anxieties, the English introduced various plants and agricultural technologies into English agrarian practices in the seventeenth century. Eager to obtain new plants and learn new planting regimens, early modern men and women integrated various foods into their diets. The rapid introduction of plants and foods at midcentury was, in part, due to the experience of royalists living abroad during the civil war. Exiles had the opportunity to try a variety of foods in France and the Netherlands, for instance, and brought new culinary tastes home with them. But it was not only movement outside of England that introduced new tastes. Because battles were fought in various locations around England, soldiers sampled regional specialties, leading, for instance, to a growing interest in, and demand for, cider.[124] Printed recipe books also introduced new preparation and preservation techniques as well as new flavors. Samuel Hartlib's work recounted how Germans preserved cabbage by pickling it as sauerkraut, for instance. A diversity of plants "from beyond the seas" were introduced into England, and various authors encouraged gardeners to experiment with new agricultural products.[125] But one of the challenges of transplantation was the acclimatization of plants into new soils and climates. Writers assured their readers that agricultural improvement would assist the economy by enabling the English to grow goods that otherwise had to be purchased at high cost from abroad.

In addition to their interest in viticulture, the Hartlib Circle urged the introduction of root vegetables as key resources in times of dearth.[126] Widely attributed to Protestant refugees carrying them into England in the late sixteenth century, root vegetables appeared in early modern England to acclaim.[127] Hartlib wrote about market gardening practices in and around London and estimated that it was "About 50 years ago . . . [when] Ingenuities first began to creep into England, into Sandwich, Fulham and other places." Hartlib was one of many authors who flagged the *newness* of many gardening practices and materials to the English. As Hartlib recounted, "Some old men in Surrey, where it flourisheth very much at present; report that they knew the first Gardiners that came into those parts, to plant Cabages, Colleflowers, and to sowe Turneps, Carrets, and Parsnips, . . . all which at that time were great rarites, we having few or none in England."[128] The fact that Adolphus Speed offered instructions about how to store root vegetables suggests they were relatively new to English consumers (or, at least his readers): "Cabbages puld up by the roots, & set in sand, in a Cellar or some other room, may be kept all the Winter, or you may hang them up with strings, and so may you keep Artichokes, and other plants, and roots, for constant use, as Carets, Parsnips, and Turnips."[129]

Of course, one of the more influential root crops introduced into British and Irish agriculture from Native American societies was the potato. As with early interest in pickled root vegetables, descriptions of the potato often focused on its hardiness, since it was undamaged by packing and could be stored all winter. Advocates celebrated such sturdy foods as the means to mitigate the threats of hunger caused by poor harvests, weather, and wartime destruction. According to Speed, potatoes "are excellent food" because they could be prepared in "several waies." They "will make very good bread, cakes, paste, and pyes," and "they will hardly be destroyed but increase of themselves in a very plentifull manner, with very little labour."[130] For some authors these rugged root vegetables, and perhaps potatoes above others, were associated with particular kinds of consumers and topographical regions. Stephen Blake, in *The Compleat Gardeners Practice* (1664), suggested the value of potatoes to food supply and described the distinctive regional agricultural patterns of the potato: "They are not known in the South parts of England, yet in the North parts they are planted in poor and rich mens Gardens, for the goodness that they yeeld . . . to their tables in the winter when no other roots are to be had." Meanwhile, in Ireland, "they are so generall and so common, that I never saw any man that had land and habitation there but that he had a store of Potatoes for his use, and those which plant them for profit have twenty or thirty acres of them, more or less according to their abilities."[131] While some writers advocated the adoption of new dietary items, including corn and potatoes, lingering anxieties about the healthfulness of unfamiliar foods remained.

Writers were interested not only in describing foods new to England but also in encouraging the production of more food. Andrew Yarranton, in *England's Improvement by Sea and Land* (1677), argued that agricultural improvement was a matter of national importance and should be taken seriously by the government. Implementing "vigorous Improvements of these unparallel'd Advantages, which the situation of our Climate, the Nature of our Soil, and the Constitution of both our People and Government affords us," would lead to "making us every way great, beyond any Nation in the world."[132] Food supply remained a topic of significant interest to governments around the Anglo-Atlantic because of the presumed connection between food access, social stability, and economic and demographic strength.

Food and Demographic Strength

Early modern governments understood the relationship between food access and political stability, while on a day-to-day basis, consumers considered what their food choices might do to their humors. Anxieties about having enough food were prevalent in the early modern world. According to Joan Thirsk, the preceding half century prior to the Restoration had witnessed several "sharp shocks" of cereal shortages.[133] Thirsk argues that the periodic scarcity of food, especially from the 1620s through the early 1650s, led to a "sense of unease and uncertainty, which offers one explanation for the significant efforts to increase basic food resources by improving land (resulting in a lot more enclosure)." Writers also sought to respond to these conditions by investigating "alternative foods for use in emergencies."[134] The proactive introduction of new plants and cultivation techniques offered some security against food scarcity.

Numerous residents of England suffered from food scarcity during civil war due to ravaged fields. Moreover, much of what remained had gone to soldiers' rations. In addition to the stresses and disruptions of war, several years of bad weather, from 1646 to 1651, had rotted harvests.[135] It is hard to overstate the fear of scarcity, even if remembered at a decade's distance. Scarcity was an ongoing feature of life for many, especially poorer families living in "chronic vulnerability to sudden change."[136] John Richards characterizes the early modern era as one in which "food supplies were always precarious. Successive harvest failures meant malnutrition for many, even outright starvation amid the horrors of famines. Often war and the breakdown of public order made the effects of food scarcities more severe."[137] Thus, it is against a backdrop of periodic shortages, as well as wartime ravages, that a growing interest in agricultural improvement emerged, and local communities routinized their responses to poverty. The impetus for implementing new technologies and planting new fruits and vegetables was to reduce dependence on a single crop. Farmers sought a diversity of crops, including root vegetables like potatoes, as well as the means by which to farm "more efficiently with the help of enclosure, the draining of fenland, and the use of new crop rotations."[138] Writers and officials also sought to learn from periods of famine, publishing texts such as Edinburgh physician Robert Sibbald's *Provision for the Poor in Time of Dearth & Scarcity* (1699), in which he explained how to procure food when ordinary provisions failed, such as "Slake," or seaweed, a "Sea-Lettuce" that grew on coastal rocks in the north of Scotland. He also looked to other places around the globe for inspiration and information and pointed out how "Millions of Peopl still, in the *East-Indies*, use no other Food but Vegetables, & live well upon them," while the Irish ate a diet of boiled "Batatas," or potatoes.[139]

If harvests after the bad years of the early 1650s were more bountiful, and fear of dearth and famine receded somewhat, England's authorities remained interested in the intertwined concerns of social order and the "alleviation of severe poverty."[140] Both local governments and the national government maintained an active interest in questions of food access due to a presumed relationship between food supply and social order. Large-scale migrations frequently resulted from famine as people traveled to find better conditions. Not only did relieving and preventing famine contribute to social stability, but access to food was also seen as critical to staving off the epidemics that frequently stalked communities already suffering from starvation conditions.[141] Officials sought to ensure access to food supplies through the introduction of new foods, innovations in gardening and farming, and experimentation with food preparation. To ensure peace, order, and stability, the Restoration government routinized local initiatives long in place, such as poor laws and dearth orders. Poor laws generally covered only extreme moments of dearth by controlling the export of grain, for instance, to counteract the worst excesses of famine. The government also charged searchers with entering storehouses and barns on private land in order to ensure that if there were supplies, they were not withheld. As Joyce Appleby has explained, there remained an "unchallenged assumption that the English government had the right and responsibility to regulate economic activities in the interest of the common good."[142] But just how to define the common good, and the manner and extent of authorities' intervention and regulation of economic activities, remained open for debate. Who was responsible for ensuring subjects around the English empire were well fed? Who should design, administer, or pay for agricultural improvement schemes?

Debates focused, in part, on questions surrounding the reach of public authority. Where, exactly, did state responsibility end and private initiative begin?[143] Responses to extraordinary events, such as famine or plague, differed from everyday poverty. Interventions by public authorities were situationally dependent, and they alternatively defined concerns as national issues, local problems, or personal responsibilities. Those "activities which were deemed to have particular bearing on security and the military potential of the nation, its security and its independence," were often the most highly regulated, including matters of food access.[144] So, for instance, soldiers expected to be fed while acting on behalf of England's interests. When deployed to "soe remote a country [as Tangier]," and when facing "soe many hazards dayly [to] have the Honour to expose their lives in his Maties service," they believed they should be assured of rewards for their labors, including access to sufficient provisions.[145] Indeed, food access was a high priority in wartime, and soldiers and ships were fitted with supplies, such as biscuits, beef, pork, peas, oatmeal, oil, and butter.[146] In addition to hazarding their lives as soldiers, subjects might require state assistance at other times. Dangers to English bodies might lie in invading armies or in cripplingly poor harvests that left subjects, including children, in desperate need of food.

As Paul Slack has argued, in the seventeenth century, "welfare had not yet been separated out as a definite subset of concerns for governments and citizens," and in the early modern era "its connotations were almost boundless."[147] In the mid-seventeenth century, writers pointed to the roles the government ought to play in fostering public welfare. Reason Melish cited the contemporary publication by Samuel Fortrey, author of *Englands Interest and Improvement* (1673), in a discourse he prepared for the Royal Society, entitled "Concerning the best ways of England's Improvement." He declared that "the greatest thing that any Prince can aime att, is to make his dominions Rich and Populous"[148] Or, in other words, wealth and population size were the most important concerns for rulers. According to Melish, it was a powerful prince who had the best hope of transforming the poor from drags on public resources into productive members of society. Who else had the power and resources to encourage such substantial transformations? Writers like Melish "firmly established in the public mind the assumptions that the rural as well as urban poor were a productive resource which could be harnessed, not a rabble to be regulated or edified."[149] Not only did he urge officials to increase wealth by harnessing the labor of inhabitants, but he schemed to encourage populousness. Melish suggested that encouraging a multitudinous nation was also a program best fostered by the government. Indeed, he urged, it should "become the care of those that sit at the helme of Governmt to use such means as may be thought conducing to encrease the number of our people."[150] These ideas gained traction, and numerous authors articulated similar strategies that they claimed might lead to England's "very great Improvement."[151]

William Petty's similar pronouncement that "fewness of people is real poverty" would have met with a great deal of approval and agreement.[152] Melish offered a similar sentiment, arguing that the population of a nation led to its strength and wealth, so that the secret to a stronger England was not so secret: "The strength of a nation consists in the multitude of people, and so likewise its wealth," and those multitudes must be "rightly Imployed."[153] Writers like Petty and Melish linked greater population size to national strength and its future productive wealth. Or, as Roger Coke asserted in A Discourse of Trade (1670): a "Multitude, and Concourse of People, Advance Trade," whereas a "Scarcity of People Diminish Trade."[154] Yet if many Restoration-era writers agreed that there was strength and wealth in numbers, it was not always clear how to ensure that people were "rightly Imployed" or how best to encourage a populous nation.

Although previous generations had feared that England was too populous, and colonial promoters had looked to the colonies as outlets for surplus populations from an overcrowded England, this attitude altered dramatically in the second half of the seventeenth century.[155] Instead of too many people, there were new fears that there were too few people to compete with more populous nations, although not everyone agreed on the strategies necessary to promote populousness at home. While colonial expansion might improve England's strength, in part, because lands in alternative climactic zones could grow foods, spices, and other goods that could not be naturalized in England, not everyone was convinced.[156] Other writers argued that improvements in farming techniques, such as the addition of nutrients to the soil to aid in acclimatization, new tools and technologies, or the introduction of new techniques, might offset or even obviate the need for expansion and the loss of populations across oceans.[157] As chapter 2 revealed, these writers claimed that the improvement and the reclamation of wastes within England, such as the fenlands, would feed the nation and improve England's demographic strength without imperial expansion.[158]

Opponents argued that further expansion was an unnecessary waste of people, money, and time. They argued that the ongoing settlement and peopling of plantations was a hurdle to economic successes.[159] They described people as the vital organs of the body politic, and many argued that, like the loss of blood, or vitality, an expansion of plantations and emigration sucked strength from the organism by depleting its strength.

To writers like Roger Coke it was not only that internal improvement would render plantations unnecessary but that actively planting colonies was actually injurious to England. For instance, Coke argued in *A Discourse of Trade* (1670) that "The Trade of England, and the Fishing Trade, are so much diminished, by how much they might have been supplied by those men who are diverted in our American Plantations."[160] Because "men are necessary to improve trade," the loss of population to the colonies led to a diminished supply of people who might otherwise have engaged in myriad useful trades in England. For writers like Coke, planting colonies was a drain on the population of England, thereby decreasing national strength and economic power. Meanwhile, it was not only the American colonies that siphoned English men and women away. Coke likewise pointed to the "Repeopling [of] Ireland, since the Late Massacre and War there," as well as deaths from plague, as additional drains on English population resources.[161] Such depopulation left England destitute of their possible contributions to labor, wealth, and knowledge. Coke portrayed colonization as the loss of human potential and a labor problem. Too many bright and capable young people left for Ireland or the American plantations and could not be readily replaced.

In response to these losses, Coke encouraged a relaxation of naturalization laws. Naturalizing foreigners would replace those lost to colonization, disease, and war, thereby improving the health and vitality of the body politic. As a legal means to incorporate foreign subjects, naturalization would boost population, a key component in any competition with other nations. Coke compared the situation in England to that of Spain. He suggested that, at first, a consolidated and powerful Spain had been able to extend and maintain a massive empire across the seas and control the riches of the West Indies. But Spain had then fallen to a weak position. Coke reasoned that no "other reason be given hereof (at least that I understand)" for this fall from power "but removing the Moors out of Granado, the transporting so many Spaniards into the West-Indies, and the Inquisition which barrs out any future supply."[162] Coke did not want to follow in the footsteps of what he viewed as the rise *and* fall of Spain over the course of its run as the once-premier international superpower. He argued that England's loss of population to the colonies coupled with harsh naturalization laws were worse than Spain's Inquisition at keeping foreigners out, to the detriment of England's demographic and economic strength.[163] Such policies damaged England's future prosperity because they barred those who might also bring in money and ideas to an island otherwise losing them at a precipitous rate. Indeed, according to Coke, the loss of bodies to the plantations, including the new colony of Carolina, was "pernicious" to the health and wealth of the nation: "In this condition I leave thee, Reader, to judg, where it will not be yet so much more pernicious to the Trade of this Nation to endeavour a further discovery of new Plantations; and that is the Project of Peopling Carolina from the Residue of the men we have left in England, if it succeeds, will not so much more enfeeble this Nation, and reduce the Trade thereof to so much less proportion by how many men shall be withdrawn from it?"[164] More plantations meant simply, and injuriously, the further loss of men, loss of trade, and the "enfeeble[ment]" of the body politic. Writers like Coke thus drew numerous connections between population and national strength and offered numerous schemes to boost both.

While varied, a common sentiment emerged to encourage demographic strength that included a broad reassessment of the nation's agricultural practices and food supply. Improvement schemes sought both to increase the arable acreage as well as to make more productive use of lands already under cultivation, to boost England's demographic strength. More unimproved "waste" lands under cultivation at home and abroad would boost food supply. One midcentury author encouraged readers to imagine "the great benefit which could accrew to this Nation, if all land which were fit to be digg'd, were so ordered, and their corne set."[165] After the Restoration, William Petty, Reason Melish, Adolphus Speed, and others, much like Samuel Hartlib and his circle of correspondents before them, asserted that England's land was woefully underused, when it might be made to sustain far higher numbers of people per acre. They singled out wetlands, bogs, and fens as landscapes that required improvement, claiming that drainage would open large swaths of waste land to arable agriculture, thus equating drainage with increased food production. To prove his point that England's population might be given a boost by his proposals, Melish first considered the quantity and quality of available acreage and attempted to estimate how many people "the yearly fruit & product of it may plentifully maintaine: And if we find the land will maintaine any considerable number of persons more then yet are in it; we shall then propose some wayes to increase our strength & wealth, that is, the number of our people."[166] Turning so-called wastelands into productive spaces was one of many stratagems for increasing national power; agrarian reforms and the introduction of new crops helped to feed armies in times of war and to ensure the health and longevity of England's populace, which were both deemed necessary to national strength. Authors of recipe books also promised longevity, healthier bodies, cures for sterility, and a boost to fertility.

Officials promoted populousness so that more people would labor and engage in economic activities. When both the land and the people in the colonies and England were "rightly Imployed," it would be a political and economic boon. A well-fed nation was not only less likely to behave riotously, it was a population more capable of expending those calories doing something productive. Andrew Yarranton argued that well-fed people could work, especially in the production of manufactures or in projects designed to benefit the public. Yarranton's *England's Improvement by Sea and land* (1676) argued for "Bank Graneries," which would do two things at once: "all the poor people that are employed in these Manufactures, shall be in the same Counties fed with bread sufficient, without any charge to the Publick; and thereby the Commodities will be manufactured cheap."[167] Thus agricultural improvement schemes were touted as improving demographic and national strength, and an increase in the laboring potential of subjects. By the end of the century, government control over the grain trade had loosened enough to allow the exportation of surpluses, suggesting a growing confidence that England was relatively safe from large-scale threats of famine.[168]

Colonial governments, too, saw strength in numbers, and in populousness a means of keeping enemies at bay. Consequently, throughout the colonies, they enacted legislation to ensure that residents grew enough grain for subsistence. As early as 1617 the governor of Virginia, Thomas Dale, decreed that tobacco cultivators must also plant ten acres of grain. The spectre of famine shaped such policies. To prevent catastrophe and ensure adequate rations, Maryland laws also demanded planters grow two acres of grain to accommodate each person working in fields of tobacco. It is likely that officials required colonists to grow corn due to stories circulating in print about earlier colonists' experiences with starvation conditions.[169] Whether in legislation from the Chesapeake or in William Petty's proposals for William Penn about his new colony of Pennsylvania, colonial officials and advisers sought to secure order and maintain the health, safety, and productivity of colonists by ensuring they had enough to eat. Stability was perhaps the most important aim of these laws. Cultivating grains and other staples of the early modern English diet encouraged colonists to craft an environment that did not allow "barbarous" activities like unsettled pastoralism. Improved and cultivated nature and national strength went hand in hand, and "notions of natural and national economy were closely linked."[170]

Planting orchards "became standard policy in the Chesapeake. When planters let out their lands to tenants, they regularly required that their new tenants plant and tend to orchards, generally specified to be seventy to one hundred trees."[171] In Maryland, the colonial courts offered guidelines for planting orchards and specified the general distances that ought to be maintained between trees.[172] As proponents of tree-planting projects had long maintained, fruit trees were a boon because after the initial planting and tending, they required little labor in relation to the amount of food they provided. The minor upkeep of fruit trees was often their selling point in colonies where they were short on labor and were anxious to ensure food supplies. The founder of Pennsylvania likewise appreciated the symbolic importance of trees. One of William Penn's earliest comments about the heterogeneous settlers along the Delaware River was a condemnation of their failure to properly cultivate, claiming, "[They] have made no great progress in culture, or propagation of fruit trees." Penn suggested that the lack of such cultivation was the result of colonists living too long in isolation among Delaware's indigenous inhabitants.[173] Orchards, in well-spaced, linear rows, expressed the kind of proper geometrical order that planners of New World colonies imagined appropriate to tame these "wilderness" places. English colonists similarly accused the indigenous residents of North America of failing to plant orchards, which was an indictment of their civility and a failure to plan ahead. Certainly, some writers, like Roger Williams, acknowledged that indigenous people managed their woodlands. As Williams wrote, the "burning of the Wood to them they count a benefit."[174] The burning was a "benefit both for destroying of vermin, and keeping downe the Weeds and thickets."[175] But for others, such evidence of woodland management was not enough.

Colonial planners were aware of the crucial importance of food to the success of a new colony, but it was not altogether clear what should be grown and how much was necessary. In the plans he designed for William Penn's new colony of Pennsylvania, William Petty advised that Penn put colonists to work the day after arrival.[176] In a document entitled "Generall Cautions concerning Pensylvania," he suggested: "Let all men bee settled to new Employment within a day after landing" and "Let all men of between 18 & 58 pay for ye keeping of all children that are borne."[177] With these proposals for Penn, Petty entered the debate about who was best charged with ensuring the bodily welfare of subjects, particularly as that welfare related to agricultural provisions. Petty's proposals might not have been implemented in Pennsylvania, let alone

England, but his schemes allow us to consider the intellectual context in which they were created. In Petty's schemes for utopian colonial projects on behalf of his "old friend" Penn, the extent to which a government might assume capacious control over the diets and welfare of subjects was quite broad. For instance, Petty suggested that a colonial proprietor should have the power to compel work regimens, and Petty offered visionary suggestions for agricultural improvement projects designed to offer the perfect ratios of acreage sown to keep every colonist in dietary comfort.[178] Petty's plans indicate that he imagined the colonies were also a place to test theories about the relationship between governments and subjects and what each owed the other.

Like many of his contemporaries who were interested in using mathematical calculations to advise governments on a variety of "curiosities" (in John Graunt's words), including "the relation between healthfull and fruitfull Seasons, the difference between the City and Country Air, &c.," or using calculations to advise about the theoretical maximum population England might sustain within its borders, Petty attempted to calculate the specific acreage necessary to sustain each new colonists' body in health.[179] His notes contain a document entitled "A Proposall concerning an American Plantation" that suggested building a walled town of 120 acres within which sixty houses should be built, thirty on each side of a main street, "the end of wch street shall abut the River." Petty then advised that each house should have a small garden and that the town should share, collectively, "2 Comon large kitchen Gardens planted with Trees, Rootes, herbs Ligumes &c to furnish something for the table every day in the yeare."[180] Thus, not only would each family have their own small plots attached to each house, but there would be large, collectively owned and operated gardens and orchards within the town walls. Beyond the walls, Petty suggested that each town might clear and plant fifteen acres of gardens and set aside 120 acres for the tillage of corn, "with Meadow" in proportion to the number of cattle.[181]

Petty further advised that with "Each of the sd 75 familys there bee a teeming woman of between 16 and 30 years old."[182] Thus, in Petty's proposals about the American colonies, he envisioned the success of any colony relied on the proprietor's ability to devise legislation and create town plans that linked the productive and reproductive potential of its environment and populace. Women's bodies were necessary to reproduce future generations and added to the colonial population. He also sought to determine mathematically how much each body was likely to consume. Thus, Petty saw reproduction, of people and seasonal harvests, as the recipe for colonial strength. If "fewness of people is real poverty," then Petty's suggestions provided clear paths toward populous, wealthy, and powerful colonies, by addressing the need for more food and more bodies. Petty's advice suggests that he believed specific, highly detailed provision instructions, mathematically set out, were the best means to ensure success for any would-be colonial proprietor. Authors like Petty understood that successful colonization required colonists who could stay alive long enough to produce saleable goods and reproduce the next generation. Thus "teeming" women were critical to his colonization proposals.

Perhaps it is no surprise that an individual trained as a physician, like Petty, translated concepts from his studies of individual bodies into his political schemes.[183] Like his contemporaries, Petty discussed the relationship of population size and national strength. Although he was unsure of the wholesale benefits of colonization, his manuscripts suggested New England added to England's strength. In his notes Petty wrote that he "hoped that New England, where few or no women are barren, and most have many Children, and where people live longer and healthfully hath provided an increase of as many people as were destroyed in the late Tumults in Ireland."[184] By arguing that fertile women in New England might make up for populations lost to violence in the Irish Rebellion of 1641 or Oliver Cromwell's incursions during the Wars of the Three Kingdoms, he linked two very different places and scenarios by turning bodies into abstract, manipulatable numbers. He imagined that in the Americas, a place associated in numerous natural history treatises and travel literature with extraordinary fertility, similarly influenced the bodies of female colonists and lengthened the lives of others, making up for lives lost in other "members" of the body politic.[185] For Petty, "The art of government was the improvement and deployment of populations."[186] But deploying successfully this "art of government" relied on intimate knowledge of the way bodies responded to various landscapes. If one of the fears about colonization was losing numbers necessary to English military and economic strength, Petty assuaged these fears by insisting on American fertility, imagining an integrated and well-functioning imperial body that spanned the Atlantic. By claiming that "teeming" women in the colonies might make up for population loss in Ireland during the war, Petty envisioned the empire as an interconnected organism. Population growth in New England might make up for population losses elsewhere in the empire. The loss of vitality in one member might be balanced by strengthening another limb.

Petty's schemes for colonial designs and improvement suggest that he saw himself as participating in the role of a "Publick-Spirited" gentlemen who studied the *Georgics*.[187] Like many politicians of the age, Petty was crucially concerned with stability. He, too, had seen the death and destruction of long, drawn-out civil war and saw in schemes of improvement a way to improve society as well as ensure law and order.[188] According to historian Ted McCormick, in the 1670s, William Petty helped to invent the concept of "political arithmetic," in part as a response to the turmoil of war, and to assist the state in fostering stability. He hoped his recommendations would "confer on the crown the power both to undo the damage of past policy and to remake both land and people—again and again, if necessary—in its own image."[189] Political arithmetic was not "an early economics" but was, instead, "an ambitious art of government by demographic manipulation."[190] Among the aims of officials interested in political arithmetic was boosting England's population. Writers of improvement schemes both before and after the Restoration desired the king and officials to be energetic reformers of the English landscape. The king might legitimate his position by acting as the "propitious and wise Authority" who promoted the "public good" with an aim to improving his subjects' "health and felicity," including supporting projects that aimed to increase the nation's demographic strength.[191]

To varying degrees, dealing with public hunger and promoting subjects' health and populousness was a matter of state interest around the Anglo-Atlantic world. One way to secure the safety and populousness of a new colony was to experiment with, and cultivate, healthful foods as well as useful and efficacious medicines. For example, "the most pressing motivation" for seeking medicines and locating cultivatable foods "was to keep European troops and planters alive in the colonies. Colonial botany was crucial to Europe's successful control" over the colonies.[192] In addition to keeping soldiers and colonists alive, officials also celebrated commodities that would cure sterility or increase fertility as an additional method to promote demographic strength and secure colonial claims. In the wake of the English conquest of Jamaica in 1655, English medical writers like William Hughes and Henry Stubbe praised chocolate, a substance relatively new to English consumers, as "a most Soveriegn Medicine." They claimed that chocolate's advantages included benefits to women's reproductive health and fertility by celebrating how cacao "confort[ed] the Womb."[193] Drinking chocolate "nourish[ed] the Child in the Womb."[194] Stubbe further claimed that chocolate's qualities enabled endless physical exertion, even when little food was available.

With chocolate, "servants" could "subsist all day, notwithstanding their great labor, and [the] heat."[195] Writers concerned with Jamaica's uncertain status in the empire touted the cultivation and consumption of chocolate as means of transforming Jamaica from a place widely associated with death into a populous, settled, and prosperous colony. It is possible that authors referencing the connection between chocolate, fertility, and labor may have been alluding to the bodies of enslaved women. Jennifer L. Morgan has revealed how planters constructed ideologies of racialized slavery that focused on the bodies of African women. Planters exploited the intertwined economic possibilities of African women performing agricultural labor as well as performing reproductive labor by bearing children as a way to increase their wealth.[196] Around the Anglo-Atlantic world, officials sought to increase population, as well as boost the labor pool, by locating new and diversified foods. In one version of that vision, writers like Hughes and Stubbe suggested cacao might foster a plantation economy and slavery.

Managing the "Publique Trust": Private and Public Improvement

New economic arguments assured projectors that private gain need not be at odds with public profit. As fen-drainer Samuel Fortrey concluded in *The History or Narrative* (1685), public profit did not preclude private profit, and this stance characterized a widespread attitude toward improvement projects.[197] The internal colonization of England by draining fenlands promoted by Fortrey, and discussed in chapter 2, was "of private Profit, and of Publick Store."[198] If it had "Begun with vertue, shall with Fortune, end, / For Profit publick thoughts do still attend."[199] Stuart improvers were in a long line of Englishmen who justified their enterprises by proclaiming their efforts were for "the general benefit of his Majesties dominions," regularly highlighting the practical application of their work and its value to the country in order to gain support for their projects.

Others were adamant that it ought to be those at the "helme of Governmt" who developed the strategies of improvement and implemented them. Numerous writers agreed that improvements were necessary and should be initiated by a caring, intervening government. They followed in the footsteps of a cohort of improvers from the 1650s, many of them correspondents of Samuel Hartlib, who discussed and proposed a range of proposals with "benefit[s] to Humane Society then hitherto we could attaine unto."[200] Hartlib and his intellectual cohort had long advocated for greater centralized control of improvement projects and argued that the government was best placed to compel people to work so that everyone who was not a benefit to the state, such as poor children, widows, the elderly, and the disabled, would have to work in some form and would thus save the nation money. Writers advocated for a strong direction and vision from a centralized source because they believed men and women had to be compelled to do the right thing. Among the many schemes laid out to improve English agricultural practices included the creation of a new office with officials charged with overseeing agricultural production methods, as well as overseeing the kinds of plants planted. Hartlib desired "Worthies" who might "manage the Publique Trust" and determine "ways of advantaging both thy selfe and the Publique." They would encourage industry and combat the "disorderly and lazy undertakings of private men."[201] According to Hartlib, however, it was not simply laziness or disorderly conduct that discouraged innovation. As other commentators similarly pointed out, new skills had to be taught or else people would continue to practice agriculture in the ways they had been taught across generations. They argued that attachment to tradition was one of the major obstacles to improvement. Tenants also resisted labor that did not have immediate benefit but instead benefited the landowner over the long term.[202]

Hartlib's "Worthies that manage the Publique Trust" would "by their Influence and Authority" encourage those who tilled the land in a range of ways, to benefit "the Publique and General Welfare of this Commonwealth." But first, people had to be encouraged to learn new skills and brought to see the benefits of new management techniques. Too often people were "wonderfully wedded to old customes, are not easily won to any new course, though never so much to their owne profit." In order to preserve critical resources, like woodlands, and to introduce new "customes" to the people, Hartlib thought it best that "two or more fit persons of approved skill and integrity may be made Publique Stewards or Surveyors; one of the Husbandry, the other of the Woods of this Common-wealth, and impowered to oversee and take care of the preservation of what is, and by all good improvement to procure and provide for what is wanting to the present age" as well as those things which it is "more then likely will be wanting to suceeding ages."[203] Hartlib thus imagined public officials empowered to instigate improvement projects on private lands, provided it was for the good of the nation. Alterations to English husbandry, managed by the appointed "Worthies," would encourage the nation's farmers and improve the commonwealth. With such improvements the nation might be better placed to weather tough times and "beare necessary and Publique burdens with more ease to our selves, and benefit to Humane Society then hitherto we could attaine unto."[204] Varied agricultural improvement schemes similarly promised to promote stability and claimed they were necessary to the public good. According to the historian Joan Thirsk, "the spirit of optimistic enterprise" and interest in food and agricultural improvement begun in the 1650s continued over the next few decades.[205] Writers continued to debate about whether a government should dictate what agricultural products were cultivated and how, thereby determining the diets of its subjects, particularly the poor. Many members of the Restoration government had expansive ideas about where the "boundaries of the public realm and the body politic" lay.[206] Restoration writers and officials opined that Charles II would prove to be the ultimate steward of the landscape, ushering in a new era of government responsiveness to agricultural innovation.[207]

Charles II and many of his advisers saw in schemes of improvement the "possibilities of social engineering."[208] These schemes reflect both continuities and transformations to ideas about what constituted the "public interest," what the government owed its subjects, and who was best placed to ensure their bodily welfare.[209] Schemes ranged from enforcing laws related to access to food to ensuring the "qualitie" of life of his subjects. In 1660 observers anticipated Charles II might be just such a reforming monarch.[210] But it was not clear what role the government should play versus that of citizens. Hartlib suggested a role for public stewards, or worthies, capable of instigating reforms, but how much power should such figures have to compel others to act? How would knowledgeable experts be found? What types of improvement should they instigate? Who would pay? While the government had long assumed "both the right and the responsibility to regulate economic and social affairs for the common good," the extent to which subjects would welcome intervention remained a question.[211] In a letter from John Beale to John Evelyn in 1670, Beale reasoned that to inspire widespread change to gardening, agriculture, and "draing bogues," they would have to make some "noyse" to catch the attention of those "active and intelligent psons [in] ye Innes of Court, those Giants who have al ye purse, power, & influence in ye Kgdome" and to unite them in action with "ye Rurall" lords.[212] Meanwhile, Evelyn confided in a letter to the Duke of Albemarle that he wrote *Sylva* (1664) under the "pretence of exciting our English Gentry to solid improvements."[213]

In order to ensure that agricultural improvement projects were useful to the empire and its many residents, contemporaries advocated for the careful observation and study of the plant world. For instance, the ability to see with a microscope what had never before been seen with unassisted eyes might uncover powerful knowledge. Some went so far as to suggest that the acquisition of scientific knowledge paralleled imperial expansion. As Royal Society Fellow Nehemiah Grew wrote in *The Anatomy of Plants* (1682) about his botanical observations, "In sum, Your Majesty will find, that we are come ashore into a new World, whereof we see no end." Grew's rhetorical flourish linked the voyages of discovery with scientific discovery. The "new World" he had discovered, and over which he suggested the king might now claim dominion, was visible only through the microscope. Grew further flattered the king, claiming that as the patron of the Royal Society, he should be applauded for promoting intellectual advancements over making territorial advancements: "Your Majesty deeming it to be a more Noble Design, To enlarge the Territories of Knowledge, than those of Dominion: and the Highest Pitch of Human Glory, not to rule, in any sort, over many but to be a Good Prince over Wise Men."[214] While Grew complimented the king's focus on knowledge accumulation, he also pointed to a new territory into which England might expand its control. Indeed, Grew dedicated this book to Charles II and claimed it provided a "Map of the Country," to aid future explorers and colonists. He linked knowledge of the structures of plants to a kind of dominion over them. While of vastly different scales—continental and microscopic—both were open to colonization by Grew's "Good Prince," who might best determine how to take advantage of both.

The Royal Society, or the king's so-called "Parliament of Nature," claimed that one of the purposes of their newly founded organization was also to promote the acquisition and compiling of useful knowledge that might be used for the benefit of the king, securing his rule over his varied dominions.[215] In February 1660 a group that included Sir Robert Moray, William Petty, Robert Boyle, Thomas Povey, John Evelyn, Ralph Austen, and Henry Oldenburg was appointed to a committee "to consider of proper Questions to be enquired of in the remotest parts of the World."[216] They sought to make themselves useful by gathering, codifying, and calculating information that might not have been traditionally collected or studied by governments. As such, they promoted themselves as a kind of arm of the government. The useful knowledge they hoped to provide about local and global agricultural practices and improvements, for example, might then be used by those "Publique Stewards or Survey-ors" for the benefit of the empire and its subjects. They later offered "Pro-posalls and Reasons for the Improving, & advancing of Planting, humbly tendered to the Lords & Comons in Parliament Assembled."[217] More-over, in March 1664, thirty-two members of the Royal Society formed the "Georgical Committee" to gather a "perfect" history of gardening and agriculture from around the country. They planned to send ques-tionnaires and solicit information "from their owne and their knowing friends observation and experience," in order to "give as full and as punc-tuall answers thereunto, as they could" and ensure "that thereby it might be knowne, what is knowne and done already, both to enrich every place with the aides, that are found in any place, and withall to consider, what further improvements may be made in all the practise of Husbandry."[218] The Royal Society hoped to direct the activities of landholders in England, to collect and codify knowledge about agricultural practices, and to provide guidelines and information. Later Restoration authors looked back approvingly at the innovations and trials of the previous decades and expansion in the quantity and quality of England's food supply. While he was doubtless overstating the extent of the transforma-tions, by 1675 John Beale commented approvingly on the "bold adven-tures in horticulture and agriculture" that had unfolded "within [his] memory" and had "become the chief relief of England."[219]

From its foundation in 1660, the Royal Society made agriculture one of its many concerns. Understanding plant growth became a focus of earnest discussion, with Robert Sharrock publishing a *History of the Propagation and Improvement of Vegetables* (1660). Other highlights included Beale's call to propagate apple trees for cider in 1662 and the publication of Evelyn's *Sylva*, appended with *Pomona*, to encourage fruit-tree cultivation in 1664. In 1663 the Royal Society also considered a proposal to plant potatoes throughout England as a future preserva-tive against famine.[220] The society resolved to plant their own potatoes and to "persuade their friends to also plant" them.[221] After the Georgical Committee was established in 1664, they met bimonthly and developed Inquires they planned to send to "experienced Husbandmen in all the Shires and Counties of England, Scotland, and Ireland."[222] The following year the committee published their inquires in the *Philosophical Trans-actions* in order to better understand the nation's soils, which grains were sown, and other details they hoped would benefit the country.[223]

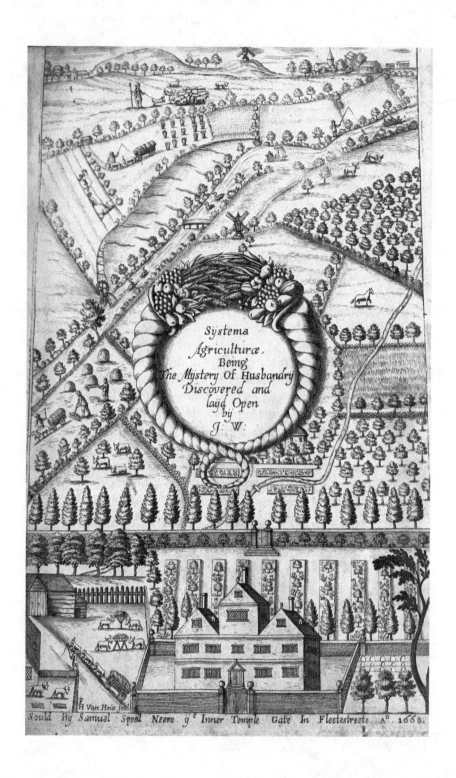

Systema
Agriculturæ,
Being
The Mystery Of Husbandrij
Discovered and
laid Open
by
J. W.

Sould By Samuel Speed Neere yᵉ Inner Temple Gate In Fleetestreete. Aᵒ. 1668.

They engaged in myriad investigations into food because "agricultural plenty was understood to be the basis of social peace."[224]

The Georgical Committee devised many inquiries about the soil. If it was insufficient to the task of growing food, they highlighted the importance of preparing the soil, "fattening" it and making it more nutritious. Soil was the first essential ingredient necessary to productive agriculture.[225] While human hands might alter the soil for the better, there were some limitations. Agriculturalists were constantly testing those limits and agricultural writers insisted that soils, like plants and people, had essential characteristics. The extent to which they were manipulatable remained an animated debate. Richard Bradley, author of numerous treatises on horticultural topics, wrote that soil type mattered a great deal to successful plant growth. For instance, Bradley discussed which soils were "natural to each Tree" and considered "how all Kinds of Soils may be mended, alter'd, or improved by proper Mixtures with each other." He worried that too few authors took up the subject of soils, "and yet the Whole depends chiefly upon it."[226] Small but significant changes to the soil might make life sustainable for a wider variety of plants.[227]

In their hopes of establishing a compilation of useful knowledge, members of the Royal Society followed in the footsteps of the collective around Samuel Hartlib, who sought to create a "Systema or compleat Book of all the parts of Agriculture."[228] The Hartlib Circle also urged the erection of a college for agricultural experiments to further develop their "compleat Book" on "Universall Husbandry."[229] Because manuring was one of the practices regularly touted as essential to improvement, they discussed it with regularity.[230] In *Samuel Hartlib his legacie*, in "A Large letter concerning the Defects and Remedies of English Husbandry written to Mr. Samuel Hartlib," the author cited various methods of dunging and manuring lands and provided descriptions of such methods used throughout England and "beyond the seas." He cited practices in Kent,

FIGURE 4.2 (opposite page). John Worlidge's text was among the many books on the "Rustick Art" of husbandry published during the 1660s and 1670s. The frontispiece pictures a landscape buzzing with the activities he associated with agricultural improvement. John Worlidge, *Systema Agriculturae, The Mystery of Husbandry Discovered; Wherein is Treated of the Several New and Most Advantagious Ways of Tilling Planting Sowing Manuring Ordering Improving All Sorts of Gardens, Orchards, Meadows, Pastures, Corn-lands, Woods, & Coppices* (London, 1669). RB 379550, The Huntington Library, San Marino, California.

Sussex, Cornwall, Canterbury, Hertfordshire, London, Flanders, France, Holland, and New England. The author also cited the practice in New England and Virginia of manuring with fish, which enabled "extraordinary" fertility.[231] Altering the soil was one way to test the mutability of the landscape by human hands. Experiments proved that soils could be improved and could impart new qualities into plants as a result.

Restoration authors continued to seek practices that were "beneficial to use" by observing European practices, such as their use of clover to produce greater agricultural yields.[232] Andrew Yarranton produced a new edition of his text to include a lengthy description of clover and its uses in *The Improvement Improved by a second Edition of the Great Improvement of land by Clover* (1663). And indeed, "clover revolutionized farming by replenishing the nitrogen at an unprecedented rate."[233] Legumes such as peas, beans, and clover "convert atmospheric nitrogen into nitrates in the soil; in effect, it makes fertilizer."[234] Numerous authors contributed testimonials about clover's uses and sang its praises. Knowledge of clover moved with people, arriving in England after travelers to other countries witnessed its uses. Writers wrote endlessly about the benefits of clover and "enthused" about the crop, "pointing to its cultivation in the Low Countries as evidence of its value."[235] Farmers' enthusiasm rested on the fact that clover had readily observable effects. The introduction of clover "permitted the arable area to expand at the expense of permanent pasture," since crops like clover yielded higher outputs.[236] Maurice Ronayne, an estate manager in County Waterford, Ireland, wrote to his employer, Lord Grandison, on January 2, 1728, to say that "I have writ to mr Percevall for A sufficient quantitie of Rye Grass Seed + Clover," which he claimed was likely to increase production. He sought to ensure that the land would be "managed according to yr Lordships doctrines."[237] Ronayne's letter suggests that among a certain subset of people who subscribed to the latest agricultural improvement knowledge, Ronayne could refer to planting clover as having reached the status of *doctrine* by the 1720s. Indeed, contemporaries were astounded by the productivity clover facilitated. According to Speed, clover "improves the ground," citing a farmer who "hath this year exceeding great buck wheat upon a piece of healthy ground, not one shilling the acre before, which hath been Clover grass three years."[238]

Because soil is a crucial foundation for plants and might bring about manifold physical changes to the plants, it mattered a great deal to agricultural improvers. Among the information solicited by the Georgical Committee of the Royal Society, and included in their questionnaires for the country's husbandmen, were accounts of their methods of manuring. One of the respondents, Mr. Howard, provided "A briefe description of the Soyle and Husbandry of Surrey and Berkshire" and dated the response November 7, 1666. The questions he sought to answer were listed in a column as "1. Of the Soyle 2. Of the Annoyances 3. Of the Improvements of the helpe of remedyes 4. Of what is sowed or planted 5. What Cattle and other living Creatures 6. What tooles or utensells with other necessarye for husbandry."[239] While this was only one response from a questionnaire widely distributed, the answers tell us something about farmers' local knowledge in the 1660s.[240] Various types of soil were richly documented by Howard, detailing about a dozen types in total.[241] Howard next enumerated the "Improvements or Remedies" deployed by the region's husbandmen to remedy the soil, including the folding in of "Dung of Cattle," "Lyme," "Marle," "Chalke," "Burning the Superficies," "Ashes," "Fferne rotted," "Hornes hooves shreds," and "steeping of Graine," into the soil. Other improvements he noted included some basic field preparation, such as "Weeding and gathering of stones," "Often mowing," or by rotating "Winter and sumer fallowes."[242] The region's farmers also managed water. They practiced "Trenching" to drain water. On other occasions they practiced "Overflowing with River or Raine water," which perhaps indicates the process of floating meadows, or keeping a shallow layer of water during the winter months, which "encouraged the growth of early grass, proving fodder, usually for sheep."[243] Among the various things sown and planted in Berkshire included wheat, rye, barley, oats, beans, peas, turnips, carrots, parsnips, potatoes, flax, buck wheat, hemp, clover, and hops. Among the improvements Howard recorded included new plantations of oak, elm, ash, beech, walnut, chestnut, birch, willow, crab apple. He likewise included blackberry's, "Darking cherryes," "Oziers," "Darking pippins," and "Darking Codlins" on his list.[244]

The Royal Society's Georgical Committee planned to compile responses like those from Howard to create a complete picture of English agricultural practices. Once compiled, they aimed to offer advice about the best practices, so that one region might learn from another. Members of the Georgical Committee, like Beale, further aimed to gather information about the husbandry practices from the American plantations.[245] The Dublin Philosophical Society, much like their London counterparts, similarly sought information about regional agricultural practices, inquiring of correspondents: "What things observable in the tillage of Ireland; & what things chiefly to be regarded for the well ordering of it for all manner of graine: and wherein the chief difference between the tillage of England and Ireland?"[246] Recognizing and collecting successful regional practices might be the first step in offering "improvement" advice or by codifying collected knowledge into digestible knowledge. While the Royal Society sought to collect knowledge from numerous sources, it was not clear how they would organize or offer advice based on the knowledge collected. Questionnaires produced by the Royal Society, much like questionnaires designed by members of the Lords of Trade and Plantation, for instance, sought useable information but lacked the effective ability to manage the information they received. Numerous authors believed that collecting such knowledge might only be useful if someone at the "helme of Governmt" had the power to consider, distill, and enforce their ideas.[247] Of course, some of the schemes and projects proposed were too expensive and elaborate to implement or featured schemes to transplant plants that could not be acclimatized.

Agrarian historians have suggested that it was often large landholders who first introduced improvements. According to Joan Thirsk, "the gentry were influential pioneers of new crops and new systems of farming," largely because they were "experienced through travel (often abroad)," and "together with the reading of books, [they] promoted agricultural improvement in widely scattered regions of the kingdom." Thirsk further suggests that the "density of innovations was highest in the counties of the south-east and East Anglia, where foreign influences were strong, and where London offered a discriminating but appreciative market near at hand."[248] Moreover, regional diversity—of soils and of demography—influenced which schemes of agricultural improvement might succeed. Many improvers insisted that "improvement" was most likely to occur under the management of an individual with the time and energy to innovate and break free of tradition and inherited wisdom, and they justified enclosures as a means to achieve this; others, however, insisted landowners would have to be forced to innovate.[249] Andrew Yarranton claimed that the gentry were "ingenious gentlemen" and were a natural fit for the role of improver, in addition to the king. The gentry had many motives for pioneering improvements. According to Thirsk, beginning in the sixteenth century the gentry became increasingly involved in their estates. Thirsk argues that it was partly due to ideological motivations, a result of the repopularized agricultural manuals by Cato, Varro, and Virgil, for instance.[250] Their innovations were also a result of travel and access to manuals.[251] Moreover, like the king, various landowners within England, along with colonial proprietors and colonial leaders, cited an ability to regulate and improve the land as evidence of their suitability to govern, or control, both the land and the people on it. When discussing the fate of the newly acquired colony of Jamaica, in 1661, for instance, the Council of Foreign Plantations sought to encourage settlers to move to the island.[252] They presumed that only people with higher-class status were capable of encouraging innovative agricultural improvement projects.[253] The Council lacked faith in the ability of people without estates and fortunes to satisfactorily improve the island. A similar ethos extended to New York, where large land grants were doled out to individuals like Robert Livingston "in order to promote the emergence of the sort of landed gentry that held the preponderance of power in England."[254]

Although agricultural improvement is often told as a tale of gentry-led innovation in England, it is also true that agricultural innovation arrived in England through many channels. For instance, newcomers, including religious refugees, frequently carried new plants and knowledge into England.[255] The introduction of certain root vegetables for consumption has been widely attributed to Protestant refugees who arrived in the late sixteenth century. Such evidence reminds us that if elite figures positioned themselves as the rightful bearers of new plants and agricultural innovation, their rhetorical claims were often an advertisement, to claim for themselves social and political power. An interest in the transformation of landscape, and the introduction of new agricultural and gardening specimens often had a didactic purpose and did not necessarily reflect what was happening on the ground.

Moreover, though male landowners have often been credited with innovative gardening, the reality of who was doing the work was often much more complicated. For instance, in 1690 Sir Arthur Rawdon, friend and correspondent of Sir Hans Sloane, both of County Down in northern Ireland, employed the gardener James Harlow (at Sloane's recommendation) to collect plant specimens from Jamaica. Harlow succeeded in bringing an astonishing shipment of hundreds of living trees, shrubs, and seeds back to Rawdon's Ireland estate, Moira, and installed them in Rawdon's newly constructed hothouses, the first of their kind in Ireland.[256] Rawdon was a second-generation English landlord in Ireland. He commissioned Harlow in the midst of the destructive Williamite Wars, during which Rawdon was nearly killed. It is possible that he saw in formal gardens the potential to make a symbolic statement about gardening and civility as the antithesis of Ireland's supposedly wild and uncultivated inhabitants.

Rawdon's gardens were a deeply collaborative effort from the beginning. The long-distance movement of Jamaican flora to northern Ireland required the participation and expertise of numerous individuals. Harlow and untold numbers of others in Jamaica, England, and Ireland assisted in gathering, packing, shipping, and caring for these plants on their long journey. This was an enormous task. Meanwhile, letters written to Rawdon from various family members indicate that the whole family was intimately involved in his botanical exploits, the female members in particular. In one letter his mother reported on the growth of his watermelons and an adjacent seed bed, while in another letter he was assured that his sister would soon send her own account of the plants under her care.[257] As Lady Isabella Graham wrote to her son: "your sister will give you an account concerning the plantes you writt to me off" as "she tooke all the care of them when they weare heare."[258] These letters illuminate the extent to which women related to Arthur Rawdon were engaged in the work for which he alone is usually remembered, and they continued their involvement for decades.[259] Transformations of the landscape in England, like histories of agricultural improvement around the Anglo-Atlantic, were often instigated by innumerable unsung innovators and caretakers.

Agricultural landscapes were places where "constructions of national identity" were played out.[260] Straight rows of grain and lines of orchard trees were just two of the ways of arranging space that was "encoded with aesthetic, cultural, and social relations—including those of class and power."[261] The orchards and fields planted in straight rows were valued for the fruits and crops they produced but also for the symmetrical rows that appeared to early modern English eyes as the most rational, practical, and civilized arrangement.[262] Residents of early modern England believed that the cultivation of the soil and the culture of plants led to cultivated and cultured people. Agricultural labor was "a dignified and morally uplifting activity."[263] These rows were likewise encouraged in the colonies. Many writers contrasted European agriculturalists to Indian agriculturalists, who had traditionally grown corn in mounds, intertwined with beans and squash. Various colonists believed that by teaching Indians to cultivate in straight rows, they might likewise inspire social reform, even though the Indian practice of growing beans together with corn was the best practice as beans added necessary nitrates to the soil. It was not only that these regulated landscapes were understood to be "a cultural force for the construction and maintenance of national and social identities" but that these material transformations likewise wrought tangible transformations in humoral bodies of individuals and societies.[264] While fields, orchards, and gardens were supposed to be arranged according to ideals of social order, a tangible, local manifestation of broader geopolitical ideals, this imposed and orchestrated order more often existed in the promotional literature about the colonies and did not accurately reflect a messier reality. Numerous writers and projectors claimed that their projects deserved support because cultivation and other agricultural improvement would lead to better-cultivated political subjects.[265] But it was the arrangement not only of fields but of their contents that concerned early modern English men and women.

Early modern schemes of improvement were also celebrated as work regimens for poor people, or a kind of enforced "cultivation." Agricultural work was considered by many as a moral act because it subdued "howling wilderness" and made it into a cultivated landscape; thus it was an act of moral reformation as well as an act of physical reformation. Alterations to the physical environment were often a product of the Restoration government's attempt to regulate people as well as plants, including the inhabitants of England and the colonies. Because "Pastoralism was equated with barbarism—an attitude that colored British attitudes toward other pastoral peoples around the world as the British empire expanded," colonists often sought to enforce agricultural regimes on other peoples.[266] Methods of improvement touted by early modern English writers included land reclamation processes that turned wastelands into productive spaces. Draining wetlands and the "watering of dry grounds" were two such methods.[267] These lands could then be made available to agricultural practices. But it was not enough merely to produce the goods; they had to be moved around in order to get products where they were wanted. Thus, making rivers and other modes of transport "Navigable" was likewise a goal of improvers.[268] Making rivers navigable ensured that a balance of trade was preserved and well regulated, like a healthy body with balanced humors and good circulation.

Although there was disagreement about how to achieve demographic health, contemporaries broadly agreed that a strong and wealthy nation was a populous nation. In *Natural and Political Observations . . . upon the Bills of Mortality* (1661), John Graunt attempted to use varied calculations to make recommendations to the Restoration government. If Graunt attempted to advise the government by utilizing numbers in new ways, others advised on new methods of agricultural improvement, promoting their new products, technologies, or knowledge as the best way to ensure the health, well-being, and populousness of the nation. Scholars such as Joan Thirsk have noted that while individuals such as John Locke are more famous for their writings on political economy and philosophy, not their interest in and writings on food, she asks what might happen if we were to think about these two seemingly disparate efforts as integrated?[269] As the story of the green children of Woolpit suggests, moreover, food consumption and food choices were about much more than ingesting calories. Consumption choice mediates the self and the collective; decisions about food allow consumers to display affiliation and belonging in a community or a nation.[270]

Writers of agricultural improvement treatises promised that their work was the best means to ensure individual bodily health, as well as national strength, with the production of more food. Projects touting agricultural improvement further promised benefits to the social body as more people could be put to work, producing more for the good of all. People with no work might have work. People with no food might have food. And if the projectors of these schemes got rich, they argued, so be it, especially if the nation and its myriad residents were well served and well fed. Ensuring access to food placed the king back at the head of the nation's table. Satiated subjects offered further evidence of his legitimacy and the legitimacy of the gentry. The restored king expanded the basis of his authority by rooting it in his skillful management of nature and by making sure that restored soils, improved agricultural techniques, and delicious and healthy foods could encourage and sustain a populous, and propagating, empire.

5 /   Naturalizing Bodies: Transplanting People and Plants to Jamaica

As the king's new Council of Foreign Plantations plotted the best methods for "peopling & settling the Island Jamaica," they recognized that developing a lucrative botanical product was necessary to ensure Jamaica's financial and demographic success.[1] While colonial promoters argued that the island would require an investment of time, money, and people, the status of the island remained an open question. Uncertainty dotted the Council's discourse on Jamaica's present condition and future status. While some voiced concerns that the island continued to be a drain on England's resources, others argued that it was worth the investment because the island was well-situated to grow lucrative and healthful plants, many of which could not be grown in England's colder climate. Not only might Jamaican plants boost the health of residents in England, but new settlers to the island suffering from a period of "seasoning," or acclimatization, might similarly benefit from locating local *materia medica*, in addition to transplanting medicinal plants to the colony, to aid in colonists' physical adjustment.

In *The American Physitian* (1672), William Hughes promised to reveal newfound American plants useful for *"Meat"* and *"Medicine"* that might *"be necessary to all which first travel to those parts."*[2] Plants with medicinal virtues would serve "to keep our Bodies sound" in the West Indies.[3] If Jamaica were to be retained and improved, English settlers would require methods of reinforcing the health of their bodies in Jamaica in addition to locating a lucrative commodity.[4] While some physicians warned about the effects of the "torrid zone" on the humors and temperaments of travelers and settlers alike, others argued that previous generations of writers had overemphasized the dangers of the climate of the West Indies.[5] One "briefe survey" of the island reassured the Council of Foreign Plantations that there was "not such an antypathy between" English constitutions and the "clyme."[6] According to Hughes, Jamaica was already "*temperate*" and "*healthful.*" He further asserted that the climate would be even more accommodating as colonists felled more trees. As woods made way to cultivated gardens and fields, Jamaica would have "as temperate a Climate as can be desired."[7] The colony could be transformed to better suit English bodies.

After conquering the island in 1655 from the Spanish, English colonial promoters debated what factors would lead to a prosperous future. In the decade following conquest, few envisioned the exclusive planting of sugarcane as the best or only way to secure Jamaican prosperity and settlement.[8] Early debates about the value of Jamaica and its place in the empire reveal it was not destined to be a sugar island from the moment of conquest. Among the numerous schemes to promote the "peopling & settling" of Jamaica—if, indeed, there were convincing reasons why "the king should keepe Jamaica in his Possession"—was a plan to plant medicinally useful plants within the king's demesne.[9] Against a backdrop of Jamaica's uncertain future, the king, a coterie of merchants, colonial officials, and members of the Royal Society exchanged letters and plans about the transplantation of plants, including the construction of two elaborate gardens, one in England, the other in Jamaica. One garden would be planted in London for the king. The other garden would be cultivated in the king's royal colony of Jamaica, a vast garden of East Indian specimens transplanted to the West.[10] The similar and simultaneous gardening schemes intended for England and Jamaica also suggest that Restoration officials saw the practical and symbolic significance of gardens—as metaphors for the state—in politically turbulent times.[11] By plotting the transplantation of medically useful plants, sweet-smelling specimens, and lucrative spices, the schemes' architects anticipated the potential of these gardens to alter subjects' health and longevity, sociopolitical character, and economic well-being. Meanwhile, attention to identifying plants indigenous to Jamaica, particularly pimiento pepper and cacao, further suggests colonists' continued interest in plants known for their healing properties, aesthetic qualities, and their potential for profit. English bioprospecting in the colonies featured regularly in the writings of colonial promoters, natural philosophers, apothecaries, and settlers.[12] Interest in medicinal plants from the East and West Indies highlights the diversification of medicinal plants available for sale in England and the emergence of what Harold J. Cook has called the "medical marketplace."[13]

With these global botanical transplantation schemes, English subjects around the Atlantic sought to acquire medicinal specimens, "to the great Advantage of Physicians and Patients," including those useful specimens that "will not approach our *Northern Beare* (and that are *incicurabiles* amongst us)."[14] In other words, plants might be cultivated in Jamaica that might not thrive in England's cooler climate. Moreover, the gardens' architects recognized the symbolic power of gardens as spaces to perform civility and sought to conceptualize and enact authority as well as define and delimit the appropriate behaviors of imperial subjects near the gardens by transforming the landscape and altering the quality of the airs, including smell. By placing the gardens in London and in Jamaica, the gardens' promoters may have targeted locations with residents perceived to be disorderly and unhealthy. Sweetly scented plantations suggested order, wealth, and civility. Moreover, the scale of the garden "plantations" suggests that these were intended as significant undertakings. While it is unlikely that the gardening schemes were undertaken, and certainly not on the scale or in the specific manner outlined in plans drafted on behalf of the king, endorsed by East India Company committee member Richard Ford, or in letters penned to colonial governors in Virginia and Barbados by the merchant, Royal Society Fellow, and member of the Council of Foreign Plantations Thomas Povey, the plans nevertheless offer a lens through which we may explore their creators' intent.[15]

Drafts of the planned garden transplantation projects remain strewn like "colonial debris" among the papers of the merchant and minor Restoration official Povey, the court book of the East India Company, and the records of the Royal Society, and scholars such as Ann Laura Stoler remind us of what can be gained by "developing historical negatives" in the archive by examining such failed schemes.[16] Although the "improbable visions" expressed in these myriad inquiries and calls for botanical experimentation may not have been undertaken, there is value in excavating and examining the "conflicting visions of the future" embedded in these letters and proposal drafts.[17] Stuart officials may have lacked the ability to plan and manage the outsized ambitions reflected in such schemes, but the plans provide a view into the expectant, but messy and uncertain, early history of English Jamaica when the legal, environmental, and even epistemological foundations of the colony remained unresolved.[18]

According to Ford's plan, the king's garden "plantations" in London and Jamaica would grow medicines, and spices, as well as colorful and aromatically pleasing plants.[19] Lucrative and alimentary plants could help to boost the wealth and health of subjects on both sides of the Atlantic. Moreover, according to Povey, the king particularly requested specimens for his gardens that could perfume the air, transforming scent into an object of statecraft in the process.[20] Indeed, in a treatise published the same year, John Evelyn called for the improvement of London's air quality, suggesting that sweet smells might waft through the riot-prone city and help to quiet residents and any lingering remnants of the chaos and "political disorder" of the previous decades.[21] Sweet-smelling airs were widely understood to have the power to infuse residents with a collective "good temper."[22] By constructing a garden in London, Evelyn suggested he might engineer new, calming "smellscapes" in the midst of England's premier city, widely acknowledged as a hotbed of unrest during the civil war and Interregnum.[23]

For the garden in Jamaica, the king, through the efforts of Ford and Povey, also sought lucrative spices and scented plant specimens to ensure that the recently acquired colony would be a viable addition to the empire. In his request for East India Company assistance the king anticipated that the success of his "experem^t" offered the "means to settle" and "impro^v ye Island of Jamaica."[24] Without a merchantable or "usefull" export commodity, and without residents to cultivate it, some members of the Council of Foreign Plantations doubted there was a compelling reason to maintain the island.[25] At stake in the scheme to transmit botanicals was Jamaica's uncertain place within the empire; the king's new Council of Foreign Plantations queried whether or not the king's interest would really be served by retaining and improving the island.[26] Making Jamaica a success would require an investment of time and money and a means of encouraging colonists. Meanwhile, residents already in Jamaica worried that the king might negotiate a return of the island to the Spanish.

Among the schemes outlined to secure Jamaica's place within the empire was the successful transplantation of lucrative and prized spices, like pepper, which could offer the means of financial survival as well as the benefits of its prized taste, aromatic, and health qualities.[27] The English had long looked to the East Indies for medicinally effective plants. Scholars estimate that over 60 percent of the drugs for sale in apothecaries' shops in England came from the East Indies.[28] By relocating East Indian drugs to Jamaica, desired spices, like pepper, would be

FIGURE 5.1. "Piper nigrum," Johann Weinmann, *Phytanthoza Iconographia* (Regensburg, 1737–45). RB 144172, The Huntington Library, San Marino, California.

more accessible. Transplantations to Jamaica would enable the English to avoid trading in a region of the world patrolled by Dutch ships. They might also cultivate for themselves what they would otherwise have to pay for at great expense.[29]

A key concern for Restoration officials and colonial promoters interested in Jamaica was how to facilitate development. They worried that

disorderly English soldiers and remnant maroon communities pre-
dominated on the island, limiting potential colonists' interest in settling.
Moreover, the island's reputation was associated with poor health and
death.[30] The gardens' architects may have intended the scented, healthful spices grown in the king's Jamaican garden to soothe the specters of
disgruntled soldiers, and perhaps even maroon communities, in Jamaica
by cultivating a civilized nature around them. For Jamaica's promoters,
ideas about health, civility, and commerce were intimately intertwined;
the new garden offered the promise of profit, medicines necessary to assist
fragile bodies through the process of seasoning, as well as an opportunity to transform the qualities of the air to aid further settlement. Such
interventions were necessary on an island whose unhealthy reputation
acted as a break on early English colonial ambitions. By transporting
medicines, planting orderly gardens, and locating drugs indigenous to
the island, officials, planters, and merchants and their agents sought to
offer potential colonists the comprehensive means of counteracting the
damaging effects of hot climates and unfamiliar foods, while simultaneously enriching planters. In Jamaica, as in London, gardens offered
officials the means to boost residents' health, refashioning the complexions and humors of subjects in both locations, and improving both locations' suitability for human residence. As a result, Restoration officials
aimed to cultivate gardens in England and Jamaica as potential sources
of wealth as well as to manipulate subjects' olfactory encounters with the
environment in order to impart a constellation of desirable qualities in
residents; it was a multifaceted approach to imperial statecraft.

While some scholars of the senses have suggested a trajectory in
which sight gained prominence in the eighteenth century, and vision
became the sense most utilized in a range of disciplinary regimes developed by modernizing bureaucratic states to control potentially unruly
populations, they have likewise traced alternative sensory hierarchies
and historical trajectories. Although in many early modern hierarchies
of the senses sight was regularly considered "the sense most closely
aligned with reason," smells were also understood to play crucial roles
in shaping health, attitude, and social behavior.[31] Odor may seem too
ephemeral to be a tool of the state, but this chapter highlights how officials imagined scent to be a medium of control during an unstable and
unsettled period. Indeed, scholars of the senses have suggested that smell
is often particularly utilized to mark or enable moments of personal and
community transition. Scenting the air can foster a sense of commu-
nion, such as during the performance of rituals.[32] The king's gardens

were more than merely metaphors of imperial improvement; they were also tools by which authorities might refashion residents' porous bodies and influence their "spongy brains" in London and Jamaica.[33] Improvers deployed aromatics in London and Jamaica to encourage social order.

Early modern gardens were thus ripe with transformative possibilities and were sites of experimentation. The king expressed his desires to transplant the spices and foods of the East Indies into Jamaica in the language of "curiosity," "tryall & enquiry," and experimentation.[34] The king's gardens in England and Jamaica might be usefully thought of as laboratories in which the king and his officials sought to successfully transplant and nurture therapeutic and salubrious substances as well as sites in which imperial officials might work out how to project English power over diverse people and places. These aims were particularly significant in unsettled Jamaica. But on both sides of the Atlantic, cultivated gardens might lead to cultivated people, suggesting, once again, the deep conceptual links between cultivation as planting or pruning fields, and cultivation as hands-on political governance.[35] Unruly plants and polities alike might be "settl[ed]" and thrive by "plowing" and cultivating gardens.[36]

According to many Restoration-era commentators, the individual best suited to oversee these multiple types of cultivation was Charles II, often celebrated by his contemporaries for his interest in gardening.[37] In Jamaica he might transform both the physical and political landscapes of the island—which former Spanish proprietors had referred to as the *garden of the Indies*—into a landscape suited to its new English proprietors.[38] Transforming the environment would not only establish property rights and ensure the colony's economic viability; it would also alter human health and community behavior. The garden schemes further highlight how medical and environmental concepts bolstered early modern sociopolitical thought. Restoration officials intended the gardens to transform residents. The creation of gardens dotted around the Anglo-Atlantic enunciated and refashioned themes of ideal kingship suited to an expanding Restoration empire, including the ideal of a merchant king overseeing plantation emporiums or that of the king as a physician or gardener curing or cultivating the body politic.

Projectors also looked to projects of botanical transplantation in Jamaica as a lens through which they might assess the likelihood of successful human settlement. Colonization and transplantation required both plant and human bodies to relocate to new climates and soils, which was a risky proposition. Successful botanical transplantations to

Jamaica mattered, then, because the transplanted plants offered evidence of the suitability and dangers awaiting human transplantation and vice versa.[39] Thus the successful naturalization of transplanted specimens might indicate that the colonial enterprise had the potential to thrive. The Council of Foreign Plantations theorized the necessity of transplanting both people and botanicals as necessary to the health, improvement, and success of the colony.[40] Yet there were also long-standing fears about the potentially deleterious effects of transplantation on both plant and human bodies.[41] It was risky to transplant porous humoral bodies to hot climates while also subjecting them to new dietary regimes.[42] Beyond fears of poor health, questions about whether or not settlers could maintain their Englishness, physically, culturally, and politically—if born and raised in different climes—haunted colonial settlement.[43] As James Robertson has suggested, "Being 'English' in late seventeenth-century Jamaica was often as much a goal as an achievement."[44] Since claims to Englishness so often deployed agricultural metaphors and pointed to a rootedness in home soil, colonists grappled with the risks to their physical health and identities by uprooting and transplanting themselves.[45]

As colonists wrestled with their health and identities abroad, English officials grappled with whether or not to extend "a general naturalization" of "aliens" into England.[46] Restoration officials debated about the legal and practical effects of the "peopling" of England at the same time as they wrestled with questions about the "peopling" of Jamaica. The question of which of the newcomers could or should be incorporated or naturalized was a pressing issue of political economy and a hot-button issue of the day, as a populous nation was believed to be a strong nation. The timing of these botanical-transplantation schemes, developed at the same time as Charles II and his Council considered the position of recently acquired Jamaica and its population, as well as the desirability of an influx of newcomers into England, is significant.[47] After all, the term "naturalization" held multiple meanings. It was both a legal term and described a physical process. While its most common usage was as a legal concept, derived from Roman law to define newcomers with specific rights in England, including property ownership, naturalization was also used in texts on gardening to suggest a process of physical adjustment to new surroundings. As agricultural writers mused about naturalizing strangers into the garden, officials debated naturalizing strangers to the nation, and colonists wondered what happened legally and physically to English bodies when they moved to new places with new soils and airs. The garden was one place to work out thorny concepts about the relationship of nature, culture, and political belonging. The king's two gardens were both sites to test the limits of mutability and heredity in the plant and human worlds. Both offered evidence about the kinds of traits that were alterable and those that were not. This mattered to officials who were concerned with how to "settle" subjects and spaces, particularly in newly acquired territories like Jamaica.[48]

Procuring Simples and Spices "Serviceable for His Maties Plantations in Jamaica & England"

On March 4, 1661, Thomas Povey, merchant and member of both the Council of Foreign Plantations and the Royal Society, drafted letters and accompanying inquiries to colonial contacts in which he requested they provide him with detailed descriptions of the local environment of Virginia and Bermuda and collect and ship specimens to England to be planted in the king's garden.[49] While the specific content and contours of the garden remained vague in his written plans, Povey claimed he wrote on behalf of the Royal Society as well as the society's patron, Charles II, who would welcome "naturall products," particularly those rarities that were "considerable either for their flower, smell, Alimentary or medicinall use."[50] Povey's queries were likely inspired by his participation as a member of a committee of the Royal Society tasked "to consider of proper Questions to be enquired of in the remotest parts of the world."[51] The committee was appointed to draft the questions in February 1661. Povey wrote his inquiries about the colonial natural world several weeks later, in March.[52]

The Royal Society desired various roots because of their tincture or for their presumed health benefits, such as "Musquasoen," (roots with a red tincture) and "Tockawouge" (roots dried and grounded up to make bread).[53] Of the many specific requests, varied names, such as the "Putchamin fruite," were drawn from Algonquian words, indicating that the knowledge of these specimens and their uses was derived from indigenous people, even if this was largely unacknowledged.[54] The form of delivery was up to the discretion of the collectors, be it seeds, roots, slips, or young versions of the plants, presumably because those individuals with local knowledge would be best suited to send them in the form "most proper for the propagation of them," as well as provide information about "their manner of culture."[55]

Povey concluded his letter with a reminder that the king particularly wanted shipments of rarities "not found in England."[56] He urged his contacts to take care to gather "Plants and Simples and varieties of that nature, and it will be most acceptable to his Matie." According to Povey, members of the Royal Society also desired specimens of various medicinal and nourishing roots, dyes, and other rarities. The medicinal specimens on his list included the "poison weede like our Ivy whose leaves by the touch do cause blisters" from Bermuda, as well as a "red reed whose juice or infusion causeth vomit" and a variety of "wood bine whose fruit like a flat beane, purgeth vehemently." Additional items with medicinal properties included "minerals, stones, Bitumens, Tinctures, Drugges & a specimen of each."[57] Early modern medicine saw immense benefits in blistering, purging, and bleeding as remedies. The expulsion of putrefaction was a coherent, visible, and satisfactory method of balancing humoral bodies. Indeed, people expected healing to be a painful process, and when these expectations were not met, the therapy was deemed suspect.[58]

The king and members of the Royal Society also sought information about plant products that might make living in hot climes more bearable, inquiring, for instance, "What kind of tree those Barkes are taken from, which are used in stead of Tile or Slet in the covering of their houses being more coole in summer & warme in winter then stone?"[59] In questionnaires later sent with Colonel Thomas Lynch on his way to become governor of Jamaica, members of the Society requested knowledge about the healing properties of the *Palma christi*, asking, "whether it be true," that the Indians, Africans, and African-descended people "make the leaves of it, applied to the head, ye remedy for their Headache."[60] They echoed earlier queries when they asked him to "observe what considerable minerals, stones, Bitumens, Tinctures, and Druggs there are in Jamaica?"[61] Knowledge that addressed the realities of living in a hot climate, like that of Jamaica, had real utility for settlers considering the move and was likewise of interest to Charles II and his advisers, who actively considered how best to settle and populate Jamaica and how to ensure colonists' survival. As Anya Zilberstein argues, colonists did not think that they were helpless in the face of climates ill-suited to their tempers and health. Colonial promoters, travel writers, and officials regularly asserted that with careful cultivation and improvement, landscapes that were too hot or too cold might be ameliorated.[62] Unlike older models that defined regions on the globe by latitude, many colonists came to argue that climate was not fixed. The detrimental effects of hot and freezing climates on humoral bodies might be mitigated by transforming the environment. As a result, moderating the climate became one of the goals of imperial officials and settlers seeking to make Jamaica more livable.

However, collecting the desired rarities and medicinal specimens from Bermuda and Virginia were not enough to satisfy the king. In another set of proposals, collected in Povey's papers, were plans to collect additional garden specimens for the king. One of the drafts outlining a scheme "concerning sending Plants . . . from the East Indies" to the West Indies was endorsed as "Richard Fords Paper." Richard Ford was a commissioner in the East India Company and later served on the Council of Trade and Plantations alongside Povey.[63] The transplantation schemes were outlined in two drafts; the first draft introduced, and the second elaborated on, a "Proposal for removing spices & other plants from the East to the West Indies," in which gardeners appointed by the king would gather plants and simples in the East Indies on his behalf.[64] The plans called for East India Company assistance in fetching additional specimens for the king's London garden from numerous locations in India and Indonesia, as well as to transport the majority of the collected East Indian spices to Jamaica. By gathering rarities and spices from around the globe, the king could position himself as a powerful merchant king, the facilitator of a global trade network as well as the cultivator of large-scale garden hubs on both sides of the Atlantic.

Ford's transplantation schemes were written in response to a royal letter penned on August 20, 1661, to a private committee of the East India Company (EIC). In the letter the king instructed the committee to experiment with transplanting spices from the East Indies and test if they could be successfully cultivated in Jamaica.[65] He wanted to know if the plants could be acclimatized to his royal colony. For his Jamaican garden, the king sought "Spices" and other plants and foods of the East Indies that "may agree with that [our] Island y^t if possible wee may hereafter receive from the growth of [our] plantations such commodities as with greate expense & inconvenience . . . Wee fetch" from distant countries.[66] The king sent his missive to the "private Comitty" of the East India Company, who were able to "transact the more private affaires" and sent Thomas Povey to deliver the letter in person and "conferre further with you" so that his plans would be "thoroughly understood."[67] The king explained that by "Tryall & enquiry" he hoped these transplantation experiments would be the "means to settle" and "impro^v" Jamaica.[68] The court minutes in the records of the East India Company reveal that on the very same day, "A proposal of secrecy" was made to the "Committee appointed for affaires of yt Nature, for them to consider if it might bee of any advantage to ye Company and it being declared to ye Court (after a strict injunction of Secrecy) the same was at large debated by them."[69] Although the injunction to secrecy means the "proposal" was not specified in the court minutes, the evidence overwhelmingly suggests they debated the king's proposals to transplant spices to Jamaica. Ten days later, on August 30, the Company considered the "businesse proposed in a letter from his Majesty" and "spent much time in the serious debating and contriveing how to accommodate his Majesty" and appointed Richard Ford, William Ryder, and Christopher Boone to "returne an answer" to the king "according to the sence" of the court.[70]

In the first draft outlining plans for transplantation, Ford proposed appointing gardeners who would be sent aboard EIC ships to locations on the western and eastern coasts of India, including Surat and the Coromandel Coast. Additional gardeners would sail to various Indonesian island ports. The proposal never specifies how this cadre of skilled gardeners would be selected or what they should seek out upon arrival. The insistence that they would get in touch with the EIC's local factors for advice about procuring plants and spices indicates an acknowledgment that on-the-ground knowledge would be necessary to the success of the scheme.[71] A second version of the proposal offered more specifics. It is likely that among those "parts of India" to which Ford proposed sending ships and gardeners was the "chiefe realme" of Malabar, the southwestern coast of India. Authors had long pointed to both the Malabar and Coromandel Coasts as notable regions for procuring pepper. The more aromatic the pepper plants, the higher price it would fetch.[72] Pepper, the only spice named outright in drafts outlining the plans for the king's gardens, was extremely significant to English EIC trade, and concerns over access to pepper drove many of their activities and plans.

After visiting "all partes of India," the gardeners were to travel to Bantam at the start of their winter, in April, and then, during "may, june, and july [they should] gather pepper plants and such others as [the] Island of Java, Sumatra, & other adjacent partes may afford."[73] At that time, specimens should be "dispatched directly for Jamaica" so that they "may arrive in a proper tyme for theire Replanting there." The proposal continued, outlining how one or two of the gardeners should travel with the specimens aboard a ship bound directly for Jamaica, to care for them on the long journey. The remaining gardeners would "bee sent from Bantam, on the first available passage to the Coast of Coromandie, Bay of Bengala and Banda Islands." In these locations they would yet again address themselves to the Company's factors to gain assistance in their work. The gardeners would then wait until EIC ships arrived in January for the next leg of their journeys.[74]

The plants from this second group, many of which were intended for the king's London garden, would return in EIC ships and were to have "all good accommodation for their persons & plants."[75] In St. Helena a planned drop-off and pickup would occur. This stop in St. Helena replicated an EIC policy in place for at least a decade, of ships gathering in St. Helena before embarking for home. Moreover, St. Helena played an even more significant role in EIC plans after they acquired a new patent in 1658. The EIC expected the island "to serve as a locus for the transshipment of commodities and for the establishment of a plantation."[76] Ford's plans on behalf of the king, therefore, made use of EIC ships and personnel and fit within the EIC's recent reimagining of the important new role to be played by St. Helena in their global schemes. According to Ford's plans, at least one of the ships traveling back with this second group would peel off from the rest. After mustering in St. Helena, some of the gardeners and their specimens would board a new ship, this one sent by the king from England to meet them. The "small ship" sent by the king to St. Helena would take aboard "such men & plantes as may be proper for Jamaica & carry them directly thither." The final leg of the journey for this "small ship" would thus bring the remainder of an astonishing botanical haul to Jamaica, in order to grow a vast garden of East Indian plants in the West. The second draft continued with an elaborate scheme to organize the funding of these journeys.[77]

In retrospect, we may read the schemes to transport East Indian plants to the West as unrealistic because they did not unfold as planned. Certainly, they would have required time, money, knowledge, cooperation, coordination, and more than a great deal of luck to succeed.[78] The logistical obstacles faced by projectors when transporting plants over long distances alone would have been a significant hurdle.[79] Similar long-distance transplantation schemes undertaken in the late seventeenth century offer a window into the challenges of transport. Due to untrustworthy sea vessels and delicate, living cargo, maintaining the physical integrity and viability of plants during transport presented a major challenge. Specimens had to be protected from the elements. For instance, roots were to "be wrapt up in mosse or light earth," "kept from dashing of sea-water; giving ym Air every day, when the weather is fair, and watering ym wth fresh water once a day."[80] One late seventeenth-century ship carrying botanical cargo to Ireland "sprang a leak" and was "forc'd to return to Jamaica."[81]

Although it does not appear that the specific schemes requested by the king, outlined by Ford, and collected among Povey's papers were undertaken, the benefits of such a plan were clear, including their critical geopolitical consequences. The transplantation schemes would bring extremely lucrative specimens to a more accessible location for English ships, to an island recently claimed by the English. It would circumvent the need to purchase high-priced items from merchants with better access, particularly the Dutch.[82] Instead of purchasing pepper at a loss, they would transplant it to an island within the English empire, which was more in line with ideals of mercantilism. Moreover, in an era in which the English and Dutch waged regular wars with one another, ensuring uninterrupted access to spices from the East Indies would have been an economic priority. The plans sought to address the fact that the English had uncertain access to key ports. Indeed, as L. H. Roper has revealed, "the situation of the English east of the Cape of Good Hope was dire in the mid-1650s."[83] The king's gardens may have been a response to these recent geopolitical concerns.[84] They were likely envisioned as the means of circumventing Dutch threats to English access to pepper, a crucial economic resource, later heralded by the governor of the East India Company, Josiah Child, as "sufficient to defray ye constant charge of a great Navy in Europe"[85] Child suggested that pepper was a commodity so critical to the English that anyone who made themselves "sole Masters" of the spice would achieve dominion over the seas and beyond.[86]

Although it is not easy to explain the EIC's willingness to consider assisting the king to carry spices into the West Indies, Ford's likely authorship of the transplantation schemes suggests, perhaps, that the EIC hoped to branch out into the Atlantic, as they had already done with the establishment of a plantation on St. Helena. Moreover, it might reflect the renewed interest from the king's brother, James, Duke of York, and his circle in the establishment of a West India Company—an idea that had itself been suggested and circulated for decades—which was a plan that aligned with York's broader aims of attacking Dutch trade and even going to war with the Dutch to ensure English trading supremacy.[87]

When Ford drafted the schemes to procure and transplant plants, he called on gardeners to procure the specimens and seeds that would be most "serviceable for his maties plantations in Jamaica & England."[88] Although the specific form, size, and content of those "plantations" remains elusive, the type of garden spaces imagined by the king, Povey, and Ford is suggestive. Moreover, as noted above, East India Company member Ford was already invested in another "plantation" that played a key role in the plans to cultivate "his maties plantations in Jamaica & England." Several months earlier, on April 3, 1661, Charles II had reconfirmed the EIC's charter and the right to build "Plantations, Forts, Fortifications, Factories or colonies, where the said Company's Factories and Trade are or shall be in the said *East-Indies*," including St. Helena.[89] In fact, the EIC had begun the work of establishing a plantation on St. Helena in 1659.[90] Thus, when the king reconfirmed the Company's patent in 1661, the EIC had already been at work establishing a plantation in St. Helena for two years. Several months later, the king inquired about transplanting East Indian specimens to the West, and Ford produced the schemes outlining how to cultivate the garden "plantations" in England and Jamaica, while suggesting St. Helena should play an important role.

Several weeks after reconfirming the patent, on April 23, 1661, Charles II processed through London, traveling from the Tower of London to Whitehall to his coronation. As he processed through London, he made an appointed ceremonial stop at the East India House on Leadenhall Street so the Company could "take occasion to express their dutiful Affections to His Majesty."[91] John Ogilby described the "entertainment": "First, a Youth in Indian Habit, attended by two Black-Moors, is sent out to bespeak the Kings Expectation, kneeling before His Horse" and thanking him by reciting a poem about a "full fraught Caravan" from India that was the king's "due Tribute." Next, "another Youth, in an Indian Vest, mounted upon a Camel, led out by two Black-Moors, & other Attendants, the Camel having two Panniers fill'd with Jewels, Spices, and Silks, to be scattered among the Spectatours," also recited a poem about goods carried from the East, including "Aromaticks." This same youth thanked the king for the EIC's "Enlarg'd . . . Charter" and for dispelling "our Fears of the incroaching Holland's Rival Force," ensuring that London would only grow in significance as an "Empory" of "All That's Rich." According to Ogilby, the two costumed "youths" who addressed the king were John Ford and Samuel Ford, sons of Richard Ford.[92]

Examining the coronation ceremony and the transplantations schemes together, suggests the king and his advisers envisioned a trade-oriented vision of imperial sovereignty in London and in the royal colony of Jamaica, with nodes of cultivated goods overseen by a powerful merchant king, or at least a king who protected and promoted merchants. As others had envisioned before him, the "plantations" in Ford's transplantation schemes were, ideally, defined as places that were "not like an *Assylum* for fugitives, a *Bellum Piraticum* for *Banditi*, or any such base *Ramas* of people; but [would be] an *Emporium* for the confluence of all Nations that love, or profess any kinde of virtue, or Commerce."[93] In other words, the plantation gardens would be emporiums that would enable the king and merchants to engage in virtuous commerce. This ideal of an empire of trade was later echoed by Francis Hanson, who called Port Royal, Jamaica, the "Storehouse or Treasury" of the West Indies, "a continual Mart or Fair where all choice Merchandizes are daily imported."[94] If the king could facilitate trade, he could bolster his authority. By relocating plant rarities and spices to particular sites within the empire, gardeners could locate "the world's exchange" in London, for instance, and projectors might make "both Indies ours."[95]

Much like the garden transplantation schemes among Povey's papers, numerous additional writers schemed about the possibility of transplanting high-priced groceries or commodities that had to be purchased from foreign merchants into England or English colonies to circumvent the need to pay high prices for them. As John Beale wrote to the intelligencer Samuel Hartlib about coffee, he believed it would be better if the English could purchase it "from our owne plantations, than from Turkye." The result would be mutually beneficial, since "our vanityes & luxury by Gods providence" would be "diverted to sustaine our forreigne bretheren."[96] In other words, English fondness for coffee could benefit the English colonists who were willing to cultivate it. He went on to suggest experimenting with the cultivation of coffee in both North American colonies and the West Indies.[97] Many saw the potential for great profit awaiting schemes of transplantation, exclaiming, like Thomas Sprat in his continued high hopes for the future of silkworm production in Virginia, that the "profit will be inexpressible."[98]

Perhaps hearing of the transplantation plans of the king and Ford from fellow Royal Society member Povey, Thomas Sprat wrote about multiple kinds of transplantation the Society encouraged in their efforts to improve the "Manual Arts" in his book *The History of the Royal Society of London* (1667). Sprat reasoned that transplantation would be successful if plants were carried from "the same scituation in respect to the *Heavens*," or from places at the same latitude. He reasoned, "This may be trid by conveying the Eastern *Spices*, and other useful *vegetables*, into our Western *Plantations*."[99] Meanwhile, the prolific garden writer and member of the Royal Society, Beale, envisioned a future for England in which sweetly scented garden emporiums grew profusely, composed of plants acquired from around the globe. In January 1663 Beale wrote hopefully to John Oldenburg about how London might become an "Emporium of the World," if only everyone would participate in the Royal Society's aims of gathering the world's knowledge together, including its botanical wonders. In a short time, London would be "a paradyse, the very ayre epidemically purifyed & sweetened," in part because the air would be aromatically conditioned by the array of botanical specimens transplanted from the world over.[100] Beale suggested that the purified and sweetened air would, in turn, fashion industrious and wealthy subjects; the scent of profit would be sweet.

Like Ford, Povey, Sprat, and the king, Beale also schemed of transplanting flora from the East Indies. In a letter written April 1, 1664, to Henry Oldenburg, he proposed transplanting East Indian spices to England.[101] It was read aloud to the Royal Society in May.[102] Beale later wrote to Oldenburg that he hoped to inspire "a new and *active spirit* in all ye gardeners about London, England, Scot, and Ireland."[103] Beale envisioned these paradisiacal gardens dotting the length and breadth of these kingdoms in addition to the aromatic "Emporium" of London. The "paradyse" he described was a market. Londoners could enjoy the botanical riches of the world in one place as strange and wonderful things from around the world entered England by ship. Odiferous scents would radiate from plantation entrepôts like London. In turn, these emporiums were connected to the wider world by trading routes. Coupling sweet scent and profit was not limited to Stuart supporters. In *Paradise Lost* (1667), the poet John Milton envisioned trade routes as akin to aromatic corridors crisscrossing oceans, tempting and drawing sailors on by ribbons of scent rather than navigation by maps or stars. He described sailing routes to the East as scented journeys, ships carried by winds with "odoriferous wings" beckoning those "who sail / Beyond the Cape of Hope, and are now past / Mozambic," with "Sabean odors from the spicy shore / Of Araby the blest."[104] Travel writers to North American colonies reported that they were aware of the scents of verdant forests long before land was visible, sure of their approach by smell, not sight.[105]

Schemes to fetch specimens from these distant "spicy" or verdant shores and then gathered into emporiums might transform an island like Jamaica from a burden into a "usefull" colony, one more worth retaining, through the transplanting of "serviceable" plants. Evelyn pointed to other Atlantic islands, such as the Canaries, which had already been vastly improved by transplanting oranges and grape vines. He claimed that transplantation had transformed the Canaries from "Rocks and Sun-burnt Ashes" into "one of the richest spots of *Ground* in the *World*."[106] "Expansionist merchants" like Povey sought to convince skeptics of Jamaica's potential value by promising that a similar transformation was possible in Jamaica.[107] Povey detailed the positive attributes of the island in voluminous writings, highlighting "the nature of its climate, fruitfulnesse of the soile, and its suitableness to English complexions."[108] Povey, like others with a personal stake in maintaining the island, sought to convince others of its value.[109] While individual self-interest certainly played a significant role in determinations about Jamaica, and in schemes of transplantation, some saw an important role for the king in overseeing such a lucrative trade in spices, fruits, and vegetables. Thomas Sprat also acknowledged an important symbolic role for the king's gardening activities. He claimed the king "has made *Plantations* enough, even almost to repair the Ruins of a Civil War," and he suggested the king, or those who claimed they acted on the king's behalf, had also cultivated a range of landscapes in and around London, proving himself to be the better steward of the land than Cromwell.[110]

According to Beale, it was the king who was best positioned to encourage a lively seed trade because "greater things may be done by ye Command, or Countenence of a Prince, then by any, or many private mens industry." As a result, the king was best suited to "To exchange ye Seedes of England, Fr, Italy & generally of Europe with ye seedes of all kinds from New-foundland, New England, Virg, Carol, Bermuda, Barbad, Jamaica &c."[111] Beale envisioned a powerful monarch collecting specimens from around the world who could bolster subjects' trading aspirations and oversee a densely interconnected commercial empire of trade. Many hoped to bolster the king's role and argued that Charles II was the very embodiment of "a London-centered global absolutism," by facilitating global commerce through putting the power of the state behind seed-trading and transplantation endeavors.[112] The result of this new political economic order would ensure the flow of goods, including botanical specimens, thereby transforming England, as in Beale's schemes, into a sweet-smelling market paradise.

Ameliorating a Disordered Public with "Sweet and Ravishing" Smells

Early modern English authorities had long claimed a range of powers over subjects' health and bodies. As discussed in chapter 1, city officials in London manipulated insalubrious air on behalf of community health, particularly in order to combat dangerous miasmas and pestilential airs; they burned aromatic materials as a therapeutic intervention. During the plague year in 1666 they built cleansing fires on city streets. Gideon Harvey instructed London's officials to burn "*Stinck pots*, or *Stinckers*, as they call them, in Contagious Lanes," in order to decontaminate infected zones of the city.[113] The aldermen and the mayor of London ordered bonfires lit in the streets in 1666 in an effort to combat infection; the famed diarist Samuel Pepys noted such public fires in early September.[114] Individuals had to stay alert to danger because contamination lurked wherever there were foul smells or unusual changes in climate or atmosphere.[115] But it was not only the dangers bad air posed to residents' health that worried Restoration officials. The association of foul odors and social disorder prompted authorities to propose a variety of reforms, such as enumerating the responsibilities of the individuals licensed to cart out London's waste or advocating the widening of streets to allow more breeze and light to penetrate and to disperse malodorous smells and pestilence while also improving surveillance.[116]

The garden schemes of Povey and Ford shared many of the same aims, but they advocated for more permanent additions to the city's smell-scapes than Harvey's antiplague "stinck pots." Among the plants Povey requested on behalf of the king were specimens considerable for their medical and "Alimentary" use.[117] Among pepper's many uses and benefits were its perceived salubrious effects on the digestive and respiratory health of those who consumed or smelled its spiced flavor and aromatic scent. The letters and schemes soliciting rare and odoriferous plants and medicinal simples for the king's Jamaican and London gardens offer an intriguing interpretative lens. Cultivating gardens of spices and medicines with aromatic and therapeutic features was a means to combat the dangerous influence of miasmas to benefit health as well as regulate temperament, providing Restoration officials with what they understood to be a powerful means of social control.[118] As a nation's healthy and sizeable population was increasingly understood to underpin national strength, officials realized that gardens had the potential to bolster these political economic ideals from the ground up.[119] The contents of the king's gardens, made up of spices and medical "simples," might boost the bodies, minds, and strength of the nation. The potential medical uses of the king's gardens are reiterated in contemporaneous and similar schemes. The Royal Society's historian, Thomas Sprat, referred to another instance of the successful transplantation of therapeutic specimens into a London garden when he praised the king, who had "incourag'd" and "provok'd" scientific progress by his own example, fostering *"Chymical Operators"* under his own roof who were resolved "to restore, to enlarge, to examine *Physick"* and had additionally "planted a Physick Garden under his own eye."[120] Sprat's claims that the king had already ordered the cultivation of a physic garden echoed transplantation schemes outlined by Povey and Ford, who had similarly sought useful drugs and scented plants for the king's gardens. Gardens did important symbolic work. The king could claim he sought to proactively preserve the bodies of his subjects and point to his skills in managing nature for the good of the people. By scenting the environs of the city, a physician king might also calm London's infamously "restless citizenry."[121]

Historians of smell have pointed to the ways in which foul odors were frequently linked in the early modern imagination to chaotic and unsettled political regimens and social disorder, whereas pleasing smells were seen to both promote and reflect a spiritually sound and stable community. Alain Corbin examines how foul odors were interpreted as a threat to society in post-Revolutionary France that required elimination. He traces how figures in the medical establishment simultaneously promoted hygienic practices and the use of fragrant scents to ensure social stability in the postwar years.[122] Pleasing fragrance was associated with health and a well-ordered community in opposition to the fetid, dangerous odors associated with disease, plague, and social disorder. Similar concerns wound their way through the texts of English writers and officials in the seventeenth century; they proposed dealing with socially and politically volatile places by ameliorating poor air quality and fetid smells. Garden writers like John Evelyn mused, for instance, that "the aire and genious of Gardens worke upon humane spirits towards virtue and Sanctitie."[123] Collectively, these texts suggested that calming smells might stabilize riot-prone populaces of political dissenters, republicans, or ex-soldiers, whether in London or Jamaica.

Claims that gardens would benefit health were a regular feature of gardening texts in the seventeenth century. Meanwhile, air and smell became subjects of study.[124] In such an intellectual climate, scent could become a tool of the state. Whereas foul smells were associated with "evil odors," demons, witches, the devil, social disorder, and poor health, sweet smells had long associations with the opposite, including sanctity. Passages in the Bible described how moral behavior, obedience, and the humble sacrifices of humanity wafted up to God as pleasant aromas.[125] Good behavior in life allowed individuals to achieve an "odour of sanctity" after death.[126] Fragrant scents counteracted a range of distempers, including the plague.[127] Perfumes, herbs, and spices were powerful agents that secured individuals' health. Air quality mattered to early modern men and women because they understood their porous bodies as "almost perpetually contiguous" with the air as they inhaled and exhaled.[128] Galen had even suggested that the structures of the nostrils, with their supposedly direct pathway to the brain, pointed to the particular importance of smell to human perception.[129] Or, as the seventeenth-century essayist Robert Burton suggested in his compendious tome *The anatomie of Melancholy* (1621), "as the Aire is, so are the inhabitants," leading to people who were, as a result of the qualities of the air, variably witty, nimble, lusty, subtle, neat, cleanly, clownish, sick or sound.[130]

The transplantation request of the king, the letters and proposals of Povey and Ford, and a proliferation of contemporaneous gardening schemes reveal the symbolic and practical importance of gardens to Restoration officials and writers. When the newly restored king encouraged John Evelyn's efforts to produce a pamphlet on how to improve the air and health of Londoners afflicted with coal-smoke inhalation by planting "the most fragrant and odoriferous" plants "aptest to tinge the *Aer* upon every gentle emission at a great distance," the underlying rationale suggested it was possible to use gardens to combat one of the perceived factors in London's high mortality rates, improving longevity and altering temperaments.[131] In response to the king's encouragement, Evelyn printed his findings in a treatise entitled *Fumifugium: or, the Inconveniencie of the Aer and Smoak of London Dissipated* (1661). As the historian Mark Jenner has argued, in the royalist Evelyn's work, the roiling black clouds of coal smoke in the text were "a metaphor of the political disorder of the Interregnum."[132] Meanwhile, Charles II's Restoration was the clearing, cleaning, cloud-dispersing sunshine that would ameliorate looming threats of political and bodily disorder. Across the Atlantic, metaphors of the gathering of "darke clouds" were regularly used in colonial North America to express fears of looming danger, including political, religious, and military threats.[133] London's recent, riotous past, particularly its broad parliamentarian support during the civil wars, was reimagined in Evelyn's text, ominously represented by a putrid, pestilential, and spiritually corrosive coal-smog atmosphere. These metaphors were especially potent for residents of London in 1661 because clouds of smog emanated from a variety of industries and household hearths and filled London's airs, settling in sooty layers on residents' clothes as well as the buildings of the capital city, making Evelyn's text doubly suggestive.[134]

Evelyn recommended planting wide "Invironing Gardens" around much of the city, particularly the "low-grounds circumjacent to the City." Planted with refreshing and "incomparably fragrant" shrubs, trees, and flowers, Evelyn anticipated the aromas would alter the well-being of the city's inhabitants.[135] Consequently, the garden was something akin to what Gillian Darley has deemed a "perfumed *cordon sanitaire*."[136] The city's residents would benefit directly from "the sweet and ravishing varieties of the perfumes" released into the air, including herbs like rosemary, which was so potent that, if planted on the coast, it could be smelled at sea. With such range, Evelyn imagined the whole city would benefit from the scents, and as the "*Aer* and *Winds* perpetually fann'd from so many circling and encompassing Hedges, fragrant Shrubs, Trees, and Flowers," the whole city would be sensible of the delightful aromas.[137] He further urged the cultivation of a garden in the yard of St. Paul's Cathedral that might become "wholesome bellowes" to that part of the city[138]

Evelyn envisioned how gardens could be powerful political tools to tamp down on disordered populations, confused by, and mired in, the smoky London atmosphere.[139] The proposal to encircle London with gardens like "*Palisad's* . . . elegantly planted, diligently kept and supply'd" with fragrant shrubs, hinted at a militant regulation of London's airs and inhabitants alike, though the aspirations to such expansive power was masked by the language of elegant gardens and scented effusions.[140] The use of the word "palisade," a gardening term also used to describe battle fortifications, suggested a potentially combative attitude toward the people corralled within the confines of the encircling garden. Evelyn's vision was consistent with mid-seventeenth-century garden ideals, in which gardens were ordered, controlled, and stylized in bounded and geometrical space.[141]

Evelyn's gardening schemes, designed to environ London and alter its airs and residents, may have been influenced by fellow member of the Royal Society Robert Boyle's work on air, even though the Society's interest in air was not universally admired. As an anonymous satirist of the Royal Society wrote in a pamphlet in 1663, instead of useful experiments, the Society busied itself with macabre experiments on the air such as utilizing Boyle's "Pneumatick Engine" to kill a cat instead of attempting something truly useful. But despite such mocking commentary, the study of air remained popular with the Royal Society. And while it might only have been intended as a send-up of Evelyn's gardening ambitions, mocking his insistence that coal smoke "doth our Lungs and *Spiritts* choake," such derision did not seem to dampen Evelyn's enthusiasm for improving Londoners' lungs and longevity through the "melioration of the Ayre" with the planting of cedar, juniper, rosemary, and roses.[142]

As Jenner has pointed out, Evelyn's plans to plant sweet-smelling specimens around London paralleled, and were likely influenced by, the writings of his friend and correspondent, and author of numerous treatises on gardening, John Beale.[143] One of Beale's many gardening schemes included a treatise on gardening that offered designs for plantations that would "rectify & purify the ayre of all the neighboring Country, both for health of body, & of minde; to prepare & dispose for Vertue, & for sanctity; & to procure longevity."[144] This powerful conception of the multivalent reaction of human bodies, minds, and spirits to the ambient air underlines its significance. Air quality had significant explanatory power for many human characteristics in the early modern era. Better air led to longer-lived and more virtuous subjects. Beale envisioned that air purified by a garden might even lead to a purified soul. By imagining the spiritual succor of smells wafting from the garden, Beale's work echoed earlier writers who had similarly linked purified airs to purified spirits. French Renaissance essayist Michel de Montaigne praised the role of pleasurable smells in raising his thoughts to God. Montaigne mused that in addition to their myriad health benefits, aromas had the power to alter his mental and spiritual state by moving his spirits, depending on their strength and quality. Scents "worke strange effects in me," he wrote, further suggesting that the use of incense and perfumes in church "had an especiall regard to rejoyce, to comfort, to quicken, to rowze, and to purifie our senses, that so we might be the apter and readier unto contemplation."[145] Garden writers, including Evelyn and Beale, would have been familiar with long-standing ideas about the transformative power of scent.

Plans for crafting fragrant smellscapes in Jamaica and London went hand in hand with other sensorial transformations. As chapter 1 detailed, in London, city officials had long advocated for the reconstruction of city streets, hoping to widen and straighten thoroughfares, anticipating that a rebuilt urban landscape might also promote reason and orderliness. As Evelyn had cautioned in 1659, London was made up of a confused maze of streets, and the buildings were as "deformed as the minds & confusions of the people."[146] Whereas linear and well-lit places led to reason and increased air flow to health, disorderly and obscure vistas were associated with confusion, stink, disease, unsociable and criminal behaviors, and deformities. Those aiming to transform London's urban landscape addressed both scent and sight. Similarly, when the future governor of Jamaica Thomas Lynch recommended transforming Jamaica's dense woods into linear and well-spaced groves, he similarly implied that there was a link between form and a transformed sensorial landscape. As naturalists' treatises on Jamaica claimed, better air flow and penetration by the sun "in clear'd open grounds" allowed for the earlier ripening of the most fragrant pimiento pepper than was possible "in thicker woods."[147] In this case, well-ordered landscapes transformed a commodity, its salable, olfactory qualities fetching higher prices for potential cultivators.

Restoration officials were wary of the political views and behaviors of London's residents, and they were likewise anxious about the residents of recently acquired Jamaica; they articulated a range of reforms to ensure order and stability. As in London, they looked to the amelioration of Jamaica's airs as a means of boosting the health of inhabitants. But ensuring the health and good behavior of Jamaican settlers was acknowledged to be a monumental challenge. Acquired at great cost in lives as part of Oliver Cromwell's Western Design in 1655, the new royal colony of Jamaica held an uncertain place in the growing empire, at once made up, in the English popular imagination, of both human death and wildly fecund plants.[148] The unhealthy reputation of the island was the result of devastating survival rates among the English. In the first six years of settlement approximately twelve thousand Englishmen arrived, but only thirty-five hundred survived.[149] Such shocking mortality might not have surprised contemporaries, long suspicious of the damaging effects of hot climates on English bodies.[150]

At the Restoration, Jamaica's legal fate remained unresolved, as Restoration officials sought to configure imperial sovereignty on the island and define Jamaica's status within the empire. Uncertainty about Jamaica's place in the growing English empire led numerous commentators to suggest the island was not worth retaining.[151] Some, like Povey, insisted on Jamaica's potential future greatness. His personal interests in the island likely influenced his prognosis. Others disagreed, such as the Venetian envoy in London who wrote home in 1660 that the island was merely "costly and useless."[152] While Jamaica's varied topography of mountains, plateaus, and coastal plains seemed to offer many possibilities for investment and future agricultural success, such heterogeneous terrain likewise presented a range of complications.

Beyond its variegated environmental features, the island was demographically, politically, legally, and economically unsettled. To promote their claims to the island, the English asserted that the island had been only sparsely populated by Spanish, free black, and enslaved residents before 1655.[153] Their declarations about Spanish inattention and lack of improvement in Jamaica served to justify English aggression and claims of possession. From their arrival, English rhetoric dismissed the legitimate possession of its previous residents. Early English commentators in Jamaica were military men who had participated in Cromwell's Western Design, and many noted a need for cultivation and greater political intervention on the island. Recounting his first impressions, the soldier Henry Whistler was wholly unimpressed by the conditions in Jamaica. He could not imagine why the Spanish had called Jamaica the "Garden of the Indges." Whistler acknowledged that it may have been an impressive garden once upon a time, "but," he wrote, "this I will say, the Gardeners have bin very bad, for heare is very litell more then that which growth naterallie."[154] Two decades later, other observers continued in the same vein, claiming that the old Spanish plantations were "less Considerable then those made by the English."[155] These and similar claims that the Spanish and free and enslaved black residents of the island had not been good gardeners, failing in their duties to transform the disordered wilderness of the Caribbean island into a cultivated garden, served as English propaganda about rightful ownership. Failure to garden, or to manipulate the landscape in certain ways, was constantly remarked upon as a failure of civility and a failure of possession.[156] Like Lynch and Whistler, Richard Blome characterized the former Spanish residents as merely *using* wild pimiento pepper but failing to labor to cultivate this potentially lucrative commodity and "very Aromatical" spice. The new English proprietors framed their criticisms of Spanish rule in gardening terms.[157] The former residents were portrayed as poor managers of Jamaica's nature for failing to improve the island and its airs. In contrast, the English sought to legitimize their rule by constructing magnificent gardens of East Indian spices. Gardening improved upon fallen nature, returning it to an idealized, Edenic state. Extensive, cultivated gardens and grounds were praised as a "'paradise' in comparison with 'Nature's shames and ills.'"[158]

The transplanted specimens in Ford's plans may have been intended for those lands that were to be set aside for a grand estate, in particular, a sprawling royal demesne of four hundred thousand acres. The Council of Foreign Plantations included instructions to set aside this vast demesne for the king's particular use in their commission to General Edward D'Oyley, in which they further urged D'Oyley, as governor, to settle the colony.[159] The demesne was intended by the king as "a marke of Our soveranity."[160] Such extensive holdings would have represented a significant percentage of the island's arable lands.[161] By referring to large swaths of the island as the king's demesne, the Council emphasized the king's personal, royal rule; he was lord over his extensive Jamaican manor. Although a garden and an empire can appear to be too distinct in scale to theorize together, the size of the king's extensive royal demesne makes the conceptual leap a little less dizzying; the king's garden corresponded with the outlines of his royal colony.

However, the rhetoric of English improvement and gardening prowess masked a very different reality on the ground. Five years after conquest, the English soldiers on the island had failed to plant enough for consumption, and D'Oyley wrote to the Commissioners of the Admiralty on February 1, 1660, that they were in "extreame necessity" and required provisions.[162] The only "mercy" that proved to D'Oyley that God had not entirely forsaken them was that some of his soldiers had the "good success of finding out ye negroes where they have lurked this four yeares undisturbed who haveinge built a Towne & planted about two hundred acres of provisions" and had been forced to hand over their crops after "submitting themselves to us."[163] Clearly the reality of who was doing the work of cultivation on Jamaica and transforming Jamaica into a productive "garden" was a different story of improvement than Whistler and his English compatriots would have liked to imagine. While African-descended communities and maroon communities residing in Jamaica readily proved they were more than capable of cultivating land to sustain themselves and their own communities, the English were barely scraping by. Among the "extreame necessit[ies]" suffered by the English, as noted by D'Oyley, was the "want of shoos and all things necessary for souldiers to March." He sought the assistance of the commissioners, whom he charged with the "neglect of this place," deploring the conditions in Jamaica.[164] He had little confidence that retaining and improving the island was worth the necessary cost and effort and regularly wrote as much to his superiors in London.[165]

In addition to English failures to cultivate and improve in order to meet their own claims about what constituted legitimate legal possession, Jamaica's status within the English empire was politically uncertain, in part because it remained demographically unsettled; a committee of the Council of Foreign Plantations questioned whether or not it should properly be called a colony.[166] Jamaica was neither entirely a military occupation nor a civilian colony of planters, but, as various commentators suggested, some hybrid of the two, failing at both.[167] Officials claimed the island had been ineffectively planted because it was host to a volatile mix of disgruntled ex-soldiers, new planters, and maroon communities. Committees of the Council of Foreign Plantations offered suggestions about how to transform this unsettled populace into a proper colony. They claimed Jamaica lacked the necessary numbers and lacked the right kind of people necessary to ensure a flourishing colony. The Council was especially wary of the soldiers who remained in Jamaica. They disdained soldiers as laborers, claiming such men were both unwilling and unapt for the work of agriculture "and that they became soulders because they would not labour."[168] For numerous reasons, the Council suggested the speedy payment and disbandment of the army.[169] Some of these definitional questions remained unresolved until the colony was declared a royal colony in February 1661. Other uncertainties remained.

As the king's new Council of Foreign Plantations plotted the best methods for "peopling & settling the Island Jamaica" in early 1661, they suggested promoting a person of status and reputation to a position of power. They declared that such a maneuver would "more fullie declare his Matyes Estimation of the place, & his purpose to settle itt, wch will encourage great numbers of people to transplant themselves."[170] Their plans reveal methods by which they might encourage those with estates and fortunes to plant the island. According to the Council, "without people of Estates, noe place can be eyther comprended or settled, for poore planters are incapable of producing any quantityes of Manufactures or goods, nor can they find out ye advantages or improve the Island."[171] The Council lacked faith in the ability of people without wealthy estates to cultivate useful goods, improve the island, or direct Jamaica's economic and political fate. According to this logic, the king and his extensive garden demesne might have been the most desirable cultivator of all, as it would reveal his "estimation" of the place, transforming Jamaica's fate in the process.[172] Whereas some officials thought "poore planters" would not properly improve the island, others saw the "large and fertile" island as a refuge for the poor of the West Indies and England alike. The island could welcome what we might call environmental refugees from neighboring plantations where they had already worn out the soil, "and their woods waste[d]," while the "multitudes of vagrants" in England might live honestly and plentifully. In this vision, all such settlers might become consumers of English manufactures, which would encourage employment in England.[173]

Residents also debated with officials about what it meant that the island was a colony of conquest and what legal implications that status might have for how residents should be governed. Even as late as 1670, long after it had become a royal colony, Governor Thomas Modyford reported to Lord Arlington that the island's planters were anxious. They worried that if Jamaica was an island of conquest, and that conquest had been paid for by the state, the king might arbitrarily levy taxes to increase royal revenue.[174] Colonial officials' letters to the "Councell for forrain Plantacõns" advised that the sooner a "Body of Lawes" for the island was assented to by the king, the better "for Incouraging Others to come, when they know what Lawes they shall be Governed by."[175] In other words, confusion over the status of Jamaica, and by what laws the colony would be governed, may have slowed rates of immigration.

Jamaica also remained unsettled in the broader geopolitical context. Spain still laid formal claim to the island until 1670, and threats of possible Spanish naval fleets aiming to return Jamaica to Spanish control dotted officials' accounts in these years.[176] Rumors continued to swirl even after Spain's formal secession in 1670. Planters feared that the king intended to sell the island back to the Spanish. Modyford reported that planters "advised their factors not to plant for as one lately expressed it is not a place to live long or get an estate in as affairs now stand betwixt England and Spain."[177]

Prior to declaring it royal colony, England's leaders debated whether it was worth the time, money, and effort to hold on to Jamaica and to continue to invest in its improvement. Five years after English forces first captured the island, D'Oyley wrote repeatedly to the Commissioners of the Admiralty and painted a bleak and unpromising picture of neglect, and extreme necessity, about "this Unhappy designe & place."[178] If he planned to hold on to Jamaica, the king's advisers encouraged Charles II to cultivate the island and promote stability. An ideal monarch was obliged to provide protection to subjects and their property if they were expected to remain loyal subjects at home or in the colonies.[179] Royalist writers like John Evelyn heralded Charles II as a good gardener of Jamaica's botanical riches. In *Sylva*, Evelyn commended the king's treatment of the island's pimiento trees, a spice used in the preparation of chocolate and a commodity he praised for its "mixture of so many *Aromatics* in *one*." According to Evelyn it was "by the most prudent, and princely care of his *Majesty* that I am assur'd of a late solemn Act of *Councel*, enjoyning the preserving of that incomparable *Spice* . . . that there is not onely prohibited the destruction of these *Trees* (for it seems some *Prodigals* us'd to cut them down for the more easie gathering) but order taken likewise for their *propagation*."[180] Thus, he praised the king for simultaneously preventing wanton deforestation and promoting afforestation of an aromatic commodity, earning Evelyn's approbation. Indeed, a good gardener preserved and propagated useful specimens but also acted immediately to control riotous weeds. According to Evelyn, a gardener was comparable to the "monarch & Generall" who must "governe this numerous or rather innumerable people, the glorious inhabitants" of the garden, and must do so with "dexterity, polity, Art, & particular oeconomie."[181] The poet Abel Evans would later similarly compare a gardener's swift action to control unruly vegetation as akin to an emperor or king pruning or rooting out political riotousness to preserve the health and safety of the kingdom.[182] Gardens, as metonyms for the kingdom, suggested that gardeners, like kings, planted, pruned, managed, and improved the residents of their green and leafy realms. Both chose which plants to naturalize in their gardens. Wild spaces were transformed into something well-ordered. The king's control over landscapes undergirded his claims of rightful stewardship of England and its empire.

Restoration writers argued that political rulers and the country's elite landholders could and should cultivate their properties to prove themselves fit for the work of cultivating their subjects and the nation alike. As Evelyn wrote to Lord Danby, who oversaw the maintenance of royal forests, he thought leaders should ideally model themselves on "Cicero, Hortensius & the purpl'd Senators in the midst of Business & State Affairs," who "went often to their *Tusculans* and Wimbledons to irrigate and refresh the *Platanus* with whose very hands they sign'd the Fate of Empires and controll'd the World."[183] He heralded cultivation as an ideal activity for leaders, and this "hortulian" way of thinking represented the capacious, if fanciful, aims of several Restoration writers and officials. The newly restored Charles II likely realized landscapes were a powerful place for political theater. Gardens were microcosms not only of the nation but of the empire. An impressive garden in London or Jamaica was an assertion of his right to the throne after his long exile. Manipulating and managing nature was a way to make his rule seem more *natural* and undergirded a belief that in domestic and colonial environments alike people and plants required careful management.[184] Ideally, Charles II could embellish and adorn the landscape with scented plants, turn "wild" plants and people into cultivated specimens, and similarly transform Jamaica into a landscape that was recognizably gardened, properly civilized, and ready for English habitation. In Jamaica the king could be the good gardener required to counter the perceived ill effects of Spanish rule and all of their perceived gardening—and political—failures.

Mitigating catastrophic loss of life and promoting the demographic health of the island was essential to the future status of Jamaica if England's leaders chose to maintain it. Efforts to preserve the lives of residents and soldiers on Jamaica began during the Interregnum, as officials sought to stem the catastrophic loss of life on the island. The committee charged with managing Cromwell's American affairs received a letter dated October 30, 1657, from Lieutenant-General William Brayne, delivered to them by Admiral William Goodsonn, who had been left in charge after Penn's departure, containing requests for "Phisicall and Chirurgicall Medicines" as well as hatchets, axes, iron, powder, pistol molds, and coal.[185] In December the committee recorded supplies sent to Jamaica, including food for two thousand men for six months, and "A proportion of medicamts both for physicke and Chirurgery to the value of one hundred pounds."[186] Officials and officers also sought local commodities to ameliorate sickness.

Interest in the medicinally efficacious commodities of Jamaica continued during the Restoration era. Jamaica's receiver-general, Thomas Tothill, identified a range of medicinally useful products on Jamaica in a report prepared for the Council of Foreign Plantations. In his survey of the island's "commodities" he affirmed the presence of cacao, indigo, salt, and sugar, as well as other products that the planters believed to be healthful drugs.[187] Tothill also mentioned *Cassia fistula*, known for its purgative qualities, growing in Jamaica. While it is unlikely that Tothill would have known it, *Cassia fistula* was indigenous to Southeast Asia and had been successfully introduced to the island by the Spanish. The English may have been busy dismissing Spanish botanical knowledge in order to further justify their capture of the island, but the Spanish had already succeeded in the transplantation of a highly desirable early modern drug to the island. The same might be said of China root, similarly native to Asia, or tamarind, indigenous to Africa, which was likely transplanted and cultivated by people of African descent on the island. Tothill also mentioned "lignum vitae," or wood of life, due to its medicinal virtues, vanilla, achiote, and "sweet-smelling and other curious woods," thereby emphasizing the valuable drugs and sweet-smelling woods found growing on Jamaica.[188] Over the next two decades, in reports back to the London, officials regularly emphasized the "abundance" of "Drugges" that "doe cure many hurts, ulcers, and distempers" in their reports on the island.[189]

In his letters on behalf of the Royal Society and the king, Povey inquired about the impact of the local environment on the bodies of its residents, collecting information that might be of use.[190] Such localized knowledge of colonial climates was considered to be critical to successful settlement; colonists "thought about the air and its impact on human life in terms of the spaces within which everyday activities occurred."[191] Qualities of the air, including scent and temperature, could be altered and colonists might craft "artificial Aire" to make up for any qualities it naturally lacked.[192] Travel writers and authors of promotional literature regularly noted salubrious airs in various colonies to induce settlers to transplant themselves, citing the "fresh ruddy Complexions" and old ages attained by residents who inhaled them.[193] If the airs of Jamaica were not yet ideally suited to English bodies, they might replicate the verdure of Carolina, for example, by cultivating "sweet smelling" cedar and cyprus trees, fragrant myrtles, bays and laurels, and sassafras, "whose Bark and Leaves yield a pleasing Smell" as well as offering a variety of healthful properties when ingested.[194] If transplanted, such aromatic botanicals might similarly condition Jamaica's airs. Elsewhere, agricultural and husbandry manuals encouraged the transplantation and cultivation of plantations of pines because they "exceedingly improve the air" with "their *odiferous* and *balsamical* emissions," while simultaneously providing ornamentation. By maintaining their verdure all year long, pines were visually refreshing; they offered eyes the relief of "a perpetual spring."[195] The writer Thomas Amy praised planters in Carolina who arranged useful trees, such as the mulberry, in "Rows and Walks . . . for Use, Ornament and Pleasure" in cultivated gardens, thereby ensuring the land was "beautified and adorned."[196] A well-ordered landscape was pleasing to both the eye and the nose.

However, not all trees were verdant and healthful. In *A Description of the Island of Jamaica* (1672) Richard Blome looked to Virginia for evidence that dangerous airs might be refashioned to better suit English humoral bodies. It was only "of late," he acknowledged, that Virginia had come to be "blest with a sweet and wholesome *Air*," as well as a clime that was "very agreeable to the *English*." Blome attributed this alteration to "the clearing of *Woods*; so that now few dyeth of the *Countreys* disease, called the *Seasoning*."[197] If the air might be made wholesome and sweet by cutting trees in Virginia, so might the English effect such a transformation in Jamaica. Blome was especially critical of the thickly wooded parts of Jamaica where "[the] *Woods* being also thick, and close, rendreth the *Aire* less agreeable, then the North and South parts, which are more plain and open."[198] Open, cultivated fields and orderly, scented gardens compared favorably to the thick, uncultivated woods of the mountainous interior. Visitors and new officials to Jamaica advised clearing this woodland, thereby alleviating the stagnant air in those dark, dense locations where maroon communities were assumed to dwell. Such actions would render the air more agreeable to English settlers, by making it less "thick, and close," while simultaneously opening the ground to the light and heat of the sun and its many perceived healthful properties.[199] In Jamaica, as in many other parts of the English empire, heavily wooded areas were regarded with suspicion. Not only were they dark, confused, overgrown, and unwholesome, they were also presumed to provide cover for a range of social outsiders living beyond the bounds of English society.[200]

In addition to manipulating the qualities of the air, the king's gardens would provide healthful medicines that might be consumed by residents and sold as commodities. Transplanting "usefull" East Indian commodities, like pepper, might ensure Jamaica's future in the empire. Creating a successful polity required people to plant and cultivate the island and to stay alive long enough to do so. Without both, a colony would founder. Jamaica's future integration into the empire thus depended upon colonists' transformation of the environment to suit English bodies, as well as cultivating commodities that would fill their pockets and tempt others to settle. However, there remained some anxiety about transplanting foreign commodities in English soil. While Povey's letters make no mention of the potential dangers in gathering various sweet-smelling specimens from around the world together in the king's "plantations" in Jamaica and England, many authors encouraged caution when importing aromatic, spicy smells into the English empire.[201] Early modern men and women associated countries to the east with warmth, fragrance, and sensorial luxuriance. But such sensory delights were simultaneously coded as overly pleasure-focused, without virtue, or lustful.[202] Or, as some writers warned when referencing Jamaica's abundant verdure, something with beautiful, ornate, and colorful exteriors might mask a rotting interior. The transplantation of varied scented spices raised questions about the potential effects of foreign scents on the bodies of residents of Jamaica and London.[203] It remained a question if the commodities associated with these regions could be repurposed or transformed to suit English bodies and society.[204]

While the particular pepper transplantation schemes outlined in this chapter may have failed to transpire, Povey maintained an active interest in promoting the cultivation of therapeutic plants in Jamaica, turning his attention to botanical goods already thriving in Jamaica in lieu of transporting them from the East Indies. Among his documents is one entitled "A briefe survey of Jamaica," in which he championed a range of potentially useful flora, such as pimiento, which "growes plentifully in Mountaines," as well as tamarind and *Cassia fistula*.[205] The Royal Society joined him in praising the health benefits of Jamaica's indigenous pimiento pepper and claimed it could be a suitable replacement for East Indian pepper.[206] The Society claimed both types of pepper offered medicinal benefits, and an anonymous author of a treatise for the Royal Society suggested that pimiento might even surpass the original.[207] Indeed the "Jamaica pepper tree" "may deservedly be counted the best & most temperate & innocent of common spices, & fit to come into greater use & to gaine more ground then yet it hath of the E. India commodities of this kind" so that it might even "far surpass" the former "by promoting the digestion of meat."[208] Blome celebrated the *"Piemente"* as a "spice in the form of *East-India Pepper*" that was "very Aromatical" as well as "of a curious *Gousto*, having the mixt taste of divers *Spices*."[209] This aromatic spice grew plentifully on the island and was celebrated as a possible replacement commodity for the desired variety from the east.[210] Henry Stubbe, author of an early English treatise on chocolate, called it the *"most delicate of Spices"* with "a most *delicate smell*" and served to *"amen[d] the breath,"* was "excellent against Wind, and helps digestion" among other benefits.[211] Stubbe further claimed other writers "recommend [pimiento] for fragrancy, and taste, beyond any Spice" and that it had "an excellent smell."[212] With or without transplantation from the East, colonial promoters continued to seek a saleable botanical product to ensure Jamaica's political, economic, and demographic success. When Thomas Tothill, receiver-general, wrote to the Council of Foreign Plantations, he affirmed the presence of pimiento and its promising status as a saleable commodity. According to Tothill, the mountains were full of pimiento, and if someone were to encourage the cultivation and trade, fifty thousand pounds might be sold annually.[213]

By the 1670s the celebrated commodities of Jamaica included innumerable medicines. In addition to pimiento, the island abounded in "Drugges," which, according to common knowledge included: "Guarum, Chinarootes, Cassiafistula, Achiote, tamarind, and divers gummes and Rootes where wth experience[d] planter doe cure many hurts ulcers, and distempers and these wee have from an intelligent Dr: . . . Contra yerva, Ciperas, assolepia Adiandum, Nigrum, Aloes, Aucumisa grestis, sumach, auacina, Miselto with any other Drugges, Balsomes, and Gumes, whose names are not remembered."[214] Collected among

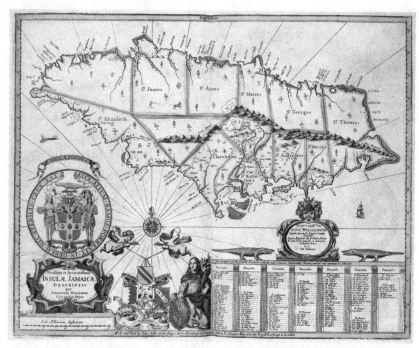

FIGURE 5.2. John Seller's map suggests the continued importance of cacao to the English in 1672. The map includes a notation of the "Cocoa Walks" in the Parish off Saint Catherine and offers a comparative account of the planters cultivating cacao, indigo, sugar, and cotton on the island. John Seller, *Novissima et accuratissima Insulae Jamaicae*, in *Atlas maritimus, or A book of charts* (London, 1672). Map reproduction courtesy of the Norman B. Leventhal Map & Education Center at the Boston Public Library.

Povey's papers, the document, "A briefe survey of Jamaica," included a subsection entitled "Some Consideracons why the king should keepe Jamaica in his Possession" that explained that Jamaica provided the empire with things that did not thrive anywhere else, including "Cocoa, Hydes, Turtleshell, Copper, and by report Silver, Woods, Dyes, Gumes, Drugges, infinite kinds of fruytes, fowl, and fish, wch they have not" in the other English plantations.[215] Sugar does not appear on that list. Tothill advised planters to plant cacao because "it will be of far more gain to the planter than indigo, cotton, ginger, or sugar."[216] Although Povey's plan to transplant pepper may never have materialized, interest in the useful "Drugges" and commodities growing in Jamaica remained critical to colonists, merchants, and court officials.

Transplanted, Naturalized, and "Indenizon'd"

Departing from their native soil was cause for some anxiety, and colonists wondered if residence in new lands would alter health, temperament, and subject status. Early modern men and women believed that soil exerted a powerful influence on health. Royal Society member Robert Boyle thought that many diseases might originate in soil and that travelers should be aware of soil quality before traveling. Boyle urged travelers to seek out "What Countrys are only or chiefly upon the account of the *soil*, the most apt to breed the Disease, whether in the Natives, or in strangers. [As Ireland does much dispose me, especially new comers to Fluxes, and Kent to Agues.]"[217] Travel and relocation to new soils posed dangers. Colonists also worried about consuming plants rooted in foreign soils. Moreover, if they were no longer residents of England, neither tilling its fields nor eating products grown in that soil, were they still English? Were there environmental dimensions of political as well as personal identity? English nationality law was often "muddled" on these questions.[218] There remained a great deal of confusion about the legal status of English colonists and their descendants as they took up residence overseas. One element of that confusion was whether or not bodily transformations associated with travel and settlement in unfamiliar climes influenced political identity and loyalties as well as health and humors. Just as plants might be naturalized to new soils, people might similarly adjust. Moreover, colloquial understandings of subject status had environmental dimensions; the departure from home soils and *naturalization* elsewhere hinted at both a new physical and legal status.

In order to better understand the potential range of physical transformations associated with transplantation overseas, colonists looked to garden plant transplantation successes and failures to draw conclusions about the possibilities and dangers awaiting their own relocation. As a result, one of the critical questions for colonists was whether or not familiar or desirable plants might be transplanted to new soils. The possibilities of plant acclimatization were critical to any number of colonial projects.[219] Colonists often desired to transplant familiar plants, in order to consume familiar foods.[220] Travel writers, officials, and early colonists pointed to the successful transplantation of plants as evidence that colonization would be a success and indicated the potential for successful human transplantation. Colonial promoters regularly touted a colony's close resemblance to England's climate and soil and suggested that plant acclimatization of English plants would be quite straightforward, enabling colonists to consume familiar foods.[221] They pointed out that even those places that were not immediately imagined as ideal for English bodies, like Jamaica, could also support a range of "*European Garden Plants*," especially in the mountains, where it was "higher" and "cooler" and there was more rain.[222] Furthermore, they promised that with human intervention and cultivation they might further transform the Jamaican environment to make it even more suitable to English plants and stomachs. Experiments that revealed which plants could be successfully transplanted provided crucial economic information but also signaled whether or not colonists could re-create their preferred diets in unfamiliar locations and by doing so stave off the potentially detrimental impacts of hot climates and unfamiliar foods on their health, complexions, behavior, and identity.[223]

Moreover, if colonists failed to find a native plant to cultivate for sale, they hoped to transplant a lucrative botanical product, such as the scheme to transplant pepper outlined in this chapter. Without a saleable native or transplanted plant, economic development might founder, and people might move to a more promising colony. Additionally, the threat lingering over all transplantation schemes was the fear that acclimatization might fail or that plants might be utterly transformed in the process (and perhaps even lose whatever quality made them valuable).[224] Gardeners acknowledged the challenges of transplantation and acclimatization. Not all plants could thrive under new environmental conditions. The color, taste, or medically efficacious qualities might be detrimentally altered. Anxieties over such potential transformations resulted in experiments to study the phenomenon.

Members of the Royal Society, like Daniel Cox, formulated experiments to study the potential effects of changing temperatures on plant life. In his "A History of Vegetables," read to the Society in 1668, Cox wondered "How the Aer might bee made to change the Nature or Properties of Plants." Cox recommended utilizing fellow-member Robert Boyle's "Pneumatick Engine" so that the plants would be "excluded from the Aer," and they might be able to determine if air was the source of nourishment and what might happen to the "Nature or Properties" of plants without it.[225] In his proposals Cox likewise suggested experimenting with how varied temperatures might affect a plant. He wanted to know

what would happen if plants were exposed to extremely cold temperatures, reflecting what would happen if plants from warmer regions were
brought "suddainly out of warme into cold places, and the Contrary."[226]
Underlying Cox's experiments were questions about plant transplantation and environmental change. If plants were moved and exposed to
alternative climates and unfamiliar "Aer," in what ways would this alter
the plant? These were not theoretical questions alone but were of critical
consequence to colonists relocating to places with unfamiliar climates
and soils.

New colonists, such as individuals on their way to Jamaica, required
information about local plants as well as those that might be successfully
transplanted and acclimatized, even if altered in the process. In a memo
entitled "Inquires Recommended to Colonel Linch going to Jamaica,"
members of the Royal Society compiled a set of questions that they sent
with Colonel Thomas Lynch, who was to return to Jamaica at the behest
of the king to serve as lieutenant governor in 1670. They instructed Lynch
"to try the raising of rice, olives, coffee-berries, currants, and the like, in
Jamaica. As also to try, whether our late-ripe fruit here in England, as
all sorts of winter-pears and the like, will not ripen in Jamaica sooner
on?"[227] The Society further wondered "whether the Potatos, yt grow in ye
saltpeter-grounds there, ripen two months sooner than elsewhere," likewise suggesting that different soils might alter the speed of ripening.[228]
Early ripening had many benefits, but there were also fears that ripe,
fecund abundance might mask rotting interiors and result in shortened
life spans. As one almanac author warned, earlier ripening or "Generation" led to earlier "Corruption."[229] Another author offered this "Friendly
Advice": "Soon ripe, soon rotten."[230]

William Hughes, author of *The American Physitian* (1672), agreed
that the particular air, soil, and climate in which a plant put down roots
changed its qualities. He mused that cacao trees growing in different
countries "differ[ed] in quality very much," particularly in accordance
with "the places whence they come; as those which grow in *Mexico*, are
not in all respects (how well soever cured) like unto them in *Jamaica*:
and so for those in *Nicaragua*, *Soconusca*, *Guatimala*, &c. by reason
these places are in somewhat different Climates and Degrees." In other
words, cocoa kernels differed in size and "quality" depending on the latitude and climate wherein they were cultivated.[231] Similarly, in his treatise on the botanical productions of Jamaica, Hans Sloane meditated on
the potentially transformative effects of the sun on transplanted European plants. Sloane suggested that colors of botanical specimens were

"*heightened by the Sun*," offering by way of example that newly sprouted tulips were white, but "*when the Sun and Light has farther acted upon them, they arrive at that variety we observe in them with pleasure.*" He went on to argue that this might also explain why they "*may have in European Gardens different Colours, from what they are in their native soil, and a warmer Sun.*" He concluded that transplantation changed the color of plants removed from their native soils.[232] Underlying the queries for Lynch, Cox's experiments on plants, and writings from Hughes and Sloane, were concerns about transplantation and transformation. If plants were moved and exposed to new soils and climates or unfamiliar "Aer," in what ways would this alter the plant and its saleable characteristics, such as its scent, taste, or medicinal properties?

The extent of the malleability of plant size, form, color, taste, and quality had long been the focus of botanical experimentation. Gardeners and natural philosophers alike recognized that many plants could not thrive if transplanted to widely varied climatic zones or might be altered in the process. As John Beale wrote to the secretary of the Royal Society, Henry Oldenburg, "I can give yu a large liste of Vegetables, wch from ye same seede do quite alter their figures, & other qualityes, in severall climates."[233] Others required careful introduction into new climates, allowing for a gradual adjustment, much like a process of "hardening off."[234] During transplantation a plant might "languish" and starve, or "grow so luxuriate," or "change their very shapes, colours, leaves, roots, and other parts," depending on the qualities of the new airs and soils.[235] New environments altered the properties of plants, even to the point of unrecognizability. As a result, gardeners sought to retain or improve the salubrious, aesthetic, or salable properties of plants during transplantation. A critical question for those scheming to transplant ships laden with East Indian plants to London and Jamaica would have to have been whether or not the desirable properties of East India pepper would be transformed in the process. If essential qualities were altered in the process, could good gardeners intervene to mitigate deleterious effects?

Early modern gardens had long taught gardeners that nature was malleable and transformable. Gardens were ripe with transformative possibilities and were sites where experimentation in plant malleability might occur. As Royal Society member Thomas Sprat acknowledged, transplantation could improve upon nature, but not necessarily. According to Sprat, "Sometimes the *Soil* and the *Air* being chang'd, will give a new force to the new *Guests*; as the *Arabian Horse*, by mingling with our *Breed*, produces a more serviceable *Race* than either of them single." But on other occasions "the alteration will be for the wors," such as grape vines transplanted from France to England or "the *Horses* and *Dogs* of *England* into *France*; both of which are found to degenerat exceedingly: Their *Soil*, of *pleasure* and *delight*; and our *Air* and our *Earth* being more proper to beget *valor* and *strength*."[236] Thus there was a range of possible outcomes during transplantation. Transplanted plants might not take root, or their desirable aesthetic or medicinal qualities might be diminished or transformed. Meanwhile, it is clear that contemporaries worried that their own bodies were similarly malleable and transformable. As the Royal Society discussed transplanting plants, they drew broader parallels to better understand "the transformation of creatures by means of the qualification of the place, wherein they are fostered" such that Europeans inhabiting Africa "turn black" while black residents of England "become white" in a process analogous to the botanical residents of gardens.[237]

Indeed, one of the many reasons the successful acclimatization of plants to Jamaica was so important to so many writers, colonists, and officials was that successfully transplanted plants reaffirmed the suitability of the soil and air to human transplants. Plants naturalized to new soils offered evidence that human transplantation might similarly succeed. Writers drew parallels between plant and human bodies. After establishing such parallels, they claimed that what happened to plants during transplantation offered evidence of what happened to human bodies. Plant and animal acclimatization—and its risks, challenges, and rewards—offered clues about the likelihood of successful human "seasoning," a period of physical adjustment that bodies suffered in a new environmental context. Looking to plants to better understand human bodies, and vice versa, was a regular feature of works on agriculture and natural history in the early modern era. Varied commentators insisted that the benefits of research into the processes of the vegetable world would have profound implications and applications in the human world.[238] Careful examination of both the plant and animal world, they argued, offered insights. Natural philosophers reasoned that the same deity had designed both plants and animals. Both were the "*Contrivances of the same Wisdom*," thus many felt confident in pursuing correlations between them.[239] Writers maintained that certain structural similarities allowed for the translation of ideas between plant and animal bodies. Members of the Royal Society—Charles II's "Parliament of Nature" in one contemporary's colorful phrasing—assessed the risks and conducted experiments to determine the influence of changing temperatures on plant bodies and often claimed that their work served to promote better understanding of parallel processes in human bodies.[240] They wanted to better understand acclimatization.[241] Officials also thought about how to use this knowledge to advance their own understanding of what happened to transplanted English subjects.

Authors debated about the extent to which people were transformed in the process of colonization. Although writers often referred to the physical adjustment to new places as a process of "seasoning," others used the evocative term "naturalize," which held within it a range of meanings. The term described a physical adjustment but was also a term used in English nationality law. Writers frequently used the terms "enfranchise" and "naturalize" to discuss the transplantation and introduction of plants into new soils and climates. Words that in other contexts were used to discuss more abstract concepts such as membership in a body politic or the granting of particular kinds of privileges were utilized to discuss a range of material processes in the garden, and vice versa. Early modern political ideology drew from and contributed to the conceptual force of garden cultivation as a metaphor for education, culture, and governance. But these metaphors worked both ways. By discussing plants as naturalizing to new soils, these metaphors infused these concepts in the political realm with new shades of meaning. Metaphors don't merely reflect reality; they create a reality.[242] The use of political concepts to explain gardening concepts, and vice versa, suggests the deeply physical, and unstable, conception of the political subject.

Among the "novell experiments" encouraged by midcentury garden writers was the attempt "to *enfranchise* such plants as are strangers" into new soils and gardens. After enfranchising strangers to the air and soil of the place, the gardener should attempt "Secondly to Civilise such as are wilde, and to amplify, & adorne . . . by alterations."[243] *Enfranchising* plants into the realm of the garden allowed gardeners to take on responsibilities normally reserved for the king or Parliament. Meanwhile, it was clear to contemporaries that not all plants traveled successfully. As the anonymous correspondent of the midcentury intelligencer Samuel Hartlib wrote, "some Plants are great Travellers," whereas others needed the help of human industry for successful transplantation, and "like the settling of new colonies," they required careful cultivation, guidance, and human industry.[244] The author claimed sugar was one such plant, which with time and effort both traveled and colonized new regions. Other plants were "strickt Citizens, onely of one Countrey or Place," and despite efforts to make them "Denizons of other Countreyes," they "have allwayes refused to dwell in any place, but their owne homes." Such plants could not be naturalized in new places or thrive beyond home soil.[245] By describing plant specimens as thriving citizens at home versus suffering denizens abroad, the author lays bare his assumptions about the environmental underpinnings of political identity and belonging.

While some plants traveled and colonized, and others always remained at home, some plants, like pepper, were "admitting of a Transplantation" but "will allwayes require one & the same, Clyme." In other words, transplanting pepper posed a challenge, but it was possible under the right constellation of climatic conditions.[246] This was also the case for cotton, indigo, and other plants that "will hardly appear or shew [themselves] at all in a colder Countrey, whereas others will admitt of severall Climates." Pepper was not a great traveler, but there was potential for transplantation, particularly if it was the right climate.

The garden writer John Evelyn similarly used political terms like "endenized" to describe the physical transformation of strange and new plants into good citizens of the garden. During transplantation a plant might "languish" and starve, or "grow so luxuriate," or "change their very shapes, colours, leaves, roots, and other parts," depending on the quality of the new airs and soils.[247] Evelyn encouraged gardeners to consider modifying the air around garden plants to assist in the process and to "make the remedy as well *regional* as *topical*."[248] In this way "Strangers yet amongst us" might become "indenizon'd amongst us, and grow every generation more reconcileable" to the region's air and soil.[249] Thus, he told a story of a slow process of acclimatization to a soil, ultimately resulting in plants "indenizon'd" to England. While some plants and people might be transplanted with success, others would "always require" a familiar climate to thrive and could not be naturalized in unfamiliar grounds. Instead, they were best suited to their native soil; it was the ground in which their identities were rooted. There were important health and environmental dimensions to the ways in which people defined a nation's political character, which explains why colonists expressed anxiety about how their bodies would react in new lands. A departure from those lands and climates might not only alter their health and character but also call their political loyalties into question.[250]

Not only did authors debate about whether or not plants might be naturalized to new soils; they also debated about the naturalization of people. To what degree would new airs alter characteristics of individual bodies, and how much did that matter to defining those bodies politically? Restoration officials grappled with questions about whether—or if—to integrate non-English inhabitants as subjects in England and within the empire. Meanwhile, as colonists debated how to naturalize plants in Jamaica, they also called for an Act of Naturalization, so that the governor could declare any foreigner settled on the island who agreed to take an oath of allegiance, as naturalized, "as if born within his Majesty's Dominions."[251] The use of the term to describe both a physical adjustment to new soils and climates as well as a legal process that transformed political status suggested that political identity was, in some ways, tied to the climate, soil, and air. As a result, it remained an open question if people were still English if acclimatized over a lifetime in a new environment and suggested that political identity might be transformed alongside health and temperament.

Almost a decade earlier, in 1661, the king issued *A Proclamation for the Encouragement of Planters in His Majesties Island of Jamaica*, in which the authors of the proclamation stipulated how they might legally define those born on the island. The proclamation asserted that "All children of our Naturall born Subjects of England to be born in Jamaica shall from their respective Births be reputed to be, and shall be free Denizons of England and shall have the same priviledge to all intents and purposes as our free born Subjects of England."[252] While children birthed by "Naturall born Subjects" would have all of the privileges of denizens of England, these were not all the rights of a subject. Raingard Esser has defined seventeenth-century denizens as "citizens with limited legal rights particularly in terms of property-ownership and inheritance patterns."[253] Therefore, the specification of Jamaica-born offspring of "Naturall" subjects as denizens, not true subjects, suggests that the authors imagined that place of birth and territorial allegiance were connected. Denizens did not have rights to property and inheritance in England, the literal ground that was defined as England, which may have imbued those who lived there with particularly English characteristics. These definitions suggest key differences between Jamaica and England. Even if the islands were legally bound to the Crown, Jamaica remained a distinct physical place, composed of distinct soils and airs. Moreover, the authors of the proclamation may have imagined that this variant place was likely to pass on some embedded—and embodied—qualities to children born there, which, cultivated since birth, would mark them as distinct subjects relative to those subjects born on English soil.

Writers recognized that colonists endured a period of physical adjustment in their new homes. For example, when Sloane asserted that certain foods, like cacao, were so medicinally efficacious that they benefited

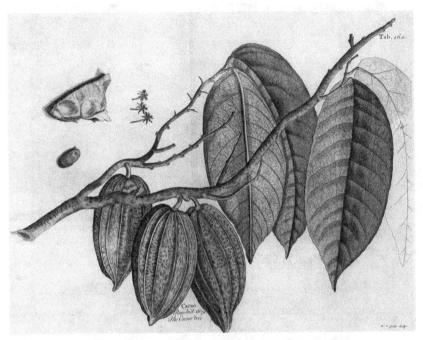

FIGURE 5.3. Hans Sloane spent fifteen months in Jamaica, 1687–88, and later hired artist and engravers to produce images of the specimens he collected. *Cacao*, in Sir Hans Sloane, *A Voyage to the Islands* (London, 1707–25). Image courtesy of the John Carter Brown Library at Brown University.

all bodies "as well Strangers as Natives, or those that are Naturaliz'd," he recognized, by making a distinction between bodies, that newcomers, those born in Jamaica, and those who had been there long enough to physically adjust to the place might require different diets or medical care.[254] Writers were deeply interested in the changes experienced by newcomers to the island and theorized about the physical process of naturalization. According to Hughes, newcomers shed thicker skins to reveal thinner skins, thereby preserving their health in the hotter climate of Jamaica. He surmised that thin skins better ensured perspiration and the transpiration and expulsion of the noxious humors from the body, and thus this process of shedding thicker skins was essential to survival. He claimed that chocolate could assist in this process and preserve health by opening pores and facilitating the body's efforts to expel ill humors. According to Hughes, "it is well observed by some, that most of those who travel from the more Northerly parts of the world

FIGURE 5.4. Hans Sloane collected many of the specimens still found in his herbarium while visiting Jamaica. He relied on enslaved people to help him collect many of his specimens. "Theobroma cacao L."— BM000589108, The Sir Hans Sloane Herbarium. Image courtesy of the Trustees of the Natural History Museum, London.

into the *Indies*, before they are Naturalized there, do, as it were, Serpent or Adder-like, change their skin; that is, the external thick skin, or scarf-skin, called the *Cuticula*, doth peel off, there coming in the place thereof another, yet more thin and lank then that was." Shedding this layer of skin was essential, Hughes argued, because "such persons as lose not their skin after this manner, so for the most part become desperately ill, and perhaps not escape death, because the fuliginous vapours want a more free transpiration." He suggested that chocolate could help with the process of "purging by Expectorations, and especially by the sweat-vents of the body," in order to prevent "unnatural fumes ascending to the head."[255] Unlike Sloane, Hughes asserted that chocolate was best suited to the bodies that had already been "Naturaliz'd to those parts, whose stomacks are more lank and weak, by reason of the external ambient heat; and therefore required something easily digested."[256] In other words, their bodies had adjusted to the climate and required a different diet, one that included chocolate.

However, Hughes warned against the frequent consumption of chocolate in England because it might accustom the stomach to lighter fare and make it less apt or able to digest heavier local foods in the future.[257] But when it came to those residents of the Indies, chocolate was the best choice. Hughes claimed that "good *Chocolate* is the only drink in the *Indies*, and I am fully perswaded is instrumental to the [p]reservation and prolonging of many an Europeans life that travels there."[258] Thus, the process of seasoning, or naturalizing, suggested everything from shedding skins to new digestive faculties. In addition to these physical processes were concomitant alterations to character. Seventeenth-century writers regularly mused about the influence of the environment on human nature and whether people might "partake somewhat of the nature of the country" where they lived.[259] Colonists to Jamaica were aware they too might "partake somewhat of the nature of the country." Investigations into the processes by which plants were transformed when they took root in the new soils of Jamaica gardens offered some insights into what sorts of transformations human bodies might undergo when they settled on the island.

It is possible that flexible meanings of the term "naturalization" show that ideas about transplanting people and plants may have merged, or emerged, from the same premises about the physical response of plants and people to nature. The plant and human denizens of the king's Jamaican gardens were both subject to transformation and acclimatization, which had economic and political ramifications. The king's two gardens were both sites to test the limits of mutability and heredity in the plant and human worlds. Both offered evidence about the kinds of traits that were alterable and those that were not. This mattered to contemporaries who were concerned with how to define "natural" subjects as they immigrated into, and emigrated from, England.

At the Restoration, Charles II sought to define imperial consolidation legally and physically. In interconnected projects on either side of the Atlantic scent was used as a political and economic tool. Concerns about human and plant transplantation to the island shaped both new legislation and gardening schemes. In considering the status of Jamaica, and in planning for its future, Restoration officials imagined that plants, people, and a viable polity must be simultaneously cultivated, and fostering smellscapes and lucrative spices was one way to do so. Meanwhile, in London, temperamental crowds living their lives in a city filled with coal smoke were imagined to similarly require scented plantations to mitigate the ill effect of sooty airs. This chapter has suggested that agents of the Restoration government sought to reshape desirable subjects by transforming climatic and aromatic environments on both sides of the Atlantic, in part, by planting royally sponsored gardens and by clearing the dense woodlands of Jamaica. There is suggestive evidence that contemporaries took seriously the connections between individuals, societies, and nature and thought about how to use this knowledge to advance their own goals of imperial reform both within England and in the American colonies. Gardens were ripe with transformative possibilities and taught gardeners that nature was malleable, as were the men and women who similarly required cultivation.

Gardens might seem too limited, and their productions and smell too ephemeral or quotidian, to offer a new perspective on early modern imperial governing strategies. But perhaps the sense of vertigo one might experience while leaning in to consider the sweetly aromatic or sharp scents of flowers, spices, herbs, or trees in a garden, then leaning out to consider Restoration officials' imperial goals, might be resolved in Jamaica itself, where the garden and the polity were much the same thing, coming together in those lands that were supposed to be set aside for a royal demesne.[260] The king's royal demesne was to encompass nearly a quarter of the island's arable land. Here the king could cultivate a garden (or gardens) that paralleled the contours of a colony. Moreover, the king might mimic those Augustinian or Ciceronian models praised by contemporaries such as Evelyn. Such hands-on manipulation of the colony, through remaking its verdure and airs, signaled that Charles II was among those classical-style leaders who irrigated with one hand and "sign'd the Fate of Empires" with the other.

English officials had long compared their efforts to the work of gardeners. In terms of establishing and regulating the empire, including Jamaica, they extended their gardening metaphors when debating if and how to incorporate the island and facilitate its success. Not only did they need to locate a lucrative plant—by transplanting one or by locating one indigenous to the island—but officials during the Interregnum and Restoration agreed that Jamaica would not succeeded without people, and thus they supported the "constant supplying" of Jamaica "with People." One recommended method was "the weeding of this Comon Wealth of Vagabond, condemned Persons and such as are heere useless" and transplanting them to Jamaica. Harmful weeds in one garden might thrive and take root in more receptive soils.[261] Another method the Stuarts turned to was the capture and transportation of enslaved men and women to labor on the island. The trade in enslaved people was included in the charter of the Company of Royal Adventurers Trading by 1663, and many of the individuals who helped devise the transplantation schemes outlined in the chapter, such as Richard Ford, were involved. Ford became the deputy governor of the company, overseeing an acceleration in England's involvement in the slave trade.

Certainly a king who aspired to intervene in the bodies and temperaments of varied imperial subjects would be deeply interested in gardening texts that dealt with theories about how plants might alter the health and character of those who consumed them, breathed the scents emitted, and enjoyed the aesthetic experience of color and shape. The medical world linked color, smell, and human malleability, and this was of great interest to early modern people, and their leaders. Charles II, as both the merchant king and the gardener king, was in a position to plant, prune, cultivate, and otherwise manage his people by planting aromatic palisades and plantation emporiums. In his royal demesnes or in his plantations the king might acquire the technical skills applicable and transposable to other endeavors. In both his political and leafy realms, he might refashion the air or transform wild and unsettled inhabitants by cultivating lucrative plants with sweet scents.

Conclusion

In *Political Arithmetick*, written in the 1670s and published posthumously by his son in 1690, William Petty acknowledged that the recent suffering endured by Londoners had been both materially and psychologically damaging and difficult to bear, including the "Slaughter and Destruction of Men by the late Civil Wars and Plague," and the property damage wrought in the capital by the Great Fire of London in 1666.[1] But notwithstanding these catastrophes, Petty remained hopeful about England's present and future. He looked around at a London that was being rebuilt and claimed that since the fire the city had grown "great and glorious." Meanwhile, "the *American* plantations employ four Hundred Sail of ships; Actions in the *East-India* Company are near double the principal Money," and the "Materials for building (even Oaken-Timber) are little the dearer, some cheaper for the rebuilding of *London*" than they had been before the fire. He likewise noted that the number of beggars had not appeared to increase, nor had more people been executed as thieves in the wake of these many disasters than had been executed in the previous decades. There were splendid coaches, "magnificent" public theaters, and the king was in possession of an even "greater Navy." Moreover, "much Land has been improved, and the Price of Food [was now] so reasonable."[2] Petty asserted that the preponderance of evidence pointed to the conclusion that while England had indeed suffered its share of calamities, the world had more or less righted itself. Although Petty acknowledged remaining inequities, and that "some are poorer than others," he dismissed this as evidence of decline because, in his opinion, inequality "ever was and ever will be." If the world was no utopia, then he at least hoped his observations would remind readers "that Men eat, and drink, and laugh as they use to do," and encouraged Petty to write and bring such "comfort [to] others, being satisfied my self, that the Interest and Affairs of England are in no deplorable Condition."[3] Yet, if he had reason to feel reassured that the world was not in a "deplorable condition," he acknowledged that much work remained to be done. Utilizing his new practice of political arithmetic to make calculations and to offer advice, he noted a number of concerns and issues that might be attended to if only the government had the right information and the proper tools.

But Petty's equanimity about how the "Affairs of England [were] in no deplorable Condition," was not shared by many of his contemporaries. A number of English men and women recorded their experience of the mid- to late seventeenth century as one of disruption, instability, and disorder. After the Restoration, events of national significance, including plague, fire, and war, proved deeply unsettling. Many writers fretted about the meaning of such catastrophes for the nation and its future. While individuals like Lady Mary Rich fasted and searched their souls to unearth their own sinful roles in bringing down such punishments on the nation, those suffering from the plague—and their families—found themselves shuttered within homes and dying behind marked doors. Indeed, Petty's approval of the "great and glorious" rebuilt city muffled the experiences of those who lost homes and more in the conflagration.

Petty was not alone in heralding "improvements," and making promises to reveal how "the Impediments to Englands Greatness, [were] but contingent and removeable" with advice gleaned from his practice of political arithmetic.[4] Indeed, Petty was among an elite network of Restoration theorists who championed a particular strand of political ecology. They encouraged the king to better manage his subjects by better managing places. Charles II looked to bodies and landscapes alike as experimental sites to reinvent a role for himself after the political upheavals of the previous decades, and his long exile, had undermined his authority. Calls for landscape improvement projects could be found in a range of publications, including promotional tracts written by Bedford Level Corporation adventurers, who promised to improve the Great Level of the fens—and the sickly pallor of its residents—by constructing extensive drainage works.[5] Among the targets of these improvement schemes were numerous residents of the Restoration empire, particularly those people whom the government believed to be disorderly and riotous, including many of the residents of the City of London and those who lived in landscapes that were not considered properly English, such as swamps.

One innovative approach to the improvement of these disorderly places and people adopted by government officials was to develop plans derived from natural philosophy and medicine. For instance, when William Petty advised the judicious application of "Politicall Medicine" in a politically and socially unstable Ireland, he was an early, but by no means singular, supporter of applying new scientific methods and concepts in new political contexts.[6] Varied Restoration theorists debated how to apply "Politicall Medicine" to major projects of landscape transformation, demographic manipulation, and public health initatives. Restoration officials' claims about sick lands and people in need of state assistance proved to be a powerful and flexible rhetoric that Restoration officials applied in numerous settings. They regarded some places as ideal sites for experimentation and had an expansive sense of their right and ability to intervene. Their projects remind us that in the early modern world, ideas about the environment and ideas about bodily health were deeply interconnected. Many also hoped that Charles II would support their wide-ranging plans for improvement and become the heralded "wise Authority" who sought only the "Publick Good."[7] While Petty anticipated that a statistical analysis of populations—his new science of statecraft—would facilitate new policies to augment "Englands Greatness," he expressed no particular concern about the ethical dimensions undergirding the "transmutation" of individuals into abstract numbers to be manipulated by his political arithmetic.[8]

An example of such detached population management among improvers included their numerous schemes to transform "waste" people into productive members of society through labor. As the poor transformed wastelands into productive landscapes, they could supposedly transform their own social value in the process.[9] Thus, writers anticipated that if such individuals could be properly managed by the government, both *waste* lands and *waste* people could be made useful to the nation through their agricultural labors.[10] By cultivating the land, they could also cultivate themselves. Moreover, by laboring to grow food, they ensured that their well-nourished bodies would be more fit for labor.[11] Restoration projectors saw in agricultural improvement projects the means to simultaneously cultivate healthy bodies, robust economies, and secure social order within the growing English empire.[12]

Petty agreed that there were "spare Hands enough among the King of England's subjects," who could be more productively employed.[13] Others worried, however, that there were too few people. They feared that if a strong nation was a populous nation, there might be an inherent tension between improvement and imperialism. Both required people. Reason Melish's calls for authorities to better manage populations to ensure that they were "rightly Imployed" doing agricultural labor in England—which he promised would "add to the strength" of the nation—were not made in isolation, for instance. They were made at the same time as the king sought the means to "settle" and "impro^v ye Island of Jamaica."[14] Indeed, as Abigail L. Swingen has argued, conflicts and debates about labor in England shaped, and were shaped by, anxieties about access to labor in the colonies. According to Swingen, it was "not merely coincidental that African slavery became an integral part of English imperial designs at the same time that economic thinkers raised the issue of the empire's impact on England's domestic labor supply."[15] If some people remained uncertain about Jamaica's place in the empire, and debated which commodities might be cultivated to make it a success, the Royal African Company, led by the Duke of York, quickly claimed that the success of the plantations, including Jamaica, depended on an investment in slavery, without which the plantations would be "utterly ruined."[16] Petty's brief mention that "much land has been improved" thus obscured complicated stories about which populations were performing the labor of improvement throughout the empire.

This book has argued that Restoration officials imagined for themselves a capacious right and ability to manipulate residents of the English empire and the environments in which they resided. However, while some crafted grandiose plans for transforming landscapes and subjects, they were frequently unable to fully enforce their visions on the ground. Moreover, the local populations they intended to manipulate and control frequently acted in ways that subverted or redirected their original plans. In numerous instances, things rarely worked out in the way they were planned. Rivers overflowed their drainage banks and salt water destroyed seeds on long journeys across the ocean. By the time Petty wrote *Political Arithmetick*, he would have seen a number of his own projects ignored, underfunded, or failed.[17] Among the many projects of environmental improvement proposed by Petty and others, few were fully realized, if at all.[18] But even those projects that failed sometimes lived curious afterlives.

Nearly a century after Thomas Povey and Richard Ford set down plans to transplant spices from the East Indies to Jamaica, the Society for the Encouragement of Arts, Manufacture and Commerce sought the assistance of individuals who could "cultivate a spot in the West Indies in which plants, useful in medicine and profitable articles of commerce might be propagated and where a nursery of the valuable products of Asia and the distant parts might be formed for the benefit of His majesty."[19] Indeed, schemes designed on behalf of the king to transplant lucrative and alimentary plants from the East Indies to awaiting nurseries in the West Indies remained an ideal worth pursuing. But perhaps one of the most famous botanical transplantation schemes, made so by the onboard mutiny on the HMS *Bounty* in 1789, was the expedition ordered by George III and organized by Joseph Banks to transplant breadfruit trees from the Pacific to Jamaica and the other sugar islands. The trees were successfully delivered four years later. Planters sought assistance from the king in retrieving a cheap source of food to feed the enslaved populations on the islands.[20] Planters in Jamaica had long since invested in the cultivation of sugar and desired the transplantation of breadfruit because the trees apparently required no labor, thus ensuring the enslaved would continue to work without interruption at the backbreaking work of sugar cultivation.

As with the numerous improvement failures, in many other ways, the "empire remained more vision than reality" in the 1660s.[21] Authorities did not succeed in stitching together "soe many remote colonies" or in bringing them under a "uniforme inspeccon."[22] Instead, the rapid and large-scale territorial expansion in the decades after the Restoration era led to an empire that Owen Stanwood has described as "diverse and diffuse" in myriad ways: "Not only in geography, but in economic livelihood, political form, and ethnic composition, each of the king's plantations was a world apart."[23] Meanwhile, in the early years of the Restoration, many contemporaries questioned whether these numerous acquisitions were worth the time, effort, and cost. A primary concern for some imperial theorists was that the nation's subjects would be spread too thin if too many settlers departed to the territories. Furthermore, the king's military would likewise be overstretched. Thus, they argued that it was not necessarily a boon to England that the territory under the king's dominion had increased. Many predicted innumerable costs and confusions.

Many Restoration writers and officials attributed the range of distinctive governing styles found throughout the empire to its widespread and diverse topographies. The multiplicity of political forms posed a troubling hurdle to the Restoration government, which sought to unify and stitch these scattered places and peoples together into a uniformly governed body politic. Charles II created a council that he hoped could accomplish this ideal of a consolidated community. Proposals for this council claimed its purpose was "for the better regulating and improving of forreigne Plantations," and declared that the council aimed to develop a unified political community. These ideals of political unity resembled a properly functioning body, whose "Head and Centre is Heere," in London. Members of the council anticipated that the dispersed colonies could and should be sutured together.[24] The colonies were akin to limbs that needed to be reattached to the body politic.

Officials debated how best to govern this topographically and jurisdictionally diverse empire and discussed what governments owed their subjects, and what subjects owed their governments, at home and abroad, both in older colonies where distance and time had accustomed colonial subjects to making local decisions about governance and in new colonies acquired by force. They debated, but they also acted, and sought to transform the environment in a multiplicity of local places by promoting a range of on-the-ground projects. Through numerous manipulations to the early modern landscape, including the diverse improvement projects examined in the preceeding chapters, agents of the English Restoration government aimed to alter and redefine the nature and boundaries of the newly expanded English empire, as well as define the kinds of bodies that might become part of the imperial body. Because porous human bodies and humorally constituted temperaments were understood to be malleable, many of the improvements undertaken by agents of the Restoration government were directed toward the tactile reshaping of various bodies as well as political identities. As the size and location of territory under English control changed dramatically during these years, contemporaries reevaluated the boundaries of the English empire and reevaluated who belonged as a subject.

A resident of the new colony of New Jersey, Robert Smythe, wrote a letter in 1680 to the new governor, Edward Byllynge, in which he articulated a range of ways that colonizers might choose to treat any residents of lands they had acquired. A government might select to "new-mold, displace, or remove, contend or quarrel with" the inhabitants.[25] While many of the possible scenarios included violent encounters, or outright removal, Smythe likewise left open the possibility that the new government might "new-mold" those who were already there. One of the ways in which a community might be *remolded* was by altering the environments in which they lived, thereby initiating a range of transmutations. Drainage projectors claimed their work could alter human health by cleansing the air of miasma, for instance. Drainage further ensured that inhabitants labored at arable agriculture in properly English ways, by planting wheat and ploughing instead of gathering reeds, fowling, and fishing. New molding, moreover, suggested a range of material and cultural attributes that the colonizers might have sought to alter in subject populations, including dress and diet, such as in the case of the green children of Woolpit. When this brother and sister of unknown provenance consumed English foods and breathed English airs, these elements remade their bodies and linguistic skills, such that they lost their green hue and began to speak English.[26] Acts of eating were the means to gain sustenance, but the choice of food was a profoundly symbolic way to express broader community belonging. Moreover, in a deeply religious society like much of the early modern English Atlantic, bodies were viewed as houses of clay, temporarily housing the spirit. Thus, spiritual renewal was often expressed through the language of remolding. Physical acts performed through the body, such as fasting, also had spiritual effects, simultaneously remaking the body and soul. Ultimately, a phrase such as Smythe's "new-mold" suggested a whole range of tactile, spiritual, political, and social remaking. In the Restoration era, ideas about profound and significant social and political transformation were often imagined and described as material processes.

While many changes wrought to malleable human bodies were believed to have been for the better, this was not always the case. Early modern men and women feared how new climates, foods, and soils might affect their bodies and characters. Like the plants that derived their natures from the ground and thrived best in certain soils, people were healthiest and happiest when in their homelands, as they were partly constituted physiologically and psychologically by those soils. A person's *native soil* was the soil to which they were best suited and colonists worried what might happen if they became naturalized in their new homes. Meanwhile, plants required a range of things to survive and thrive. They required an agreeable climate—or "air"—as well as the right kind of soil. However, with the right kind of assistance, both plants and people might overcome these environmentally based limitations.

Merchants, writers, and officials angled for support for their projects by rhetorically framing their schemes as beneficial to the nation as a whole. They claimed that Charles II should manipulate the empire's nature to its advantage, thereby naturalizing his territorial ambitions at home and abroad. His ability to manage nature was also a way to establish a new basis for political authority in a tumultuous and changing world. These Restoration writers articulated a close relationship between the careful stewardship of land and the management and improvement of residents; they argued that numerous domestic and colonial places and people would benefit from the restorative "healing Balm" of Charles II.[27] Their plans relied on enduring ideas about the relationship between individuals' health and character and the environments they inhabit, to argue for ambitious environmental engineering projects. Stuart officials may have lacked the ability to plan and manage the outsized ambitions reflected in such schemes, but their plans provide insight into the political ecology of Restoration theorists and their beliefs about how subjects of their expanding empire should be rearranged morally, healthfully, and spatially.

Acknowledgments

It is a particular pleasure to write the acknowledgments at the conclusion of this years-long project because it underscores the truly collaborative nature of a historian's work. Many generous individuals and institutions have supported the research and writing of this book. I am particularly grateful for the patient mentorship of Karen Ordahl Kupperman. She has read drafts of this project over the span of many years and I am grateful for her guidance and incisive critiques. I continue to admire her wide-ranging curiosity about worlds past and present. A supportive community of scholars and mentors at NYU offered critical feedback during the early stages of research and writing. I benefited immensely from my conversations about environmental history and the history of science and medicine with Karl Appuhn. I am also grateful for constructive criticism from Martha Hodes and Guy Ortolano. The NYU Atlantic World workshop participants read and commented on numerous early drafts and taught me to be a better writer by example. Thank you to Karen Auman, Greg Childs, Christian Crouch, Nicole Eustace, Daniel Kanhofer, Andrew Lee, Alexander Manevitz, Timo McGregor, Jeppe Mulich, Hayley Negrin, Marin Odle, Emma Otheguy, Gabriel Rocha, Samantha Seeley, Jenny Shaw, Anelise Shrout, Katy Walker, and Jerusha Westbury. I was lucky to find a whole cohort of thoughtful and engaging scholars at NYU. Many of them also became friends, including Natalie Blum-Ross, Thomas Fleischman, Laura Honsberger, Larissa Kopytoff, and Carmen Soliz.

Research for this book was generously supported by several different institutions and grants. I appreciate the financial support of the Doris G. Quinn Foundation and the Colonial Dames of America. A short-term residency at Dumbarton Oaks Research Library and Collection gave me access to numerous rare books on early modern gardening practice and theory and introduced me to a diverse collection of scholars who asked great questions and stretched my imagination. The months spent at University College Cork as a Glucksman Fellow reminded me, in vivid colors, that place matters. As a Provost's Global Research Initiative Fellow at NYU London, I was able to write and complete crucial archival research. I was lucky to work side by side with Jonathan Mullins and Shannon McHugh in our offices overlooking the British Museum.

Fellowships at the American Antiquarian Society and at Winterthur Museum, Garden, and Library introduced me to many remarkable collections and knowledgeable staffs. I am particularly grateful to Ashley Cataldo for her imaginative and unexpected suggestions about where to look next. In both locations I was lucky to have many dinner conversations on the porch about the day's archival finds, and enjoyed delightful summer strolls swapping ideas and watching fireflies with the other fellows, including Jennifer Chuong, Nicholas Cooley, and Christy Pottroff. I had the opportunity to present parts of this work to a handful of helpful audiences over the years, including at the annual Omohundro Institute of Early American History & Culture Conference, a McNeil Center for Early American Studies Brown Bag Session, the Forum on European Expansion and Global Interactions Biennial Conference, the International Water History Association, and the American Society for Environmental History. I had the good fortune of meeting Katherine Johnston and Noel Edward Smyth at a summer workshop in Williamsburg, Virginia. I hope we continue to share our works-in-progress in the years to come. I am grateful for their detailed feedback and encouragement of my work. I am even more grateful for their friendship.

A few years ago, I found a home in California and a job teaching at California State University, Bakersfield. Support from the Dean's office enabled me to take a final research trip to London to track down several critical sources in the archives. The Provost's Research, Scholarship, and Creative Activity Initiative lowered my course load for two semesters so I could complete the manuscript. All of my colleagues in the History Department at CSUB have been extremely supportive, but I am particularly grateful to Stephen Allen, Mustafa Dhada, Jeanne Harrie, Clíona Murphy, Christopher Tang, Miriam Raub Vivan, and Sean Wempe for reading and commenting on proposals and portions of my work as members of the Historical Research Group. Many of my students, and their excellent questions, inspired me to rethink portions of this book. Tim Vivan generously read and edited several chapters.

For permission to incorporate a revised portion of a previously published chapter into the book, I thank Brill. The chapter, "The Aromas of Flora's Wide Domains: Cultivating Gardens, Airs, and Political Subjects in the Late-Seventeenth Century English Atlantic" appeared in *Empire of the Senses: Sensory Practices of Colonialism in Early America*, edited by Daniella Hacke and Paul Musselwhite (Leiden, NL: Brill, 2017). At New York University Press, Clara Platter helped shepherd this project from proposal to completed manuscript with well-timed reminders and expert advice. Thank you also to Sarah Bode, Mary Beth Jarrad, Veronica Knutson, Susan Murray, and Tim Roberts for all of the additional work and support. I have learned so much about the team of people who labor to bring a book to press. I am also very grateful to the three anonymous external readers who read drafts of this manuscript and offered incisive and generous advice. They have made this a much better book.

And, of course, I'd like to thank the friends and family who supported this journey from outside of academia. Their kindness and their confidence in me made me believe I could actually write a book. But they also reminded me to set down my work and to look up from the computer. I thank them for introducing me to my first redwoods, driving with me across the country, and hiking with me to the tops of mountains to remind me that sometimes we all need to look at the world from another perspective. I am grateful to Laine Clark-Balzan, Matt and Regin Davis, Johanna Kleingeld, Claire Levenson, Jennifer Macmillan, Allison Pieja, and Caroline Yao who, from Oxford to Los Angeles, offered me excellent company and places to sleep on my many travels.

A very special thank you is due to Daniel Leinker, who cheers me on and thinks I can do anything. I am immensely grateful for his laughter and his love. I also want to thank my three incredible sisters, Claire Mulry, Ryan Mulry, and Carrie Ellis, who inspire me with their kindness, wisdom, and humor. I look forward to many more adventures with them and with their beautiful families. The final acknowledgement goes to my parents, Philip and Susan Mulry. Their love, patience, support, and guidance have shaped the whole course of my life. This book is dedicated to them.

Notes

Introduction

1. The improvement literature in this period was vast. For several examples, see Walter Blith, *The English improver improved, or, The Survey of husbandry surveyed discovering the improveableness of all lands* (London, 1653); Samuel Fortrey, *England's Interest and Improvement* (London, 1663); Carew Reynell, *The True English Interest* (London, 1674); A. N., *Londons Improvement* (London, 1680); and Andew Yarranton, *England's Improvement by Sea and Land* (London, 1677). Historians such as Paul Slack have discussed the prominence of the idea of "improvement" in later seventeenth-century England. Although the term first referred to land management and securing greater profits from the land, its use eventually broadened "to apply to every aspect of human and social endeavour" (Slack, *The Invention of Improvement: Information and Material Progress in Seventeenth-Century England* [Oxford: Oxford University Press, 2014], 4, 7). Additional scholars who have examined the history of the concept of improvement, including its relationship to imperial ideology, include Richard Drayton, *Nature's Government: Science, Imperial Britain, and the "Improvement" of the World* (New Haven, Conn.: Yale University Press, 2000); Toby Barnard, *Improving Ireland?: Projectors, Prophets and Profiteers, 1641–1786* (Dublin, Ireland: Four Courts Press, 2008); and Paul Warde, "The Idea of Improvement, c. 1520–1700," in *Custom, Improvement and the Landscape in Early Modern Britain*, ed. R. Royle (Farnham: Ashgate, 2011).

2. *Philosophical Transactions of the Royal Society* 9, no. 101 (1674): 19.

3. "Overtures touching a Councell to bee erected by his Matie for the better regulating and improving of forreigne Plantations," Egerton MS 2395, ff. 272–73, British Library; A letter to the Comitte of ye East India Company for an Experim^{t} in Jamaica, Sloane MS 856, f. 37b, British Library.

4. Cited in Ted McCormick, *William Petty and the Ambitions of Political Arithmetic* (Oxford: Oxford University Press, 2009), 73.

5. John Evelyn, *Fumifugium: or, the Inconveniencie of the Aer and Smoak of London Dissipated Together with Some Remedies Humbly Proposed* (London, 1661), "To the Reader."

6. According to Paul Slack, "Unlikely as it might have seemed later, Charles II could persuasively present himself as a reforming monarch in 1660" because he engaged in a number of public works projects and backed a range of social reforms (Slack, *From Reformation to Improvement: Public Welfare in Early Modern England* [New York: Oxford University Press, 1998], 88).

7. "Overtures touching a Councell to bee erected by his Matie for the better regulating and improving of forreigne Plantations," Egerton MS 2395, ff. 272–73, British Library.

8. As numerous scholars have pointed out, describing the state in terms of its resemblance to a natural body had a long history. See A. D. Harvey, *Body Politic: Political Metaphor and Political Violence* (Cambridge: Cambridge University Press, 2007). As Katherine Bootle Attie has argued, even though it was "numbingly cliché," James I found that "it was precisely the trope's familiarity and conventionality that made it suitable . . . as a vehicle for his new defense of royal prerogative." According to James I, "the proper office of a king towards his subjects, agrees very wel with the office of the head towards the body" by directing the other members (Attie, "Re-Membering the Body Politic: Hobbes and the Construction of Civic Immortality," *ELH* 75, no. 3 [Fall 2008]: 497–98).

9. William Petty, *Political Arithmetick, or, A Discourse Concerning the Extent and Value of Lands, People, Buildings; Husbandry . . . As the Same Relates to Every Country in General, but more Particularly to the Territories of His Majesty of Great Britain* (London, 1690), 87.

10. Petty, *Political Arithmetic*, 87–88.

11. Petty, *Political Arithmetic*, 88.

12. Edward Randolph, "The Present State of New England," September 20, 1676, Add MS 28089, f. 9, British Library.

13. Petty, *Political Arithmetick*, preface.

14. John Romeyn Brodhead, *Documents Relative to the Colonial History of the State of New-York: Procured in Holland, England, and France* (Albany, N.Y.: Weed, Parsons, 1853–87), 32–33.

15. "His Majesty's Commission for a Councill for Foreign Plantations," cited in Walter W. Woodward, *Prospero's America: John Winthrop, Jr., Alchemy, and the Creation of New England Culture, 1606-1676* (Chapel Hill: Published for the Omohundro Institute of Early American History and Culture by the University of North Carolina Press, 2010), 254–55.

16. Owen Stanwood, *The Empire Reformed: English America in the Age of the Glorious Revolution* (Philadelphia: University of Pennsylvania Press, 2011), 3.

17. L. H. Roper has questioned the usefulness of using the Restoration "as a benchmark of English imperial history" (Roper, *Advancing Empire: English Interests and Overseas Expansion, 1613-1688* [Cambridge: Cambridge University Press, 2017], 8). Similarly, Carla Gardina Pestana has argued that the Restoration of the monarchy did not mark a significant departure from what came before. Instead, she emphasizes continuities, highlighting, for instance, how the king "silently adopt[ed]" the "imperial apparatus" built by revolutionaries and Oliver Cromwell to systematize

and centralize control over the colonies, including the committees created to oversee and develop legislation for colonial governance and commerce (Pestana, *The English Conquest of Jamaica: Oliver Cromwell's Bid for Empire* [Cambridge, MA: The Belknap Press of Harvard University Press, 2017], 11–12). Similar claims about continuities across this "rigid historiographical divide" have been made concerning English culture and society (Janet Clare, ed., *From Republic to Restoration: Legacies and Departures* [Manchester: Manchester University Press, 2018], 1). This project does not seek to return to or reinforce the periodization these works have questioned. Indeed, the individuals discussed in the following chapters, like the ambitious merchant Thomas Povey, who retained and expanded his influence after the king's Restoration, was valued for his expertise and experience even if it was gained during the Interregnum. But if there were continuities, there were also adaptations and innovations, particularly in officials' emphasis on healing languages when boosting claims of sovereignty and possession.

18. According to Gary S. De Krey, "More land had changed hands than at any time since the dissolution of the monasteries in the reign of Henry VIII" (De Krey, *Restoration and Revolution in Britain: A Political History of the Era of Charles II and the Glorious Revolution* [New York: Palgrave Macmillan, 2007], 27–28).

19. De Krey, *Restoration and Revolution in Britain*, 28.

20. Joan Thirsk has estimated, for example, that the lands of fifty royalists in southeastern England had been purchased by 257 individuals (Thirsk, "The Restoration Land Settlement," *The Journal of Modern History* 26, no. 4 [1954]: 315).

21. Ted McCormick, *William Petty and the Ambitions of Political Arithmetic* (Oxford: Oxford University Press, 2009), 116–17. According to McCormick the English took about 8,400,000 acres from Ireland's Catholic residents.

22. Daniel K. Richter, *Before the Revolution: America's Ancient Pasts* (Cambridge: Harvard University Press, 2013), 254–55. In London after the Restoration, for instance, descendants of the original proprietors of the Province of Maine and the Province of New Hampshire, Sir Ferdinando Gorges and John Mason, brought forward claims against the Massachusetts Bay Colony, and sought to undo the colony's annexation of their province in the 1650s (Hannah Farber, "The Rise and Fall of the Province of Lygonia, 1643–1658," *The New England Quarterly* 82, no. 3 [September 2009]: 490–513). Walter Woodward tracks the efforts of Connecticut's governor, John Winthrop, Jr., to acquire a charter for the Connecticut colony (Woodward, *Prospero's America: John Winthrop, Jr., Alchemy, and the Creation of New England Culture, 1606–1676* [Chapel Hill: Published for the Omohundro Institute of Early American History and Culture by the University of North Carolina Press, 2010]).

23. Early modern Europeans resorted to a "scattershot approach to legal rationales" for acquiring sovereignty, including their claims to possession through occupation (Lauren Benton and Benjamin Straumann, "Acquiring Empire by Law: From Roman Doctrine to Early Modern European Practice," *Law and History Review* 28, no. 1 [February 2010]: 3). Meanwhile, earlier work by Patricia Seed discusses how the English justified the displacement of Native Americans by pointing to their supposed failures to demonstrate permanent habitation and improvement, which was the English colonists' preferred ceremony of possession (Seed, *Ceremonies of Possession in Europe's Conquest of the New World, 1492–1640* [Cambridge: Cambridge University Press, 1995]). But Seed did not discuss how a similar strategy was also, at times, used to

further justify the conquest of imperial rival's colonies in the aftermath of conquest. The English made similar claims about their rivals' failures to improve the landscape and community health to justify their possession, as this book argues.

24. Allan Greer, *Property and Dispossession: Natives, Empires and Land in Early Modern North America* (New York: Cambridge University Press, 2018), 202. Some of these records were created in response to the Duke of York, for instance, who revealed plans to inspect and reissue land patents in order to assess quitrents in his new colony.

25. Greer, *Property and Dispossession*, 355.

26. Greer, *Property and Dispossession*, 357.

27. Tim Harris, "What's New about the Restoration?" *Albion* 29, no. 2 (Summer 1997): 194.

28. "Overtures touching a Councell to bee erected by his Matie for the better regulating and improving of forreigne Plantations," Egerton MS 2395, f. 273, British Library.

29. There is a growing literature on public health and welfare charting the willingness of early modern states to intervene, broadly conceived, in the bodily welfare of subjects (see Douglas Biow, *The Culture of Cleanliness in Renaissance Italy* [Ithaca, N.Y.: Cornell University Press, 2006]; Kristy Wilson Bowers, *Plague and Public Health in Early Modern Seville* [Rochester, N.Y.: University of Rochester Press, 2013]; Harold Cook, "Policing the Health of London," *Social History of Medicine* 2 [1989]: 1–33; Ole Peter Grell and Andrew Cunningham, eds., *Health Care and Poor Relief in Protestant Europe, 1500–1700* [London: Routledge, 1997]; and Slack, *From Reformation to Improvement*). "Nasty folks" were discussed in Gideon Harvey, *A discourse of the plague containing the nature, causes, signs, and presages of the pestilence in general, together with the state of the present contagion* (London, 1665), 15–16.

30. Laura Lunger Knoppers and Joan B. Landes, eds., *Monstrous Bodies/Political Monstrosities in Early Modern Europe* (Ithaca, N.Y.: Cornell University Press, 2004), 1–4; Karyn Valerius, "'So Manifest a Signe from Heaven': Monstrosity and Heresy in the Antinomian Controversy," *New England Quarterly* 83, no. 2 (June 2010): 179–82; Lorraine Daston and Katherine Park, "Unnatural Conceptions: The Study of Monsters in Sixteenth- and Seventeenth-Century France and England," *Past and Present* 92 (August 1981): 20–54. Royalist writers regularly described the republic as monstrous, as either a headless body, or a body with too many heads. During his coronation Charles II marched past actors riding on a hydra, "personating Rebellion," similarly connecting monstrosity and political disorder (Ogilby, *The Entertainment of his most excellent majestie Charles II*, 13).

31. Rebecca Earle, *The Body of the Conquistador: Food, Race and the Colonial Experience in Spanish America, 1492–1700* (New York: Cambridge University Press, 2012), 30–31.

32. Trudy Eden, *The Early American Table: Food and Society in the New World* (DeKalb: Northern Illinois University Press, 2008), 12, 15.

33. John Archer, *Every man his own doctor* (London, 1672); Robert Burton, *The anatomie of Melancholy* (London, 1621), 259; Nicholas Culpepper, *Pharmacopoeia Londinensis; or, the London Dispensatory Further Adorned by the Studies and Collections of the Fellows now living, of the said Colledg.* (London, 1672), A4.

34. Sarah Covington, *Wounds, Flesh, and Metaphor in Seventeenth-Century England* (New York: Palgrave Macmillan, 2009), 2.

35. Nancy Shoemaker, "Body Language: The Body as a Source of Sameness and Difference in Eighteenth-Century American Indian-European Diplomacy East of the Mississippi," in *A Centre of Wonders: The Body in Early America*, ed. Janet Moore Lindman and Michele Lise Tarter (Ithaca, N.Y.: Cornell University Press, 2001), 213.

36. Attie, "Re-Membering the Body Politic," 498. For the classic discussion of the two bodies of the king, see Ernst H. Kantorowicz, *The King's Two Bodies: A Study in Mediaeval Political Theology* (Princeton, N.J.: Princeton University Press, 1957).

37. John Ogilby, *The Entertainment of his most excellent majestie Charles II, in his passage through the city of London to his coronation* (London, 1662), 13.

38. Gideon Harvey, *The Disease of London: or, A New Discovery of the Scorvey* (London, 1675), "The Epistle Dedicatory"; John Bird, *Ostenta Carolina: Or the Late Calamites of England with the Authors of them. The Great Happiness and Happy Government of K. Charles II Ensuing, Miraculously Foreshewn by the Finger of God in two wonderful Diseases, the Rekets and Kings-Evil* (London, 1661), preface. See also Stephen Brogan, *The Royal Touch in Early Modern England: Politics, Medicine and Sin* (London: Royal Historical Society, 2015), 68.

39. Harvey, *The Disease of London*, "The Epistle Dedicatory."

40. *His Maities Letter, To the Generals of the Navy at Sea Together with His Majesties most gratious Declaration* (London: Printed by James Fletcher, Printer to the Honorable City of London, 1660), 3.

41. *His Maities Letter, To the Generals of the Navy at Sea*, 8.

42. *A common-Councell Holden the first day of May 1660* (London: Printed by James Fletcher, Printer to the Honorable City of London, 1660), 8–9.

43. *His Maiesties Letter, To the Generals of the Navy at Sea*, 3–4.

44. Bird, *Ostenta Carolina*, 69.

45. Ogilby, *The Entertainment of his most excellent majestie Charles II*, 13.

46. John Ogilby, *The Relation of His Majestie's Entertainment Passing through the City of London, to His Coronation: With a Description of the Triumphal Arches, and Solemnity* (London: Printed by Tho. Roycroft, for Rich. Marriott, 1661), 13, 18.

47. Ogilby, *The Entertainment of his most excellent majestie Charles II*, 135.

48. While many drugs, spices, and groceries streamed into England during this period and were celebrated for their flavor and salubriousness, the English were often suspicious and fearful of what new tastes or medicines might do to their humoral bodies. For more on these European anxieties, see Peter C. Mancall, "Tales of Tobacco Told in Sixteenth-Century Europe," *Environmental History* 9, no. 4 (October 2004): 648–78; and Daniela Bleichmar, "Books, Bodies, and Fields: Sixteenth-Century Transatlantic Encounters with New World *Materia Medica*," in *Colonial Botany: Science, Commerce, and Politics in the Early Modern World*, ed. Londa Schiebinger and Claudia Swan (Philadelphia: University of Pennsylvania Press, 2005).

49. Brogan, *The Royal Touch*, 68.

50. Brogan, *The Royal Touch*, 68.

51. Thomas Hobbes claimed that the body politic was an artificial body, not a natural body. This book wonders if the state's attention may have turned to the actual bodies of subjects as a way to "naturalize" itself as the idea of an organic body politic lost traction.

52. Elaine Scarry, *The Body in Pain: The Making and Unmaking of the World* (Oxford: Oxford University Press, 1985), 14.

53. Pamela H. Smith, *The Body of the Artisan: Art and Experience in the Scientific Revolution* (Chicago: The University of Chicago Press, 2004).

54. For instance, Harold J. Cook tracks the ideas of a group of early modern political theorists in the Netherlands, including Spinoza, and demonstrates how they "grounded their views" in "new claims about the body that flowed from the recent anatomical discoveries and theories, in a time and place comfortable with materialism" (Cook, "Body and Passions: Materialism and the Early Modern State," *Osiris*, 2d ser., 17 [2002]: 25). An example of this would be how early modern understandings of the circulation of blood helped writers explain the flow of trade and circulation of money. According to Henry Pollexfen, "Trade is to the Body Politick as Blood to the Body Natural," suggesting trade, like blood, carried necessary nutrients to both bodies through circulation (Pollexfen, *Discourse of trade, coyn, and paper credit, and of ways and means to gain, and retain riches to which is added the argument of a learned counsel upon an action of a case brought by the East-India-Company against Mr. Sands the interloper* [London, 1697], 107).

55. Peter Anstey suggests that John Locke's philosophical work was shaped by contemporary developments in natural history, medicine, and the experimental investigations of Royal Society member, Robert Boyle, for instance. Likewise, Ted McCormick has argued that William Petty's formulation of "political arithmetic," and his interest in transforming society and political policy, related to his other intellectual enterprises, including his background in medicine and the broader social and scientific context of which he was a part (see Anstey, *John Locke and Natural Philosophy* [Oxford: Oxford University Press, 2011]; and Ted McCormick, *William Petty and the Ambitions of Political Arithmetic* [Oxford: Oxford University Press, 2010]). Similarly, a recent collection of essays has asked why so many important political economists had backgrounds in medicine, moving from studies of the natural body to writing about the body politic (Peter Groenewegen, ed., *Physicians and Political Economy: Six Studies of the Work of Doctor Economists* [London: Routledge, 2012]).

56. There is a robust literature that investigates the ways in which scientific concepts of examinations of natural phenomena shaped social and political ideas and vice versa, including when and which ideas moved or were translated "across domains of activity" (Henry S. Turner, "Lessons from Literature for the Historian of Science [and Vice Versa]: Reflections on Form," *Isis* 101, no. 3 [September 2010]: 581). In a classic text by Charles Webster, for instance, Webster traces the interconnections between the intellectual and religious climate of early modern England and suggests that the fervent millenarianism of Puritans fueled a particular kind of scientific inquiry, including the kinds of questions they asked and answered. In other words, their approach to science was shaped indelibly by social context (Webster, *The Great Instauration: Science, Medicine, and Reform, 1626–1660* [London: Duckworth, 1975]). Scholars have also examined how new modes of inquiry, such as empiricism, prized by groups like the Royal Society, were intellectually indebted to medical practitioners and anatomists, for whom empiricism had long held "epistemological primacy" (Charles T. Wolfe and Ofer Gal, eds., *The Body as Object and Instrument of Knowledge* [Dordrecht, Netherlands: Springer, 2010], 2). Scholars who are interested in how social contexts shape scientific ideas include Barbara J. Shapiro, who has identified a fascinating story of the adoption of "facts," long part of the English legal tradition, into the language and practice of experimental philosophy (Shapiro, *A Culture of Fact:*

England, 1550–1720 [Ithaca, N.Y.: Cornell University Press, 2000]). Londa Schiebinger suggests that eighteenth-century scientists mapped their cultural assumptions, ideas about gender, and customs onto plants and the natural world. As she argues, "who does science affects the kinds of science that gets done" (Schiebinger, *Nature's Body: Gender in the Making of Modern Science* [New Brunswick, N.J.: Rutgers University Press, 1995], 3).

57. John Rose, *The English Vineyard Vindicated* (London, 1666), dedication.

58. William Lawson, *A New Orchard* (London, 1683), 49.

59. Henry Oldenburg, *Philosophical Transactions* 9, no. 101 (1674), "The Epistle Dedicatory."

60. Oldenburg, *Philosophical Transactions* 9, no. 101 (1674), "The Epistle Dedicatory."

61. For recent works that examine different elaborations of early modern political ecological thinking see Molly Warsh, "A Political Ecology in the Early Spanish Caribbean," *The William and Mary Quarterly* 71, no. 4 (October 2014): 517–48; and Keith Pluymers, "Atlantic Iron: Wood Scarcity and the Political Ecology of Early English Expansion," *The William and Mary Quarterly* 73, no. 3 (July 2016): 389–426.

62. Among the scholars whose work falls in the "intellectual-cultural mode" of environmental history (quote from James D. Rice, "Early American Environmental Histories," *The William and Mary Quarterly* 75, no. 3 [July 2018]: 401–32): Keith Thomas, *Man and the Natural World: Changing Attitudes in England, 1500–1800* (New York: Penguin Books, 1984); Karen Ordahl Kupperman, "Fear of Hot Climates in the Anglo-American Colonial Experience," *The William and Mary Quarterly* 41, no. 2 (April 1984): 213–40; Simon Schama, *Landscape and Memory* (New York: A. A. Knopf, 1995); and John R. Gillis, *Islands of the Mind: How the Human Imagination Created the Atlantic World* (New York: Palgrave Macmillan, 2004). Several scholars of early modern environmental history have emphasized how changing land use connected with the emergence of a capitalist economy. They discuss these transformations as the de-spiritualization or commodification of the landscape into easily exploited materials: William Cronon, *Changes in the Land: Indians, Colonists, and the Ecology of New England* (New York: Hill and Wang, 1983); Carolyn Merchant, *Ecological Revolutions: Nature, Gender, and Science in New England* (Chapel Hill: University of North Carolina Press, 1989); and Donald Worster, *Nature's Economy: A History of Ecological Ideas* (Cambridge: Cambridge University Press, 2004). This book argues that the many schemes to refashion subjects' health and behavior by transforming environments reveals Stuart assumptions and anxieties about authority and order.

63. For more on the history of individuals known as "projectors" see Eric H. Ash, *Power, Knowledge, and Expertise in Elizabethan England* (Baltimore: Johns Hopkins University Press, 2004). If Stuart projectors promised a balance between private and public gain, however, their motives were sometimes suspect. But suspicious or not, the proliferation of discourses promising to improve, heal, and transform the nation's landscapes and subjects demonstrates that there was a ready audience for such proposals.

64. Recent work by Anya Zilberstein examines British colonial officials' confidence that they could craft a more temperate climate that would better suit their bodies (Zilberstein, *A Temperate Empire: Making Climate Change in Early America* [New York: Oxford University Press, 2016]). This work parallels some of Zilberstein's arguments

about British officials' efforts to remake colonial climates while highlighting many additional environmental changes Stuart elites endeavored to make. Moreover, this book examines the close links Restoration theorists made between the environment, behavior, health, and authority.

65. As Anabel Brett has argued, although early modern subjects were, theoretically, only "civilly obliged" to the commonwealth in early modern natural law, this definition obscures the "relationship of the state to its subjects as necessarily physically embodied beings," which meant that subjects often experienced even this abstract political relationship "*through* their bodies" (Brett, *Changes of State: Nature and the Limits of the City in Early Modern Natural Law* [Princeton, N.J.: Princeton University Press, 2011], 143–44). This project examines how Charles II sought to secure his position, and reinforce his legitimacy, by healing the diseased and unhealthy bodies of his subjects.

66. This assessment of the Restoration court's knowledge of the American plantations was made by Walter Woodward, *Prospero's America: John Winthrop, Jr., Alchemy, and the Creation of New England Culture, 1606–1676* (Chapel Hill: Published for the Omohundro Institute of Early American History and Culture by the University of North Carolina Press, 2010), 8.

67. Michael Braddick, *State Formation in Early Modern England, c. 1550–1700* (Cambridge: Cambridge University Press, 2000), 103; Ralph Paul Bieber, *The Lords of Trade and Plantations 1675–1696* (Allentown, Pa.: H. R. Haas, 1919), 16.

68. Bieber, *The Lords of Trade and Plantation*, 17.

69. For inspiration, the English scrutinized imperial intelligence activities undertaken by the Spanish. The use of circulars and questionnaires was a method of investigating used by the Spanish to collect knowledge about their dispersed and expansive empire. In an effort to gather information about colonial resources, Spanish officials sent out the "Relaciones geográficas" (Jorge Cañizares-Esguerra, "Iberian Colonial Science," *Isis* 96, no. 1 [2005]). Meanwhile, Antonio Barrera-Osorio has argued that the innovative practices of collecting and organizing natural knowledge by institutions like the Casa de la Contratación in Seville served as inspiration for Francis Bacon and later Royal Society members (Antonio Barrera-Osorio, *Experiencing Nature: The Spanish American Empire and the Early Scientific Revolution* [Austin: University of Texas Press, 2006]).

70. John Romeyn Brodhead, Esq., ed., *Documents Relative to the Colonial History of the State of New-York*, vol. 3 (Albany: Weed, Parsons and Company, Printers, 1853), 35. The commission was dated December 1, 1660.

71. Much like the Council of Foreign Plantations, the Royal Society used questionnaires and circulars as instruments of inquiry, and sought to harness the potential wealth and power that knowledge of colonial environments and resources might afford. Interest in the *materia medica* and economically viable products from around the world, for instance, had long been high. For more on early modern collecting practices and cultures of collecting see Paula Findlan, *Possessing Nature: Museums, Collecting, and Scientific Culture in Early Modern Italy* (Berkeley: University of California Press, 1994); Daniela Bleichmar, Peter Mancall, and Cecile Fromont, eds., *Collecting Across Cultures: Material Exchanges in the Early Modern Atlantic World* (Philadelphia: University of Pennsylvania Press, 2013).

72. "His Majesty's Commission for a Council for Foreign Plantations," December 1, 1660, in *Documents Relative to the Colonial History of the State of New-York*, ed. Brodhead, 33.

73. John Romeyn Brodhead, *Documents Relating to the Colonial History of the State of New York*, vol. III (Albany: Parsons and Company, 1853), 35; "Overtures touching a Councel to bee erected by his Matie for the better regulating and improving of forreigne Plantations," Egerton 2395, f. 237, British Library. In order to secure such "experienced persons," the king directed the Privy Council to send letters to the East India Company "as well as others" to nominate members to be appointed to the "Committee for establishinge, and promotinge, of Trade." East India Company Court Book, August 29, 1660, IOR/B/26, f. 285, British Library.

74. Raymond Phineas Stearns, *Science in the British Colonies of America* (Urbana: University of Illinois Press, 1970), 90; John Beale, *Nurseries, orchards, profitable gardens, and vineyards encouraged ... for the general benefit of His Majesties dominions* (London, 1677); Henry Oldenburg, *The Philosophical Transactions*, vol. 1 (March 1665), introduction.

75. Stearns, *Science in the British Colonies of America*, 90.

76. Robert Iliffe, "Foreign Bodies: Travel, Empire and the Early Royal Society of London. Part II. The Land of Experimental Knowledge," *Canadian Journal of History* (1999): 28.

77. Woodward, *Prospero's America*, 8.

78. "Overtures touching a Councell to bee erected by his Ma[tie] for the better regulating and improving of forreigne Plantations," Egerton MS 2395, ff. 272–73, British Library.

79. "Overtures touching a Councell to bee erected by his Ma[tie] for the better regulating and improving of forreigne Plantations," Egerton MS 2395, ff. 272–74 , British Library.

80. Ken MacMillan, "Imperial Constitutions: Sovereignty and Law in the British Atlantic," in *Britain's Oceanic Empire: Atlantic and Indian Ocean Worlds c. 1550–1850*, ed. H. V. Bowen et al. (Cambridge: Cambridge University Press, 2012), 5.

81. Overtures touching a Councell to bee erected by his Ma[tie] for the better regulating and improving of forreigne Plantations, Egerton MS 2395, f. 273, British Library.

82. Mr Reason Melish his discourse, Concerning the best ways of England's Improvement, Cl.P/10iii, f. 16, Royal Society Library.

83. Royal Society, Cl.P/10iii/16.

84. Mr Reason Melish his discourse, Concerning the best ways of England's Improvement, Cl.P/10iii, f. 16, Royal Society Library. In addition to promoting national interest through "conducing" cycles of production and reproduction, Melish suggested jump-starting this population growth by inviting refugees into England, especially if they had desirable economic skills.

85. Ash, *The Draining of the Fens*, 4.

86. John Graunt called the king a "*Prince of Philosophers* and of *Physico-Mathematical* Learning." He claimed the king had many interests beyond the typical interests in government and trade, such as natural history and philosophy, in which he might productively dabble (Graunt, *Natural and Political Observations . . . Made upon the Bills of Mortality* [London, 1662]).

87. Brooke N. Newman has argued that white colonists began to take advantage of "evolving definitions of and ongoing uncertainties surrounding British subjecthood and to whom precisely the legal inheritance of freeborn Englishmen applied" and began to define British subject status as an inheritance carried in the blood. These ideas of Britishness as something in the blood combined with "racialized notions of blood lineage" to include some and exclude others (Newman, *A Dark Inheritance*, 9).

88. Van Horn, *The Power of Objects in Eighteenth-Century British America* (Chapel Hill: University of North Carolina Press, 2017), 19.

89. Linguists suggest that metaphors have "the power . . . to create a reality rather than simply to give us a way of conceptualizing a preexisting reality." The degree to which the adoption of the same term to describe both an abstract political concept as well as a physical readjustment of garden plants shaped the conceptualization of both processes is one of the questions this book explores (George Lakoff and Mark Johnson, *Metaphors We Live By* [Chicago: University of Chicago Press, 1980], 144).

90. In *An Essay Concerning Human Understanding* (1689), John Locke argued "for a mutable self that was heavily influenced by exterior environment" (Jennifer Van Horn, *The Power of Objects*, 23.

91. J. M. Ross, "English Nationality Law: Soli or Sanguinis?," in *Studies in the History of the Law of Nations*, ed. Charles Henry Alexandrowicz (New York: Springer, 1970), 5.

92. Ross, "English Nationality Law," 7–9.

93. According to Jennifer Van Horn, for instance, residents of the "British Atlantic world expected identity to be visible and flexible and assumed that even seemingly fixed characteristics, such as race or gender, might be manipulated or altered through changes in costume or climate." By assembling material objects like clothing, furniture, and cosmetics, colonists asserted visibly their membership in a polite, civil transatlantic society, while excluding those whom they claimed lived in a state of nature, such as African Americans and Native Americans. This book argues that in addition to objects, early modern projectors, colonial officials, and natural philosophers sought to reconstruct identities through managed landscapes (Van Horn, *The Power of Objects*, 9, 23). Sophie White, too, has argued for the power of material objects, such as textiles, to shape emerging ideas about race and identity in the early French Atlantic (see White, *Wild Frenchmen and Frenchified Indians: Material Culture and Race in Colonial Louisiana* [Philadelphia: University of Pennsylvania, 2012]).

94. According to Brooke N. Newman, "formal rules regarding the conferral and transmission of British subject status overseas did not crystallize until the late eighteenth century," and thus the status of British subjects abroad was often "muddled" (Brooke N. Newman, *A Dark Inheritance: Blood, Race, and Sex in Colonial Jamaica* [New Haven: Yale University Press, 2018], 11, 14).

95. As one scholar has suggested of medieval British community formation, "Welding dissonant heterogeneity and hybridity into some harmonious collective is not easy to accomplish." Jeffrey Jerome Cohen argues that in this period "the process typically proceeded through exclusion" (Jeffrey Jerome Cohen, *Hybridity, Identity, and Monstrosity in Medieval Britain: On Difficult Middles* [New York: Palgrave Macmillan, 2006], 35).

96. Anon., *An Abstract or abbreviation of some few of the many (later and former) testimonys from the inhabitants of New-Jersey* (London, 1681), 27.

97. The work of Joyce E. Chaplin argues that colonists interpreted epidemics decimating Native American populations as evidence that their own bodies were more suited to North America's nature (Chaplin, *Subject Matter: Technology, the Body, and Science on the Anglo-American Frontier, 1500–1676* [Cambridge: Harvard University Press, 2001]). Meanwhile, Rachel Herrmann has argued that anxiety about starvation, and literature on starvation, shaped perceptions and policies in early Virginia (Herrmann, "The 'Tragicall Historie': Cannibalism and Abundance in Colonial Jamestown," *William and Mary Quarterly* 68, no. 1 [January 2011]: 47–74).

98. The phrase is derived from Raymond Williams, *Marxism and Literature* (Oxford: Oxford University Press, 1977), 128–34.

99. In his article entitled "What's New about the Restoration?," Tim Harris discusses those scholars who tend to emphasize continuity or discontinuity at the Restoration. See, for example, Alan Houston and Steven Pincus, eds., *A Nation Transformed: England after the Restoration* (Cambridge: Cambridge University Press, 2001); and Jonathan Scott, *Algernon Sidney and the Restoration Crisis* (Cambridge: Cambridge University Press, 1991). This book suggests that Charles may have used an older language of healing so prevalent in the postwar period but applied it in innovative ways in order to grapple with a large and expanding imperial context.

100. Rob Iliffe, "The Masculine Birth of Time: Temporal Frameworks of Early Modern Natural Philosophy," *British Journal for the History of Science* 33, no. 4 (2000): 442, 445. The millenarian beliefs espoused before and during the Interregnum celebrated social and personal reform as the means to bring about the return of God's rule over earth. Many scholars have explored the connections between the scientific activities and religious aims of midcentury Protestant reformers and Puritans like the members of the so-called Hartlib Circle: Charles Webster, *The Great Instauration: Science, Medicine and Reform, 1626–1660* (London: Duckworth, 1975); Mark Greengrass, Michael Leslie, and Timothy Raylor, eds., *Samuel Hartlib and Universal Reformation: Studies in Intellectual Communication* (Cambridge: Cambridge University Press, 1994); and J. T. Young, *Faith, Medical Alchemy and Natural Philosophy: Johann Moriaen, Reformed Intelligencer, and the Hartlib Circle* (Aldershot: Ashgate, 1998). Protestant reformers often pointed to a range of material practices that could reform the spirit, including fasting. William Lawson, author of *A New Orchard and Garden* (1631), suggested that spirits, like trees, needed to be regularly pruned of their "disorderly" and "beastly" appendages. These examples of the way in which social reform was connected to material practies like eating and gardening suggests continuities with the Restoration-era projects dicussed in this volume. William Lawson, *A New Orchard and Garden* (London, 1631).

101. Stanwood, *The Empire Reformed*, 4, 27–28.

102. Literature grappling with anxieties about bodily reaction of new climates and environments includes Rebecca Earle, *Body of the Conquistador: Food, Race and the Colonial Experience in Spanish America, 1492–1700* (Cambridge: Cambridge University Press, 2014); and Karen O. Kupperman, "Fear of Hot Climates in the Anglo-American Colonial Experience," *William and Mary Quarterly* 41, no. 2 (1984). The work of Joyce E. Chaplin argued that colonists interpreted epidemics decimating Native American populations as evidence that their own bodies were more suited to North America's nature (Chaplin, *Subject Matter: Technology, the Body, and Science on the Anglo-American Frontier, 1500–1676* [Cambridge: Harvard University Press, 2001]).

103. Graunt, *Bills of Mortality*, Dedicatory.

104. Ann Laura Stoler, *Along the Archival Grain: Epistemic Anxieties and Colonial Common Sense* (Princeton: Princeton University Press, 2009), 21.

105. Stoler, *Along the Archival Grain*, 106.

106. Philippa Levine, *The British Empire: Sunrise to Sunset* (Harlow, U.K.: Pearson, 2007), 1.

107. Samuel Fortrey, *The History or Narrative of the Great Level of the Fenns, Called Bedford Level* (London, 1685), 75. William Petty was one of the many writers from this period to link imperial expansion to domestic improvement projects. For instance, he linked the acquisition of new territories to the draining (and the revealing of) new land in the fens (Add MS 72,865, ff. 83–84, Petty Papers, British Library).

108. "Husbandry of England," Ephemerides 1651, Part I, 28/2/2B, Hartlib Papers.

109. Add MS 72,865, ff. 83–84, Petty Papers, British Library; Egerton MS 2395, ff. 272–73, British Library.

110. Oldenburg, *Philosophical Transactions* 9, no. 101 (1674): "The Epistle Dedicatory."

111. Not all writers, however, envisioned an uncomplicated relationship between imperial expansion and domestic improvement. Some saw these as projects at odds with one another. If desirable commodities could be cultivated at home, or if apples could substitute for sugar, why risk losing populations to lengthy sea voyages and unhealthy colonial climates? Although domestic projects were often understood as concurrent and operating within a broader frame of imperial-wide schemes of improvement, they could also serve as safer alternatives. This book further also explores this tension.

112. Jack M. Sosin, *English America and the Restoration Monarchy of Charles II: Transatlantic Politics, Commerce and Kinship* (Lincoln: University of Nebraska Press, 1980); Richard R. Johnson, *Adjustments to Empire: The New England Colonies, 1675–1715* (New Brunswick, N.J.: Rutgers University Press, 1981); Stanwood, *The Empire Reformed*; Stephen Saunders Webb, *1676: The End of American Independence* (Syracuse, N.Y.: Syracuse University Press, 1995).

113. Paul Warde, *Ecology, Economy and State Formation in Early Modern Germany* (Cambridge: Cambridge University Press), 3.

114. Charles II, *A Proclamation for a General Fast through England and Wales, and the Town of Barwick upon Tweed, on Wednesday the Tenth of October next* (London, 1666).

115. Karen Ordahl Kupperman, "Controlling Nature and Colonial Projects in Early America," in Hans-Jürgen Grabbe, ed., *Colonial Encounters: Essays in Early American History and Culture*, American Studies 109 (Ersch-Termin, 2003), 78.

116. In the mid-seventeenth century, many writers suggested that "waste" people could be put to use to improve national strength and to make them "serviceable to the Common-wealth" (Samuel Hartlib cited in Braddick, *State Formation in Early Modern England*, 133).

117. Mark Jenner, "The Politics of London Air: John Evelyn's Fumifugium and the Restoration," *The Historical Journal* 38, no. 3 (September 1995): 540.

118. Victoria Henshaw, *Urban Smellscapes: Understanding and Designing City Smell Environments* (New York: Routledge, 2014), 5; J. Douglas Porteous, *Landscapes*

of the Mind: Worlds of Sense and Metaphor (Toronto: University of Toronto Press, 1990), chap. 2.

119. This project has been inspired by calls from historians such as Kevin Sharpe, who has urged "a move from politics conceived (anachronistically) as the business of institutions, bureaucracies and officers to the broader politics of discourse and symbols, anxieties and aspirations, myths and memories." Sharpe argues that cultural acts can "embody and signify political codes and values," including, for instance, the king's claims about healing diseased bodies, or the cultivation of sylvan symbols of royal authority, such as oak trees, on Restoration-era estates (Sharpe, *Remapping Early Modern England: The Culture of Seventeenth-Century Politics* [New York: Cambridge University Press, 2000], 3, 17).

1 / Sinful, Sick, and Misbehaving Bodies

1. Jeremiah Wells, "On the Rebuilding of London," in *London in Flames, London in Glory: Poems on the Fire and Rebuilding of London, 1666–1709*, ed. Robert Arnold Aubin (New Brunswick, N.J.: Rutgers University Press, 1943), 123.

2. Charles II, *A Proclamation for a General Fast through England and Wales, and the Town of Barwick upon Tweed, on Wednesday the Tenth of October next* (London, 1666).

3. Early modern men and women understood catastrophe and contagion as a punishment from God. Bodily corruption was thought to be divine retribution for sin (Jennifer C. Vaught, ed., *Rhetorics of Bodily Disease and Health in Medieval and Early Modern England* [Farnham, U.K.: Ashgate, 2010], 6).

4. Margaret Healy, *Fictions of Disease in Early Modern England: Bodies, Plagues and Politics* (New York: Palgrave, 2001), 233.

5. Wells, "On the Rebuilding of London," 123.

6. Gideon Harvey urged his readers to "shun all publick meetings, where people promiscuously conversing with one another, do readily propagate the infection." He argued that the "steams and breaths" emitted during conversation in close proximity to other people could amplify the rate of contagion, especially if those bodies were "nasty folks, as beggars, and others: whence those houses happen to be soonest infected, that are crowded with multiplicity of lodgers and nasty families" (Harvey, *A discourse of the plague containing the nature, causes, signs, and presages of the pestilence in general, together with the state of the present contagion* [London, 1665], 15–16). During plague outbreaks, officials sought to control peoples' movements. For instance, towns could deny entry to those without passes. Meanwhile, physicians, and the officials they advised, were authorized to extend penal measures over London's residents. Those who were ill, or lived in the same house as someone who was, might be locked within.

7. Environmental history scholarship that focuses on the urban environment includes William Cavert, *The Smoke of London: Energy and Environment in the Early Modern City* (Cambridge: Cambridge University Press, 2016); Andrew Isenberg, ed., *The Nature of Cities* (Rochester, N.Y.: University of Rochester Press, 2006); Martin V. Melosi, "The Place of the City in Environmental History" *Environmental History Review* 17, no. 1 (Spring 1993): 1–23.

8. John Evelyn, *A character of England, as it was lately presented in a letter to a noble man of France* (London, 1659), 43.

9. Cited in E. S. De Beer, ed., *John Evelyn: London Revived: Consideration for Its Rebuilding in 1666* (Oxford: Clarendon, 1938), 54–55.

10. Harvey, *A discourse of the plague*, 5; De Beer, ed., *John Evelyn*, 11–12.

11. Knowing about a country's air quality was considered key to understanding the people and place, as well as information critical for travelers. Interest in the effects of travel on bodies led to published queries such as in Robert Boyle, "General Heads for a Natural History of a Countrey, Great of small, imparted likewise by Mr. Boyle" (*Philosophical Transactions of the Royal Society of London* 1 [1665]: 187).

12. Adriaen van der Donck, *A Description of the New Netherlands* (New York: Printed for the New York Historical Society, 1841), 180.

13. Robert Boyle, *New Experiments Physico-Mechanical, Touching the Spring of the Air, and Its Effects* (Oxford, 1660), 2; Mark Jenner, "The Politics of London Air: John Evelyn's *Fumifugium* and the Restoration," *Historical Journal* 38 (1995): 545; Richard Blome, *Cosmography and Geography* (London, 1682), "To the Reader."

14. Physicians prescribed travel and breathing new air in order to alleviate medical conditions (Michael Hunter, ed., *Robert Boyle's 'Heads' and 'Inquiries,'* Robert Boyle Project Occasional Papers no. 1 [Birkbeck: University of London, 2005], 33).

15. According to De Beer, Evelyn, "demanded regularity, uniformity, [and] architectural discipline" in a rebuilt London, because they were the "qualities possessing a sort of moral beauty" and indicated "civic self-respect," which were both "essential for the architecture of display" (De Beer, *John Evelyn*, 13).

16. Historians have mapped out the growing importance of sight in the eighteenth century. Sight facilitated "the great panoptic dream" (see Roy Porter, introduction to *The Foul and the Fragrant: Odor and the French Social Imagination*, trans. Miriam L. Kochan, Porter, and Christopher Prendergast [Cambridge, Mass.: Harvard University Press, 1986], v).

17. Samuel Rolle, *Londons Resurrection or the Rebuilding of London Encouraged, Directed, and Improved, in Fifty Discourses* (London, 1668), preface.

18. Rolle, *Londons Resurrection*, preface.

19. In his treatise, Samuel Rolle emphasized the cloud-dispersing sunshine shining on the rebuilt London. Rolle wrote, "the Author is a friend to publick order, and Ordinances." His words suggest that for Rolle and others, visibility was linked to public control (Rolle, *Londons Resurrection*, preface).

20. According to Constance Classen, "sight, as the most detached sense (by Western standards), provide[d] *the* model for modern bureaucratic society" (Classen, David Howes, and Anthony Synnott, *Aroma: The Cultural History of Smell* [New York: Routledge, 1994], 3–5).

21. W. Noel Sainsbury, ed., *Calendar of State Papers, Colonial Series, America and West Indies, 1669–1674* (London: Printed for her Majesty's Stationary Office by Eyre and Spottiswoode, 1889), vol. 7, 111.

22. According to the act, skilled laborers, such as bricklayers and masons, even those "who are not freemen of the said City," could work to rebuild London and "have and enjoy such and the same liberty of working . . . as the freemen of the City of the same trades and professions have and ought to enjoy; Any usage or custom of the City to the contrary notwithstanding" (cited in Leonard W. Cowie, *Plague and Fire: London 1665–66* [New York: G. P. Putnam's Sons, 1970], 113).

23. Paul D. Halliday has argued that maybe we should think less about top-down attempts to wrest control and more about how "the growth of royal institutions resulted from the needs of persons, groups, and communities in the provinces" (Halliday, *Dismembering the Body Politic: Partisan Politics in England's Towns, 1650–1730* [Cambridge: Cambridge University Press, 1998], xii). In this case, however, the needs of the city, in times of plague and postfire, required so much capital and coordination that the king stepped in to fill a need.

24. The practice of medicine linked private bodies and corporate bodies. Each was believed to impact the other. Sick individuals might infect the body politic, and this was especially evident during epidemics. Thus, both were subject to control (Healy, *Fictions of Disease in Early Modern England*, 18).

25. Annabel Brett in Charles Tilly, *Cities and the Rise of States in Europe, A.D. 1000–1800* (Boulder, Colo.: Westview, 1994).

26. Thomas D. Wilson, *The Ashley Cooper Plan: The Founding of Carolina and the Origins of Southern Political Culture* (Chapel Hill: University of North Carolina Press, 2016), 11, 35, 67. Other historians have suggested Spanish influence on the grid patterns implemented in urban design plans (Matthew Mulcahy, "'That Fatall Spott': The Rise and Fall—And Rise and Fall Again—of Port Royal, Jamaica," in *Investing in the Early Modern Built Environment: Europeans, Asians, Settlers and Indigenous Societies*, ed. Carole Shammas [Leiden, Netherlands: Brill, 2012], 198).

27. Elizabeth Fay and Leonard von Morzé, eds., *Urban Identity and the Atlantic World* (New York: Palgrave Macmillan, 2013), 1; Leonard von Morzé, ed., *Cities and the Circulation of Culture in the Atlantic World: From the Early Modern to Modernism* (Palgrave Macmillan, 2017); Jorge Cañizares-Esguerra, Matt D. Childs, and James Sidbury, eds., *The Black Urban Atlantic in the Age of the Slave Trade* (Philadelphia: University of Pennsylvania, 2016).

28. Wilson, *The Ashley Cooper Plan*, 68, 100–101.

29. Cited in *Historic Philadelphia: Historic, Central, Metropolitan, Industrial* (Philadelphia: Public Ledger Company, 1922), 2.

30. Wilson suggests that responses to plague and fire resulted in a "pivotal moment in English history after which city planning acquired greater importance" (Wilson, *The Ashley Cooper Plan*, 11).

31. Both Spanish and English colonists sought to cultivate gardens as a means to combat hostile, satanic wildernesses. Virtuous horticulturalists saw gardens as evidence of the spread of Christianity (Jorge Cañizares-Esguerra, *Puritan Conquistadors: Iberianizing the Atlantic, 1550–1700* [Stanford: Stanford University Press, 2006], 178–214).

32. Paul Warde, *Economy, Ecology and State Formation in Early Modern Germany* (Cambridge: Cambridge University Press, 2006), 3, 5. See also Steve Sturdy, *Medicine, Health and the Public Sphere in Britain, 1600–2000* (London: Routledge, 2002).

33. Harvey, *A discourse of the plague*, 15; Cowie, *Plague and Fire*, 17.

34. Cited in G. Huehns, ed., *Clarendon: Selections from "The History of the Rebellion and Civil Wars," and "The Life by Himself"* (Oxford: Oxford University Press, 1955), 410.

35. Cited in Huehns, ed., *Clarendon*, 410.

36. Cowie, *Plague and Fire*, 20–21. While members of the court and parliament fled, "the Captain-General [Monck] stayed on in his Whitehall lodgings, the only

representative of national government left in the capital. He ruled the western suburbs and, together with the lord mayor, Sir John Lawrence, he maintained public order and ensured that each night the fires were lit in the streets to ward off the contagion" (Adrian Tinniswood, *By Permission of Heaven: The True Story of the Great Fire of London* [New York: Riverhead, 2004], 126).

37. Samuel Pepys, *Diary and Correspondences of Samuel Pepys, F.R.S.*, ed. Richard, Lord Braybrooke (Philadelphia: John D. Morris, 1910), April 30, 1665.

38. Pepys, *Diary*, May 27, 1665.

39. Pepys, *Diary*, June 7, 1665.

40. Cowie, *Plague and Fire*, 27.

41. Harvey, *A discourse of the plague*, 22.

42. Cowie, *Plague and Fire*, 48.

43. Tinniswood, *By Permission of Heaven*, 10.

44. Tinniswood, *By Permission of Heaven*, 8–9; Cowie, *Plague and Fire*, 17, 56.

45. Harvey, *A discourse of the plague*, 15, 21.

46. Healy, *Fictions of Disease*, 89.

47. Harvey, *A discourse of the plague*, 9–11, 15.

48. Harvey, *A discourse of the plague*, 5.

49. Ari Kelman, "New Orleans's Phantom Slave Insurrection of 1853: Racial Anxiety, Urban Ecology, and Human Bodies as Public Spaces," in *The Nature of Cities*, ed. Andrew Isenberg (Rochester, N.Y.: University of Rochester Press, 2006), 17.

50. Healy, *Fictions of Disease*, 3.

51. T.D., *Food and Physick, for every Householder, & his Family, During the Time of the Plague* (London, 1665), 13, 18.

52. T.D., *Food and Physick, for every Householder*, 15.

53. Rev. E. Heath, *A full account of the late dreadful earthquake at Port Royal in Jamaica written in two letters from the minister of that place* (London, 1692), n.p.

54. Heath, *A full account of the late dreadful earthquake at Port Royal*.

55. Healy, *Fictions of Disease*, 58.

56. Harvey, *A discourse of the plague*, 1–2.

57. Theophilus Garencieres, *A Mite Cast into the Treasury of the Famous City of London: Being a Brief and Methodical Discourse of the Nature, Causes, Symptoms, Remedies and Preservatives from the Plague, in the Calamitous Year, 1665*, 3rd ed. (London, 1666), 4, 14.

58. Harvey, *A discourse of the plague*, 5.

59. Harvey, *A discourse of the plague*, 5.

60. Thomas Cocke, *Advice for the Poor by way of Cure & Caution* (London, 1665), 8.

61. Harvey, *A discourse of the plague*, 6–7.

62. Harvey, *A discourse of the plague*, 7.

63. Harvey, *A discourse of the plague*, 6.

64. Harvey, *A discourse of the plague*, 13.

65. Harvey, *A discourse of the plague*, 7–8.

66. Healy, *Fictions of Disease*, 93–94.

67. T.D., *Food and Physick, for every Householder*, 5.

68. Garencieres, *A Mite Cast into the Treasury*, 6.

69. T.D., *Food and Physick, for every Householder*, 5.

70. Cocke, *Advice for the Poor by way of Cure & Caution*, 4.

71. T.D., *Food and Physick, for every Householder*, 9.

72. Harvey, *A discourse of the plague*, 20.

73. Evelyn Papers, Add MS 78343, f.1, British Library.

74. T.D., *Food and Physick, for every Householder*, 9.

75. The author likewise suggested engaging other sense against the plague by chewing foods with strong flavors, like cinnamon, vinegar, sorrel, and garlic (T.D., *Food and Physick, for every Householder*, 6, 9).

76. Harvey, *A discourse of the plague*, 19.

77. Harvey, *A discourse of the plague*, 13–14.

78. Harvey, *A discourse of the plague*, 14.

79. Harvey, *A discourse of the plague*, 20.

80. Garencieres, *A Mite Cast into the Treasury*, 12.

81. Harvey, *A discourse of the plague*, 16.

82. Harvey, *A discourse of the plague*, 29.

83. Harvey, *A discourse of the plague*, 29.

84. Neil Hanson, *The Great Fire of London in that Apocalyptic Year, 1666* (Hoboken, N.J.: Wiley and Sons, 2002), 38.

85. Cowie, *Plague and Fire*, 49.

86. Garencieres, *A Mite Cast into the Treasury*, 6–7.

87. Cowie, *Plague and Fire*, 53–54.

88. Harvey, *A discourse of the plague*, 9.

89. Harvey, *A discourse of the plague*, 21–22.

90. Healy, *Fictions of Disease*, 3.

91. This was part of a larger project of control over bodies and their acts (see Norbert Elias, *The Civilizing Process* [New York: Blackwell, 1986]).

92. Healy, *Fictions of Disease*, 16–17.

93. Pepys, *Diary*, May 1, 1667.

94. Sheldon Watts offers a list of regulations and prohibitions from around the world (Watts, *Epidemics and History: Disease, Power and Imperialism* [New Haven: Yale University Press, 1997], 18–25).

95. According to Jonathan Gil Harris, "the recurrent representations of Catholics, Jews and witches as pathogenic infiltrators responsible for England's social 'ills' resonate with Paracelsus's and others' emergent proto-microbiological conception of disease as a malign, invading entity" (Harris, *Foreign Bodies and the Body Politic: Discourses of Social Pathology in Early Modern England* [Cambridge: Cambridge University Press, 1998], 15).

96. Cocke, *Advice for the Poor by way of Cure & Caution*, preface.

97. Healy, *Fictions of Disease*, 70.

98. England was late to instate regulations, and those they did utilize were borrowed from elsewhere, generally Italy. Watts cites the development of an "Ideology of Order" which were first developed by Italian city states, "which during epidemic crises justified intervention into the lives of ordinary people" (Watts, *Epidemics and History*, 15–18).

99. Healy, *Fictions of Disease*, 13–14.

100. Cowie, *Plague and Fire*, 17–19.

101. Cowie, *Plague and Fire*, 35–36.

102. Cowie, *Plague and Fire*, 38.

103. Cowie, *Plague and Fire*, 37; W. G. Bell, *The Great Plague in London* (Bodley Head, 1924), 333–34.

104. Cocke, *Advice for the Poor by way of Cure & Caution*, 4–6.

105. Harvey, *A discourse of the plague*, 15–16. T.D. acknowledged that sin was the "first Cause of this *Sickness*" and that sins were "the Parents of this *Pestilence.*" Because Londoners had neglected to be charitable to their poor neighbors, the poor lived in conditions that led to contagion. Because the poor lived where "multitudes are pestered together in a little room" their "nakedness," "filthinesse," "noysomeness," resulted in contagion (T.D., *Food and Physick, for every Householder*, 18).

106. See, for instance, Harvey, *A discourse of the plague*; Cocke, *Advice for the Poor by way of Cure & Caution*; T.D., *Food and Physick, for every Householder*; Garencieres, *A Mite Cast into the Treasury*.

107. T.D., *Food and Physick, for every Householder*, 13, 15.

108. John Evelyn and M. de Sainte-Marie cited in Steve Pincus, *1688: The First Modern Revolution* (New Haven, Conn.: Yale University Press), 66.

109. Tinniswood, *By Permission of Heaven*, 3; Evelyn, *A Character of England*, 4.

110. Evelyn, *A Character of England*, 7. Evelyn wrote the text as a satire, as if he were a visitor to London. He complained that there were too many "raskally warehouses, and so sordidly obscur'd and defac'd, that an argument of greater avarice, malice, meanness, and deformity of mind, cannot possibly be expressed" (John Evelyn, *The Miscellaneous Writings of John Evelyn*, ed. William Upcott [London: Henry Colburn, New Burlington Street, 1825], 151).

111. Evelyn, *The Miscellaneous Writings of John Evelyn*, ed. Upcott, 157.

112. Mulcahy, "That Fatall Spott," 198.

113. Francis Heeson, *The Laws of Jamaica . . . to which is added a Short Account of the Island and Government thereof* (London, 1683), "To the Reader."

114. Cited in James Robertson, "Late Seventeenth-Century Spanish-Town Jamaica: Building an English City on Spanish Foundations" *Early American Studies* 6, no. 2 (October 2008): 389.

115. Robertson, "Late Seventeenth-Century Spanish-Town Jamaica," 366.

116. "Overtures touching a Councell to bee erected by his Ma[tie] for the better regulating and improving of forreigne Plantations," Egerton MS 2395, ff. 272–73, British Library.

117. Evelyn was certainly neither the first nor the last to look at coal smoke as deeply problematic to the health and appearance of London. For medieval efforts to control the burning of coal, see Peter Brimblecombe, *The Big Smoke: A History of Air Pollution in London since Medieval Times* (London: Methuen, 1987), 9.

118. Evelyn suggested these plantations in *Fumifugium or, the Inconveniencie of the Aer and Smoak of London Dissipated* (London, 1661). For further discussion of this scheme, see chapter 5.

119. Cowie, *Plague and Fire*, 11.

120. Kenelm Digby "postulated that the damaging effects of coal smoke arose from the fact that the atoms were sharp and pointed." Meanwhile, John Graunt suggested in his *Natural and Political Observations . . . Made upon the Bills of Mortality* (1662) that coal smoke resulted in "suffocations which many could not endure" (cited in Peter Brimblecombe, *The Big Smoke: A History of Air Pollution in London since Medieval Times* [New York: Routledge, 1987], 44, 55).

121. Various midcentury writers suggested the coal smoke in London posed a danger to human health (Brimblecombe, *The Big Smoke,"* 43–47).

122. Cited in Tinniswood, *By Permission of Heaven*, 11. Evelyn not only lambasted coal smoke but pointed to various industries that caused bad smells and air pollution that needed to be removed outside of the city limits.

123. Cavert, *The Smoke of London*, 200.

124. Cited in Pincus, *1688*, 66.

125. Edward Earl of Clarendon, *The Life of Edward Earl of Clarendon, Lord High Chancellor of England* (Oxford: Clarendon, 1827), 3:101.

126. For books on the Great Fire, see Neil Hanson, *The Great Fire of London In That Apocalyptic Year, 1666* (Hoboken, N.J.: John Wiley, 2002); and Tinniswood, *By Permission of Heaven*.

127. Huehns, ed., *Clarendon*, 419.

128. Evelyn, *Diary*, September 4, 1666.

129. Evelyn, *Diary*, September 7, 1666.

130. Charles II, *By the King, A Proclamation for the keeping of Markets to supply the City of London with Provisions, and also for prevention of Alarms and Tumults, and for appointing the Meeting of Merchants* (London, 1666).

131. Charles II, *A Proclamation for a General Fast through England and Wales*.

132. Cited in Cowie, *Plague and Fire*, 107.

133. Edward Waterhous, *A Short narrative of the Dreadful Fire in London* (London, 1667), 47–48.

134. Huehns, ed., *Clarendon*, 413.

135. The king also issued two royal proclamations in the aftermath of the fire; they concerned providing provisions and setting up markets. Meanwhile, any surviving structures, like churches and taverns, were quickly set up as temporary shelters. In many of the city's open spaces, like Moorfields and the Finsbury artillery grounds, the army set up tents and other temporary shelters (Hanson, *The Great Fire of London*, 166, 171).

136. Rolle, *Londons Resurrection*, preface.

137. Plans were developed by Christopher Wren, John Evelyn, Sir William Petty, Captain Valentine Knight, and Peter Mills, who was an "ex-Bricklayer to the City, and a surveyor and architect with a considerable reputation" (Tinniswood, *By Permission of Heaven*, 198–99).

138. According to Lawrence N. Powell, there were rare opportunities to entirely remake European cityscapes, which had often grown organically and thus did not fit emerging ideals of an Enlightenment city grid. It was only after "major calamities like fires and earthquakes, or the edicts of emperors" that city planners could engineer new urban settings (Powell, *The Accidental City: Improvising New Orleans* [Cambridge: Harvard University Press, 2012], 62).

139. Jeremiah Wells, "On the Rebuilding of London," in *London in Flames, London in Glory: Poems on the Fire and Rebuilding of London, 1666–1709*, ed. Robert Arnold Aubin (New Brunswick, N.J.: Rutgers University Press, 1943), 128.

140. Simon Ford, "Londons Resurrection, Poetically represented, and humbly presented To His Most Sacred Majesty" in *London in Flames*, ed. Aubin, 149.

141. Wells, "On the Rebuilding of London," 127.

142. Wells, "On the Rebuilding of London," 127–28.

143. London's streets were regularly commented on disparagingly, but so were the streets of other English cities. Henry Chapman described Bath in 1673: "He thought the streets were mostly 'of the Narrowest size' and were the 'greatest Eyesore to its Beauty, and Cumber to its accommodation'" (Emily Cockayne, *Hubbub: Filth, Noise & Stench in England 1600–1770* [New Haven: Yale University Press, 2007], 11–12).

144. Ford, "Londons Resurrection, Poetically represented, and humbly presented To His Most Sacred Majesty," 149.

145. Cited in De Beer, *John Evelyn*, 49. Evelyn also advocated for green spaces for London, including a band of sweet-smelling shrubs around the city (cited in Cowie, *Plague and Fire*, 110–11).

146. De Beer, *John Evelyn*, 33.

147. De Beer, *John Evelyn*, 37.

148. De Beer, *John Evelyn*, 37.

149. De Beer, *John Evelyn*, 36–37.

150. Cowie, *Plague and Fire*, 109. Scholars have suggested that Evelyn's emphasis on greenery and the creation of garden cities shaped proprietors' visions when developing urban designs in the colonies. De Beer further suggests that Evelyn's brief stint as a commissioner "for the Repairing the High-Wayes and Sewers, and for Keeping Clean of the Streets, in, and about the City of London and Westminster" from May 1662 through November 1663 may have given him "some practical experience" in urban design, including an understanding of street paving (De Beer, *John Evelyn*, 11–12). However, Thomas D. Wilson points to Richard Newcourt's plan, not Evelyn's, as the inspiration for Charles Town, Philadelphia, and Savannah (Wilson, *The Ashley Cooper Plan*, 102).

151. De Beer, *John Evelyn*, 50.

152. Cowie, *Plague and Fire*, 108.

153. Tinniswood, *By Permission of Heaven*, 220.

154. The Royal proclamation of September 13, 1666, in *Historical Charters and Constitutional Documents of the City of London*, ed. Walter Gray de Birch (London: Whiting, 1887), 66.

155. De Beer, *John Evelyn*, 25.

156. De Beer, *John Evelyn*, 31.

157. Francis Willmoth, *Sir Jonas Moore: Practical Mathematics and Restoration Science* (Rochester: Boydell & Brewer, 1993), 88, 130. Moore was appointed surveyor to the 5th Earl of Bedford's fen drainage company in late summer 1650. He lived and worked in the fenland for the next seven years. He was surveyor general for the first four years.

158. Willmoth, *Sir Jonas Moore*, 138.

159. Willmoth, *Sir Jonas Moore*, 130.

160. Tinniswood, *By Permission of Heaven*, 191–93.

161. Cowie, *Plague and Fire*, 111; T. F. Reddaway, *The Rebuilding of London after the Great Fire* (London: Jonathan Cape, 1940), 55. According to Tinniswood, the king selected three surveyors to be "Commissioners of Rebuilding" on October 3: Roger Pratt, Hugh May, and Christopher Wren. Civic commissioners then matched his selections with three of their own: Robert Hooke, Peter Mills (City Surveyor), and Edward Jerman, "a City carpenter with an interest in architecture and 'an experienced man in building'" (Tinniswood, *By Permission of Heaven*, 211–12).

162. Rolle, *Londons Resurrection*, preface.

163. This was also the era of the uptick in spies and the growing post office and other means of monitoring the lives of English women and men around the country (see Pincus, *1688*, 70–72; and Edward Higgs, *The Information State in England: The Central Collection of Information on Citizens since 1500* [New York: Palgrave Macmillan, 2004]).

164. Robert Hooke, *The Diary of Robert Hooke F.R.S., 1672–1680*, ed. Henry W. Robinson and Walter Adams (London, 1935); Lisa Jardine, *The Curious Life of Robert Hooke: The Man Who Measured London* (London: Harper Collins, 2003).

165. Powell, *The Accidental City*, 63.

166. Many writers sought to express a range of political and social ideals through the design and construction of urban environments (Powell, *The Accidental City*, 63).

167. De Beer, *John Evelyn*, 37.

168. De Beer, *John Evelyn*, 34. Placing ecclesiastical buildings on raised ground was a way to promote their importance. To be always able to see St. Paul's, to have a constant view, was perhaps also imagined as a way to always have God's eyes on you and your actions.

169. De Beer, *John Evelyn*, 39.

170. De Beer, *John Evelyn*, 39.

171. De Beer, *John Evelyn*, 48.

172. De Beer, *John Evelyn*, 48–49.

173. *An Act of Common Council by the Commissioners for Sewers, Pavements, &c., Touching the Paving and Cleansing the Streets, Lanes and Common Passages within the City* (London, 1671), 16.

174. There may have been a range of practical reasons why people bearing burdens might not be allowed on the pavement. For instance, there could have been a risk that they would damage the works.

175. *An Act of Common Council by the Commissioners for Sewers, Pavements, &c.*, 7–8.

176. *An Act of Common Council by the Commissioners for Sewers, Pavements, &c*, 9–11.

177. Cowie, *Plague and Fire*, 113.

178. In Evelyn's third plan for rebuilding London, Evelyn outlined that major thoroughfares should be forty to sixty feet wide (De Beer, *John Evelyn*, 26–27).

179. De Beer, *John Evelyn*, 26–27; Tinniswood, *By Permission of Heaven*, 224–25. The Rebuilding Act was passed in February. It insisted on standardized building practices, such as height and building materials. A copy of the First Rebuilding Act is in Reddaway, *Rebuilding of London*, 6.

180. Corporation of London, *Proclamation, Additional Act of Parliament for Rebuilding the City of London* (London, 1673).

181. Corporation of London, *Proclamation, Additional Act of Parliament for Rebuilding the City of London*.

182. *An Act of Common Council by the Commissioners for Sewers, Pavements, &c.*, title page.

183. For a more in-depth discussion of the links between smell, health, and character, see chap. 5.

184. *An Act of Common Council by the Commissioners for Sewers, Pavements, &c.*, 27.

185. *An Act of Common Council by the Commissioners for Sewers, Pavements, &c.,* 29.

186. Garencieres, *A Mite Cast into the Treasury,* 6.

187. For instance, car-man Robert Simonds lived in Tower, operated three carts, and was a caretaker of Horsly-Down. William Pinchbanck of Candlewick operated one car and cleared Blackmanstreet. Chistopher Rose of Cheapside owned two carts that operated on Whitecross Street (*An Act of Common Council by the Commissioners for Sewers, Pavements, &c.,* 34).

188. Mondays through Fridays from October 11 until February 11, they were expected to be on the streets by 5:00 a.m. and finished with their work by 9:00 a.m. However, from February 11 through October 11, they were supposed to begin by 4:00 a.m. and to be off the streets by 8:00 a.m. On Saturdays they began cleaning on the afternoon and were to complete their work by nighttime (*An Act of Common Council by the Commissioners for Sewers, Pavements, &c.,* "Paving and Cleansing the Streets," 20).

189. *An Act of Common Council by the Commissioners for Sewers, Pavements, &c.,* 3–5.

190. Pincus, *1688,* 66–67. According to Pincus, streetlights, gas lamps, were installed in the final decades of the seventeenth century, and "London soon required that the new lights be placed outside all public buildings" in order "to make towns safer and to encourage a variety of evening cultural activities." This chapter further argues that manipulating sensory experiences—with light and scent—were also intended to have physiological impact.

191. De Beer, *John Evelyn,* 47.

192. Cowie, *Plague and Fire,* 12.

193. Wilson, *The Ashley Cooper Plan,* 68.

194. Wilson, *The Ashley Cooper Plan,* 111.

195. Wilson, *The Ashley Cooper Plan,* 100.

196. *A short advertisement upon the situation and extent of the city of Philadelphia* (London, 1683), 10.

197. Wilson, *The Ashley Cooper Plan,* 111.

198. Wilson, *The Ashley Cooper Plan,* 101–3. According to Wilson, it is likely that Ashley Cooper's position in Charles II's government would have given him access to the various plans put forward to redesign London. He may have taken these plans into consideration when designing plans for Carolina.

199. "Proposals in order to the improvement of the county of Albemarle in the Province of Carolina in point of Townes, trade and Coyne," and "Proposalls concerning building of towns in Virginia," Egerton MS 2395, ff. 661, 666, British Library.

200. "Proposals in order to the improvement of the county of Albemarle in the Province of Carolina in point of Townes, trade and Coyne," Egerton MS 2395, f. 661, British Library.

201. "Proposalls concerning building of towns in Virginia," Egerton MS 2395, f. 666, British Library.

202. Mulcahy, "That Fatall Spott," 200.

203. Mulcahy, "That Fatall Spott," 200.

204. Mulcahy, "That Fatall Spott," 209.

205. Cowie, *Plague and Fire,* 12.

206. Cited in De Beer, *John Evelyn*, 47–48.

207. Cristobal Silva, *Miraculous Plagues: An Epidemiology of Early New England* (Oxford: Oxford University Press, 2011), has argued that in early New England bodily health was a key sign of an individual's and a community's status before God and influenced perceptions of community identity.

208. Rolle, *Londons Resurrection*, preface.

209. Rolle, *Londons Resurrection*, preface.

210. Although postfire, urban development in London was a local phenomenon, the ideas circulating in print about the causes and the aftermath of plague and fire were read and discussed by people beyond the city. What role did catastrophe play in cultivating a sense of shared, imagined community?

211. Although Harvey had published his ideas about the circulation of blood in human bodies several decades prior, it was still a revolutionary idea. The adoption of circulation as a metaphor for trade, infusing the body with good health, requires explanation.

212. John Graunt addressed concerns that the great metropolis of London was "perhaps a Head too big for the Body, and possibly too strong" because it had become so populous. He further observed that "this Head grows three times as fast as the Body unto which it belongs" (Graunt, *Natural and Political Observations . . . made upon the Bills of Mortality* [London, 1662], title page).

213. As the nearest town to the Scottish border, Barwick-upon-Tweed was a point of contention between England and Scotland. I suppose this was the king's way of trying to define his outermost borders and territories.

214. Charles II, *A Proclamation for a General Fast through England and Wales*.

215. Charles II, *A Proclamation for a General Fast through England and Wales*.

216. Charles II, *A Proclamation for a General Fast through England and Wales*.

217. Certainly fasting was a way to establish inclusion and exclusion within spiritual communities. It appears that fasting proclamations by early modern leaders like Charles II were engaged in a similar community-building project.

218. Lady Mary Boyle (sister to Robert Boyle and Catherine, Countess of Ranelagh) married Charles Rich, who became the 4th Earl of Warwick. She lived in Essex at Leighs Park. Throughout her diary she writes about praying outdoors in the "wilderness" at Leighs Priory, but when in London, she did so in the gardens of Sir Hans Sloane.

219. Warwick's residence, Leighs Priory, was near the Thames River on the coast in Essex. She may have heard sea battles in the North Sea. She might also have been referencing the sea battle from June 3 that killed her brother. The events were described by Pepys on June 8: "The Earl of Falmouth, Muskerry, and Mr. Richard Boyle killed on board the Duke's ship, The Royall Charles, with one shot: their blood and brains flying in the Duke's face and the head of Mr. Boyle striking down the Duke, as some say." With such a horrible account of the events the previous year, she might have been meditating on her personal connections to the event (Pepys, *Diary*, June 8, 1665).

220. Diary of Lady Warwick, Add MS 27,351, f. 8, British Library.

221. Diary of Lady Warwick, Add MS 27,351, f. 13, British Library.

222. Diary of Lady Warwick, Add MS 27,351, f. 22, British Library.

223. Diary of Lady Warwick, Add MS 27,351, f. 22, British Library.

224. Diary of Lady Warwick, Add MS 27,351, f. 22, British Library.

225. Warwick was an extremely elite woman who did, indeed, have close contact with powerful figures who regularly dined at her table and visited her home. On November 29, 1666, she dined with Lord Berkley, and after dinner she received a visit from the archbishop of Canterbury. After a visit with the Duchess of York she recorded in her diary that she could not concentrate on prayer because her "mind was discomposed and like Martha I was trobled with worldly busines and the Duches of Yorke being to com and supp at my house with in two or three dayes I was full of feare how to entertaine her" (Diary of Lady Warwick, Add MS 27,351, ff. 41, 83, British Library).

226. Cited in Reddaway, *The Rebuilding of London*, 300.

227. According to Bliss, "there were definite stirrings of progressive change in the areas which, today, we might call public policy. . . . [T]here was also a sense of deliberate purpose to public policy during this period which foreshadows the emergence of the modern state" (Robert M. Bliss, *Restoration England: Politics and Government, 1660–1685* [London: Taylor & Francis, 1985], 22).

228. Healy, *Fictions of Disease*, 13–14.

2 / Taming Fenland Bodies

1. For the myth of web-footed fen residents, see Oliver Rackham, *The History of the Countryside* (London: Phoenix Press, 2000); for their pallid complexions and sickly appearance, see Mary J. Dobson, *Contours of Death and Disease in Early Modern England* (Cambridge: Cambridge University Press, 1997). Meanwhile, contemporary documents include comparisons of residents to animals, such as in an account of travel through the "Westerne Counties" written by Lieutenant Hammond (Lansdowne MS 213/27, ff. 381–82 [1635], British Library). Still others lambasted fenlanders' supposed laziness, incivility, and spiritual ineptitude, such as in Samuel Fortrey, *The History or Narrative of the Great Level of the Fenns, Called Bedford Level* (London, 1685), 72.

2. Anon., "Enquiries Concerning Agriculture," *Philosophical Transactions of the Royal Society* 5 (1665): 94.

3. For more on pro-drainage rhetoric, see Eric H. Ash, *The Draining of the Fens: Projectors, Popular Politics, and State Building in Early Modern England* (Baltimore: Johns Hopkins University Press, 2017), 8–9, 17–18.

4. William Dugdale, *The History of Imbanking and Draining of Diverse Fens and Marshes, Both in Foreign Parts and in This Kingdom* (London, 1662), 145.

5. Keith Lindley, *Fenland Riots and the English Revolution* (London: Heinemann, 1982); Ash, *The Draining of the Fens*, 217–48.

6. Oliver Cromwell was a native of the fen region and had defended fenlanders' rights in the late 1630s against the Crown and the first Great Level drainage adventurers (see Ken Hiltner, "Early Modern Ecology," in *A New Companion to English Renaissance Literature and Culture*, ed. Michael Hattaway, 2 vols. [Oxford, U.K.: Wiley-Blackwell, 2010], 2:1645–46; and Lindley, *Fenland Riots and the English Revolution*, 95).

7. Chandra Mukerji, *Impossible Engineering: Technology and Territoriality on the Canal du Midi* (Princeton, N.J.: Princeton University Press, 2009), 2; Chandra Mukerji, *Territorial Ambitions and the Gardens of Versailles* (Cambridge: Cambridge University Press, 1997).

8. Mukerji, *Impossible Engineering*, 2.

9. According to Dorothy Summers: "The very nature of fen life made some form of organized effort essential. A complex system of communal regulations, designed to ensure a careful utilization of the land at all times, gradually evolved" (Summers, *The Great Level: A History of Drainage and Land Reclamation in the Fens* [Newton Abbot, Vt.: David and Charles, 1976], 34).

10. For scholarship included in the "new coastal history," see David Worthington, ed., *The New Coastal History: Cultural and Environmental Perspectives from Scotland and Beyond* (Cham, Switzerland: Palgrave Macmillan, 2017), v; Andrew Lipman, *The Saltwater Frontier: Indians and the Contest for the American Coast* (New Haven, Conn.: Yale University Press, 2015); and Christopher L. Pastore, *Between Land and Sea: The Atlantic Coast and the Transformation of New England* (Cambridge, Mass.: Harvard University Press, 2014).

11. Lieutenant Hammond, "A relation of a short survey of the westerne counties" (1635), Lansdowne MS 213/27, f. 381, British Library.

12. Karen Ordahl Kupperman, "Controlling Nature and Colonial Projects in Early America," in *Colonial Encounters: Essays in Early American History and Culture*, ed. Hans-Jürgen Grabbe, American Studies 109 (Ersch-Termin, 2003), 78. The word "wilderness" was likely a reference to uncultivated land but may also have suggested a spiritual state.

13. Mary Dobson, "'Marsh Fever'—the Geography of Malaria in England," *Journal of Historical Geography* 6, no. 4 (1980): 367–70.

14. For the reference to the petrified wood of Lough Neagh, see Royal Society, *Philosophical Transactions*, August 22, 1685; for the bird, see MS 883, vol. 1, f. 8, Trinity College Dublin Library; for examples of water cures, see MS 883, vol. 1, f. 2, Trinity College Dublin Library.

15. Ash, *The Draining of the Fens*, 217–48.

16. *Arts Improvement* (London, 1725), 158.

17. Robert Burton described the impact of marshlands air on residents, claiming such airs led to people who were "dull, heavy, and subject to many infirmities" (Burton, *The Anatomie of Melancholy* [London, 1621], 259).

18. Richard Franck, *Northern Memoirs, calculated for the meridian of Scotland wherein most or all of the cities, citadels, seaports, castles, forts, fortresses, rivers and rivulets are compendiously described* (London, 1694), 108.

19. The presence of wetlands was regularly deployed as evidence that the residents were uncivilized. Pastoralists were assumed to have any number of undesirable characteristics. Take, for instance, Richard Franck's descriptions of Scotland as "besieged" with bogs (Franck, *Northern Memoirs*, 108).

20. Lindley, *Fenland Riots and the English Revolution*, 1.

21. John Maynard, *The Picklock of the Old Fenne Projects* (London, 1650).

22. Margaret Albright Knittl, "The Design for the Initial Drainage of the Great Level of the Fens: An Historical Whodunit in Three Parts," *Agricultural History Review* 55, no. 1 (2007): 47.

23. Knittl, "The Design for the Initial Drainage of the Great Level," 49.

24. Lindley, *Fenland Riots and the English Revolution*, 223.

25. Ash, *The Draining of the Fens*, 10.

26. Francis Mathew, *Of the Opening of Rivers for Navigation* (London, 1656), 2.

27. Scholars such as Jane Ohlmeyer have argued that English colonization in Ireland was neither governance at home nor governance in the colonies but a more complicated category (Ohlmeyer, "'Civilizinge of Those Rude Parts': Colonization within Britain and Ireland, 1580–1640s," in *The Oxford History of the British Empire*, vol. 1: *The Origins of Empire: British Overseas Enterprise to the Close of the Seventeenth Century*, ed. Nicholas Canny [Oxford: Oxford University Press, 1998], 124–47). With Ireland effectively a "laboratory of empire," decisions made and tested there were often exported elsewhere. Meanwhile, scholars have long debated how best to analyze English activity in Ireland. Should Ireland be discussed as a kingdom within a Three Kingdoms framework or as a colony within an Atlantic framework? (see John Patrick Montaño, *The Roots of English Colonialism in Ireland* [Cambridge: Cambridge University Press, 2015]).

28. Michel Foucault, *Discipline and Punish: The Birth of the Prison*, trans. Alan Sheridan (New York: Random House, 1995); Constance Classen, David Howes, and Anthony Synnott, *Aroma: The Cultural History of Smell* (New York: Routledge, 1994), 3–5.

29. Lieutenant Hammond, "A relation of a short survey of the westerne counties" (1635), Lansdowne MS 213/27, ff. 381–82, British Library.

30. Eve Darian-Smith, "Beating the Bounds: Law, Identity and Territory in the New Europe," *Political and Legal Anthropology Review* 18, no. 1 (May 1995): 63–73.

31. William Dugdale, *The History of Embanking and Draining of Divers Fens and Marshes* (London, 1662), mentions fenlanders on stilts.

32. Allan Greer, *Property and Dispossession: Natives, Empires and Land in Early Modern North America* (New York: Cambridge University Press, 2018), 355.

33. Greer, *Property and Dispossession*, 202.

34. An example of the type of person involved in both domestic improvement and imperial ventures is Bedford Level Corporation member Samuel Fortrey. Fortrey's cousin John Josselyn wrote two books on the natural history of New England and thanked Fortrey for his financial assistance. Fortrey's position as "Clerk of the Deliveries" for the Board of Ordnance Office required his knowledge of both domestic and imperial possessions. Similarly, Arthur Annesley, Earl of Anglesey, was one of the bailiffs of the Bedford Level and was deeply engaged in colonial activities, including as one of the founding members of the Council of Foreign Plantations. The office had Josselyn's two texts on their book shelves ("A List of all Books (in the Plantation Office) Treating of New England," Egerton MS 2395, f. 573, British Library). Annesley was also treasurer of Ireland after the Restoration and was the recipient of a letter containing William Petty's introduction of the concept of "political arithmetic," which suggested that new, mathematical concepts might rationalize governance. Finally, Thomas Colepeper, 2nd Baron of Culpeper of Thoresway, was a bailiff of the Bedford Level Corporation and later served as a governor of Virginia, for example.

35. Scholars had begun to investigate the conceptional and chronological links between external colonization and internal state building, and to flesh out concepts such as "internal colonialism" (see Robert Bartlett, *The Making of Europe: Conquest, Colonization and Cultural Change, 950–1350* [Princeton, N.J.: Princeton University Press, 1993]; and Phillipa Levine, *The British Empire: From Sunrise to Sunset* [Edinburgh: Pearson, 2007]).

36. Adolphus Speed, *Adam out of Eden, or, An abstract of divers excellent Experiments touching the advancement of Husbandry* (London, 1659), "To the Reader."

37. An older but still informative text on fenland draining is H. C. Darby, *The Draining of the Fens* (Cambridge: Cambridge University Press, 1940).

38. Cornelius Vermuyden, *A discourse touching the drayning the Great Fennes* (London, 1642), 5.

39. Summers, *The Great Level*, 18–22.

40. Vermuyden, *A discourse touching the drayning the Great Fennes*, 5–6.

41. Summers, *The Great Level*, 18–22.

42. Vermuyden, *A discourse touching the drayning the Great Fennes*, 5.

43. Summers, *The Great Level*, 34.

44. Vermuyden, *A discourse touching the drayning the Great Fennes*, 6

45. The fenlander song cited in Ken Hiltner, *What Else Is Pastoral? Renaissance Literature and the Environment* (Ithaca, N.Y.: Cornell University Press, 2011), 133.

46. Lieutenant Hammond, "A relation of a short survey of the westerne counties" (1635), Lansdowne MS 213/27, f. 381, British Library

47. Summers, *The Great Level*, 83.

48. Hiltner, "Early Modern Ecology," 1643.

49. Hiltner, "Early Modern Ecology," 1643.

50. Hiltner, "Early Modern Ecology," 1643.

51. Hiltner, "Early Modern Ecology," 1.

52. Hiltner, "Early Modern Ecology," 2.

53. Hiltner, "Early Modern Ecology," 1.

54. According to Eric Ash, most of the major drainage works were undertaken after Charles I ascended to the throne because of his "willingness to frame things in terms of the royal will versus selfish local interests, with the good of the commonwealth at stake" (Ash, *The Draining of the Fens*, 175).

55. Knittl, "The Design for the Initial Drainage of the Great Level," 35.

56. Knittl, "The Design for the Initial Drainage of the Great Level," 36.

57. Ash, *The Draining of the Fens*, 216.

58. Francis Willmoth, *Sir Jonas Moore: Practical Mathematics and Restoration Science* (Rochester: Boydell & Brewer, 1993), 91.

59. Gregory Kennedy, "Marshland Colonization in Acadia and Poitou during the 17th Century," *Acadiensis* 42, no. 1 (2013): 40.

60. Mathew, *Of the Opening of Rivers for Navigation*, 1.

61. Willmoth, *Sir Jonas Moore*, 91.

62. Hiltner, "Early Modern Ecology," 1643.

63. Lindley, *Fenland Riots and the English Revolution*, 1.

64. Lindley, *Fenland Riots and the English Revolution*, 1.

65. Ken Hiltner, "Early Modern Ecology," 1644. Ultimately, scholars such as Keith Lindley see these popular protests against drainage as a contributing factor to civil war.

66. Willmoth, *Sir Jonas Moore*, 91.

67. The full text of the act can be read in Samuel Wells, *The History of the Drainage of the Great Level of the Fens, Called Beford Level* (London, 1830), 173–74.

68. Willmoth, *Sir Jonas Moore*, 92; Summers, *The Great Level*, 66.

69. Summers, *The Great Level*, 66.

70. For instance, John Cotton noted a shipment to Boston of "sundry Scots" taken at Dunbar who "had arrived there and been sold, not for slaves to perpetual servitude,

but for six or seven or eight years." An agent for Massachusetts likewise purchased others from jail in London (cited in James Davie Butler, "British Convicts Shipped to American Colonies," *American Historical Review* 2, no. 1 [1896]: 13).

71. Charles II, *A Proclamation for the Preservation of the Great Level of the Fens, called Bedford Level, and of the Works made for the Dreining of the same* (London, 1662).

72. Charles II, *A Proclamation for the Preservation of the Great Level of the Fens.*

73. Fortrey, *Englands Interest and Improvement*, "To the Reader."

74. According to John Richards, *The Unending Frontier: An Environmental History of the Early Modern World* (Berkeley: University of California Press, 2003), the English regularly framed their imperial ventures and the "extension of state power" as a means to civilize "pastoral peoples around the world," whom they believed were uncivilized for their failures to cultivate extensively (198).

75. Summers, *The Great Level*, 46.

76. The printer of *The History or Narrative of the Great Level of the Fenns* claimed that the manuscript had "come into my hands." While it is frequently attributed to Sir Jonas Moore because his famous maps of the Great Level accompanied the text, his involvement with the Great Level had long since ended. Likewise, textual clues have made the possibility unlikely. Yet the general attribution to Fortrey made by numerous scholars is also a little puzzling. The text includes information from the new administration of the Great Level in 1684, two years after Fortrey's death. It is possible that he wrote the text and this new information was added after the fact. Indeed, despite Samuel Fortrey's death in 1682, the Fortrey family did remain involved with fen drainage. Their properties in Cambridge, Byall Fenn, required embanking, continued upkeep, and investments in improvements, such as the installation of an engine to pump out water (see Add MS 26,082, f. 41, British Library).

77. Fortrey, *The History or Narrative*, 60–63. Fortrey was involved in the Bedford Scheme as early as 1649. Investors in the drainage had seven years to complete the draining. Investors would receive about ninety-five thousand acres, and twelve thousand were reserved for Cromwell. The "Act for the draining of the Great Level of the Fens" was passed on May 29, 1649. The full text is in Wells, *History of Drainage*, 1:173–74. After the Restoration, the Beford Level Corporation sought a permanent renewal of its powers, but it was at first prevented from obtaining this by several former investors who demanded readmission to the corporation. As part of a campaign to gain support, the company published William Dugdale's *History of Imbanking and Drayning of Divers Fenns and Marshes* in 1662, a text that celebrated the benefits of drainage. The good press worked, and the Bedford Level Corporation was founded in 1663.

78. Lindley, *Fenland Riots and the English Revolution*, 253.

79. Ash, *The Draining of the Fens*, 146.

80. Ash, *The Draining of the Fens*, 205.

81. Fortrey, *The History or Narrative*, 59–60.

82. Fortrey, *The History or Narrative*, 57.

83. Charles II, *A Proclamation for the Preservation of the Great Level of the Fens*, 2.

84. Cited in Summers, *The Great Level*, epigraph.

85. Annabel Brett, *Changes of State: Nature and the Limits of the City in Early Modern Natural Law* (Princeton, N.J.: Princeton University Press, 2011), 5.

86. However, William Dugdale supported the drainage works. The purpose of the inclusion of the fenlander song in the text is not necessarily a straightforward one. Perhaps the work of the poem is to imagine the fenlanders' displacement, hoping reality would soon catch up to fantasy.

87. The author went on to remind the readers that while "The feather'd fowls have wings, to fly to other nations; / But we have no such things, to help our transportation; / we must give place (oh grievous case) to horned beasts and cattle, / Except that we can all agree to drive them out by battle" (cited in Hiltner, *What Else Is Pastoral?*, 133).

88. Fortrey, *The History or Narrative*, 2–3.

89. Joyce Appleby, *Economic Thought and Ideology in Seventeenth-Century England* (Princeton, N.J.: Princeton University Press, 1978), 76; N. A. M. Rodger, *The Command of the Ocean: A Naval History of Britain, 1649–1815* (New York: Norton, 2005), 99.

90. Rodger, *The Command of the Ocean*, 97.

91. As Keith Pluymers has argued, however, "scarcity and abundance" were "disputed concepts" (Pluymers, "Atlantic Iron: Wood Scarcity and the Political Ecology of Early English Expansion," *William and Mary Quarterly* 73, no. 3 [July 2016]: 426).

92. John Evelyn, *Sylva, or, A discourse of forest-trees, and the propagation of timber in His Majesties dominions* (London, 1664), 114.

93. Of course, as Walt Woodward has argued in *Prospero's America*, Winthrop, Jr. later seems to have regretted his openness in sharing stories of the resources available in the colonies. He became increasingly reluctant to share details about the natural world when he began to realize that this information in the wrong hands could put Connecticut, and London's relatively lax oversight of the colony, at risk (Woodward, *Prospero's America: John Winthrop, Jr., Alchemy, and the Creation of New England Culture, 1606–1676* [Chapel Hill: Published for the Omohundro Institute of Early American History and Culture by the University of North Carolina Press, 2010]).

94. John Josselyn, *New-Englands Rarities Discovered in Birds, Beasts, Fishes, Serpents, and Plants of that Country* (London, 1672), 4.

95. Josselyn, *New-Englands Rarities Discovered*, 63–64

96. Pluymers, "Atlantic Iron," 392.

97. Fortrey, *The History or Narrative*, 2–3.

98. See, for instance, MS 883, f. 316, Dublin Philosophical Society Papers, vol. 1, Trinity College Library Dublin. Bogs were thought to have special preservative properties: "The Bog Itself: Enlightenment Prospects and National Elegies," in *Bardic Nationalism: The Romantic Novel and the British Empire*, ed. Katie Trumpener (Princeton, N.J.: Princeton University Press, 1997).

99. Such reports of ancient tree growth below wetlands came from numerous sources, including the Isle of Orkney, Scotland. Observers reported that "it seems there hath been Woods growing in this Country, for in the Mosses they find Trees with their Branches intire of 20 or 30 foot in length." These trees in the "Mosses" provided evidence that such magnificent trees had once existed in Orkney. "The Author of the following Description of the Orkney Isles, was the Reverend Mr. James Wallace Minister of Kirkwall, the only Town in these Isles." A DESCRIPTION of the ISLES of ORKNEY; By Master JAMES WALLACE, late Minister of KIRK WALL, Published after his Death by his Son (Edinburgh, 1693), 19.

100. Hot spring in Logh Neagh, MS 883, f. 2, Dublin Philosophical Society Papers, vol. 1, Trinity College Library Dublin.

101. MS 883, f. 299, Dublin Philosophical Society Papers, vol. 1, Trinity College Library Dublin.

102. MS 883, f. 316, Dublin Philosophical Society Papers, vol. 1, Trinity College Library Dublin.

103. MS 883, f. 316, Dublin Philosophical Society Papers, vol. 1, Trinity College Library Dublin.

104. The anonymous author further suggested that "to this I may add that the antient appellation of this Countrey speaks no less, for it was called by name which Imports the Forest of the blackhogg suggesting woodlands" (cited in MS 883, f. 316, Dublin Philosophical Society Papers, vol. 1, Trinity College Library Dublin).

105. "Customes and Manners," MS 883, f. 331, Dublin Philosophical Society Papers, vol. 1, Trinity College Library Dublin.

106. MS 883, ff. 316, 331, Dublin Philosophical Society Papers, vol. 1, Trinity College Library Dublin.

107. Lieutenant Hammond, "A relation of a short survey of the westerne counties" (1635), Lansdowne MS 213/27, f. 381, British Library.

108. Fortrey, *The History or Narrative*, 72.

109. Fortrey, *The History or Narrative*, 72.

110. Fortrey, *The History or Narrative*, 75.

111. Fortrey, *The History or Narrative*, 75.

112. Scholars like Patricia Seed have illuminated how improvement schemes functioned as a way to assert both political and personal possession (Seed, *Ceremonies of Possession in Europe's Conquest of the New World*). But the same discourse was utilized in internal colonization, such as the land grabs by adventurers in the fenlands.

113. Fortrey, *The History or Narrative*, 71–81.

114. Critics have suggested that Denham's description of the overflowing Thames from earlier versions in the 1640s stood for the unrestrained and uncontained behavior of the king's rule. However, in the version from 1655 it has been broadly understood as having an altered meaning (Hiltner, "Early Modern Ecology," 1631).

115. Denham rewrote it several times through the 1640s and 1650s, and it "can certainly be read as revealing much about contemporary political and cultural landscape" (Hiltner, "Early Modern Ecology," 1642).

116. Cited in Julie Bowring, "Between the Corporation and Captain Flood: The Fens and Drainage after 1663," in *Custom, Improvement and the Landscape in Early Modern Britain*, ed. Richard W. Hoyle (Farnham, U.K.: Ashgate, 2011), 235–61.

117. A report on the location and condition of the forts in and around Ireland, MS 883, f. 84, Dublin Philosophical Society Papers, vol. 1, Trinity College Library Dublin.

118. A report on the location and condition of the forts in and around Ireland, MS 883, f. 84, Dublin Philosophical Society Papers, vol. 1, Trinity College Library Dublin.

119. Nicola Whyte, *Inhabiting the Landscape: Place, Custom and Memory, 1500–1800* (Oxford: Oxbow, 2009), 25–26.

120. Roberta Gilchrist, *Contemplation and Action: The Other Monasticism* (London: Leicester University Press, 1995), 115.

121. Dugdale, *The History of Imbanking and Drayning*, 7.

122. Mary Dobson, *Contours of Death and Disease in Early Modern England* (Cambridge: Cambridge University Press, 1997), 295.

123. Thomas Stafford, *Pacata Hibernia. Ireland Appeased and Reduced* (London, 1633), 355.

124. Of course, not all watery environments were the same. According to Dr. John Armstrong's poem *The Art of Preserving Health* (London, 1744), running water was far healthier than still, stagnant water, which was corrupt. Water at rest he described "with vegetation green / squalid with generation, and the birth / Of little monsters."

125. Dobson, "Marsh Fever," 364.

126. A poem written by a fenlander suggested: "The moory soil, the watry atmosphere / With the damp, unhealthy moisture chills the air. / Thick, stinking fogs, and noxious vapours fall, / Agues and coughs are epidemicall; / Hence every face presented to our view / Looks of a pallid or a sallow hue" (Dobson, "Marsh Fever," 364–66).

127. Samuel Purchas, *Hakluytus Posthumus or Purchas his Pilgrimes, containing a History of the World in Sea Voyages and Lande Travells Purchas his pilgrims* (Glasgow: Printed by Robert Maclehose and Sons for the University of Glasgow, 1902), 1374.

128. Everett Emerson, *Letters from New England: The Massachusetts Bay Colony, 1629–1638* (Amherst: University of Massachusetts Press, 1976), 23.

129. M. Bromfield, *A Brief Discovery of the chief Causes, Signs, and Effects of the most Reigning Disease, the Scurvy* (London, 169[?]), 6.

130. Lieutenant Hammond, "A relation of a short survey of the westerne counties" (1635), Lansdowne MS 213/27, f. 382, British Library.

131. Bromfield, *A Brief Discovery*, 6.

132. Lieutenant Hammond, "A relation of a short survey of the westerne counties" (1635), Lansdowne MS 213/27, f. 381, British Library.

133. Cited in Dobson, *Contours of Health and Disease in Early Modern England*, 295.

134. Dobson, "Marsh Fever," 367–70.

135. Dobson, "Marsh Fever," 368.

136. Dobson, "Marsh Fever," 368.

137. Cited in Dobson, "Marsh Fever" 368.

138. Burton, *The anatomie of melancholy* (London, 1621), 259.

139. Burton, *The anatomie of melancholy*, 259.

140. Dobson, "Marsh Fever," 312.

141. Lieutenant Hammond, "A relation of a short survey of the westerne counties" (1635), Lansdowne MS 213/ 27, f. 381, British Library.

142. Richards, *The Unending Frontier*, 218.

143. Rev. James Brome, *Three Years' Travels in England, Scotland and Wales* (London, 1700), 115.

144. Lansdowne MS 213/27, f. 381, British Library.

145. Brett, *Changes of State*, 5. Meanwhile, this book suggests that a metaphor like this perhaps held such power, such force, because of contemporaries' recognitions that bodies and temperaments really might change in new places. It works as a metaphor because it is meant to describe a conceptual, political space, not a real space, but relies on the physical and material world to give it its abiding power as a concept. Porous bodies might very well become—if not animal—then *animal like*, in certain places. For contemporaries, behavior, much like health, was influenced by environment.

146. James David Drake, *The Nation's Nature: How Continental Presumptions Gave Rise to the United States of America* (Charlottesville: University of Virginia Press, 2011), 19.

147. Andrew Wear, *Knowledge and Practice in Early Modern English Medicine, 1550–1680* (Cambridge: Cambridge University Press, 2000), 184–85.

148. Wear, *Knowledge and Practice in Early Modern English Medicine*, 186.

149. Kupperman, "Fear of Hot Climates," 216.

150. "The Irish Report that Railes towards winter turn to water Hens," MS 883, f. 8, Dublin Philosophical Society Papers, vol. 1, Trinity College Dublin Library.

151. "The Irish Report that Railes towards winter turn to water Hens," MS 883, f. 8, Dublin Philosophical Society Papers, vol. 1, Trinity College Dublin Library.

152. Hot spring in Logh Neagh, MS 883, f. 2, Dublin Philosophical Society Papers, vol. 1, Trinity College Dublin Library.

153. Hugh Todd, "An Account of a Salt Spring, and Another Medicinal Spring, on the Banks of the River Weare, or Ware in the Bishoprick of Durham in a Letter to the Publisher . . . ," *Philosophical Transactions* 14 (January 1684): 726–29.

154. Joan Thirsk, *Food in Early Modern England: Phases, Fads, Fashions 1500–1760* (New York: Hambledon Continuum, 2007), 129.

155. Alexandra Walsham, *The Reformation of the Landscape: Religion, Identity, and Memory in Early Modern Britain and Ireland* (Oxford: Oxford University Press, 2011). According to Walsham, in England, the association of healing springs and wells was often linked to a much older pre-Reformation culture of religious healing.

156. William Petty, "Some Queries Whereby to Examine Mineral Waters by the Learned Sir William Petty Knight," *Philosophical Transactions* 14 (January 1684): 802–3.

157. Clonuffe Waters by Mr King, MS 883, f. 18, Dublin Philosophical Society Papers, vol. 1, Trinity College Dublin Library.

158. Clonuffe Waters by Mr King, MS 883, f. 18, Dublin Philosophical Society Papers, vol. 1, Trinity College Dublin Library.

159. Clonuffe Waters by Mr King, MS 883, f. 18, Dublin Philosophical Society Papers, vol. 1, Trinity College Dublin Library.

160. Daston and Park, *Wonders and the Order of Nature*, 216.

161. Fortrey, *History or Narrative*, 72.

162. Cited in Keith Pluymers, "Taming the Wilderness in Sixteenth-and Seventeenth-Century Ireland and Virginia," *Environmental History* 16, no. 4 (October 2011): 613.

163. Fortrey, *The History or Narrative*, 71–81.

164. John Josselyn's father was twice married. His first son by his first marriage, Torrell, had a daughter, Theodora, who was married to Samuel Fortrey. John and his elder brother Henry were sons of the second marriage. John Josselyn's brother was a colonist in Black Point, Maine.

165. Ash, *The Draining of the Fens*, chap. 8, note 103.

166. Samuel Hartlib, *Samuel Hartlib his legacie* (London, 1651), 53.

167. Cited in Michael Garibaldi Hall, *Edward Randolph and the American Colonies, 1676–1703* (Chapel Hill: University of North Carolina Press, 1960), xi.

168. Fortrey was not alone in making such an argument. According to the economic historian Ellen Meiksins Wood, numerous early modern writers asserted that

anyone improving wastelands held in common "has *given* something to humanity, not taken it away" (Wood, *The Origin of Capitalism* [New York: Monthly Review Press, 1999], 111).

169. Scholars have begun to note how the reaction to contact with the wider world often spurred Englishmen to turn inward. Alix Cooper has argued that the proliferation of far-flung spices, drugs, and exotic plants in England inspired a newfound interest in England's own plant productions (Cooper, *Inventing the Indigenous: Local Knowledge and Natural History in Early Modern Europe* [Cambridge: Cambridge University Press, 2007]).

170. The focus on extractive colonization is often seen as an early model of colonization that was replaced by settlement models. But Fortrey, among others, retained a sense that colonization ought to be prosecuted in limited circumstances, particularly when that place could grow certain useful or lucrative items. The persistence of multiple colonization models works to disrupt any easy characterization of colonial models in later periods. The ongoing fishing industry in Newfoundland serves as an example (Peter E. Pope, *Fish into Wine: The Newfoundland Plantation in the Seventeenth Century* [Chapel Hill: University of North Carolina Press, 2004]).

171. Agricultural improvement was perceived to solve many domestic problems. It had the potential to inject some life into the economy, by growing goods that had to be purchased at high cost from abroad.

172. Andrew Yarranton, *England's Improvement by Sea and Land* (London, 1677).

173. Speed, *Adam out of Eden*, "To the Reader."

174. According to Eric Ash, midcentury reform advocates such as Samuel Hartlib, Robert Child, and Cressy Dymock had also claimed that fen drainage "represented a unique tabula rasa" on which to conduct experiments in agricultural improvement and that "such sweeping improvements as these were the best and godliest way for England to prosper, because they increased the size and productivity of the nation through peaceful means, rather than conquest" (Ash, *The Draining of the Fens*, 282, 285).

175. Cameralist theory sought to avoid the issues associated with colonization and with imbalanced trade by planting what was needed at home. Linnaeus's economic strategy for Sweden rested on "import substitution" (Lisbet Koerner, *Linnaeus: Nature and Nation* [Cambridge, Mass.: Harvard University Press, 1999], 6, 139). Fredrik Albritton Jonsson has tracked the emergence of civil cameralism in eighteenth-century Scotland, wherein "schemes of import substitution undercut both colonial and foreign trade in favor of an economic strategy of national autarky within the British Isles" (Albritton Jonsson, "Scottish Tobacco and Rhubarb: The Natural Order of Civil Cameralism in the Scottish Enlightenment," *Eighteenth-Century Studies* 49, no. 2 [Winter 2016]: 130). Both Koerner and Jonsson have tracked how cameralists saw in import substitution "a cheaper and morally superior alternative to external commerce and conquest" (Jonsson, "Scottish Tobacco and Rhubarb," 131).

176. Carew Reynell, *The True English Interest* (London, 1679), 90.

177. Vermuyden, *A discourse touching the drayning the Great Fennes*, 2.

178. Summers, *The Great Level*, 71.

179. Summers, *The Great Level*, 71.

180. Lansdowne MS 213/27, f. 382, British Library.

181. Greer, *Property and Dispossession*, 355.

182. MS 72,865, ff. 83–84, Petty Papers, British Library. Yet elsewhere William Petty espoused a negative assessment of colonization in New England. According to Ted McCormick, Petty thought that the "colonies were not simply a source of competition or a drain on population in an absolute sense; by creating divisions they increased the costs of government while diminishing the value of population through geographic dispersal, economic dissociation, political disaffection, and ultimately—as in Ireland—degeneration" (McCormick, *William Petty and the Ambitions of Political Arithmetic* [Oxford: Oxford University Press, 2010], 231).

183. Add MS 72,865, f. 84, Petty Papers, British Library.

184. Kupperman, "Controlling Nature and Colonial Projects in Early America," 81.

185. Early drainage efforts employed Dutch surveyor generals. The Dutch were considered the reigning experts on drainage works. However, during the Anglo-Dutch Wars, this was no longer a possibility. The Bedford Corporation hired the English mathematician Sir Jonas Moore to oversee the drainage works. Moore later oversaw engineering projects along the Thames and in Tangiers and was patronized by the Duke of York.

186. Summers, *The Great Level*, 95.

187. Cited in David Alff, *The Wreckage of Intentions: Projects in British Culture, 1660–1730* (Philadelphia: University of Pennsylvania, 2017), 110.

3 / Bodies of Water

1. Dutch efforts at colonization along the western banks of the Delaware River began in the 1630s. It initially failed in the face of conflict with Lenape Indians. A disgruntled former employee of the Dutch West India Company then assisted with the organization of a New Sweden company. New Sweden was populated by a number of Finns, who sometimes had been forcibly sent to America. English colonists also moved to the region. The results of this history was scattered, polyglot settlement along the western banks of the river. For an overview of the early history of the region, see Robert C. Ritchie, *The Duke's Province: A Study of New York Politics and Society, 1664—1691* (Chapel Hill: University of North Carolina Press, 1977).

2. Edmund Andros is generally acknowledged to have been a strong executive, taking his lead from the proprietor James, Duke of York. York was the architect of the controversial political unit of the Dominion of New England during his brief reign. Michael J. Braddick has called James II "a more convincing absolutist than Charles II" but still questioned his ability to exert such power in England, and by extension, the colonies (Braddick, *State Formation in Early Modern England, c. 1550–1700* [Cambridge: Cambridge University Press, 2003], 415).

3. Charles T. Gehring, ed., *New York Historical Manuscripts: Dutch*, vols. 20–21, *Delaware Papers (English Period): A Collection of Documents Pertaining to the Regulation of Affairs on the Delaware, 1664–1682* (Baltimore: Genealogical Publishing Co., 1977), 78 (hereafter cited as *DPEP*). The language of *nuisance* is significant as it had specific meaning in English tort law.

4. For a brief account of the so-called "Dike Mutiny" and its potential connections to earlier protests against a Swedish governor who tried to force the inhabitants to perform labor (1653) and the Long Finn's Rebellion (1669), see Evan Haefeli, "The Revolt of the Long Swede: Transatlantic Hopes and Fears on the Delaware, 1669,"

Pennsylvania Magazine of History and Biography 130, no. 2 (April 2006): 152–53. See also Mark L. Thompson, *The Contest for the Delaware Valley: Allegiance, Identity, and Empire in the Seventeenth Century* (Baton Rouge: Louisiana State University Press, 2013), 191–95.

5. *DPEP*, 92–93.

6. Chandra Mukerji, *Territorial Ambitions and the Gardens of Versailles* (Cambridge: Cambridge University Press, 1997), Abstract.

7. For a sample of the vast literature discussing the connections between cultivating, "improving," or transforming the environment as a means of expressing or promoting national or imperial identities, or expressing particular cultural values, see Michael Leslie and Timothy Raylor, eds., *Culture and Cultivation in Early Modern England: Writing and the Land* (Leicester, U.K.: University of Leicester Press, 1992); Alan Lester, "Reformulating Identities: British Settlers in Early Nineteenth-Century South Africa," *Transactions of the Institute of British Geographers* 23, no. 4 (1998): 515–31; Jorge Cañizares-Esguerra, "Colonization as Spiritual Gardening," in *Puritan Conquistadors: Iberianizing the Atlantic, 1550–1700* (Stanford: Stanford University Press, 2006); Chandra Mukerji, *Impossible Engineering: Technology and Territoriality on the Canal du Midi* (Princeton, N.J.: Princeton University Press, 2009); and Joanna Brück, "Landscapes of Desire: Parks, Colonialism, and Identity in Victorian and Edwardian Ireland," *International Journal of Historical Archaeology* 17, no. 1 (March 2013): 196–223.

8. The phrase is derived from Patricia Seed, *Ceremonies of Possession in Europe's Conquest of the New World, 1492–1640* (Cambridge: Cambridge University Press, 1995). Additional books that examine the myriad English debates, arguments, and justifications for their occupation and possession of American lands (or the rhetoric of claiming colonial possession though "improvement" narratives) include Ken MacMillan, *Sovereignty and Possession in the English New World: The Legal Foundations of Empire, 1576–1640* (New York: Cambridge University Press, 2006); Lauren Benton and Richard J. Ross, eds., *Legal Pluralism and Empires 1500–1850* (New York: New York University Press, 2013); Andrew Fitzmaurice, *Sovereignty, Property and Empire, 1500–2000* (Cambridge: Cambridge University Press, 2014); and Allan Greer, *Property and Dispossession: Natives, Empires and Land in Early Modern North America* (New York: Cambridge University Press, 2018).

9. Robert Burden and Stephan Kohl, eds., *Landscape and Englishness* (New York: Rodopi, 2006), 18.

10. Peter R. Christoph, ed., *New York Historical Manuscripts: English*, vol. 12, *Administrative Papers of Governors Richard Nicolls and Francis Lovelace, 1664–1673* (Baltimore: Genealogical Publishing Co., 1980), 122 (hereafter cited as *AP*).

11. According to Robert Ritchie, both Nicolls and Lovelace faced the challenge of how to organize and centralize a varied landscape dotted with heterogeneous peoples, cultural traditions, and legal systems: "The resulting patchwork of administrative units was unmatched elsewhere in the colonies" (Ritchie, *The Duke's Province: A Study of New York Politics and Society, 1664–1691* [Chapel Hill: University of North Carolina Press, 1977], 25).

12. It was during war with the Dutch that Admiral Penn went into debt on behalf of the Crown. Instead of asking Charles II to pay back eleven thousand pounds, William Penn secured his new colony (Richard S. Dunn, "William Penn and the Selling

of Pennsylvania, 1681–1685," *Proceedings of the American Philosophical Society* 127, no. 5 [October 1983]: 323). In 1684 New Castle was the site of William Penn's landing.

13. Mark L. Thompson, *The Contest for the Delaware Valley: Allegiance, Identity, and Empire in the Seventeenth Century* (Baton Rouge: Louisiana State University Press, 2013), 74–78, 180–89.

14. Peter R. Christoph and Florence A. Christoph, eds., *New York Historical Manuscripts: English, Books of General Entries of the Colony of New York, 1664–1673, Orders, Warrants, Letters, Commissions, Passes and Licenses Issued by Governors Richard Nicolls and Francis Lovelace* (Baltimore: Genealogical Publishing Co., 1982), 5. At the same time colonial officials arbitrated between the towns of Gravesend and New Utrecht, the Restoration court sought to gain a clear understanding of colonial boundaries. Charles II put together a commission for "Setling Boundarys between Neighbouring Colonyes."

15. Brian Donahue, *The Great Meadow: Farmers and the Land in Colonial Concord* (New Haven, Conn.: Yale University Press, 2004).

16. Officials also collected fines and fees secured funding for public works projects.

17. John E. Pomfret, *Colonial New Jersey: A History* (New York: Scribner's Sons, 1973), 28.

18. Residents were unsure of the manner in which they held land. William Tom wrote to the governor because he "wish[ed] to Know by what tenure wee hold our land not being expressed in our patents." He queried if the lands were held "In common Soccage as the Duke held his, as of the maanor of East Greenwich" (*DPEP*, 23). In other words, residents wanted "a secure freehold title to land which was freely alienable and devisable" (B. H. McPherson, "Revisiting the Manor of East Greenwich," *American Journal of Legal History* 42, no. 1 [January 1998]: 56).

19. Amy C. Schutt, *Peoples of the River Valleys: The Odyssey of the Delaware Indians* (Philadelphia: University of Pennsylvania Press, 2007), 8.

20. For the central role played by gender in Lenape life, see Gunlög Fur, *A Nation of Women: Gender and Colonial Encounters among the Delaware Indians* (Philadelphia: University of Pennsylvania Press, 2009).

21. Jill Lepore, *The Name of War: King Philip's War and the Origins of American Identity* (New York: Vintage, 1999), 85–89.

22. William Penn later accused Dutch and Swedish settlers on the western banks of the Delaware of failing to properly cultivate orchards or fruit trees. Penn attributed their agricultural failures to the fact that they had lived so long in isolation among the Lenape Indians (Gunlög Fur, *Colonialism in the Margins: Cultural Encounters in New Sweden and Lapland* [Boston: Brill Academic, 2006], 244). For a history of the idea that occupation justified ownership over colonial territories, see Fitzmaurice, *Sovereignty, Property and Empire, 1500–2000.*

23. Scholars such as Anya Zilberstein have examined colonists' confidence that they could transform New World environments to better suit their bodies (Zilberstein, *A Temperate Empire: Making Climate Change in Early America* [New York: Oxford University Press, 2016]).

24. In the early modern world, wetlands were often seen as a problem associated with a postlapsarian world, which was decayed and inundated with water due to human laziness and sin. Turning wasteland into land available to arable agriculture was the means to restore and reform the fallen world and redeem it. Thus, improvements were

often undertaken in this *restorative* mode (Rob Iliffe, "The Masculine Birth of Time: Temporal Frameworks of Early Modern Natural Philosophy," *British Journal for the History of Science* 33, no. 4 [2000]: 427–53).

25. *AP*, 32.

26. The idea that people might be "new-mold[ed]" comes from a pamphlet outlining how a conquering empire, in this case England, might deal with conquered people, such as the Dutch settlers along the Delaware River, outlined in a letter to the governor of West Jersey in the late seventeenth century (Anon., *An Abstract or abbreviation of some few of the many (later and former) testimonys from the inhabitants of New-Jersey* [London, 1681], 27).

27. Mark L. Thompson, *The Contest for the Delaware Valley: Allegiance, Identity, and Empire in the Seventeenth Century* (Baton Rouge: Louisiana State University Press, 2013), 6. This chapter suggests that the English held a capacious sense of the transformations they wished to see, targeting landscapes as well as dictating certain behaviors, as a means of incorporating communities into the body politic and ensuring good behavior and loyalty.

28. Benjamin Franklin, *The Papers of Benjamin Franklin*, ed. Leonard W. Labaree, vol. 3 (New Haven, Conn.: Yale University Press, 1961), 469–72.

29. Paul Warde traces the word "improvement" over the period 1520–1700 and finds that it went through distinct phases. He argues in the mid-seventeenth century the term "emerged as a leading concept among those describing and promoting novel agricultural practices" (Warde, "The Idea of Improvement, c. 1520–1700," in *Custom, Improvement and the Landscape in Early Modern Britain* [Farnham, U.K.: Ashgate, 2011], 128).

30. As the empire expanded and incorporated new places and peoples, Restoration officials debated about how to maintain the integrity of the newly restored English body politic. They were unsure how to integrate non-English inhabitants. Some writers warned that certain types of people could *infect* the body politic, particularly populations with inclinations toward riotousness (Jonathan Gil Harris, *Foreign Bodies and the Body Politic: Discourses of Social Pathology in Early Modern England* [Cambridge: Cambridge University Press, 1998]). In an effort to project English authority in the region, the English did more than rename the towns and geographical features of the colony and introduce new law. They also instigated a range of other methods, including drainage and maintaining roads.

31. Brian Donahue, *The Great Meadow: Farmers and the Land in Colonial Concord* (New Haven, Conn.: Yale University Press, 2004); Gregory Kennedy, "Marshland Colonization in Acadia and Poitou during the 17th Century," *Acadiensis* 42, no. 1 (2013): 65–66.

32. Delaware Wild Lands, the state's first land trust, was established in 1961 and manages many of Delaware's wetlands. They are in the process of reforesting some of these wetlands (see http://www.dewildlands.org/).

33. For example, consider the *Caert vande Svydt Rivier in Niew Nederland*, or *Map of the South River in New Netherland* drawn in 1639 by the Dutch cartographer and West India Company employee Joan Vinckeboons.

34. Weslager, *The Swedes and Dutch at New Castle*, 11.

35. Ted Steinberg, *Gotham Unbound: The Ecological History of New York* (New York: Simon and Schuster, 2014), 12–13.

36. Kennedy, "Marshland Colonization in Acadia and Poitou during the 17th Century," 37.

37. According to Delaware's Department of Natural Resources and Environmental Control's online wetlands directory: http://www.dnrec.delaware.gov/Admin/DelawareWetlands/Pages/Page7Other.aspx.

38. For more on the different classifications of wetlands, see the report produced by R. W. Tiner et al., *Delaware Wetlands: Status and Changes from 1992 to 2007*, Cooperative National Wetlands Inventory Publication. U.S. Fish and Wildlife Service, Northeast Region, Hadley, MA, and the Delaware Department of Natural Resources and Environmental Control, Dover, 35 pp. (2011), http://www.dnrec.delaware.gov/Admin/DelawareWetlands/Documents/Delaware%20Wetlands%20Status%20and%20Changes%20from%201992%20to%202007%20FINAL2012.pdf.

39. For wet meadow descriptions, see www.dnrec.state.de.us/fw/observer/eob-spo2mc1.pdf. The great challenge is figuring out from these depictions what the particular habitat of New Castle might have been in the late seventeenth century. It is possible that a coastal plain pond or wet meadow might account for the seasonal nature of flooding and the habitat described by my historical sources. See also Department of Natural Resources and Environmental Control, www.dnrec.delaware.gov/Admin/DelawareWetlands/Pages/default.aspx.

40. Steinberg, *Gotham Unbound*, xvi.

41. Goodwin, *Dutch and English*, 28.

42. Weslager, *The Swedes and Dutch*, 2. According to Weslager, this place-name was fairly common.

43. Weslager, *The Swedes and Dutch*, 3.

44. Weslager, *The Swedes and Dutch*, 3.

45. Anon., *An Abstract or abbreviation of some few of the many (later and former) testimonys from the inhabitants of New-Jersey* (London, 1681), preface, 9–12.

46. Veronica Strang, "The Social Construction of Water," in *Handbook of Landscape Archaeology*, ed. Bruno David and Julian Thomas (Walnut Creek, Calif.: Left Coast, 2008), 123.

47. The work in this chapter is inspired by landscape archaeologists, who excavate "not only the physical environment onto which people live out their lives, but also the meaningful location in which lives are lived. This includes the trees and the rocks and the stars, not as abstract objects but as meaningful things that are located ontologically and experientially in people's lives and social practices (praxis)" (see Bruno David and Julian Thomas, "Landscape Archaeology: Introduction," in *Handbook of Landscape Archaeology*, ed. David and Thomas [Walnut Creek, Calif.: Left Coast, 2008], 38).

48. Annabel S. Brett, *Changes of State: Nature and the Limits of the City in Early Modern Natural Law* (Princeton, N.J.: Princeton University Press, 2011), 223. The power of water to alter the environment destabilized claims to private property. Meanwhile, according to Allan Greer, "the colony's role was one of providing a legal framework for property making" (Greer, *Property and Dispossession*, 202). If colonies failed at the task of making property, were they also unmade?

49. Brett, *Changes of State*, 224.

50. Brett, *Changes of State*, 224.

51. According to Ted Steinberg, the "fore-shore . . . as a form of property" emerged alongside a "shift toward a world economy centered more on trade," which "brought

the coast increasingly into consciousness," as well as the "space between the high-and low-watermark" (Steinberg, *Gotham Unbound*, 401–2n4). Meanwhile, Massachusetts Bay Colony "had an ordinance on the books since the 1640s permitting landowners to colonize the intertidal area" (Steinberg, *Gotham Unbound*, 23).

52. Keith Thomas, *Man and the Natural World: A History of the Modern Sensibility* (New York: Pantheon, 1983), 195. Although in this case Keith Thomas wrote of the "savage" forest, but this trope held true for various sorts of "inaccessible" environments.

53. Richard Gilpin, *Demonologia sacra, or, A treatise of Satan's temptations in three parts* (London, 1677), chap. 6.

54. Daniel Denton, *A brief description of New-York, formerly called New-Netherlands with the places thereunto adjoyning: together with the manner of its situation, fertility of the soyle, healthfulness of the climate, and the commodities thence produced . . . likewise a brief relation of the customs of the Indians there* (London, 1670), 7.

55. Nicola Whyte has urged scholars to consider the experiences of people living in a physical landscape that would have been infused with a multitude of meanings. People in the past interacted with the world around them in more than material, transactional ways (Whyte, *Inhabiting the Landscape: Place, Custom and memory, 1500–1800* [Oxford: Oxbow, 2009], 20). In the colonies, colonial settlers' experiences and encounters, violent and nonviolent, with Lenape men and women, may have taught them something about how the indigenous inhabitants viewed riverine and swamp landscapes, layering these spaces with meaning.

56. Charles Wolley, *A Two Year's Journal in New York and Part of Its Territories in America*, ed. Edward Gaylord Bourne (1902; repr., Harrison, N.Y.: Harbor Hill, 1973), 64.

57. Sir Ferdinando Gorges, *America painted to the life* (1658), 110, 115.

58. Sir Ferdinando Gorges, *America painted to the life*, 110, 115.

59. Strang argues that water is "of interest at a theoretical level" because "the cross-cultural commonality in the themes of meaning encoded in water raises key questions about universalities in human experience." She argues that because it imbued with such powerful meanings, water bodies—of any kind—unsurprisingly tend to be among the most important elements in every cultural landscape / fluidscape" (Strang, "The Social Construction of Water," 124–25).

60. According to Haefeli, these were not outlandish accusations. Many of the same individuals who later refused English instructions to construct a dike had also been involved in the Long Finn's Rebellion several years prior (Haefaeli, "The Revolt of the Long Swede," 153).

61. For a re-creation of the complex events from a fragmented and incomplete documentary record, see Haefeli, "The Revolt of the Long Swede," 137–80.

62. Thompson, *Contest for the Delaware Valley*, 187.

63. *DPEP*, 465. In the letter from Governor Lovelace to Captain John Carr and the other magistrates of New Castle relating to the Long Finn's Rebellion, he wrote that he was waiting on instructions from England, which was "that breath that must animate this little body Politique of ours." He expected a ship at any moment carrying "severall Instructions" which would outline the "whole frame of ye Governmnt standing at this tyme."

64. Karen Ordahl Kupperman, "The Puzzle of the American Climate in the Early Colonial Period," *American Historical Review* 87, no. 5 (1982): 1266; Karen Ordahl

Kupperman, "Fear of Hot Climates in the Anglo-American Colonial Experience," *William and Mary Quarterly*, 3d ser., 41, no. 2 (1984): 213–40.

65. Mary Dobson, *Contours of Death and Disease in Early Modern England* (Cambridge: Cambridge University Press, 1997), 295.

66. For instance, see MS 883, f. 2, Dublin Philosophical Society Papers, vol. 1, Trinity College Dublin Library.

67. Colonists regularly identified mosquitoes as a problem. C. A. Weslager described an episode in which a fort was deserted and the deserters claimed it was because the multitudes of mosquitoes had made life at the fort unbearable (Weslager, *The Swedes and Dutch at New Castle* [New York: Bart, 1987], 85).

68. Thompson, *Contest for the Delaware Valley*, 110–11.

69. Per Lindeström, *Geographia Americae*, 86–87, cited in Thompson, *Contest for the Delaware Valley*, 110–11.

70. Charles Wolley, *A Two Year's Journal in New York and Part of Its Territories in America* (reprinted from the original edition of 1701; Harrison, N.Y.: Harbor Hill Books, 1973), 30.

71. Denton, *A brief description of New-York*, 5.

72. Anon., *An Abstract or abbreviation*, 5.

73. Anon., *An Abstract or abbreviation*, 30.

74. Anon., *An Abstract or abbreviation*, 30. To live "scatteringly" at this time is to live without settled, civil communities.

75. Wolley, *A Two Year's Journal in New York*, 30.

76. Wolley, *A Two Year's Journal in New York*, 30.

77. Mary Dobson, "'Marsh Fever'—the Geography of Malaria in England," *Journal of Historical Geography* 6, no. 4 (1980): 364.

78. A poem written by a fenlander suggested: "The moory soil, the watry atmosphere / With the damp, unhealthy moisture chills the air. / Thick, stinking fogs, and noxious vapours fall, / Agues and coughs are epidemicall; / Hence every face presented to our view / Looks of a pallid or a sallow hue" (cited in Dobson "Marsh Fever," 364–46).

79. Denton took pains to point out that while proximity to the ocean may well have historically been understood to be a danger to a person's health, this was not so in New York. According to Denton, an "evil fog or vapour doth no sooner appear, but a North west or westerly winde doth immediately dissolve it, and drive it away" (Denton, *A brief description of New-York*, 19). This quote suggests that Denton was contradicting a well-known truism that life at the coast led to poor health.

80. Samuel Purchas, *Hakluytus Posthumus or Purchas his Pilgrimes, containing a History of the World in Sea Voyages and Lande Travells Purchas his pilgrims* (Glasgow: Printed by Robert Maclehose and Sons for University of Glasgow, 1902), 1374.

81. Everett Emerson, *Letters from New England: The Massachusetts Bay Colony, 1629–1638* (Amherst: University of Massachusetts Press, 1976), 23.

82. M. Bromfield, *A Brief Discovery of the chief Causes, Signs, and Effects of the most Reigning Disease, the Scurvy* (London, 169[?]), 6.

83. Wolley, *A Two Year's Journal in New York*, 27.

84. Wolley, *A Two Year's Journal in New York*, 29.

85. Anya Zilberstein has suggested that settlers to Nova Scotia and New England quickly realized that assumptions about the climate based on claims about

the location of the temperate zone were highly inaccurate (Zilberstein, *A Temperate Empire,* chap. 1).

86. *DPEP,* 24.

87. *DPEP,* 25–26.

88. *DPEP,* 76.

89. *DPEP,* 1.

90. *DPEP,* 2.

91. *DPEP,* 2. In the Articles of Agreement it outlines how "the present Magistrates shall be Continued in their Offices, and Jurisdictions to Exercise their Civil power As formerly" and that "the Scout [*schout*] the Burgomasters Sherriff and other Inferior Magistrates Shall use and Exercise their Customary power in Administration of Justice, within their precincts for Six months or until his Majesties pleasure is further Known."

92. Thompson, *The Contest for the Delaware Valley,* 7.

93. For a comprehensive history of the complicated colonization of the region, see Mark L. Thompson, *The Contest for the Delaware Valley: Allegiance, Identity, and Empire in the Seventeenth Century* (Baton Rouge: Louisiana State University Press, 2013).

94. Thompson, *The Contest for the Delaware Valley,* 3.

95. Delays meant they did not establish a court of sessions until 1671 (one commissary from each village and the justice of the peace). The name change took place on September 25, 1669 (*AP,* 121–29).

96. *New York Historical Manuscripts: Dutch: Kingston Papers,* trans. Dingman Versteeg, ed. Peter R. Christoph et al. (Baltimore: Genealogical Publishing Co., 1976), introduction, 121, 125.

97. *New York Historical Manuscripts: Dutch: Kingston Papers,* 2:435.

98. *AP,* 120–21.

99. *AP,* 125.

100. *AP,* 127–28.

101. *AP,* 127–28. Meanwhile, "And whereas Mr Christopher Berrisford is chosen Chiefe Magistrate for the Townes of Hurley and Marbleton, hee is hereby empowered to Command the Overseers of each Towne to take the like care for the mending and repaireing of the High-wayes in those two last mencioned Townes; and to Fine all the Overseers of both places or any of them as shall neglect their Duty in 20 Skepple of Wheat . . . [etc.]."

102. *AP,* 21–22.

103. Cited in Maud Wilder Goodwin, *Dutch and English on the Hudson: A Chronicle of Colonial New York* (New Haven, Conn.: Yale Univeristy Press, 1919), 140–42.

104. *AP,* 122.

105. Seed, *Ceremonies of Possession in Europe's Conquest of the New World*; Andrew Fitzmaurice, *Sovereignty, Property and Empire, 1500–2000* (Cambridge: Cambridge University Press, 2014); Greer, *Property and Dispossession.*

106. Fitzmaurice, *Sovereignty, Property and Empire, 1500–2000,* 119.

107. *AP,* 125–26.

108. *AP,* 125.

109. *Conduce* suggests that an act will directly lead to a conclusion. *Contribute* suggests it is just one of several causes. The language of the second version is stronger.

110. *AP*, 126.

111. *AP*, 126.

112. *New York Historical Manuscripts: Dutch: Kingston Papers*, 2:435.

113. Perhaps there was not as much anger because the drainage orders required neither days nor labor nor was the property owned by an individual who might benefit from their collective labor.

114. Allan Greer has reflected on the way in which state formation and property formation were mutually constitutive: "Felling trees, moving stones, building houses, introducing pigs and cattle, physically occupying the land, they marked the face of the earth as English, while the deeds, mortgages and litigation-related records accumulating in the courts constituted a growing archival edifice of property and jurisdiction" (Greer, *Property and Dispossession*, 202).

115. *AP*, 162.

116. *AP*, 162.

117. *AP*, 209.

118. *AP*, 211

119. *AP*, 211.

120. Kennedy, "Marshland Colonization in Acadia and Poitou during the 17th Century," 37.

121. As several scholars have revealed, centralizing state emerged in response to repeated local demands. For instance, Braddick, has suggested that a desire for arbitration by the "center" at the "periphery" brought the Crown and its agents to those locations. Or, in other words, local actors invited the English state to moderate their differences, subverting top-down narrative about the consolidation and centralization of authority in England (Michael Braddick, *State Formation in Early Modern England, c. 1550–1700* [Cambridge: Cambridge University Press, 2003]).

122. *AP*, 134–35. In colonial Pennsylvania the proprietor William Penn also kept watch over settlers' activities and property because the land would revert to him if left unimproved for the space of three years.

123. *AP*, 144.

124. The Duke of York did not have proprietary rights to the western side of the Delaware.

125. *DPEP*, 78. The language of *nuisance* is significant as it had specific meaning in English tort law.

126. *DPEP*, 76–78.

127. If they did not report to work for "two days at the dike," they could send laborers in their place or pay ten guilders in sewant [wampum] for each day missed (*DPEP*, 85–86).

128. Wetlands challenged the English in a number of ways. Due to their inaccessibility, and the regular inundation of water, it was likewise hard to map boundaries in such spaces. This might help explain why an anonymous tract written in support of NJ colonization, *An Abstract or abbreviation*, reported on the widespread but "Disingenuous and False reports of some Men" that the "Methods of Settlement were Confused and Uncertain, no Man knowing his Own Land, and several such idle Lying stories." Anxieties over establishing clear property ownership was critical to colonial promoters who wished to make their colonies a success (Anon., *An Abstract or abbreviation*, preface, 28).

129. It is referred to as Zwaenwyck in this document.

130. *DPEP*, 89. This document was entitled "Magistrates' Justification for Constructing Dikes" and "Reasons which induced us to order all the inhabitants of the district of new Castle to help construct both of the outer dikes." It was signed by H. Block, John Moll, Derck Albertsen. This memo was originally written in Dutch and I have used the translations provided. While many of the documents in the *New York Historical Manuscripts* are written in English, I have relied on Gehring's translation of those documents in Dutch. In other documents the residents of the Delaware River regularly wrote to English governors reiterating their anxiety about their inability to defend themselves in case of Indian attack, and their desire for the governor to "treate with the Sachems" to prevent war. For a mention of travel prevented by the frozen river, see *DPEP*, 97.

131. *DPEP*, 78.

132. For a good discussion of landscapes as sites of competition between colonizers and the colonized, see the work of the historical geographer William J. Smyth, *Map-making, Landscapes and Memory: A Geography of Colonial and Early Modern Ireland c. 1530–1750* (Cork, Ireland: Cork University Press, 2006). For a helpful discussion of the connections between altered landscapes, customs, laws, and industries, see Toby Barnard, "Gardening, Diet, and Improvement in Later Seventeenth-Century Ireland," in *Irish Protestant Ascents and Descents, 1641–1770*, by Barnard (Dublin, Ireland: Four Courts, 2004). For more work considering landscape as a site for the display of local social and political relationships, see Denis E. Cosgrove, *Social Formation and Symbolic Landscape* (Totowa, N.J.: Barnes and Noble, 1985).

133. Making "improvements" to land was crucial to claiming ownership. Land could be subject to forfeiture if the land wasn't improved. These issues are not only relevant to the events in question but were also relevant to land purchased from Indians. For instance, in September 1675, Andros purchased land from the "Indyan Sachems Mamarakickan and Auricktan with [ ]ko[ ]ewan, and Naneckos" and was anxious that someone go claim the land and make improvements when it had not been done by the following year. Otherwise, as he claimed, the Indians, knowing the law, might rightfully demand it back again.

134. *DPEP*, 480.

135. *DPEP*, 78.

136. *DPEP*, 76–78.

137. *DPEP*, 85.

138. *DPEP*, 85.

139. *DPEP*, 85–86.

140. *DPEP*, 86.

141. *DPEP*, 92.

142. *DPEP*, 88.

143. *DPEP*, 88. The "humble petition" was signed by several individuals, each representing their communities, who left their mark.

144. *DPEP*, 88.

145. *DPEP*, 76.

146. Residents were accustomed to paying taxes for public projects, and participating in public works projects, but they were not willing to work if they gained no benefit from their efforts or payments. The Dutch also declared work orders. For example,

Stuyvesant "authorized an excise tax to pay for a Pier for the convenience of the Merchants and Citizens' and a bulkhead to ward off erosion along the East River" (Steinberg, *Gotham Unbound*, 17–18).

147. *DPEP*, 88.

148. For an additional account of the "Dike Mutiny," see Thompson, *The Contest for the Delaware Valley*, 191–94.

149. *DPEP*, 87.

150. *DPEP*, 92.

151. *DPEP*, 92.

152. Munroe, *History of Delaware*, 33.

153. *DPEP*, 93.

154. *DPEP*, 87.

155. Jaspar Dankers and Peter Sluyter, *Journal of a Voyage to New York and a Tour in Several of the American Colonies in 1679–80*, trans. and ed. Henry C. Murphy (Brooklyn: Long Island Historical Society, 1867), 111.

156. Dankers and Sluyter, *Journal of a Voyage to New York*, 295.

157. Daniel Leeds, *An Almanack for the Year of Christian Account 1700* (New York: Printed by William Bradford, 1700).

158. Titian Leeds, *The American Almanack for the Year of Christian Account 1714* (New York: Printed by William Bradford, 1714).

159. Cited in Haefeli, "The Revolt of the Long Swede," 171. As Haefeli points out, in 1669 the English ordered that patents should be renewed and others issued so the English could better determine the quitrents due.

160. Goodwin, *Dutch and English on the Hudson*, 43.

161. It was not only the Dutch, Swedish, Finnish, or Lenape residents of the region who were troubled by questions about land security. English officials were also often confused about their own land tenure. As William Tom had written to Governor Nicolls several years earlier, he "wish[ed] to Know by what tenure wee hold our land not being expressed in our patents." He queried if land owners held their land "In common Soccage as the Duke held his," as in the manor of East Greenwich (*DPEP*, 23). Tenure in common socage was the legal way to say that colonists held a freehold title and could sell it (McPherson, "Revisiting the Manor of East Greenwich," 56).

162. *DPEP*, 481.

163. *DPEP*, 481. Their response to Carr: "Lastly as to ye tenure of ye Land at Delaware, It is to be held in free & comon Soccage as his Royll Highness by his Maties Patent holds all his Territoryes in America, that is to say according to ye Custome of ye Mannor of East Greenwch, only wth this Provisoe that they likewise pay ye Quitt Rents, reserved in their severall Patents as an Acknowledgemt to his Royall Highness."

164. Samuel Clarke, *A true and faithful account of the four chiefest plantations of the English in America* (London, 1670), 29.

165. Denton, *A brief description of New-York*, 5.

166. Donahue, *The Great Meadow*, 4.

167. Donahue, *The Great Meadow*, 1.

168. *DPEP*, 88.

169. Margaret Albright Knittl, "The Design for the Initial Drainage of the Great Level of the Fens: An Historical Whodunit in Three Parts," *Agricultural History Review* 55, no. 1 (2007): 25.

170. *DPEP*, 92.

171. Peter R. Christoph and Florence A. Christoph, eds., *New York Historical Manuscripts: English, Books of General Entries of the Colony of New York, 1664–1673, Orders, Warrants, Letters, Commissions, Passes and Licenses Issued by Governors Richard Nicolls and Francis Lovelace* (Baltimore: Genealogical Publishing Co., 1982), 125.

172. Cited in Ned C. Landsman, *Crossroads of Empire: The Middle Colonies in British North America* (Baltimore: Johns Hopkins University Press, 2010), 36.

173. See Seed, *Ceremonies of Possession in Europe's Conquest of the New World*; and Anthony Pagden, *Lords of All the World: Ideologies of Empire in Spain, Britain and France c. 1500–c. 1800* (New Haven, Conn.: Yale University Press, 1995), for more on the early modern theories underpinning the connection between improvement and ownership.

174. Ellen Wood, *The Origin of Capitalism*, 167. Contemporaries debated the comparative benefits of acquiring more land versus the intensive improvement of property already owned.

175. As I have discussed, the residents along the Delaware were at the uncertain edge of three different proprietary colonies, and it was not altogether clear to which colony they properly belonged. Thus, the improvements ordered by New York's Governor Andros offered a means to assert possession on behalf of the duke and his colony of New York.

176. Anon., *An Abstract or abbreviation*, 27.

177. For a deeply religious society, words phrases like *new-molded* suggested a range of tactile, spiritual, and social remaking. Bodies were houses of clay, and were continually remolded over a lifetime's pursuit of spiritual discipline. Quests for spiritual well-being could be deeply material, such as fasting as a means to remake the spirit, as discussed in chapter 1.

178. Cited in Fur, *Colonialism in the Margins*, 244.

179. Denton, *A brief description of New-York*, 15.

180. Denton, *A brief description of New-York*, 15–16.

181. Jean R. Soderlund, *Lenape Country: Delaware Valley Society before William Penn* (Philadelphia: University of Pennsylvania Press, 2014).

182. *DPEP*, 66.

183. Of course, Indian and Dutch relations in the region had often been strained. Several decades earlier these strained relationships had erupted in violence (Ned C. Landsman, *Crossroads of Empire: The Middle Colonies in British North America* [Baltimore: Johns Hopkins University Press, 2010], 25).

184. *DPEP*, 11.

185. Burden and Kohl, eds., *Landscape and Englishness* (New York: Rodopi, 2006), 16.

186. Burden and Kohl, eds., *Landscape and Englishness*, 18.

187. Robert Blair St. George, *Conversing by Signs: Poetics of Implication in Colonial New England Culture* (Chapel Hill: University of North Carolina Press, 1998), 65; Christina Folke Ax, ed., *Cultivating the Colonies* (Athens: Ohio University Press, 2011). Although Jennifer Van Horn has argued that objects helped Anglo-Americans create an identity, as communities coalesced around material artifacts, this chapter suggests transformed landscapes were the artifacts through which English officials and settlers sought to express national identity (Van Horn, *The Power of Objects in*

Eighteenth-Century British America [Chapel Hill: University of North Carolina Press, 2017], 29).

188. Of course, Dutch names, laws, currency, and ways of life persisted. Steinberg has tracked how the English continued to use Dutch names for water topography, including "kill" for river.

189. Steinberg, *Gotham Unbound*, 8.

190. Steinberg, *Gotham Unbound*, 14.

191. Steinberg, *Gotham Unbound*, 20. Steinberg wrote, "Filling in land under water eventually burgeoned into a fixation for the English colonists," and cited, specifically, the Dongan Charter of 1686 as a critical turning point. According to Steinberg, "from an environmental perspective, the single most important aspect of the Dongan Charter was its grant of all vacant land on 'Manhattans Island aforesaid Extending and reaching to the Low water marke.' A later section conferred the right to 'take in fill and make up and laye out' land along the coast." He further asserts: "Unlike in England or the Netherlands, where pumps and dikes drained existing lands, New Yorkers created new ground by building retaining structures and depositing material behind them. The English colonists called it 'wharfing out'" (Steinberg, *Gotham Unbound*, 23–24). Matthew Mulcahy describes a similar process of reclaiming coastal land, or "Shoal water" in Port Royal, where land was at a premium. Residents were granted "Shoal Water . . . to be recovered for Warfe Ground" and used pilings to do so (Mulcahy, "The Port Royal Earthquake and the World of Wonders in Seventeenth-Century Jamaica," *Early American Studies* 6, no. 2 [2008]: 391–421).

192. Steinberg, *Gotham Unbound*, 19.

193. Peter R. Christoph and Florence A. Christoph, eds., *New York Historical Manuscripts: English, Books of General Entries of the Colony of New York, 1664–1673, Orders, Warrants, Letters, Commissions, Passes and Licenses Issued by Governors Richard Nicolls and Francis Lovelace* (Baltimore: Genealogical Publishing Co., 1982), 125.

194. Chandra Mukerji argues that in seventeenth-century France, political position was increasingly defined in territorial terms, not just as a relationship to the monarch (Mukerji, *Impossible Engineering: Technology and Territoriality on the Canal du Midi* [Princeton, N.J.: Princeton University Press, 2009]).

195. Elizabeth DeLoughrey and George B. Han, eds., *Postcolonial Ecologies: Literatures of the Environment* (Oxford: Oxford University Press, 2011), 4.

196. Kennedy, "Marshland Colonization in Acadia and Poitou during the 17th Century," 64–66.

197. *DPEP*, 153.

198. *DPEP*, 366. The following year New Castle's magistrates resolve "towards the farther defraying of publick Charges in the Towne of Newcastle, as also up the River, and in the Bay, there bee a Levy made of one penney in the pound upon every mans Estate, to bee taxt by indifferent persons." This suggests that, learning from the fracas from the previous year, the magistrates were not going to require labor but would collect a tax for public works.

4 / Improving the Body

1. John Evelyn, *The Diary*, ed. William Bray, 2 vols. (Oxford: Clarendon, 1955), 1:43. Evelyn expressed some disappointment at the taste. The lyrical descriptions of

the flavor written by other writers led to very high expectations that, in his opinion, were not met. He acknowledged that the long journey on the boat may have altered the taste.

2. "Natural history intrigued princes and merchants because it was a tangible sign of their ability to roam the globe" (or to have others do so on their behalf). Exotic nature regularly served as gifts among early modern nobility (Paula Findlen, "Courting Nature," in *Cultures of Natural History*, ed. Nicholas Jardine, James Secord, and Emma Spary (Cambridge: Cambridge University Press, 1996), 71).

3. Anna Keay, *The Magnificent Monarch: Charles II and the Ceremonies of Power* (London: Continuum, 2008).

4. Numerous scholars have explored the relationships between imperial expansion and the transformation of domestic consumption habits, including: Sidney W. Mintz, *Sweetness and Power: The Place of Sugar in Modern History* (New York: Penguin, 1986); Troy Bickham, "Eating the Empire: Intersections of Food, Cookery, and Imperialism in Eighteenth-Century Britain" *Past & Present*, no. 198 (February 2008): 71–109.

5. Historians have tracked the circulation of accounts that emphasized starvation, among other miseries, in early English American colonies. Although these accounts were often biased and served a purpose beyond recounting the actual experience of early colonists, writers' emphasis on starvation cast a long shadow (Kathleen Donegan, *Seasons of Misery: Catastrophe and Colonial Settlement in Early America* [Philadelphia: University of Pennsylvania Press, 2013]; Rachel Herrmann, "The 'Tragicall Historie': Cannibalism and Abundance in Colonial Jamestown," *William and Mary Quarterly* 68, no. 1 [January 2011]: 47–74).

6. Joan Thirsk, *Food in Early Modern England: Phases, Fads, Fashions 1500–1760* (New York: Continuum, 2007), 97–98.

7. 51/61A-64B, Hartlib Papers.

8. Brian Cowan, *The Social Life of Coffee: The Emergence of the British Coffeehouse* (New Haven, Conn.: Yale University Press, 2005) explores some of the anxieties consumers experienced when choosing to drink coffee. Marcy Norton's work emphasizes how Europeans learned how to consume chocolate and tobacco by emulating Mesoamerican practices before introducing them to Europe (Norton, *Sacred Gifts, Profane Pleasures: A History of Tobacco and Chocolate in the Atlantic World* [Ithaca, N.Y.: Cornell University Press, 2008]).

9. John Worlidge, *Systema Agriculturae, The Mystery of Husbandry Discovered* (London, 1669), title page.

10. Anonymous, *Archimagirus Anglo-Gallicus: Or, Excellent & Approved Receipts and Experiments in Cookery . . . Copied from a Choice Manuscript of Sir Theodore Mayerne, Knight, Physician to the late K. Charles* (London, 1658), A2v.

11. Anonymous, *Archimagirus Anglo-Gallicus*, A2v.

12. Laura Lunger Knoppers, "Opening the Queen's Closet: Henrietta Maria, Elizabeth Cromwell, and the Politics of Cookery," *Renaissance Quarterly* 60, no. 2 (2007): 464–99.

13. Joan Thirsk, ed., *The Agrarian History of England and Wales*, vol. 5: *1640–1750, I. Regional Farming Systems* (Cambridge: Cambridge University Press, 1984), 562–64; cited in Reginald Lennard, "English Agriculture under Charles II: The Evidence of the Royal Society's 'Enquiries,'" *Economic History Review* 4, no. 1 (October 1932): 23–25.

14. Thirsk, *Food in Early Modern England*, 103.

15. Michael A. LaCombe, *Political Gastronomy: Food and Authority in the English Atlantic World* (Philadelphia: University of Pennsylvania, 2012), 23–24.

16. Richard Grove has outlined fears of political instability, food scarcity, and jobless migrants, during the commonwealth (Grove, "Cressy Dymock and the Draining of the Fens: An Early Agricultural Model," *Geographical Journal* 147, no. 1 [1981]: 29).

17. William Petty, *A Discourse of Taxes and Contributions* (London, 1662), 6.

18. James C. Scott, *Seeing Like a State: How Certain Schemes to Improve the Human Condition Have Failed* (New Haven, Conn.: Yale University Press, 1998), 29.

19. Cited in Lennard, "English Agriculture," 25; Royal Society, *Philosophical Transactions* 9, no. 101 (1674), "The Epistle Dedicatory."

20. Michael J. Braddick, *State Formation in Early Modern England, c. 1550–1700* (Cambridge: Cambridge University Press, 2003), 104.

21. Braddick, *State Formation in Early Modern England*, 116.

22. Paul Slack, *From Reformation to Improvement: Public Welfare in Early Modern England* (Oxford: Clarendon, 1999), 1–2.

23. Worlidge, *Systema Agriculturae*, preface.

24. Cited in Grove, "Cressy Dymock," 36.

25. Henry Stubbe, *The Indian Nectar, or a Discourse Concerning Chocolata* (London, 1662), 31; Proposalls and Reasons for the Improving, & advancing of Planting, humbly tendered to the Lords & Comons in Parliament Assembled, Cl.P/10iii/7, Royal Society Library.

26. Many of the Hartlib Circle letters dealt with foodstuff, such as a memo advertising a new oven that could "bee used with very great advantages, esp in Armies & Navies." The author was concerned with ensuring that fighting men would be well fed, suggesting the importance of soldiers and food access (55/9/1A, undated, Hartlib Papers).

27. Thirsk, *Food in Early Modern England*, 120, 137.

28. At midcentury, various European countries devised "laws that encouraged early marriage, energetic procreation, and immigration." Population size was believed to enhance the economy and was necessary to military strength (Daniel Statt, *Foreigners and Englishmen: The Controversy over Immigration and Population, 1660–1760* [Newark: University of Delaware Press, 1995], 49).

29. John Winthrop, "Reasons for the Plantations in New England," ca. 1628; Patricia Seed, *Ceremonies of Possession in Europe's Conquest of the New World, 1492–1640* (Cambridge: Cambridge University Press, 1995), 16–40.

30. In the mid-seventeenth century many writers suggested that "waste" people could be put to use to improve national strength. According to Samuel Hartlib, petty criminals and the poor alike might be forced to work, "the better to make them serviceable to the Common-wealth, by reforming their ungodly life." Moreover, orphaned children might likewise be shaped into useful citizens "under a godly and civill Government, to the great joy of good peopl" (Samuel Hartlib, *Londons Charity Inlarged Stilling The Orphans Cry* [London, 1650], cited in Braddick, *State Formation in Early Modern England*, 133).

31. Timothy Sweet, "Economy, Ecology, and Utopia in Early Colonial Promotional Literature," *American Literature* 71, no. 3 (1999): 408. Vittoria Di Palma has similarly argued that a moral imperative had been introduced to the concept of "wasteland" and its improvement. Improving wastes was a means of cultivating both "soil and soul." I'd

add that calls for improvement were also about health and healing (Di Palma, *Wasteland: A History* [New Haven: Yale University Press, 2014], 50).

32. Ralph Austen, *A Treatise of Fruit Trees* (London, 1653), "The Analysis."

33. King James Bible, John 15, "Jesus the True Vine," lines 1–2.

34. This was an era characterized in many ways by an abiding interest in a set of ideas bundled under the title of "improvement." Terms like "projector" and "project" "characterized the new era" and suggest their confidence that these were realizable goals. Many of them were undertaken (Joan Thirsk, *Economic Policy and Projects: The Development of a Consumer Society in Early Modern England* [Oxford: Clarendon, 1978], 1–2).

35. As Evelyn wrote in his dedication: "For To whom, Sir, with equal right ought I to Present this Publique Fruit of your ROYAL SOCIETY, then to its Royal FOUNDER? And this Discourse of Trees, then to your Sacred Majesty . . . as having once your Temple, and Court too under your Presence, and We celebrate with just Acknowledgement to God for your Preservation" (John Evelyn, *Sylva, or, A discourse of forest-trees, and the propagation of timber in His Majesties dominions* [London, 1664], dedication).

36. Evelyn, *Sylva*, 64. Moreover, this transplantation from the New World would have served as evidence of the king's ability to act as a careful steward of both colonial and English nature.

37. Diana Wells, *Lives of the Trees: An Uncommon History* (Chapel Hill, N.C.: Algonquin Books of Chapel Hill, 2010), 11. According to Wells, "'cassie' is a basic ingredient of French perfumes" and was made from the blooms of the acacia tree.

38. David Jacques and Arend Jan Van Der Horst, eds., *The Gardens of William and Mary* (London: Christopher Helm, 1988), 27.

39. Scholars have tracked how other states recognized the necessity of managing tree resources (Chandra Mukerji, *Territorial Ambitions and the Gardens of Versailles* [Cambridge: Cambridge University Press, 1997], 73–76; John T. Wing, *Roots and Empire: Forests and State Power in Early Modern Spain, c. 1500–1750* [Leiden: Brill, 2015]).

40. "Notes on Irish Natural History," MS 5926, f. 1, Trinity College Library Dublin. This document was part of a reply to Hartlib's "An Interrogatory relating more particularly to the husbandry and natural history of Ireland" (1652).

41. Evelyn, *Sylva*, dedicatory material.

42. Evelyn, *Sylva*, letter to the reader.

43. Evelyn, *Sylva*, letter to the reader. According to Evelyn, not even the ancient army led by Xerxes had violated groves of trees, believing that "the Gods did never permit him to escape unpunish'd who was injurious to Groves." Thus, according to Evelyn, at least this historical marauding army was a respecter of trees, giving them a leg up on Cromwell.

44. David Jacques et al., *The Gardens of William and Mary* (London: C. Helm, 1988), 27.

45. Evelyn, *Sylva*, 26.

46. Evelyn, *Sylva*, 50. Two years earlier Evelyn had written and presented a manuscript draft of what would become *Sylva*. At that time, he thought the government ought to regulate private citizens' plantation efforts. Depending on the size of the property, individuals should either plant ten, twenty, or more fruit trees, "& so in proportion for greater quantities of Land." Such plantations would be especially suitable

in hedges (Proposalls and Reasons for the Improving, & advancing of Planting, humbly tendered to the Lords & Comons in Parliament Assembled, Cl.P/ 10iii/ 7, Royal Society Library).

47. Evelyn, *Sylva*, 119.

48. In his manuscript version Evelyn imagined that a system of punishments must be in place to discourage people from digging up or otherwise destroying newly planted trees. They would be "punished" because they had damaged "the good & welfare of the kingdom" (Cl.P/ 10iii/ 7, Royal Society Library).

49. Evelyn, *Sylva*, 119–20. Several sources recommended looking to the Venetians for inspiration on how to manage their forests and tree resources.

50. Proposalls and Reasons for the Improving, & advancing of Planting, humbly tendered to the Lords & Comons in Parliament Assembled, Cl.P/ 10iii/ 7, Royal Society Library.

51. Proposalls and Reasons for the Improving, & advancing of Planting, humbly tendered to the Lords & Comons in Parliament Assembled, Cl.P/ 10iii/ 7, Royal Society Library.

52. Proposalls and Reasons for the Improving, & advancing of Planting, humbly tendered to the Lords & Comons in Parliament Assembled, Cl.P/ 10iii/ 7, Royal Society Library.

53. Directions and Inquiries concerning Virginia recommended to Edw Diggs Esq., July 22, 1669, Cl.P/ 19/ 48, Royal Society Library.

54. "Fruit of the orchard" was often left to widows in wills in Massachusetts in the seventeenth century. It may be that their former husbands thought that fruit trees required little labor and provided food. For several examples, see George Francis Dow and Mary G. Thresher, eds., *Records and Files of the Quarterly Courts of Essex County, Massachusetts* (Salem: Essex Institute, 1911–75), 340, 357–59.

55. Proposalls and Reasons for the Improving, & advancing of Planting, humbly tendered to the Lords & Comons in Parliament Assembled, Cl.P/ 10iii/ 7, Royal Society Library.

56. Ralph Austen composed *A Treatise of Fruit Trees* (1653).

57. Thirsk, *Food in Early Modern England*, 93–94.

58. Thirsk, *Food in Early Modern England*, 101.

59. Nicholas Dowdall, "A Description of the County of Longford," MS 10224, dated 1682, National Library of Ireland.

60. Patrick Kelly, "The Improvement of Ireland," *Analecta Hibernica*, no. 35 (1992): 63.

61. "A Description of the County of Longford," MS 10224, p. 2, National Library of Ireland.

62. "A Description of the County of Longford," MS 10224, p. 4, National Library of Ireland.

63. Paul Cloke and Owaine Jones, *Tree Cultures: The Place of Trees and Trees in Their Place* (New York: Berg, 2002), 16.

64. "A Description of the County of Longford," MS 10224, p. 5, National Library of Ireland.

65. As Smyth has argued, "Reformation is a central theme in early modern England—and not just a religious reformation. The drive is to re-*form*, to give new shape and meaning to old societies, economies and landscapes, which to the 'alien' modernizing eye appear formless and uncouth. Notions of 'progress', 'development',

'improvement', and 'modernity' become part of this reforming agenda" (William J. Smyth, *Map-making, Landscapes and Memory: A Geography of Colonial and Early Modern Ireland c. 1530–1750* [Cork, Ireland: Cork University Press, 2006], 15).

66. Mr Keough of the County of Roscomon and Connaguht MS 883, f.102, Dublin Philosophical Society Papers, vol. 1, Trinity College Library Dublin.

67. For in-depth accounts on myriad efforts "to make Ireland English" during the seventeenth century, see Jane Ohlmeyer, *Making Ireland English: The Irish Aristocracy in the Seventeenth Century* (New Haven, Conn.: Yale University Press, 2012), 9.

68. Patricia Seed, *Ceremonies of Possession in Europe's Conquest of the New World, 1492–1640* (Cambridge: Cambridge University Press, 1995).

69. The subtitle is a reference to Ken Albala, *Eating Right in the Renaissance* (Oakland: University of California Press, 2002).

70. Jeffrey Jerome Cohen suggests that William of Newburgh's inclusion of this tale in his text is evidence of Newburgh's anxiety about the "cultural diversity from which the kingdom had been formed," and "the hybridity it had long disowned," long after contemporaries claimed that the previous residents of the island had been subdued and had vanished after the Norman Conquest (see Cohen, "Green Children from Another World, or the Archipelago in England," in *Cultural Diversity in the British Middle Ages: Archipelago, Ireland, England*, ed. Cohen [New York: Palgrave Macmillan, 2008], 75).

71. Cohen, *Cultural Diversity in the British Middle Ages*, 82–83.

72. Cohen, *Cultural Diversity in the British Middle Ages*, 77.

73. Francis Godwin, *The Man in the Moone: Or a Discourse of a Voyage Thither* (London, 1638). When the protagonist, Domingo Gonsales, arrives on the moon, the race of Lunars offers him green plants to eat, ostensibly their green diet of choice. Other early modern sources that alluded to the story of the green children included Richard Burton, *The Anatomie of Melancholy* (London, 1621); and William Camden, *Britannia* (London, 1586). The latter was later translated into English, with numerous editions.

74. Paul Nuget, "Do Nations Have Stomachs? Food, Drink and Imagined Community in Africa," *Africa Spectrum* 45, no. 3 (2010): 89.

75. Nicholas Culpepper, *Pharmacopoeia Londinensis; or, the London Dispensatory Further Adorned by the Studies and Collections of the Fellows now living, of the said Colledg.* (London, 1672), A4.

76. Richard Bradley, *New Improvements of Planting and Gardening* (London, 1717), 28.

77. Mary Floyd-Wilson and Garrett A. Sullivan Jr., *Environment and Embodiment in Early Modern England* (Basingstoke: Palgrave Macmillan, 2007), 4.

78. Bradley, *New Improvements*, 28. Meanwhile, the interchangeability between medical and culinary recipes is evident in many manuscript cookbooks from this period that contained recipes for food and medicine on back-to-back pages: Lady Frescheville's Receipt Book, 1669, Fol. 0164, Winterthur Library. For a printed example, consider a title such as T.D., *Food and Physick, for every Householder, & his Family, During the Time of the Plague* (London, 1665). For more on the relationship of food to health and temperament, see Trudy Eden, *The Early American Table: Food and Society in the New World* (DeKalb: Northern Illinois University Press, 2008); and Ken Albala, *Food in Early Modern Europe* (Westport, Conn.: Greenwood, 2003).

79. Eden, *The Early American Table*, 4.

80. John Archer, *Every man his own doctor, completed with an herbal*, 2nd ed. (London, 1673), title page.

81. Anxieties about the potentially deleterious effects of unfamiliar foods on colonists' bodies in the Americas has been demonstrated by Karen O. Kupperman "Apathy and Death in Early Jamestown," *Journal of American History* 66, no. 1 (1979): 24–40; and Rebecca Earle, *The Body of the Conquistador: Food, Race and the Colonial Experience in Spanish America* (Cambridge: Cambridge University Press, 2014).

82. Hans Sloane, *A Voyage to the Islands Madera, Barbados, Nieves, S. Christophers and Jamaica, with the Natural History of the Herbs and Trees ... of those Islands* (London, 1707), preface. Others wrote about the growing consumption of chocolate, relatively new to England until the conquest of Jamaica, for instance, Stubbe, *The Indian Nectar*.

83. As Jonathan Eacott has pointed out, English writers expressed anxieties about the impact of the consumption of East Indian luxuries on English society, fearing a loss of English virtue and masculinity (see Eacott, *Selling Empire: India in the Making of Britain and America, 1600–1830* [Chapel Hill: University of North Carolina, 2016], 23–25).

84. "A Cup of Coffee: Or, Coffee in its Colors" (London 1663).

85. Cited in Steve Pincus, "'Coffee Politicians Does Create': Coffeehouses and Restoration Political Culture," *Journal of Modern History* 67, no. 4 (December 1995): 826.

86. Pincus, "Coffee Politicians Does Create," 812.

87. Pincus, "Coffee Politicians Does Create," 826.

88. Pincus, "Coffee Politicians Does Create," 826.

89. Kristen G. Brooks, "Inhaling the Alien: Race and Tobacco in Early Modern England," in *Global Traffic: Discourses and Practices of Trade in English Literature and Culture from 1550 to 1700*, ed. Barbara Sebek and Stephen Deng (New York: Palgrave Macmillan, 2008), 157.

90. Iliffe, "Foreign Bodies," 28.

91. Alix Cooper, *Inventing the Indigenous: Local Knowledge and Natural History in Early Modern Europe* (Cambridge: Cambridge University Press, 2007), 6.

92. Richard Burton, *The anatomy of melancholy* (London, 1621), 327.

93. Robert Hooke, *Migrographia* (London, 1665). In this text he described the vegetation of a lunar vale as seen through his telescope. In his tale *Discovery of a World in the Moone* (1638), John Wilkins suggested that astronauts might transplant moon plants for profit and to fund future lunar colonization. This scheme was repeated in Wilkins's *Discourse concerning a New World* (London, 1640).

94. As Alix Cooper has noted, European experiences with foreign spices, drugs, and exotic plants actually inspired a turn inward, back to local nature. With renewed interest, early modern men and women looked more carefully at the plants growing in their own backyards, partly inspired by the belief that English plants might be best suited to English bodies (Cooper, *Inventing the Indigenous*).

95. Samuel Hartlib, *The Compleat Husband-man: or, A Discourse of the Whole Art of Husbandry; Both Forraign and Domestick* (London, 1651), 71.

96. Kupperman, "Fear of Hot Climates in the Anglo-American Colonial Experience," 213–40.

97. Earle, *The Body of the Conquistador*, 2.

98. William Hughes, *The American Physitian; or, A Treatise of the Roots, Plants, Trees, Shrubs, Fruit, Herbs, &c. Growing in the English Plantations in America* (London, 1672), 109.

99. Bradley, *New Improvements*, 28.

100. Lady Frescheville's Receipt Book, 1669, Fol. 0164, Winterthur Library.

101. John Worlidge, *Vinetum Britannicum: Or, A Treatise of Cider, and Such Other Wines and Drinks that Are Extracted From All Manner of Fruits Growing in this Kingdom. Together with the Method of Propagating all sorts of Vinous Fruit-Trees* (London: Printed by J.C. for Tho. Dring, 1676), 1.

102. Eden, *The Early American Table*, 4.

103. Mary Anne Caton, ed., *Fooles and Fricassees: Food in Shakespeare's England* (Seattle: University of Washington Press, 1999), 10.

104. Beale to Oldenburg, January 31, 1663, EL/B1/21; Beale to Evelyn, April 16, 1663, EL/B1/29; Beale to Brereton, EL/B1/35, all in Royal Society Library.

105. John Beale, July 1, 1664, EL/B1/44, Royal Society Library.

106. Beale further promised that a "Botanicall diet" was the best way to live to the "age of Mathusalah" (Beale, "On cooking muchrooms" [1659], Add MS 4292, f. 82, British Library).

107. Daniel Cox read "A History of Vegetables" on June 4, 1668 (Cl.P/10i/8, Royal Society Library).

108. Cited in Thirsk, *Food in Early Modern England*, 141.

109. Thirsk, *Food in Early Modern England*, 141–42.

110. Earle, *The Body of the Conquistador*, 5.

111. "Concerning maize by Mr. Winthrop," December 31, 1662, Cl.P/10i/3, Royal Society Library.

112. Lois Green Carr, Russell R. Menard, and Lorena S. Walsh, *Robert Cole's World: Agriculture & Society in Early Maryland* (Chapel Hill: Published by the Omohundro Institute of Early American History and Culture and the University of North Carolina Press, 1991), 34. Regarding the fear of corn consumption in the earliest years of Virginian colonization, see Karen O. Kupperman "Apathy and Death in Early Jamestown," *Journal of American History* 66, no. 1 (1979): 24–40.

113. Carr, *Robert Cole's World*, 34.

114. Carr, *Robert Cole's World*, 34.

115. "Concerning maize by Mr. Winthrop," December 31, 1662, Cl.P/10i/3, Royal Society Library.

116. Walter W. Woodward, *Prospero's America: John Winthrop, Jr., Alchemy, and the Creation of New England Culture, 1606-1676* (Chapel Hill: University of North Carolina Press, 2010).

117. 12/190A, Hartlib Papers.

118. 12/190A, Hartlib Papers.

119. "Concerning maize by Mr. Winthrop," December 31, 1662, Cl.P/10i/3, Royal Society Library.

120. "Concerning maize by Mr. Winthrop," December, 31, 1662, Cl.P/10i/3, Royal Society Library.

121. Earle, *The Body of the Conquistador*, 56.

122. Copy of the Journall book of ye Royall Society, Sloane MS 244, f. 52, British Library.

123. "Concerning maize by Mr. Winthrop," December 31, 1662, Cl.P/10i/3, Royal Society Library.

124. Thirsk, *Food in Early Modern England*, 103.

125. Samuel Hartlib, *Samuel Hartlib his legacie* (London, 1651), 11–12. Hartlib went on to claim that gardening was "but of a few years standing in England, and therefore not deeply rooted." The art of gardening "began to creepe into England" about five years prior. The author urged readers to keep an open mind about what might grow.

126. Malcolm Thick, "Root Crops and the Feeding of London's Poor in the Late Sixteenth and Early Seventeenth Centuries," in *English Rural Society, 1500–1800: Essays in Honour of Joan Thirsk*, ed. John Chartres and David Hey (Cambridge: Cambridge University Press, 1990), 279.

127. Thirsk, *Food in Early Modern England*,

128. Hartlib, *Samuel Hartlib his legacie*, 8–9.

129. Adolphus Speed, *Adam out of Eden, or, An abstract of divers excellent Experiments touching the advancement of Husbandry* (London, 1659), 101.

130. Speed, *Adam out of Eden*, 48.

131. Stephen Blake, *The compleat gardeners practice, directing the exact way of gardening in three partsL the garden of pleasure, physical garden, kitchin garden* (London, 1664), 148.

132. Andrew Yarranton, *England's Improvement by Sea and Land* (London, 1677).

133. Thirsk, *Food in Early Modern England*, 59.

134. Thirsk, *Food in Early Modern England*, 60. However, Thirsk is quick to point out that it can be difficult to generalize about food shortages as local and class differences influenced the ways people experienced famine.

135. Thirsk, *Food in Early Modern England*, 97–98.

136. Braddick, *State Formation in Early Modern England*, 105. See also John Richards, *The Unending Frontier: An Environmental History of the Early Modern World* (Berkeley: University of California Press, 2003), 11.

137. Richards, *The Unending Frontier*, 11.

138. Thirsk, *Food in Early Modern England*, 93.

139. Robert Sibbald, *Provision for the Poor in Time of Dearth & Scarcity*, 2nd ed. (Edinburgh, 1709), 6–9.

140. Keith Wrightson, *Earthly Necessities: Economic Lives in Early Modern Britain* (New Haven, Conn.: Yale University Press, 2000), 249.

141. Margaret Pelling, *The Common Lot: Sickness, Medical Occupations, and the Urban Poor in Early Modern England: Essays* (London: Longman, 1998), 39.

142. Joyce Appleby, *Economic Thought and Ideology in Seventeenth-Century England* (Princeton, N.J.: Princeton University Press, 1978), 99.

143. Slack, *From Reformation to Improvement*, 13.

144. Wrightson, *Earthly Necessities*, 249.

145. Nathaniel Lukes, A wastbooke of all Tanger affaires 1661, Sloane 1956, ff. 30b–36, British Library.

146. Nathaniel Lukes, A wastbooke of all Tanger affaires 1661, Sloane 1956, f. 6, British Library.

147. Slack, *From Reformation to Improvement*, 1.

148. Mr Reason Melish his discourse, Concerning the best ways of England's Improvement, Cl.P/10iii/16, Royal Society Library.

149. Slack, *From Reformation to Improvement*, 97.

150. Mr Reason Melish his discourse, Concerning the best ways of England's Improvement, Cl.P/10iii/16, Royal Society Library.

151. Cl.P/10iii/16, Royal Society Library.

152. Cited in Slack, *From Reformation to Improvement*, 96.

153. Mr Reason Melish his discourse, Concerning the best ways of England's Improvement, Cl.P/10iii/16, Royal Society Library.

154. Roger Coke, *A Discourse of Trade* (London, 1670), 4–5.

155. Among the sixteenth-century colonial promoters who claimed England was too crowded was Richard Hakluyt. He advocated for prisoners to be sent to the colonies (see Donald A. Yerxa, *Recent Themes in Early American History: Historians in Conversation* [Columbia: University of South Carolina Press, 2008], 47–48).

156. William Petty saw internal improvements and external acquisitions as working hand in hand to make everyone healthier; improved domestic lands and new lands in different climatic zones improved food supply and diversified diets (Add MS 72,865, f. 84, Petty Papers, British Library).

157. Coke, *A Discourse of Trade*.

158. Samuel Fortrey, *The History or Narrative of the Great Level of the Fenns, Called Bedford Level* (London, 1685), 71–81.

159. Others argued that population was a key component in any competition with other nations and encouraged efforts to expand the size of the population. Numbers were crucial to successful plantations: "people are the foundation and Improvement of all Plantatons" (Certaine Propositions for the better accommodating ye Forreigne Plantations with Servants reported from the Comitee to the Councell of Forreigne Plantations, Egerton MS 2395, f.277, British Library).

160. Coke, *A Discourse of Trade*, 7.

161. Coke, *A Discourse of Trade*, 8.

162. Coke, *A Discourse of Trade*, 11.

163. Coke, *A Discourse of Trade*, 43.

164. Coke, *A Discourse of Trade*, 10.

165. Hartlib, *Samuel Hartlib his legacie*.

166. "Mr Reason Melish his discourse, Concerning the best ways of England's Improvement," Cl.P/10iii/16, Royal Society Library.

167. Andrew Yarranton, *England's Improvement by Sea and land* (London, 1676), 113.

168. On improving crop yields, see Craig Muldrew, *Food, Energy, and the Creation of Industriousness: Work and Material Culture in Agrarian England, 1550–1780* (Cambridge: Cambridge University Press, 2011), 3.

169. According to the authors of *Robert Cole's World*: "A rule of thumb in the early Chesapeake, expressed in Maryland law, guarded against shortages by requiring that two acres be put into corn for each hand that raised tobacco." The last prosecutions under the act occurred in the 1660s (Carr, *Robert Cole's World*, 37).

170. Emma Spary, "Political, Natural and Bodily Economies," in *Cultures of Natural History*, ed. Nicholas Jardine, James Secord, and Spary (Cambridge: Cambridge University Press, 1996), 179.

171. Carr, *Robert Cole's World*, 35.

172. Carr, *Robert Cole's World*, n. 15. In John Worlidge's *Systema Agiculturae*, 130–31, he offered advice about the ideal distance to maintain between plantings.

Maryland's courts also offered guidelines for suggested distances between trees, which echoed Worlidge's advice.

173. Gunlög Fur, *Colonialism in the Margins: Cultural Encounters in New Sweden and Lapland* (Boston: Brill Academic, 2006), 244.

174. Roger Williams, *A Key into the Language of America* (London, 1643), 125.

175. Williams, *A Key into the Language of America*, 126.

176. In the opening of one of his letters to William Petty, William Penn referred to Petty as "my old friend." In another letter to Petty, Penn suggested Petty purchase shares in his new colony. Their friendship, and this potential investment opportunity, might explain Petty's reasons for writing up the plans for Pennsylvania. Petty eventually purchased shares (Add MS 72850, ff. 234, 290, William Petty's Letters, British Library).

177. Add MS 72867, f. 72, Petty Papers, British Library.

178. While one document is entitled "Generall Cautions concerning Pensylvania," others allude generally to the colonies, such as "A Proposall for Planting 40m acres in america" (Add MS 72867, ff. 72, 78, 79, Petty Papers, British Library).

179. John Graunt, *Natural and Political Observations, Mentioned in a following Index, and made upon the Bills of Mortality. By John Graunt, Citizen of London. With reference to the Government, Religion, Trade, Growth, Ayr, Diseases, and the several Changes of the said CITY* (London, 1662), dedicatory material.

180. Add MS 72867, f. 79, Petty Papers, British Library.

181. Add MS 72867, f. 79, Petty Papers, British Library.

182. Add MS 72867, f. 79, Petty Papers, British Library.

183. For instance, among his many propositions for quieting Ireland, which he saw as a troublesome island, he suggested sending ten thousand English women each year into Ireland in order to transform the population from within, so that children of such unions might be equally influenced by their English mothers while reared in childhood. He proposed that children of such unions would be culturally and physically transformed, particularly over generations. In Petty's thinking, alterations at a "corpuscular" level could thereby alter an entire island. Ideas about the "transmutation" of elements inspired his proposal. He imagined that the Irish might, over time, be transmuted into English subjects. Petty utilized Boyle's account of transmutation, which included an account of alchemy derived from corpuscularian principles (Ted McCormick, *William Petty and the Ambitions of Political Arithmetic* [Oxford: Oxford University Press, 2010], 202–3).

184. Add MS 72,865, f. 84, Petty Papers, British Library.

185. Daniel Denton, *A brief description of New-York, formerly called New-Netherlands with the places thereunto adjoyning: together with the manner of its situation, fertility of the soyle, healthfulness of the climate, and the commodities thence produced ... likewise a brief relation of the customs of the Indians there* (London, 1670), 19.

186. McCormick, *William Petty*, 214.

187. Speed, *Adam out of Eden*, "To the Reader."

188. McCormick, *William Petty*, 9.

189. McCormick, *William Petty*, preface.

190. McCormick, *William Petty*, 10.

191. Hartlib Papers [HP, 53/36/Ia] cited in Ted McCormick, *William Petty and the Ambitions of Political Arithmetic* (Oxford: Oxford University Press, 2009), 73; John

Evelyn, *Fumifugium or, the Inconveniencie of the Aer and Smoak of London Dissipated* (London, 1661).

192. Londa Schiebinger, *Plants and Empire: Colonial Bioprospecting in the Atlantic World* (Cambridge, Mass.: Harvard University Press, 2004), 74.

193. Stubbe, *The Indian Nectar*, 48.

194. Anonymous, "The Virtues of Coffee, Chocolette, and Thee or Tea, Experimentally known in this our Climate," n.d.

195. Stubbe, *The Indian Nectar*, 31.

196. Jennifer L. Morgan, *Laboring Women: Reproduction and Gender in New World Slavery* (Philadelphia: University of Pennsylvania Press, 2004).

197. Fortrey, *The History or Narrative*, 80.

198. Fortrey, *The History or Narrative*, 72

199. Fortrey, *The History or Narrative*, x.

200. Hartlib, *Samuel Hartlib his legacie.*

201. Hartlib, *Samuel Hartlib his legacie.*

202. Cited in Grove, "Cressey Dymock," 35.

203. Hartlib, *Samuel Hartlib his legacie*, letter of dedication.

204. Hartlib, *Samuel Hartlib his legacie*, letter of dedication.

205. Thirsk, *Food in Early Modern England*, 128.

206. Slack, *From Reformation to Improvement*, 2.

207. Writers often pointed to Charles II as the ultimate steward of the land, best suited to the tasks of improvement on a grand scale, because he could support their projects with money and legislation and had the circumspection necessary to such endeavors (see Graunt, *Natural and Political Observations . . .* , [dedication]).

208. Slack, *From Reformation to Improvement*, 97.

209. Michael Hunter, *Establishing the New Science: The Experience of the Early Royal Society* (Woodbridge, Suffolk, U.K.: Boydell and Brewer, 1989), 7.

210. Slack, *From Reformation to Improvement*, 88.

211. Wrightson, *Earthly Necessities*, 249.

212. John Beale to John Evelyn, November 26, 1670, Add MS 78312/3, f. 32, British Library.

213. Evelyn to the Duke of Albemarle, September 24, 1665, Add MS 78298, f. 146, British Library.

214. As Grew wrote, "Your Majesty hath bee pleased to be the Founder, and to style Your Self the Patron of that Society, of which I have the honour to be a Member" (Nehemiah Grew, *The Anatomy of Plants. With an Idea of a Philosophical History of Plants* [London, 1682], letter of dedication).

215. John Graunt, *Natural and Political Observations Made Upon the Bills of Mortality* (London, 1663), "The Epistle Dedicatory."

216. Copy of the Journal book of ye Royall Society, Sloane MS 244, ff. 5–6, British Library.

217. Proposalls and Reasons for the Improving, & advancing of Planting, Cl.P/10iii/7, Royal Society.

218. Cited in Reginald Lennard, "English Agriculture under Charles II: The Evidence of the Royal Society's 'Enquiries,'" *Economic History Review* 4, no. 1 (1932): 24.

219. Thirsk, *Food in Early Modern England*, 122, 128.

220. Thirsk, *The Agrarian History*, 562–63; Copy of the Journal book of ye Royall Society, Sloane MS 244, f. 53, British Library.

221. Copy of the Journall book of ye Royall Society, Sloane MS 244, f. 54, British Library.

222. Cited in Lennard, "English Agriculture," 24.

223. "Enquires Concerning Agriculture," *Philosophical Transactions of the Royal Society* 5 (1665): 94.

224. Richard Drayton, *Nature's Government: Science, Imperial Britain, and the "Improvement" of the World* (New Haven, Conn.: Yale University Press, 2000), 52–53.

225. Steven Stoll, *Larding the Lean Earth: Soil and Society in Nineteenth-Century America* (New York: Hill and Wang, 2002), 13.

226. Bradley, *New Improvements*, preface.

227. Bradley, *New Improvements*, 8.

228. Hartlib, *Samuel Hartlib his legacie*, 105.

229. Hartlib, *Samuel Hartlib his legacie*, 81.

230. Bradley advised that different type of soil required different actions, different additions, and different timelines. For instance, "stiff soil" required the addition of "sharp sand"—mixed together with "the *Ashes* of *burnt Furzes, Gorse, Fern, Weeds* or *Wood*"—in September or October (Bradley, *New Improvements*, 28–29).

231. Hartlib, *Samuel Hartlib his legacie*, 42–47.

232. Many European countries were also focused on devising new agricultural methods. English horticultural and agricultural writers studied these efforts (Mauro Ambrosoli, *The Wild and the Sown: Botany and Agriculture in Western Europe, 1350–1850* [Cambridge: Cambridge University Press, 2009]).

233. Mark Overton, *Agricultural Revolution in England: The Transformation of the Agrarian Economy, 1500–1850* (Cambridge: Cambridge University Press, 1996), 17.

234. Overton, *Agricultural Revolution in England*, 3.

235. Overton, *Agricultural Revolution in England*, 110.

236. Overton, *Agricultural Revolution in England*, 99.

237. Villiers-Stuart Papers, C/5/26, Boole Library, University College Cork.

238. Speed, *Adam out of Eden*, 37.

239. Cl.P/19/21, Royal Society Library.

240. Donald Woodward, "'An Essay on Manures': Changing Attitudes to Fertilization in England, 1500–1800," in *English Rural Society, 1500–1800: Essays in Honour of Joan Thirsk*, ed. John Chartres and David Hay (Cambridge: Cambridge University Press, 1990), 251–52.

241. Cl.P/19/21, Royal Society Library.

242. Cl.P/19/21, Royal Society Library.

243. Overton, *Agricultural Revolution in England*, 112.

244. Cl.P/19/21, Royal Society Library.

245. EL/OB/128, Royal Society Library.

246. "An Interrogatory Relating more particularly to the Husbandry and Naturall History of Ireland," MS 5926a, Trinity College Library.

247. Cl.P/10iii/16, Royal Society Library.

248. Joan Thirsk, gen. ed., *The Agrarian History of England and Wales*, vol. 5: *1640–1750, I. Regional Farming Systems* (Cambridge: Cambridge University Press, 1984), xxiii.

249. Yarranton suggested that English cultivators had to be forced into innovation.

250. Michael Leslie and Timothy Raylor, eds., *Culture and Cultivation in Early Modern England: Writing and the Land* (Leicester, U.K.: Leicester University Press, 1992), 6–7.

251. Thirsk, *The Agrarian History of England and Wales*, xxiii.

252. Egerton MS 2395, ff. 272–73, 288, British Library.

253. Egerton MS 2395, f. 288, British Library.

254. Sara Gronim, *Everyday Nature: Knowledge of the Natural World in Colonial New York* (New Brunswick, N.J.: Rutgers University Press, 2007), 30.

255. Joan Thirsk, "Rural Migration in England: The Long Historical Perspective", in *Migrants in Agricultural Development: A Study of Intrarural Migration*, ed. J. A. Mollett (London: Macmillan Academic and Professional LTD, 1991), 44–47.

256. Harlow was an experienced traveler and gardener and had successfully gathered Virginian flora only several years before. This prior experience almost certainly helped him to succeed in his Jamaica transplantation scheme.

257. Lady Isabella (Bramhall) Graham to Sir Arthur Rawson, April 28, 1690, Box 9, HA 14835, Irish Papers, Hastings Manuscripts, Huntington Library, San Marino, Calif.

258. Lady Isabella (Bramhall) Graham to Sir Arthur Rawdon, January 21, 1691, Box 9, HA 14839, Irish Papers, Hastings Manuscripts, Huntington Library, San Marino, Calif.

259. Rawdon's early death, only several years after the gardens were planted, could have presaged their destruction, but for the various individuals who continued to take an active interest in the specimens. As late as 1722 Rawdon's sister, Dorothy, visited the proposed site of a new physic garden at Trinity College in Dublin and pledged the donation of several specimens from Moira on behalf of Rawdon's son, John (Dorothy Rawdon to Sir John Rawdon, July 6, 1722, IE TCD MS 3741, Trinity College Library Dublin).

260. Robert Burden and Stephan Kohl, eds., *Landscape and Englishness* (Rodopi: New York, 2006), 16.

261. Burden and Kohl, eds., *Landscape and Englishness*, 18.

262. In his recent monograph Walter Johnson discusses another reason for the English desires for straight rows of agriculture: the incarceral feature of rows in fields worked by enslaved laborers. The enslaved were separated, visible, and presumed controllable in such a formation (Johnson, *River of Dark Dreams: Slavery and Empire in the Cotton Kingdom* [Cambridge, Mass.: Harvard University Press, 2013]).

263. Earle, *The Body of the Conquistador*, 81.

264. Burden and Kohl, eds., *Landscape and Englishness*, 24.

265. Historians have argued that there were links between agricultural cultivation and education reform. "The members of the Hartlib Circle, whose activities are central to debates on the proper organization of agriculture and horticulture in the seventeenth century, were also profoundly concerned with the remaking of education: place-making and the making of individuals and societies were inextricably linked in their thought" (Michael Leslie and Timothy Raylor, eds., *Culture and Cultivation in Early Modern England: Writing and the Land* [Leicester, U.K.: Leicester University Press, 1992], 4).

266. Richards, *The Unending Frontier*, 19.

267. Add Ms 72,865, ff. 83–84, Petty Papers, British Library.

268. Add Ms 72,865, ff. 83–84, Petty Papers, British Library.

269. When he lived in Holland, John Locke was part of a network of individuals trading seeds and plants, including turnips, parsnips, carrots, and root vegetables from the Netherlands (Thirsk, *Food in Early Modern England*, 129).

270. Paul Nuget, "Do Nations Have Stomachs? Food, Drink and Imagined Community in Africa," *Africa Spectrum* 45, no. 3 (2010): 89.

5 / Naturalizing Bodies

1. Consideracons about the peopling & settling the island of Jamaica, Egerton MS 2395, f. 288, British Library.

2. William Hughes, *The American Physitian; or, A Treatise of the Roots, Plants, Trees, Shrubs, Fruit, Herbs, &c. Growing in the English Plantations in America* (London, 1672), "To the Reader."

3. Hughes, *The American Physitian*, "On Mr. Hughes's Treatise of American Plants."

4. Hans Sloane later claimed that the principal design of his treatise on Jamaica's flora was to help newcomers to Jamaica "understand what Uses the Plants they have growing *Sponte* or in Gardens with them" so that they could use them to combat illnesses with local plants. He acknowledged that it had been difficult to "carry thither such *European* Simples as are proper for the Cure of all sorts of Diseases" colonists might encounter (Hans Sloane, *A Voyage to the Islands Madera, Barbados, Nieves, S. Christophers and Jamaica, with the Natural History of the Herbs and Trees ... of those Islands* [London, 1707], preface).

5. For more on the idea that people in "torrid zones" behaved differently due to latitude and climate, see Felicity A. Nussbaum, *Torrid Zones: Maternity, Sexuality, and Empire in Eighteenth-Century English Narratives* (Baltimore: Johns Hopkins University Press, 1999), 7–11; and Hughes, *The American Physitian*, "To the Reader."

6. A brief survey of Jamaica, Egerton MS 2395, ff. 609–18, British Library.

7. According to Hughes, Jamaica's *"breezes"* and *"gales of Winde . . . do there continually blow and qualify the Sulpherous Air,"* making it *"as temperate, healthful and beneficial, as most places are in the* Temperate Zone" to English bodies (Hughes, *The American Physitian*, 139–40). According to Anya Zilberstein, early American colonists were confident that they could craft a more temperate climate by cultivating the landscape (Zilberstein, *A Temperate Empire: Making Climate Change in Early America* [New York: Oxford University Press, 2016]).

8. Jamaica's promoters offered varied schemes to settle and secure the island, and sugar was only one of the many cultivars mentioned (Kate L. Mulry, "The Aromas of Flora's Wide Domains: Cultivating Gardens, Airs, and Political Subjects in the Late-Seventeenth Century English Atlantic," in *Empire of the Senses: Sensory Practices of Colonialism in Early America*, ed. Daniella Hacke and Paul Musselwhite [Leiden, Netherlands: Brill, 2018], 259–60, 286; and Carla Gardina Pestana, *The English Conquest of Jamaica: Oliver Cromwell's Bid for Empire* [Cambridge, Mass.: Belknap Press of Harvard University Press, 2017], 13, 139, 148–49).

9. A brief survey of Jamaica, Egerton MS 2395, f. 614, British Library.

10. Early modern rulers and individuals regularly schemed to transplant lucrative spices from the east to the west, arguing this was a key to economic success. Long

before the English made any such attempts, the Spanish sought to transplant lucrative botanicals from the East Indies to the West Indies, among them *Cassia fistula* (see Pratik Chakrabarti, *Medicine & Empire: 1600–1960* [New York: Palgrave Macmillan, 2014], 24). Meanwhile, the Spanish Crown supported the transplantation, cultivation, and trade in spices, including cinnamon, pepper, ginger, and nutmeg, from both China and the Spice Islands into New Spain (Mexico) and colonies in the Caribbean beginning in the 1550s (see Paula De Vos, "The Science of Spices: Empiricism and Economic Botany in the early Spanish Empire," *Journal of World History* 17, no. 4 [December 2006]: 403, 417–18). The English regularly sought out information about the Spanish empire in order to replicate its successes. Among the schemes envisioned by English projectors over the course of two centuries included the transplantation of citrus, mulberry trees, cinnamon, cloves, and grape vines. As Karen Ordahl Kupperman has pointed out, despite the repeated failure of transplantation this did not dampen enthusiasm for such schemes (Kupperman, "The Puzzle of the American Climate in the Early Colonial Period," *American Historical Review* 87 [1982]: 1262–89).

11. Anna Svensson, "'And Eden from the Chaos Rose': Utopian Order and Rebellion in the Oxford Physick Garden," *Annals of Science* 76, no. 2 (2019): 1.

12. For a thorough examination on the practice of imperial "bioprospecting," see Londa Schiebinger, *Plants and Empire: Colonial Bioprospecting in the Atlantic World* (Cambridge, Mass.: Harvard University Press, 2007).

13. Harold J. Cook, *The Decline of the Old Medical Regime in Stuart London* (Ithaca, N.Y.: Cornell University Press, 1986), 28–69.

14. Sloane, *A Voyage to the Island of Jamaica*, preface; John Evelyn, *Sylva* (London, 1664), 131.

15. While the schemes may not have been undertaken, or at least not on the scale outlined above, the gardens were merely one among many ambitious projects dreamed up in the early modern era (see, for instance, Maximillian Novak, ed., *The Age of Projects* [Toronto: University of Toronto Press, 2008]).

16. Ann Laura Stoler, *Along the Archival Grain: Epistemic Anxieties and Colonial Common Sense* (Princeton, N.J.: Princeton University Press, 2009), 105, 138.

17. Stoler, *Along the Archival Grain*, 108, 110.

18. Recent scholarship has stressed the importance of "dismantling" the assumption that colonial administrators could easily and efficiently use information sought by administrators to improve governance, particularly scientific knowledge (Loïc Charles and Paul Cheney, "The Colonial Machine Dismantled: Knowledge and Empire in the French Atlantic," *Past & Present* 219 [2013]: 127–63).

19. "A Proposal for removing spices & other plants from the East to the West Indies," Egerton MS 2935, f. 337, British Library.

20. Enquires concerning those several kind of things which are reported to be in Virginia & ye Bermudas, not found in England, Egerton MS 2935, f. 297, British Library. Scholars of the senses reminds us that we must historicize sensory experiences. A sense of smell, for instance, is not merely biological but is conditioned by residence in a particular time, place, and culture. Sensory scholarship also emphasizes how sensory markers were often associated with regulatory aspirations (Paul Rodaway, *Sensuous Geographies: Body, Sense, and Place* [London: Routledge, 1994]; David Howes, ed., *Empire of the Senses: The Sensual Cultural Reader* [London: Bloomsbury Academic, 2005]).

21. Mark Jenner, "The Politics of London Air: John Evelyn's *Fumifugium* and the Restoration," *Historical Journal* 38 (1995): 540. Jenner has suggested the importance of reading texts like Evelyn's *Fumifugium* at once as a text on air pollution as well as on politics, which emphasized the king's ability to cleanse the air of real and metaphorical pollutants, like smog and dissonant political views.

22. John Evelyn, *Fumifugium, or, the Inconveniencie of the AER of London* (London, 1661), 22.

23. Victoria Henshaw defines "smellscape" as referring to a "smell environment," although she recognizes that there may be temporal, cultural, and biological limitations to what we can scent at any moment. Although smell may seem ephemeral, a smellscape may be a composite of smells from the past and present, because "we may carry a mental image or memory of the smellscape in its totality" (Henshaw, *Urban Smellscapes: Understanding and Designing City Smell Environments* [New York: Routledge, 2014], 5).

24. A letter to the Comitte of ye East India Company for an Experim[t] in Jamaica, Sloane MS 856, f. 37b, British Library.

25. Among the categories deemed essential to officials evaluating England's empire was the category of *use*. The new king was advised to apply "all prudentiall meanes for the recovering those Dominions usefull to England, and England helpful to Them." Perhaps unsurprisingly, it appears that identifying a lucrative, salable commodity was a key feature of this designation (see "Overtures touching a Councel to bee erected by his Matie for the better regulating and improving of forreigne Plantations," Egerton MS 2395, ff. 272–73, British Library).

26. "Overtures touching a Councel to bee erected by his Matie for the better regulating and improving of forreigne Plantations," Egerton MS 2395, f. 272, British Library.

27. According to Richard Blome, physicians' knowledge of "Drugs and Medicaments, transported from Foreign Parts" was even more essential to the ultimate success of colonizing projects in foreign climes than armies. This was because merely staying alive was necessary in the first instance (Blome, *Cosmography and Geography* [1682], "To the Reader"). Meanwhile, spices had long been of great interest to Europeans. In addition to their valued flavor, spices were also often valued as medicines (Chakrabarti, *Medicine & Empire*, 21).

28. Chakrabarti, *Medicine & Empire*, 13.

29. For more on early modern English economic though, see Joyce Appleby, *Economic Thought and Ideology in Seventeenth-Century England* (Princeton, N.J.: Princeton University Press, 1978).

30. Vincent Brown, *The Reaper's Garden: Death and Power in the World of Atlantic Slavery* (Cambridge, Mass.: Harvard University Press, 2008). Moreover, early modern London was also characterized as a place hazardous to human health, as a kind of cancerous growth in the kingdom, or like a head grown too large for its body.

31. There is a long scholarly tradition that focuses on the techniques of modern discipline in which sight was associated with the "unequal gaze" and observation by the state as a means of social control, such as is recounted in Michel Foucault, *Discipline and Punish: The Birth of the Prison*, trans. Alan Sheridan (New York: Random House, 1995). According to Constance Classen, David Howes, and Anthony Synnott, the Western world increasingly valued sight and devalued smell during the eighteenth and nineteenth centuries. They suggests that this is why "sight, as the most detached

sense (by Western standards), provides *the* model for modern bureaucratic society" (Classen, David Howes, and Anthony Synnott, *Aroma: The Cultural History of Smell* [New York: Routledge, 1994], 3–5). See also Mark P. Leone and Silas D. Hurry, "Seeing: The Power of Town Planning in the Chesapeake," *Historical Archaeology* 32, no. 4 (1998): 34–62. However, as David Howes reminds us, various senses, including smell, offered an alternative sensory hierarchy. For instance, terms such as "'nose-wise,' a word now obsolete, could mean either 'clever' or 'keen-scented'" (Benoist Schaal, Catherine Rouby, and Andri Holley, eds., *Olfaction, Taste, and Cognition* [Cambridge: Cambridge University Press, 2002], 68–69).

32. David Howes and Marc Lalonde, "The History of Sensibilities: Of the Standard of Taste in Mid-Eighteenth Century England and the Circulation of Smells," *Dialectical Anthropology* 16 (1991): 126. Moreover, according to David Howes, the burning of incense enables or creates an "'intersubjective we-feeling' among the participants in a rite as each is forced to introject particles of the odour. One cannot but participate in the effervescence (or fellow-feeling) of the situation, because it participates in *you*" (David Howes, "Olfaction and Transition: An Essay on the Ritual Uses of Smell," *Canadian Review of Sociology* 24, no. 3 (August 1987): 403).

33. Early modern medical treatises claimed the brain was a particularly difficult organ to discipline and easily affected by smells (John Sutton, "Spongy Brains and Material Memories," in *Environment and Embodiment in Early Modern England*, ed. Mary Floyd-Wilson and Garrett A. Sullivan Jr. (Basingstoke, U.K.: Palgrave Macmillan, 2007), 18.

34. A letter to the Comitte of ye East India Company for an Experim^t in Jamaica, Sloane MS 856, f. 37b, British Library.

35. See Michael Meranze, "Culture and Governance: Reflections on the Cultural History of Eighteenth-Century British America," *William and Mary Quarterly*, 3d ser., 65 (2008): 714; Rebecca Bushnell, *Green Desire: Imagining Early Modern English Gardens* (Ithaca, N.Y.: Cornell University Press, 2003), 1.

36. A letter to the Comitte of ye East India Company for an Experim^t in Jamaica, Sloane MS 856, f. 37b, British Library.

37. Scholars have noted Charles II's interest in gardening since a child (Anna Keay, *The Magnificent Monarch: Charles II and the Ceremonies of Power* [London: Continuum, 2008], 21).

38. Many colonial promoters feared the transformative effects of new airs and soils on both plant and animal bodies (see Karen Ordahl Kupperman, "Fear of Hot Climates in the Anglo-American Colonial Experience," *William and Mary Quarterly*, 3d ser. 41, no. 2 [1984]: 213–40). Fears about the risks involved in travel prompted Royal Society Fellow Robert Boyle to collect and codify information about which climates or soils were "aptest" to "breed disease." Boyle hoped he might gather enough information to aid travelers. See "Topics for the History of Disease" in Michael Hunter, ed., *Robert Boyle's 'Heads' and 'Inquiries,'* Robert Boyle Project Occasional Papers no. 1 (Birkbeck: University of London, 2005), 33–34).

39. Naturalists frequently cited those plants that had been successfully transplanted, perhaps as evidence that human transplantation might likewise be possible (Hans Sloane, *A Voyage to the Islands* [London, 1707], lxxiv–lxxv).

40. Martin Noell, Thomas Povey's business partner in the 1650s, helped fund the Western Design fleet that captured Jamaica for England. Noell was then granted

licenses to transport criminals to the colonies. While Povey schemed to transplant plants, Noell planned to transplant people.

41. Garden writer and member of the Royal Society, John Beale, encouraged projects of transplantation but also warned that transplants might lose their best qualities in the process (EL/B1/38–39, Royal Society Library).

42. Karen Ordahl Kupperman, "Fear of Hot Climates in the Anglo-American Colonial Experience," *William and Mary Quarterly*, 3d ser., 41, no. 2 (1984): 213–40.

43. Court officials and colonists alike wondered if English settlers were still English, physically and politically, if living at such a distance. The legal theorist Edward Coke had been "equivocal about whether the rights of Englishmen had traversed the Atlantic. Coke's work implied that "common law had territorial limits." This must have raised questions about whether or not English culture and temperament might likewise have topographical limits (Craig Yirush, *Settlers, Liberty, and Empire: The Roots of Early American Political Theory, 1675–1775* [Cambridge: Cambridge University Press, 2011], 11). See also Raingard Esser, "Citizenship and Immigration in 16th- and Early 17th-Century England," in *Citizenship in Historical Perspective*, ed. Steven G. Ellis et al. (Pisa, Italy: Pisa University Press, 2006). According to Coke, some core liberties were transplantable into newly conquered lands, such as property rights (Daniel J. Hulsebosch, "The Ancient Constitution and the Expanding Empire: Sir Edward Coke's British Jurisprudence," *Law and History Review* 21, no. 3 [2003]: 466).

44. James Robertson, "Making Jamaica English: Priorities and Processes," in *The Torrid Zone: Caribbean Colonization and Cultural Interaction in the Long Seventeenth Century*, ed. L. H. Roper (Columbia: University of South Carolina Press, 2018), 117.

45. For more on "soil's historical and national properties," see Hillary Eklund, *Ground-Work: English Renaissance Literature and Soil Science* (Pittsburgh: Duquesne University Press, 2017), 6, 16.

46. For the proposed general naturalization bill in 1664, see Daniel Statt, *Foreigners and Englishmen: The Controversy over Immigration and Population, 1660–1770* (Newark: University of Delaware Press, 1995), 60–61.

47. As David Armitage has argued, "the demands of extending the nation oceanically tested their political imaginations, just as the internal conflict in Europe did." He likewise asks how English "nationhood was defined by the experience of empire?" He imagines that "the great process of the seventeenth century had been the internal union of the three kingdoms" (Armitage, "Greater Britain: A Useful Category of Historical Analysis?," *American Historical Review* 104, no. 2 [1999]: 441).

48. A letter to the Comitte of ye East India Company for an Experimᵗ in Jamaica, Sloane MS 856, f. 37b, British Library.

49. Thomas Povey's working knowledge of the colonies was invaluable to the Restoration government. During the final years of the protectorate Povey had served on Cromwell's Council of Trade as well as the Council for America. He and Martin Noell had helped supply Cromwell's Western Design fleet. Two of Povey's brothers, Richard and William Povey, sailed with the fleet and remained in the Caribbean in Jamaica and Barbados as commissioner general for provisions and provost general, respectively. Meanwhile, Povey's father had been engaged in colonial affairs as a commissioner to the Caribbee Islands in 1637. Thus, dealing with England's colonial ventures was something of a family business. After the Restoration, Povey was granted a number of positions, which suggests the growing importance of colonial experience

among colonial officials (see A. P. Thornton, *West-India Policy under the Restoration* [Oxford: Oxford University Press, 1956]). For the grant of Provost Marshall of Barbados to William Povey, see Egerton MS 2395, f. 131, British Library. See also Barbara Murison, *Oxford Dictionary of National Biography*, online ed. (Oxford: Oxford University Press, 2008).

50. Letter from Mr. Povey concerning the natural products of Virginia in behalf of the Royall Society; Enquires concerning those several kind of things which are reported to be in Virginia & ye Bermudas, not found in England, Egerton MS 2395, ff. 296, 297, British Library.

51. Copy of the Journal book of ye Royall Society, Sloane MS 244, ff. 5–6, British Library.

52. Thomas Povey proceeded to write many additional letters to solicit information about the natural world on behalf of the Royal Society. For instance, in May he was "intreated to send to Bantam" about a poison that turned "a mans blood suddanly into Gelly." In September he "proposed to the society to procure Correspondence in Africa." In January 1661 he requested "four or five copies of Inquiries for forraine parts" (Copy of the Journall book of ye Royall Society, Sloane MS 244, ff. 15, 32, 38).

53. The Royal Society, "Inquires for Virginia and the Bermudas," *Philosophical Transactions* 2 (1666): 420–21. In this publication they spell "Musquasoen" as "*Musquaspenn*, a Root of a red tincture." The "Tockawouge" root is likely a Tuckahoe plant, a root regularly referred to in colonial sources as the ingredient of Indian bread. References to Indian consumption of these plants in sixteenth- and seventeenth-century texts are in texts ranging from John Smith, to Mark Catesby, to John Ogilby. For more on Powhatan women's collection and preparation of Tuckahoe tubers as food, see Helen C. Rountree, "Powhatan Indian Women: The People Captain John Smith Barely Saw," *Ethnohistory* 45, no. 1 (Winter 1998): 13.

54. The "Putchamin fruit" is likely persimmon, derived from the Powhatan for "dry fruit" (*Oxford English Dictionary*). Scholars have recently brought attention to the key role that various, often unnamed, Native Americans and Africans would have played in similar information-gathering projects (Susan Scott Parrish, *American Curiosity: Cultures of Natural History in the British Colonial Atlantic World* [Chapel Hill: University of North Carolina Press, 2006]).

55. Enquires concerning those several kind of things which are reported to be in Virginia & ye Bermudas, not found in England, Egerton MS 2395, f. 297, British Library.

56. Enquires concerning those several kind of things which are reported to be in Virginia & ye Bermudas, not found in England, Egerton MS 2395, f. 297, British Library.

57. Povey encouraged his contacts to send his queries amongst their friends, especially those with local influence, such as the governor, Sir William Berkeley. He chose Berkeley not only because he was "known to bee a Person of most imminent Ingenuitie and one that hath made verie many Tryalls and Experiments" but because he might, "by his generous Example and his Influence recomend [Povey's questionnaires] to individuale persons who in those severall Quarters and Plantations may pursue those Disquisitous, and may make returns of them to him, under their hands" (Egerton MS 2395, ff. 296–97, British Library).

58. Andrew Wear, *Knowledge and Practice in English Medicine* (Cambridge: Cambridge University Press, 2000), 414–15. However, it is not appropriate to make clear distinctions between medicinal and nonmedicinal specimens sought in this list as items that smelled nice, or were aesthetically pleasing, might likewise have emotional, mental, and physical health benefits. Neither were there clear distinctions between food and medicine.

59. Enquires concerning those several kind of things which are reported to be in Virginia & ye Bermudas, not found in England, Egerton MS 2395, f. 296, British Library.

60. Inquires Recommended to Colonel Linch going to Jamaica, Sloane MS 3984, f. 194, British Library.

61. Inquires Recommended to Colonel Linch going to Jamaica, Sloane MS 3984, f. 195, British Library.

62. According to Zilberstein, early Americans understood climate change as "a consequence of economic development." The "industrious activity" of fellow cultivators would moderate the climate (Zilberstein, *A Temperate Empire*, 15).

63. A Proposal for removing spices & other plants from the East to the West Indies; A Proposal for Removing spices and other plants to the west Indies, Egerton MS 2935, ff. 337–39, British Library.

64. Richard Ford likely authored, or coauthored these proposals. On the back of the first proposal is the notation, "Richard Fords Paper concerning sending Plants [&c] from the East Indies." Since the two drafts of this plan appear in Povey's papers, but only the first was endorsed by Ford, it is likely that Povey was deeply involved. The transplantation schemes would have required the assistance of Ford and the East India Company since the plans sought to use "our Companys shippes" to carry the plants. The king sent Povey, a commissioner of the Council of Foreign Plantations, to confer with Ford and the Company. Ford was a highly connected merchant and politician. He held a number of positions in the East India Company, served as and alderman and as lord mayor of London, had many court connections. He is mentioned in the charter of the Royal African Company (Brian Weiser, *Charles II and the Politics of Access* [Woodbridge, Suffolk, U.K.: Boydell, 2003], 126; Ritchie, *The Duke's Province: A Study of New York Politics and Society, 1664–1691* [Chapel Hill: University of North Carolina Press], 15–17). The East India Company had also established connections with the Royal Society (Povey, and later, Ford, were both members) and the Society of Apothecaries, with whom they experimented on commodities like tea or opium and suggests that the East India Company was willing to collaborate (Anna Winterbottom, "An Experimental Community: The East India Company in London, 1600–1800," *British Journal for the History of Science* 52 [June 2019]: 330–32).

65. Sloane MS 856, f. 37b, British Library. This letter was written a few weeks after sending a letter to Jamaica's Council alerting them that he had appointed a new governor, Thomas, Baron Windsor (Sloane MS 856, f. 37, British Library).

66. A letter to the Comitte of ye East India Company for an Experim^t Experimt in Jamaica, August 20, 1661, Sloane MS 856, f. 37b, British Library.

67. A letter to the Comitte of ye East India Company for an Experim^t in Jamaica, August 20, 1661, Sloane MS 856, f. 37b, British Library.

68. A letter to the Comitte of ye East India Company for an Experim^t in Jamaica, August 20, 1661, Sloane MS 856, f. 37b, British Library.

69. August 20, 1661, Court Minutes, East India Company, IOR/B/26, f. 383, British Library.

70. August 30, 1661, Court Minutes, East India Company, IOR/B/26, f. 387, British Library.

71. Egerton MS 2935, ff. 337–39, British Library. Meanwhile, Europeans trading and living in the East Indies regularly relied on on-the-ground knowledge of local inhabitants (see Harold J. Cook, *Matters of Exchange: Commerce, Medicine, and Science in the Dutch Golden Age* [New Haven, Conn.: Yale University Press, 2007]).

72. Pierre d'Avity, sieur de Montmartin, *The estates, empires, & principallities of the world Represented by ye description of countries, maners of inhabitants, riches of provinces, forces, government, religion . . . Translated out of French by Edw: Grimstone, sergeant at armes* (London, 1616), 766. Although the English first landed in 1615, they did not construct a fort until 1665.

73. Despite pepper's significance, it is likely that many of the references to "pepper plants" in these texts referred to a broader array of spices and not to pepper alone. K. N. Chaudhuri has noted that at the mid-seventeenth century pepper remained an extremely significant commodity for the Dutch East India Company. Moreover, beyond its value on the markets in Europe, pepper's physical presence aboard East India Company ships played a key role as ballast cargo, balancing the ships on the return journey (Chaudhuri, *The Trading World of Asia and the English East India Company 1660–1760* [Cambridge: Cambridge University Press, 1978], 313).

74. Egerton MS 2395, f. 339, British Library.

75. Egerton MS 2395, f. 339, British Library.

76. L. H. Roper, *Advancing Empire: English Interests and Overseas Expansion, 1613–1688* (Cambridge: Cambridge University Press, 2017), 169.

77. Egerton MS 2395, f. 339, British Library.

78. These plans may have been related to the proposal developed by Thomas Lynch (later governor of Jamaica) in November 1660 that encouraged the king to set up his own plantation in Jamaica to set a good example for his countrymen (Thornton, *West-India Policy*, 43).

79. Scholars have examined the difficulty in transporting specimens, such as Kathleen S. Murphy and Christopher M. Parsons, "Ecosystems under Sail: Specimen Transport in the Eighteenth-Century French and British Atlantics," *Early American Studies* 10, no. 3 (October 2013): 503–29.

80. Cl. P. 19/ 48, f. 92, Royal Society Library.

81. Sloane MS 4036, f. 119, British Library.

82. Ritchie, *The Duke's Province*, 9–10. Initial publications on the natural products of Asia, published in Portuguese, reflected the Portuguese domination of trade in the region, including texts from Garcia D'Orta, *Colóquios do simples e drogas he cousas medicinais da Índia* (1563) and Cristobal Acosta, *Tractado de los drogas y medicinas de las Indias Orientales* (1578). But by the seventeenth century, the Dutch East India Company's control over the spice trade was likewise reflected in the various texts published in this period that dealt with the flora of Asia, including Henry van Rheede, *Hortus Indicus Malabaricus* (1678).

83. Roper, *Advancing Empire*, 161.

84. So significant was the pepper trade to Europe's traing companies that it was recognized as "the main cause for 'the great Firmentation between the Dutch and us'"

(Chaudhuri, *The Trading World of Asia and the English East India Company*, 314–15, 317).

85. Sir Josiah Child, governor of the East India Company, cited in Batchelor, *London: The Selden Map and the Making of a Global City* (Chicago: University of Chicago Press, 2014), 8.

86. Batchelor, *London*, 8.

87. For more on the numerous schemes to establish an English West India Company, see Shinsuke Satsuma, *Britain and Colonial Maritime War in the Early Eighteenth Century: Silver, Seapower and the Atlantic* (Woodbridge, Suffolk, U.K.: Boydell, 2013), 20–27.

88. Egerton MS 2395, f. 337, British Library.

89. John Shaw, *Charters Relating to the East India Company from 1660 to 1761* (Madras, 1887), 44.

90. Roper, *Advancing Empire*, 169. They sought colonists willing to settle in St. Helena. The court minutes of the EIC in the spring of 1662 discussed affixing "bills . . . in convenient places to encourage men and women to goe for St Helena" as "free planters" with free passage and "land to plant on" (April 21, 1662, Court Minutes, East India Company, IOR/B/26, f. 483, British Library).

91. John Ogilby, *The Relation of His Majestie's Entertainment Passing through the City of London, to his Coronation: With a Description of the Triumphal Arches, and Solemnity* (London: Printed by Tho. Roycroft, for Rich. Marriott, 1661), 9–10.

92. According to Ogilby, Ford was one of nine aldermen on the committee planning the coronation-day procession and the "entertainments" performed for the king along the way (Ogilby, *The Relation of His Majestie's Entertainment*, 9–10, 37).

93. Fulke Greville, *Life of Sir Philip Sidney etc. First Published 1652* (Oxford: Clarendon, 1907), 118–19.

94. Francis Hanson, *The Laws of Jamaica* (London, 1683), preface.

95. Ken Hiltner, "Early Modern Ecology," in *A New Companion to English Renaissance Literature and Culture*, ed. Michael Hattaway (Oxford: Wiley-Blackwell, 2010), 1639.

96. Cited in Brian Cowan, *The Social Life of Coffee: The Emergence of the British Coffeehouse* (New Haven, Conn.: Yale University Press, 2005), 27.

97. Cowan, *The Social Life of Coffee*, 27.

98. Thomas Sprat, *The History of the Royal Society in London* (London, 1667), 387.

99. Sprat, *The History*, 385.

100. Robert Iliffe, "Foreign Bodies: Travel, Empire and the Early Royal Society of London. Part II. The Land of Experimental Knowledge," *Canadian Journal of History* 34 (1999): 41.

101. EL/B1/38, Royal Society Library.

102. EL/B1/37, Royal Society Library.

103. Beale to Oldenburg, April 3, 1675, in *The Correspondence of Henry Oldenburg*, ed. and trans. A. Rupert Hall and Marie Boas Hall, 13 vols. (Madison: University of Wisconsin Press, 1965–73; and London: University of Wisconsin Press, 1975–86), 11:251.

104. John Milton, *Paradise Lost . . . The Sixth Edition* (London, 1763), 265, book IV, lines 157–63.

105. Colonial promoters in New York claimed that "besides the sweetness of the Air, the Countrey it self sends forth such a fragrant small, that it may be perceived at Sea" long before making land, for example (Daniel Denton, *A brief description of New-York, formerly called New-Netherlands with the places thereunto adjoyning: together with the manner of its situation, fertility of the soyle, healthfulness of the climate, and the commodities thence produced . . . likewise a brief relation of the customs of the Indians there* [London, 1670], 19).

106. Evelyn, *Sylva*, 131.

107. David Buissieret, "Studying the Natural Sciences in Seventeenth-Century Jamaica," *Caribbean Quarterly* 55, no. 3 (September 2009): 74.

108. Cited in Buissieret, "Studying the Natural Sciences in Seventeenth-Century Jamaica," 74.

109. For their role in financing the Western Design, Noell and Povey were granted twenty thousand acres of land. Richard Povey, Thomas's bother, was the commissioner general of provisions at Jamaica and often acted as their man-on-the-ground. Thomas wrote to his brother to "buy upon our account any Cocoa, or any other good bargaine." He added, "wee are now contriving to raise a joint stock of about 20,000 *l* for the carrying on some Affairs relating to Jamaica, which will be principally intrusted to you as our Agent there." But these schemes collapsed with the death of Cromwell (cited in Richard B. Sheridan, *Sugar and Slavery: An Economic History of the British West Indies, 1623–1775* [1974; Kingston, Jamaica: Canoe Press, University of the West Indies, 1994], 92–94). Sheridan goes on to suggest that "Noell and Povey withdrew from their affairs in the West Indies"; however, this chapter follows Povey as he claimed a place for himself as an adviser to Charles II, worked to get together a new council in charge of plantation affairs of which he was a member, and wrote a series of letters suggesting vast transplantations of east Indian plants to the west. He remained deeply interested in Jamaica.

110. Sprat, *The History of the Royal Society*, 149. John Michael Vlach reminds us that the use of the word "plantation" had long meant simply the "act of planting," and only in the early eighteenth century did it come to mean "an estate or farm producing a crop with servile labor." The term had also been used in the context of Ireland in the sixteenth century to designate colonial settlements. The word had many meanings and transformed over time and place (Vlach, *Back of the Big House: The Architecture of Plantation Slavery* [Chapel Hill: University of North Carolina Press, 1993], 2–3).

111. Beale to Oldenburg, April 3, 1675, and Beale to Oldenburg, April 17, 1675, in *The Correspondence of Henry Oldenburg*, ed. Hall and Hall, 11:250, 279–80.

112. Batchelor, *London*, chap. 4.

113. Gideon Harvey, *A discourse of the plague containing the nature, causes, signs, and presages of the pestilence in general, together with the state of the present contagion* (London, 1665), 29.

114. Leonard W. Cowie, *Plague and Fire: London 1665–66* (New York: G. P. Putnam's Sons, 1970), 49; Neil Hanson, *The Great Fire of London In that Apocalyptic Year, 1666* (Hoboken, N.J.: Wiley and Sons, 2002), 38.

115. Dangerous smells abounded in the early modern world. Miasmas wafted above still and fetid water, swamps, and rotting materials and risked anyone who had the unfortunate luck to breathe in such foul odors (Peter Thorsheim, *Inventing Pollution:*

Coal, Smoke, and Culture in Britain since 1800 [Athens: Ohio University Press, 2006], 10).

116. See, for instance, *An Act of Common Council by the Commissioners for Sewers, Pavements, &c., Touching the Paving and Cleansing the Streets, Lanes and Common Passages within the City* (London, 1671); Reddaway, *The Rebuilding of London*, 300. From flowers planted in widow boxes to major city-planning works, proposed alterations to the city's air ranged from fleeting to more permanent solutions. For more on regulating the smells of London, see chapter 1.

117. Egerton MS 2395, ff. 296, 297, British Library.

118. Evelyn argued that it was essential to ensure that the air had a "good temper" because "we, who are compos'd of the Elements" were deeply influenced by its qualities. Thus, control over air was necessary to keep control over the people who breathed it in, or were constantly immersed in it (Evelyn, *Fumifugium*, 22). There is a growing literature on the willingness of early modern states to intervene in the welfare and health of its subjects (see Paul Slack, *From Reformation to Improvement: Public Welfare in Early Modern England* [Oxford: Clarendon, 1999]; Harold Cook "Policing the Health of London," *Social History of Medicine* 2 [1989]: 1–33; and Andrew Cunningham and Ole Peter Grell, *Health Care and Poor Relief in Protestant Europe, 1500–1700* [London: Routledge, 1997]). Meanwhile, Mark S. R. Jenner has suggested that in early modern England officials were so invested in "the extirpation of stench and noisome air" that "the olfactory drove social policy with regard to the regulation of London's public space" (Jenner, "Civilization and Deodorization?," in *Civil Histories: Essays Presented to Sir Keith Thomas*, ed. Peter Burke et al. [Oxford: Oxford University Press, 2000], 131).

119. To some contemporaries, however, plantations, by sapping England of its population, merely weakened England. Instead of imperial acquisitions, they argued, people should focus on internal improvements. Therefore, projects of "improvement" and colonization had in some circles a fraught, even antithetical, relationship.

120. Thomas Sprat, *The History of the Royal Society* (London, 1667), 149.

121. Gary S. De Krey, *London and the Restoration, 1659–1683* (Cambridge: Cambridge University Press, 2005), 16; James I, *A Counterblaste to Tobacco* (London, 1604), preface.

122. Alain Corbin, *The Foul and the Fragrant: Odor and the French Social Imagination*, trans. Aubier Montaigne (Cambridge, Mass.: Harvard University Press, 1986). See also Jonathan Reinarz, *Past Scents: Historical Perspectives on Smell* (Champaign: University of Illinois Press, 2014), 2–3.

123. John Evelyn, *The Letterbooks of John Evelyn*, ed. Douglas D. C. Chambers and David Galbraith, vol. 1 (Toronto: University of Toronto Press, 2014), 271.

124. Evelyn, *Sylva*, 126, 130–31. For more on experiments on air, see Steven Shapin and Simon Schaffer, *Leviathan and the Air-Pump: Hobbes, Boyle, and the Experimental Life* (Princeton, N.J.: Princeton University Press, 1985).

125. Constance Classen, "The Witch's Senses: Sensory Ideologies and Transgressive Femininities from the Renaissance to Modernity," in *Empire of the Senses: The Sensual Cultural Reade*, ed. David Howes (London: Bloomsbury Academic, 2005), 72–74; Ian D. Ritchie, "The Nose Knows: Bodily Knowing in Isaiah 11.3," *Journal for the Study of the Old Testament* 25 (2000): 59–61.

126. Ritchie, "The Nose Knows," 60.

127. Thomas Cocke, *Advice for the Poor by way of Cure & Caution* (London, 1665), 4.

128. Cited in Jayne Elizabeth Lewis, *Air's Appearance: Literary Atmosphere in British Fiction, 1660-1794* (Chicago: University of Chicago Press, 2012), 48.

129. Galen "regarded the nostrils to be directly linked with the brain, allowing unmediated information, or vaporous, to reach the brain's ventricles and be processed without the need of an intervening sensory nerve" (Reinarz, *Past Scents*, 9). However, according to Mark Jenner, anatomists after Harvey questioned these earlier ideas about smell and the permeability of the brain. By the end of the seventeenth century, physicians instead pointed to nerves in the brain as enabling smell, and no longer asserted the permeability of the membranes between the nose and the brain (see Jenner, "Civilization and Deodorization?" 134-36).

130. Robert Burton, *The anatomie of Melancholy* (London, 1621), 259.

131. Evelyn, *Fumifugium*.

132. According to Mark Jenner, Evelyn presented the cleaning of London's air as an act that "would render the people of London 'the most happy upon earth.'" Such atmospheric cleansing had deeply political meanings because contemporaries likened the restored king to the light and sun whereas they presented "the Interregnum as being an eclipse or a cloud which had temporarily obscured his lustre" (Jenner, "The Politics of London Air," 537, 540-43).

133. Owen Stanwood, *The Empire Reformed: English America in the Age of the Glorious Revolution* (Philadelphia: University of Pennsylvania Press, 2011), 17-18.

134. For a thorough examination of the problems of coal smoke in London, and residents' attitudes about the smoke, see William Cavert, *The Smoke of London: Energy and Environment in the Early Modern City* (Cambridge: Cambridge University Press, 2016).

135. Evelyn, *Fumifugium*, 24-25.

136. Gillian Darley, *John Evelyn: Living for Ingenuity* (New Haven, Conn.: Yale University Press, 2006), 176.

137. Evelyn, *Fumifugium*, 24-25.

138. Evelyn Papers, December 11, 1668, Add MS 78343, f.79, British Library.

139. Evelyn's plans were twofold. The garden plants would first fill the air daily with sweet scents. The mature plants, particularly the trees, might then be burned instead of coal, which would result in a "more benign *Smoake*" that would neither fill Londoners' lungs with corrosive substances nor cloud their brains (Evelyn, *Fumifugium*, 25).

140. Evelyn, *Fumifugium*, 24. Evelyn's plans likewise called for "Contra'spaliers," likely suggesting the gardening technique, espalier, which is a method of tying or pruning branches of bushes or trees to control growth, often highly decorative and carefully and artfully arranged. In addition, Evelyn used words like *fence* and *enclose*, suggesting layers of enclosures and control, a world of fences designed to establish property and power.

141. According to Edward Malins, formal, baroque gardens were popular in England and Ireland alike in the seventeenth century. In addition to intricate French styles, a geometrical, compartmentalized Dutch style was likewise popular in landscaping (Malins and The Knight of Glin, *Lost Demesnes: Irish Landscape Gardening, 1660-1845* [Chatham, U.K.: W & J Mackay Ltd., 1976], 1-8).

142. Anonymous, "Ballad of Gresham College" (London, 1663).

143. Jenner, "The Politics of London Air," 547-48.

144. Cited in Jenner, "The Politics of London Air," 547.

145. Michel de Montaigne encouraged physicians to take note and make greater use of good smells in their work (Montaigne, *Essays*, trans. John Florio, http://pages. uoregon.edu/rbear/montaigne/).

146. John Evelyn, *A character of England as it was lately presented in a letter to a noble man of France* (London, 1659), 43.

147. Hans Sloane, "A Description of the Pimienta or Jamaica Pepper-Tree," *The Philosophical Transactions*, vol. 17 (1693): 462-63.

148. As the eighteenth century progressed, Jamaica was widely famous as the "grave of the Europeans" (Brown, *The Reaper's Garden*, 4). Meanwhile, the parallel of plant fecundity and human death posed a conceptual problem for authors of natural histories. On the one hand, "*Drugs* are here in great abundance," yet, such salubrious verdure did not seem to halt the frightening death toll. Later authors resolved this tension by asserting that it was the disorderly behaviors of early residents, not Jamaica's climate, that was to blame. According to one observer, provisioning failures, soldiers' refusal to labor, and widespread "discontent," led to the high mortality rates (Blome, *A description of the island of Jamaica*, 13-14, 26-27).

149. Kay Dian Kriz, "Curiosities, Commodities, and Transplanted Bodies in Hans Sloane's 'Natural History of Jamaica,'" *William and Mary Quarterly*, 3d ser., 57 (2000): 35.

150. Kupperman, "Fear of Hot Climates," 213-40.

151. One of the biggest challenges facing the Restoration government in Jamaica was that "there were no precedents to follow, or even to adapt," as prior to the Western Design the island was Spain's possession (Thornton, *West-India Policy*, 39).

152. Thornton, *West-India Policy*, 43.

153. Participants in Cromwell's Western Design took the island from a sparse population of Spanish and black residents, both enslaved and free, of the island. Maroon communities retreated and continued a series of attacks on the English forces from the hills. Jamaica was not formally ceded by Spain until 1670. For scholarship on the lives of early settlers in Jamaica, see Kristen Block, *Ordinary Lives in the Early Caribbean: Religion, Colonial Competition, and the Politics of Profit* (Athens: University of Georgia Press, 2012).

154. Richard S. Dunn, *Sugar and Slaves: The Rise of the Planter Class in the English West Indies, 1624-1713* (Chapel Hill: University of North Carolina Press, 1972), 151. Early commentators may have refused to see the agricultural work done by both Spanish and black residents of the island.

155. A brief survey of Jamaica, Egerton MS 2395, f. 610, British Library.

156. Seed, *Ceremonies of Possession in Europe's Conquest of the New World*, 16-40. Seed argues that the English sought to legitimate taking possession of others' lands by "improving" it.

157. Richard Blome, *A description of the island of Jamaica . . . Taken from the Notes of Sr. Thomas Linch Knight, Governor of Jamaica* (London, 1672), 13.

158. David Cooper, *A Philosophy of Gardens* (Oxford: Clarendon, 2006), 22. See John Dixon Hunt, *Greater Perfections: The Practice of Garden Theory* (Philadelphia: University of Pennsylvania Press, 2000).

159. "Instructions to D'Oyley, 8 Feb. 1661," CO 138/1, cited in Thornton, *West-India Policy*, 45-46.

160. Cited in Robert M. Bliss, *Revolution and Empire: English Politics and the American Colonies in the 17th Century* (New York: Manchester University Press, 1990), 141.

161. In total, Jamaica is 4,243 square miles (or, approximately 2,715,500 acres). Of course, the diverse terrain, much of it mountainous or unsuitable for arable farming, would have made the king's portion of arable land proportionately greater.

162. "Col. Edward D'Oyley to the Commissioners of the Admiralty, Feb. 1, 1660," UK National Archives, CO 1/33 no. 67, accessed through Colonial State Papers Online: http://gateway.proquest.com/openurl?url_ver=Z39.88-2004&res_dat=xri:csp-us:&rft_dat=xri:csp:rec:A09-E000371.

163. "Col. Edward D'Oyley to the Commissioners of the Admiralty, Feb. 1, 1660," UK National Archives, CO 1/33 no. 67.

164. "Col. Edward D'Oyley to the Commissioners of the Admiralty, Feb. 1, 1660," UK National Archives, CO 1/33 no. 67.

165. Sugar remained just one of many possible cultivars, which included cacao and indigo. For more on the development of the sugar plantation economies in the Caribbean and its connection with Atlantic slavery, see Dunn, *Sugar and Slaves*; Sheridan, *Sugar and Slavery*; Russell Menard, *Sweet Negotiations: Sugar, Slavery, and Plantation Agriculture in Early Barbados* (Charlottesville: University of Virginia Press, 2006).

166. Egerton MS 2395, f. 272, British Library.

167. Egerton MS 2395, f. 157, British Library. The primary purpose of the new governor sent to Jamaica in 1662 was "to convert the military occupation established by Edward d'Oyley into a civilian form of government" (see Buissieret, "Studying the Natural Sciences in Seventeenth-Century Jamaica," 72).

168. Blome agreed that an army was "the worst kind of people to plant" (Blome, *A description of the island of Jamaica*, 54).

169. Egerton MS 2395, f. 288, British Library. The council also believed that it was not enough to disband the army. To encourage settlement, they thought there should be some positive economic incentives, including offering four or five years of free trade. According to Thornton, Jamaica caused such anxiety because "Containing the stragglers of an army, about 2,000 masterless men, the Island presented a formidable study in anarchy and confusion" (Thornton, *West-India Policy*, 39).

170. Egerton MS 2395, ff. 272–73, 288, British Library.

171. Egerton MS 2395, f. 288, British Library.

172. A decade later, however, Governor Thomas Modyford wrote to the Lords for Trade and Plantation that small plantations were a critical part of the island. Those plantations ranging from five to thirty acres tended to be the producers of provisions, and he wanted such small planters to be encouraged (W. Noel Sainsbury, ed., *Calendar of State Papers, Colonial Series, America and West Indies, 1669–1674* [London: Printed for her Majesty's Stationary Office by Eyre and Spottiswoode, 1889], 95–96).

173. Egerton MS 2395, f. 615, British Library.

174. Sainsbury, ed., *Calendar of State Papers Colonial*, 7:94–95.

175. Egerton MS 2395, f. 523, British Library.

176. Rumors of Spanish soldiers threatening Jamaica were a regular feature of the early months of the Restoration (see, for instance, Sainsbury, ed., *Calendar of State Papers Colonial*, 1:479–80, 490).

177. Sainsbury, ed., *Calendar of State Papers Colonial*, 7:94.

178. "Col. Edward D'Oyley to the Commissioners of the Admiralty, Feb. 1, 1660," UK National Archives, CO 1/33 no. 67.

179. According to H. V. Bowen, "a subject's allegiance to the monarch was reciprocated by the crown's legal obligation to provide protection to both the bodies of subjects and the land they occupied overseas" (Bowen et al., eds., *Britain's Oceanic Empire: Atlantic and Indian Ocean Worlds c. 1550–1850* [Cambridge: Cambridge University Press, 2012], 5).

180. Evelyn, *Sylva*, 131. Evelyn explained that although residents of Jamaica called it pepper, "in truth it be a mixture of so many *Aromatics* in *one*," seeming to be made up, at once, of cinnamon, nutmeg, and mace.

181. John E. Ingram, ed., *Elysium Britannicum, or The Royal Gardens* (Philadelphia: University of Pennsylvania Press, 2001), 397.

182. Abel Evans, *Vertumnus. An Epistle to Mr. Jacob Bobart* (1713).

183. Douglas Chambers, "'Elysium Britannicum not printed neere ready &c': The *Elysium Britannicum* in the Correspondence of John Evelyn," in *John Evelyn's 'Elysium Britannicum' and European Gardening*, ed. Therese O'Malley and Joachim Wolschke-Bulmahn (Washington, D.C.: Dumbarton Oaks Research Library and Collection, 1998), 112.

184. Christine Folke Ax et al., eds., *Cultivating the Colonies: Colonial States and their Environmental Legacies* (Athens: Ohio University Press, 2011), 2; Keay, *The Magnificent Monarch*, 1; Richard Drayton, *Nature's Government: Science, Imperial Britain, and the "Improvement" of the World* (New Haven, Conn.: Yale University Press, 2000); Robert Blair St. George, *Conversing by Signs: Poetics of Implication in Colonial New England Culture* (Chapel Hill: University of North Carolina Press, 1998), 65.

185. Egerton Manuscript 2395, f. 138, British Library.

186. Egerton Manuscript 2395, f. 141, British Library.

187. Sainsbury, ed., *Calendar of State Papers Colonial*, 7:104–5.

188. Sainsbury, ed., *Calendar of State Papers Colonial*, 7:104–5.

189. Egerton MS 2395, f. 611, British Library.

190. Egerton MS 2395, ff. 296–98, British Library.

191. Jan Golinksi, "Debating the Atmospheric Constitution: Yellow Fever and the American Climate," *Eighteenth-Century Studies* 49, no. 2 (Winter 2016): 148.

192. The phrase "artificial Aire" is drawn from Burton, *The Anatomie of Melancholy*, 263.

193. According to Thomas Amy, Carolina was such a place where the air had "so serene and excellent a temper, that the *Indian* Natives prolong their days to the Extremity of Old Age." He went on to claim that the airs ensured English bodies were free from epidemics, and children would be born "strong and lusty" with "fresh ruddy Complexions" (Amy, *Carolina, or, A description of the present state of that country and the natural excellencies thereof viz. the healthfulness of the air, pleasantness of the place* [London, 1682], 4).

194. Amy, *Carolina*, 6.

195. Bradley, *Husbandry and Trade Improv'd* (London, 1727), 31.

196. Amy, *Carolina*, 8, 12–13.

197. Blome, *A description of the island of Jamaica*, 141–42.

198. Blome, *A description of the island of Jamaica*, 6.

199. In the preface to his text, Blome wrote that his friend Thomas Lynch gave him notes "about the Description of the Island of *Jamaica*, whose Worth and Ingenuity hath lately merited from his Majesty the Government of the said Isle." Thereby Blome linked Lynch's natural knowledge of Jamaica to his suitability for a position of governance. According to Blome, Lynch both recognized the need to alter the Jamaican air and was understood to have the position and ability to do so (Blome, *A description of the island of Jamaica*, preface, 6).

200. Thomas, *Man and the Natural World*, 195.

201. Alix Cooper suggests that suspicions about the deleterious effects of exotic plants and foods on European society drove many Europeans to begin to catalogue their own local nature (Cooper, *Inventing the Indigenous: Local Knowledge and Natural History in Early Modern Europe* [Cambridge: Cambridge University Press, 2009]).

202. As Thomas Herbert wrote, "Chastity is no virtue here," a place where people think "pleasure to be a delightful conqueror" (Herbert, *Some Years Travel into Diverse Parts* [1677]).

203. As Jonathan Eacott has argued, English merchants suggested replanting East Indian commodities in the Americas in order to remove certain products from the cultural and religious associations and make them more palatable to an English consumer (see Eacott, *Selling Empire: India in the Making of Britain and America, 1600–1830* [Chapel Hill: Published for the Omohundro Institute of Early American History and Culture by the University of North Carolina Press, 2017]).

204. Contemporaries were also worried about importing the "effeminacy and luxury of absolutist monarchy" when importing goods from particular regions of the globe (see Batchelor, *London*, 173).

205. Pimiento was described as having an intriguing taste, like the "mixt tast" of diverse spices. According to the author of this survey of Jamaican commodities, the pimiento was "much valued by ye Spaniard and by them Exported as a Choise Comoditie" (Egerton MS, ff. 609–15, British Library).

206. The interest in plants indigenous to Jamaica, and their uses, inspired numerous letters and publications. For examples, see William Hughes, *The American Physitian* (London, 1672); Thomas Trapham, *A Discourse of health in the island of Jamaica* (London, 1678); and Hans Sloane, *A Voyage to the Islands* (London, 1707, 1725).

207. The Jamaican pepper, or allspice, tree is not related to the black pepper native to Southeast Asia (*Piper nigrum*). English settlers called the dried fruit and the powdered product of the *Pimento dioica* plant, native to the Greater Antilles, "pepper," because when the berries were dried they resembled peppercorns. Both could be ground, used as seasoning, and utilized as medicines. The *Pimento dioica* is a tree, whereas the *Piper nigrum* is a flowering vine.

208. It was likewise considered serviceable for "Strengthening the stomack, expelling wind, doing those friendly offices to ye bowels wee generally expect from spices" (Cl.P/10i/28, Royal Society Papers).

209. Blome, *A description of the island of Jamaica*, 13.

210. Interest in experimental gardening in Jamaica did not wane. Instead, interest turned to experimentation with indigenous Jamaican spices. Only one year after Povey drafted his transplantation schemes he sent some pepper indigenous to Jamaica—pimiento—to fellow Royal Society member Robert Boyle (likely obtained from one of Povey's contacts in Jamaica) and asked if Boyle would "thoroughly examine it, by

making such experiments that the qualities of it may be discovered and understood, for I am ready to believe that it is not of a lowe or ordinarie degree" (see Povey to Boyle, May 8, 1661, in *The Correspondence of Robert Boyle, 1636–1691*, ed. Michael Hunter, Antonio Clericuzio, and Lawrence M. Principe [London: Routledge, 2001]).

211. Henry Stubbe, *The Indian Nectar, or a Discourse Concerning Chocolata* (London, 1662), 47–48.

212. Stubbe, *The Indian Nectar*, 48, 50.

213. Sainsbury, ed., *Calendar of State Papers, Colonial Series*, 7:94–110.

214. Egerton MS 2395, f. 611, British Library.

215. Egerton MS 2395, f. 615, British Library.

216. Sainsbury, ed., *Calendar of State Papers, Colonial Series*, 7:xxii–xxiii.

217. My italics. Hunter, "Robert Boyle's 'Heads,'" 33.

218. Brooke N. Newman, *A Dark Inheritance: Blood, Race, and Sex in Colonial Jamaica* (New Haven, Conn.: Yale University Press, 2018), 11, 14.

219. Daniel Denton highlighted a range of "common" English foods that flourished in New York when he published his promotional treatise about the colony (Denton, *A brief description of New-York*, 3).

220. Rebecca Earle, *The Body of the Conquistador: Food, Race and the Colonial Experience in Spanish America, 1492–1700* (Cambridge: Cambridge University Press, 2012).

221. Daniel Denton, in promotional literature about New York, wrote of Long Island: "The Island is most if it of a very good soyle, and very natural for all sorts of English Grain; which they sowe and have very good increase of, besides all other Fruits and Herbs common in England" (Denton, *A brief description of New-York*, 3).

222. Sloane, *A voyage to the Islands*, lxxiv–lxxv.

223. As Rebecca Earle has argued, early Spanish colonists believed that European foods, particularly wheat bread, wine, and olive oil, were essential to preserving both the health of their bodies as well as their identities as Spaniards and Christians (Earle, *The Body of the Conquistador*, 16, 54).

224. Sprat, *The History of the Royal Society*, 386.

225. "A History of Vegetables by Daniel Cox" was read to the Royal Society on June 4, 1668 (Cl.P/10i/8, Royal Society Library).

226. Cl.P/10i/8, Royal Society Library.

227. Sloane MS 3984, f. 195, British Library.

228. Sloane MS 3984, f. 194, British Library.

229. Daniel Leeds, *An Almanack . . . 1700* (New-York: William Bradford, 1700).

230. Tryon, *Friendly Advice to the Gentlemen-Planters of the East and West Indies*, 49.

231. Hughes, *The American Physitian*, 109.

232. Sloane, *A Voyage to the Islands*, preface.

233. See, for instance, the *Hartlib Papers*, 8/22/2B; Beale to Oldenburg, April 3, 1675, in *The Correspondence of Henry Oldenburg*, ed. Hall and Hall, 11:250.

234. Stephen A. Harris, *Planting Paradise: Cultivating the Garden, 1501–1900* (Oxford: The Bodleian Library, University of Oxford, 2011), 32.

235. John Evelyn, *A philosophical discourse of earth relating to the culture and improvement of its vegetation* (London, 1676), 47–49.

236. Sprat, *The History of the Royal Society*, 386.

237. These discussions took place on April 12, 1682 (Thomas Birch, *The history of the Royal Society for Improving of Natural Knowledge*, vol. 4 [London, 1757], 141–43).

238. Early modern people regularly compared human society to the botanical residents of gardens (Rebecca Bushnell, *Green Desire: Imagining Early Modern English Gardens* [Ithaca, N.Y.: Cornell University Press, 2003], 135–36).

239. Nehemiah Grew, *The Anatomy of Vegetables Begun* (London, 1682).

240. Cl.P/10i/8, Royal Society Library.

241. Zilberstein, *A Temperate Empire*, 91–117. According to Zilberstein, acclimatization theories of the eighteenth century suggested that human bodies would fare best when relocating to places with similar climates.

242. George Lakoff and Mark Johnson, *Metaphors We Live By* (Chicago: University of Chicago Press, 1980), 144.

243. *The Hartlib Papers: A Complete Text and Image Database of the Papers of Samuel Hartlib (c. 1600–1662)*, 25/6/4B.

244. *Hartlib Papers*, 8/22/2A.

245. *Hartlib Papers*, 8/22/2A.

246. *Hartlib Papers*, 8/22/2A–2B.

247. Evelyn, *A philosophical discourse of earth*, 47–49.

248. Evelyn, *A philosophical discourse of earth*, 47–49.

249. Evelyn, *A philosophical discourse of earth*, 47–49.

250. Newman, *A Dark Inheritance*, 13.

251. An Act for Naturalization (1670) *in Calendar of State Papers Colonial, America and West Indies*, vol. 7, *1669–1675*, ed. W. Noel Sainbury (London: Her Majesty's Stationary Office, 1889), 94–110.

252. Cited in David Barry Gaspar, "'Rigid and Inclement': Origins of the Jamaican Slave Laws of the Seventeenth Century," in *The Many Legalities of Early America*, ed. Christopher L. Tomlins and Bruce H. Mann (Chapel Hill: University of North Carolina Press, 2001), 80.

253. Raingard Esser, "Citizenship and Immigration in 16th- and Early 17th-Century England," 238. However, Esser's work traces the legal definitions of children born in England to foreign parents. Until the General Naturalization Act in 1709, these children were made denizens. In his work, he seems to suggest that it was not enough to be born in England, but that somehow a blood inheritance prevented the full incorporation of the child as a subject. Perhaps both were in operation.

254. Hughes, *The American Physitian*, 113.

255. Hughes, *The American Physitian*, 143.

256. Hughes, *The American Physitian*, 145–46.

257. Hughes, *The American Physitian*, 146.

258. Hughes, *The American Physitian*, 147, 155.

259. Jaspar Dankers and Peter Sluyter, *Journal of a Voyage to New-York and a Tour in Several of the American Colonies in 1679–80*, trans. and ed. Henry C. Murphy (1867; repr., Ann Arbor: University Microfilms, 1966), quotes on 111, 295, 299.

260. Cited in Thornton, *West-India Policy*, 45–46.

261. Egerton Manuscripts, f. 86, British Library.

Conclusion

1. William Petty, *Political arithmetick, or, A discourse concerning the extent and vaue of lands, people, buildings* (London, 1690), preface.

2. Petty, *Political arithmetick*, preface.

3. Petty, *Political arithmetick*, preface.

4. Petty, *Political arithmetick*, chapter v.

5. For more on the complexions and sickly appearance of the residents of the fens, see Mary J. Dobson, *Contours of Death and Disease in Early Modern England* (Cambridge: Cambridge University Press, 1997). Meanwhile, travelers offered ngative assessments of the appearance of fenlanders, such as in an account of travel through the "Westerne Counties" written by Lieutenant Hammond (Lansdowne MS 213/27, ff. 381–82 [1635], British Library).

6. The phrase "Politicall Medicine" comes from a letter from William Petty to Arthur Annesley, Earl of Anglesey, in 1672. This letter was cited in Ted McCormick, *William Petty: And the Ambitions of Political Arithmetic* (Oxford: Oxford University Press, 2009), 8. Annesley was deeply engaged in colonial activities, including as one of the founding council members of the Council of Foreign Plantations and was likewise a bailiff of the Bedford Level Corporation. According to McCormick, "Implicit in Petty's account . . . was the notion that there were natural laws behind political no less than physical phenomena, laws that might be discovered and . . . employed by human art for human benefit" (McCormick, *William Petty*, 116).

7. John Evelyn, *Fumifugium: or, the Inconveniencie of the Aer and Smoak of London Dissipated Together with Some Remedies Humbly Proposed* (London, 1661), "To the Reader."

8. Petty, *Political arithmetick*, chapter v.

9. Hartlib was a proponent of transforming "waste" people through labor to make them "serviceable to the Common-wealth" (Samuel Hartlib cited in Braddick, *State Formation in Early Modern England*, 133).

10. Timothy Sweet, "Economy, Ecology, and Utopia in Early Colonial Promotional Literature," *American Literature* 71, no. 3 (1999): 408. Contemporaries drew connections between "improvement" and spiritual reformation and renewal. By improving wastelands, a person could rehabilitate both the soil and their souls (Di Palma, *Wasteland: A History* [New Haven: Yale University Press, 2014], 50).

11. Samuel Hartlib proposed that petty criminals and the poor alike should be forced to work, "the better to make them serviceable to the Common-wealth, by reforming their ungodly life." Moreover, orphaned children might likewise be shaped into useful citizens "under a godly and civill Government, to the great joy of good peopl" (Samuel Hartlib, *Londons Charity Inlarged Stilling The Orphans Cry* [London, 1650], cited in Braddick, *State Formation in Early Modern England*, 133).

12. This was an era characterized in many ways by an abiding interest in a set of ideas bundled under the title of "improvement." Terms like "projector" and "project" "characterized the new era" and suggest their confidence that these were realizable goals. Many of them were undertaken (Joan Thirsk, *Economic Policy and Projects: The Development of a Consumer Society in Early Modern England* [Oxford: Clarendon, 1978], 1–2).

13. Petty, *Political arithmetick*, chapter viii.

14. A letter to the Comitte of ye East India Company for an Experim[t] in Jamaica, Sloane MS 856, f. 37b, British Library.

15. Abigail L. Swingen, *Competing Visions of Empire: Labor, Slavery, and the Origins of the British Atlantic Empire* (New Haven: Yale University press, 2015), 2.

16. Cited in L. H. Roper, *Advancing Empire: English Interests an Overseas Expansion: 1613–1688* (Cambridge: Cambridge University Press, 2017), 192-93.

17. Paul Slack, *From Reformation to Improvement: Public Welfare in Early Modern England* (Oxford: Oxford University Press, 1998), 88.

18. According to Paul Warde, early modern governments may have made grandiose plans, but they often implemented them on an ad hoc basis (Warde, *Ecology, Economy and State Formation*, 165).

19. Stephen Harris, *Planting Paradise: Cultivating the Garden 1501–1900* (University of Oxford, 2011), 83.

20. Elizabeth DeLoughrey, "Globalizing the Routes of Breadfruit and Other Bounties," *Journal of Colonialism and Colonial History* 8, no. 3 (2007).

21. Daniel K. Richter, *Before the Revolution: America's Ancient Pasts* (Cambridge: Harvard University Press: 2013). 255.

22. John Romeyn Brodhead, *Documents Relative to the Colonial History of the State of New-York: Procured in Holland, England, and France* (Albany, N.Y.: Weed, Parsons, 1853–87), 32–33.

23. Owen Stanwood, *The Empire Reformed: English America in the Age of the Glorious Revolution* (Philadelphia: University of Pennsylvania Press, 2011), 27–28.

24. The king's new council "for the better regulating and improving of forreigne Plantations" was to inform the colonies that "that they are to bee look'd upon as united, and Embodied: and that their Head and Centre is heere" (Egerton MS. 2395, f. 273, British Library).

25. Anon., *An Abstract or abbreviation of some few of the many (later and former) testimonys from the inhabitants of New-Jersey* (1681), 27.

26. See Jeffrey Jerome Cohen, "Green Children from Another World, or The Archipelago in England," in *Cultural Diversity in the British Middle Ages: Archipelago, Ireland, England*, ed. Cohen (New York: Palgrave Macmillan, 2008), 75.

27. John Ogilby, *The Entertainment of his most excellent majestie Charles II, in his passage through the city of London to his coronation* (London, 1662), 13.

Index

About the Author

Kate Luce Mulry is Assistant Professor of History at California State University, Bakersfield. She received her B.A. from Princeton University and her Ph.D. from New York University. Her research and writing investigate the intersections of environmental history, the history of science and medicine, and ideas about the body in the early modern Atlantic world.